NATIONALISM AND IMPERIALISM
IN THE HITHER EAST

HANS KOHN

NATIONALISM AND IMPERIALISM IN THE HITHER EAST

HOWARD FERTIG

NEW YORK · 1969

First published in English in 1932
by George Routledge and Sons Ltd.

HOWARD FERTIG, INC. EDITION 1969
Published by arrangement with Routledge & Kegan Paul Ltd.

Preface to the 1969 edition

Copyright © 1969 by Hans Kohn

Library of Congress Catalog Card Number: 68-9622

PRINTED IN THE UNITED STATES OF AMERICA
BY NOBLE OFFSET PRINTERS, INC.

TO
MY WIFE AND FAITHFUL COLLABORATOR

PREFACE TO THE 1969 EDITION

This book was written in the years 1930-31, when I traveled widely in several Middle Eastern countries, from Egypt to Iraq, as a correspondent for the *Frankfurter Zeitung* and the *Neue Zürcher Zeitung.* It was published in German in 1931 and in an English translation in 1932. It deals primarily with the 1920's, when the Arab lands formed one of the centers of diplomatic interplay between the strategic interests of the then Great Powers; with the growing international interest in the oil resources of the region; and with the aspirations for national independence of the Arab people. All the problems of the 1960's were by then in the making. Without a clear understanding of the problems of the post-World War I period, the problems of the post-World War II Middle East cannot be seen in true perspective.

The 1920's brought new elements into the complex interplay of interests and emotions, of the search for dignity and identity, for profit and economic progress. In 1922 Britain recognized, at least in principle, the independence of Egypt. She took the first step here, as she did for Asia in India in 1947 and for Africa in Ghana in 1957. The Arab provinces of the defeated Ottoman Empire were organized as (British and French) mandates under Article 22 of the League of Nations Covenant, for the official purpose of fulfilling the aspiration of the majority of the populations for independence. The Balfour Declaration of November, 1917 promised the Jewish people—part of whom Theodor Herzl had organized twenty years before in a modernized Zionist movement—British sympathy for the creation of a Jewish national home in Palestine, thus introducing political Zionism as a new element into the awakening Arab East. The experience of the 1920's made it appear most improbable that a Jewish immigration into Palestine would assume proporations threatening the majority position of the native (mostly Arab) population. This

vii

situation was only changed in the following decade by the rise of National Socialism to power in Germany and for a short while in most of Europe. The unspeakable brutalities committed by the Germans against the Jews as their chief victims, but also against other people, changed the situation in world Jewry and in Palestine fundamentally. Many came to see Hitler's fanaticism bordering on insanity as a normal and perhaps recurrent phenomenon, which threatened the emancipation of Jews in all countries. What the Arabs had feared immediately after 1917, and even before, became after 1947 a reality.

At the same time the Arab peoples, formerly separated by immense distances and deserts, subject to various foreign rulers, and hardly known to each other, began to feel the desirability of a union from the Atlantic Ocean to the Indian Sea. This desire was partly stimulated by the development of modern communications and by the wave of nationalism sweeping (unexpectedly for many European observers) the civilizations and tribes of Asia and Africa, and even of the Afro-Americans. The dynasty of the Hashemites of Mecca, the standard bearers of the unification of the Western Arabs in the early 1920's, was defeated by the more energetic Wahabis from the interior of the Arabian Peninsula under the Ibn Saud dynasty. After World War II, republican and vaguely socialist trends—aiming at the economic improvement of the peasantry and at a political and social awakening from age-old apathy by means of education and health services—made themselves felt in the Middle East as in all underdeveloped countries of the earth.

When this book was written, all that seemed still far in the future. Yet the possible outlines were there, and on the whole the events after World War II have confirmed what this book foresaw. The 1960's and the coming decades are grounded in the great revolution which started in 1914 and still takes its course; they can be the better understood in the light of the 1920's.

H. K.

Philadelphia, Pa., 1968

viii

CONTENTS

LIST OF MAPS

ERRATA

Page   82, line 9 from bottom: "Kemal" should read "Kamil"
Page 115, line 13: "Kemal" should read "Kamil"
Page 337: "Mustafa Kemal Pasha, 82, 115" should read
          "Mustafa Kamil Pasha, 82, 115"

NATIONALISM AND IMPERIALISM IN THE HITHER EAST

INTRODUCTION

FROM WEST TO EAST

THE area between the Nile Valley on the western margin of the Arabian desert and Mesopotamia on the eastern margin constitutes the oldest centre of civilization amongst the Western races. All that we know of the history of antiquity down to the relatively late appearance of the Greeks took place in this region, in the clash between its peoples and their cultural interchange. The foundations of Greek civilization had their origins in Egypt, Phœnicia, and Mesopotamia, whose native civilizations, petrified and exhausted after flourishing for centuries, were stirred under Greek influence to a new and unique life and dominated the concluding era of antiquity in the form of Hellenism. Hellenism gave place to Islam, whose centres, Damascus, Baghdad, and Cairo, were again within this region. The exhaustion and petrifaction of Islam and the shifting of the great trade routes, and therewith of the political centre of gravity of the human race, then thrust the countries of Hither Asia for centuries from the foreground of world history into an insignificant corner. It is only within the last few decades that this world, forgotten by mankind and almost by itself, has re-emerged. It began with the excavation and exposure there of the traces of ancient civilization. Modern inventions of means of transit gave new life and new importance to the trade routes whose day had seemed finally past. Like the Greeks in a former age, so now European notions and ideas exercised a revolutionary influence upon the petrified existence of these countries. European penetration began to evoke new forms in the political, cultural, and social order. The difference between the development of Egypt and of the Arab countries is due to the fact that Egypt came in contact with Europe some decades

1

earlier than the lands east of the Suez Canal. For Egypt acquired importance to world communications with the invention of the steamship, Arabia only in the age of motor and air transit.

Arabia and Egypt do not constitute a national unit. The fellaheen of the Nile Valley are the descendants of the Pharaohs' subjects ; when the glories laid bare by excavation stir in them a consciousness of their ancient origin, a barrier rises to divide them from their neighbours on the east. Yet all memories of those ancient days are but the outcome of artificial reflection reaching back far beyond anything that is living and present in the Egyptians' consciousness. To-day Arabia and Egypt are united by language, religion, and culture. And though the religious tie has begun to lose its virtue in recent decades when confronted with particular national consciousness, yet Cairo, thanks to the wealth and progressive spirit of the country, constitutes a centre of Arabian culture. The new Arabian literature which arose in Syria in the middle of last century found a refuge and a field of activity in Cairo, just like the first champions of Arab national liberation at the beginning of the twentieth century. The great Cairo dailies were and are read in all Arab countries. The Egyptian nationalist movement, with its demand for democracy and independence, served as a model to the progressive elements in the Arab nationalist movement. Stimulated by the economic impetus which foreign capital gave to Egypt, and the consequent pre-dominance and influential position of foreigners in the country, Egyptian politicians were the first to realize that economic emancipation must go hand in hand with political liberation. The Banque Misr, founded by Talaat Harb Bey, defined by its statutes as a purely Egyptian concern, marked the beginning of the struggle for economic emancipation, and rendered pioneer service in the establishment of independent Egyptian manufacture and industry. In 1929 the bank extended its activities, with a similar aim, to Arabia. With the co-operation of Syrian capital, it founded the Banque Misr-Syrie-Libanon, and the Prime Minister of Iraq, Nuri es Said Pasha, stated at the beginning of July, 1930, how greatly he desired the Banque Misr to extend its activities to Iraq. Geographical proximity and economic necessity will lead to economic co-operation between Egypt and the Arab countries.

At the present day, since the secularization of Turkey, Egypt and Arabia are the chief Islamic centres. In Syria and in Egypt there are also culturally and economically strong Christian minorities. This oriental Christianity is much more closely akin in its historical tradition, in its manner of life, and in its intellectual stamp, to its own neighbours, than to the Christian peoples of the West. Since the World War the overwhelming majority of these Christians have taken part fully in the political movements of their Mohammedan fellow-citizens, and religious barriers are beginning to lose their importance in public life. Islam itself is undergoing a process of transformation in these countries, very far removed from the revolutionary pace forced upon it in the Turkish Republic and the Soviet Union, but yet bringing about a relatively speedy change and rejuvenation. Egypt, Syria, Iraq, and Palestine are in the midst of a process of cultural and social transformation from which Inner Arabia is still far removed, since it is only just touched by the first waves of the rising flood of European influence. Beyond the lingual, cultural, religious, and social bonds which unite Egypt and Arabia, is that of their position in world politics. The region between the Mediterranean Sea and the Persian Gulf is the bridge across which pass sea, land, and air communications from Europe to southern and eastern Asia. More and more it is becoming the vital junction of the great transcontinental lines of communication which, thanks to the undreamed-of acceleration of transit between remote and hitherto utterly inaccessible regions, will exercise such an influence on the political and social development of the Old World as did once the discovery of sea routes across the Atlantic Ocean ; only to-day this process of transformation is taking place far more rapidly and over a far wider area, for no part of the earth's surface seems to be excluded from the great human society that is in process of formation.

The present book seeks to present the history of this region during the past decade, in which the political structures created by the World War and the Peace Conferences have been seeking consolidation and the evolution of their own life. The problems raised by the War and the Peace had not reached solution even by the end of the first decade. But the outlines of the new structure that is in process of formation may be discerned with increasing plainness. The bases of this new structure have been set out in my *History of Nationalism in the East,* and the problems involved have been briefly summed up in my *Orient und Okzident.* The events of the World War and the Peace Conferences are not the subject of the present book. Its story begins where, after the immediate consequences of the War had been liquidated, the civil and political administration of the several countries was established. It, too, is intended as a contribution to the endeavour to understand the historical and sociological character of nationalism and of the forces which are determining the history of our own day.

Geopolitically the Arabo-Egyptian region lies at the meeting-point of three continents, right before the most important gateways to the Indian Ocean, on the road along which from time immemorial material and intellectual interchange between East and West has passed. Historically it is in the midst of a process involving the passage from a world moulded by mediaeval religion to one of modern thought. Socially and economically it is emerging from a world bound by tradition to one of individual freedom, from the feudal era to that of middle-class capitalism and the dawning consciousness of the working classes. Moreover, there is a peculiar fascination attaching to the region under consideration because the countries which make it up are at the most various stages in this process : from Nejd, which seems to belong wholly to the world of religious bonds and where the significance of Ibn Saud's personality is precisely that he recognizes the necessity of making an approach towards that other world, and is paving the way with great and statesmanlike wisdom, to Egypt whose leading circles sometimes think that their country no longer lies at the meeting-point of two worlds, but already belongs entirely to Europe.

The social, political, and cultural movements in these countries, the struggle between imperialism and nationalism which is going on there—these throw light upon processes which extend far beyond the region under consideration. They are part of the transformation of the East and of the remoulding of its relation to the West. To the future historian the first decade after the World War will be marked by the beginning of Europe's relative loss in world importance, and he will see the three decisive events of the period in the economic domination of the United States of North America, the revolutionary erection of the Soviet Union, and the recent entry of the East into world politics as an active factor, the " awakening of the nations of the East, hitherto without a history ". Only the future historian will be able to say to which of these three factors we must ascribe the greatest importance in moulding the future of mankind.

I

ANCIENT ROUTES OF WORLD COMMUNICATIONS REVIVED

THE ROAD TO THE EAST

AFTER the Crusades, Egypt and Arabia faded beyond the ken of Europe. The Crusades had been the last great attempt on the part of the West to force access to the fabled treasures of the Far East by way of Egypt and Arabia. In itself there was nothing particularly attractive about this region. Only at certain places are desert and arid steppes broken up by fertile patches, and there is little mineral wealth. That is why, right down to the nineteenth century, Arabia and Egypt were never the object of European colonizing activities. The roads to America and India lay far removed from Hither Asia, across the Atlantic Ocean. Napoleon was the first who was sufficiently far-sighted as a world-politician to discern the importance of the land route to India through Hither Asia and to enter upon a struggle with England for it, first in Egypt and Palestine, later in a still more ambitious scheme across Russia and through the Central Asian desert. In that struggle Napoleon was defeated. The route that he had descried was opened up by his victorious opponents. England turned her attention to Egypt, Arabia, and the Persian Gulf, Russia to the more easterly route across the Caucasus, Persia, and Turkistan. Hither Asia recovered its world-wide importance as a bridge from the Mediterranean to the Indian Ocean, and the ancient trade routes advanced towards a period of new and undreamed-of activity.

Thanks to their geographical situation, these countries came once more into contact with Europe in the nineteenth century. Hardly any attempt at actual colonization was made, although they are situated in the temperate zone. Their relatively low grade of fertility and the war-like hostility to strangers and comparatively high level of civilization of their inhabitants offered no incentive to such

6

a course. The European Powers were content to establish their influence, which guaranteed the security of their communications with the wealth of India and South-Eastern Asia and the sources of raw materials in tropical Africa, and ensured political and financial privileges for themselves. The sea passage to India in a sailing ship round the Cape of Good Hope had taken many months, and was exposed to the vagaries of the weather. At the end of the eighteenth century the Indian Government had set up a postal service by camel from the Persian Gulf to the Mediterranean across the Syrian desert, but with the coming of the steamship the sea passage across the Atlantic to the Indian Ocean gained the advantage of greater speed and safety.

A new era began in this region with the completion of the Suez Canal, which was opened in November, 1869. Originally Great Britain was hostile to this undertaking, for she regarded it as a menace to the British command of the seas and an attempt on the part of France to gain influence in the East. Of the 400,000 shares in the company, whose concession expires ninety-nine years after the opening of the Canal and passes to the Egyptian Government, French shareholders own more than half, whilst it was not till 1875 that Great Britain, thanks to Lord Beaconsfield's foresight, secured 176,602 shares at the price of nearly £4,000,000. This sum has since been repaid to Great Britain many times over in dividends. Since 1923 the British Government has received more than £1,000,000 annually in dividends. Although the French Government holds no shares, the company was constituted as a French one. But this French Canal on Egyptian territory represents a British imperial route. From the outset British ships have formed not only a relative, but a decided absolute majority of those passing through the Canal. After the interruption caused by the World War, traffic through the Suez Canal has been steadily increasing. In 1929 6,274 ships, with a tonnage of 36,466,014, passed through it. Of these 19,114,282 tons were British. Holland occupied the second place, with 3,544,416 tons, closely followed by Germany. France only came fourth on the list.[1] The Suez Canal connects and separates two worlds. To-day it is the most important route for the political, economic, and cultural interchange between East and West. The

Panama Canal, likewise, connects two oceans, but it does not separate two worlds. The countries bordering it on either side are wholly similar. The Suez Canal, on the other hand, is bordered immediately on the north-west and south-east by two different worlds.

Right on into the twentieth century British policy has been directed towards the protection of the Suez Canal and the sea route to India. In order to secure that route the attempt was made to make the Indian Ocean and its approaches, the Red Sea and the Persian Gulf, into British waters. But since the World War there has emerged beside the sea route the land and air route across Egypt and Arabia, beside the steamship the motor-car, aeroplane, and railway. The result has been a tendency gradually to shift the centre of gravity of communications. In addition to Alexandria and Cairo on the western margin of Hither Asia, Baghdad has become a junction on its eastern margin. The Caliph's city, barely accessible only a few years earlier, has been brought within a few hours of the Mediterranean. Thanks to the technical changes in the system of communications, Baghdad has become the focus of the forces at work in Central Asia. Thence five routes lead in all directions, open to motor transit and aircraft, and in part to the railway as well. To the west a route leads across the Syrian desert to the Mediterranean, to Beirut, Haifa, and Egypt. To the north one follows the course of the Tigris and leads to Constantinople by way of Aleppo. To the north-east the connection with the Soviet Union is established via Tehran. Two further routes lead to India through southern Persia and via Basra, across the Persian Gulf. The Oriental policy of the European Powers in the twentieth century has consisted in a struggle for the possession of these routes, and has been determined by their course and by consideration for their security. It was the development of these routes and the substitution of modern means of transit for the camel that first opened up the Middle East. Even before the World War the construction of two railways began to mark out the main lines of communication, which were destined after the end of the War to open the countries of the Middle East to economic and cultural penetration in a manner undreamed of a few years earlier.

THE RAILWAY SYSTEM OF HITHER ASIA

Both intended railway lines ran through Ottoman territory. The first, the Baghdad railway, was an enterprise of German capital and conceived as a push on the part of German world policy towards Asia. The second, the Hejaz railway, was built exclusively by Mohammedan capital, and served Ottoman and Pan-Islamic ends. It was to connect Constantinople with western Arabia and the Red Sea. Strategically it enabled Turkey to hold Medina with her military forces, and even to send troops rapidly to the distant Yemen. Neither of these routes to-day serve the interests for which they were originally devised, but instead British imperial policy and the opening out and consolidation of the road to India. Both have lost in economic importance because the politically united Ottoman territory which they formerly crossed has been broken up into a number of independent political units which frequently sever the economic hinterland from its natural centres. Neither railway has yet been completed. But the ambition to make them part of a great, unified network of railways linking Europe, Asia, and Africa, is plainly discernible. Their completion is only a question of a few years.

The Hejaz Railway was traced by its constructors some distance from the coast of the Mediterranean and the Red Sea. This diminished its economic value, since it runs mainly through desert, but increased its strategic security, since it was safe from naval guns. Only at two points did branch lines lead to the Mediterranean coast, from Damascus to Beirut along a narrow-gauge mountain railway, difficult of access and unequal to carrying much traffic, and from Deraya to Haifa, which was thus transformed from an insignificant fishing village into a seaport which rapidly outstripped the older and more famous Acre, situated on the same bay. At present the Hejaz Railway has no connection with the Red Sea, but connections have been planned from Maan to Akaba and from Medina to its seaport of Yenbo, besides a continuation of the railway to Mecca and Jidda.

The Hejaz Railway is politically important to Arabia. Originally it was Mohammedan ecclesiastical property, a Wakf under unified management. To-day it is under three separate administrations, the French mandatory administration in Syria, the British in Palestine and Trans-Jordan, and the Kingdom of the Hejaz, where, however, there has been no regular traffic since the devastations of the World War. The possession of Maan, at the point where the Hejaz Railway turns aside from a course parallel with the Mediterranean coast to one parallel with the Red Sea coast, is the subject of disputes still unsettled. Maan and its seaport, Aqaba, at the north-eastern extremity of the Red Sea, belonged till 1925 to the Kingdom of the Hejaz which, like Trans-Jordan, was subject to the dynasty of King Hussein ibn Ali. Negotiations had been in progress since 1922 concerning the possession of both places. Philby, the British representative in Trans-Jordan, handed over the line from Amman, the capital of Trans-Jordan, to Maan to the administration of the Hejaz. The British Government revoked this step, recalled Philby, and in 1925, after the fall of King Hussein, proclaimed the annexation of Maan and Aqaba by Trans-Jordan.

Nor is the problem of the ownership and general management of the Hejaz Railway settled. The Hejaz demands Mohammedan control of the railway, which is primarily intended to serve for the transit of pilgrims, and its administration by a Mohammedan Board in Mecca. The Pan-Islamic Congress summoned by Ibn Saud in Mecca in June, 1926, discussed this question at its eighth session on June 15th. On that occasion the mover of the resolution pointed out that during the negotiations the French and British Governments, in a joint statement made on January 27th, 1923, had acknowledged the religious character of the Hejaz Railway, and had agreed to the formation of a Board of Administration for the whole line. This Board was to consist of four Mohammedan members nominated by the Governments of Syria, Palestine, Trans-Jordan, and the Hejaz, and two representatives of the rest of the Mohammedan world, and was to meet in Medina. France and Great Britain were prepared to devote all the profits from the sections running through their mandated territories to the extension of the whole railway and the assistance of the pilgrims. These intentions have never been carried out. The Islamic Congress was unanimous in declaring that all sections of the

Hejaz Railway should be administered by the Hejaz, and that these demands should be pressed before the League of Nations and the International Court of Justice at the Hague.[2]

More important for world communications than the Hejaz Railway is the parallel line built along the Mediterranean coast during the World War from the Suez Canal to Haifa. At the Suez Canal it links up with the Egyptian railway system and with the projected line from Alexandria to Cape Town, the great north-to-south connection of the East African continent. For the time being its northern extremity is at Haifa, thus connecting that port with southern Palestine and Egypt, in addition to its connection with the hinterland by means of the Hejaz Railway. At the present time the port of Haifa is being extended at a cost of more than 20 million marks (roughly £1,000,000), part of the loan which the Palestinian Government floated in London in the autumn of 1927 under British guarantee.[3] Probably the potash and the various salts from the Dead Sea will also be exported from Haifa ; the exploitation of these was entrusted to a British-Zionist company, which is to build a railway northwards from the Dead Sea through the Jordan Valley to meet the branch line of the Hejaz Railway turning off at Haifa. The main line is to be extended from Haifa northwards through Beirut to Tripoli, where the railway from Constantinople and Anatolia through Aleppo and Homs now ends. As soon as this line is built, the Paris–Cairo express of the Sleeping Car Company will be able to complete the transcontinental land connection without any assistance from motor coaches. The old plan for a direct connection between the three continents will be realized. Aleppo will become the railway junction of the Hither East, and there the express trains from Europe will branch off to Cairo and Baghdad. Hitherto the line from Aleppo to Baghdad has not been constructed. On the section from Nesibin to Kirkuk the Taurus express of the Sleeping Car Company from Paris to Baghdad has to be supplemented by motor transport. But the missing section via Mosul is soon to be completed, so that the line from the Bosphorus to the Persian Gulf will be unbroken, like that to the Suez Canal.

THE MIDDLE EASTERN EMPIRE

From the British point of view, this whole Hither Asian railway system, consisting of the Baghdad Railway, the Hejaz Railway, and that connecting the Suez Canal with Tripoli, has the drawback that vital portions of it run through French mandated territory, and Haifa, which was to become the great British port in the eastern Mediterranean, does not occupy a predominant position compared with the more favourably situated ports of Beirut and Alexandretta. Great Britain, therefore, is contemplating the construction of a transverse line to run from Haifa exclusively through territory under British influence—Northern Palestine, Trans-Jordan, and Iraq—to Baghdad and the Persian Gulf, connecting with the Egypto-African railway system. This would establish a direct railway connection from Egypt to the gateways of India. If the oilfields of Mosul prove rich enough, Great Britain and Iraq intend to convey the oil by pipe-line to Haifa, whilst Syria and France have contemplated Tripoli as the end of the pipe-lines. France, too, means to build a transverse line from Tripoli via Deir ez Zor on the Upper Euphrates to Mosul. The conflict concerns not only the conveyance of oil to the Mediterranean, but also the traffic of the awakening Persian hinterland. Haifa and Basra, the terminal points of the great British railway in the Middle East, have been selected from the outset as British strategic points on the Indian route from the Mediterranean to the Persian Gulf. The development of Haifa and the construction of the " all-British " railway are the fulfilment of plans harboured by British imperial policy for decades. For the sake of that line, Britain waged her campaigns in Palestine and Mesopotamia and worked for years in order to secure appropriate frontiers with Turkey on the north and with the kingdom of Ibn Saud on the south. This was the aim pursued in her struggle with Turkey for Mosul and with Ibn Saud for the security of Iraq's south-western frontier, for the possession of the district of Maan, and the creation of a corridor uniting Trans-Jordan and Iraq. The plan of connecting the Mediterranean with the Persian Gulf by a land route has been cherished for decades. In the thirties of last century the English Lieutenant-Colonel F. R. Chesney did surveying work in Mesopotamia for that purpose. In the agreements about the division of Turkey after the World War, Great Britain endeavoured to secure Haifa and Basra. In the secret agreement with France of 1916, when Palestine was to be internationalized and there was no talk of a British mandate, Great Britain received the Bay of Acre in order to build a railway from it to Baghdad. Since the end of the World War the belt of desert stretching from the Gulf of Kuwait to the Gulf of Aqaba and forming the transition from the fertile coastal region to the Arabian desert proper, has become a great international highway which, when the British railway is built, will rival the Suez Canal in importance as a British imperial route and a bridge between two worlds.

In order that this route might lead exclusively through territory under direct British control or allied to Great Britain, it was necessary to establish a united block of territories from the Mediterranean to the Persian Gulf. In the years immediately following the World War English statesmen harboured more far-reaching intentions. To realize old imperialistic aims, Lloyd George, Winston Churchill, and Lord Birkenhead schemed for a Middle Eastern Empire, which was to extend from Egypt to India, to include Arabia and Persia, and to be protected on the north by the possession of Constantinople and by influence in the Caucasus and Trans-Caspia. In 1919 and 1920 the realization of this scheme did not appear distant. There were English troops in Constantinople, in the Caucasus, in Trans-Caspia, in Persia ; Greek troops were advancing, paving the way for Britain, into Asia Minor where, moreover, the newly created States of Armenia and Kurdistan were designed to serve the same end ; Egypt, Palestine, and Mesopotamia were under direct British administration ; and Great Britain was at that time endeavouring to prevent France from establishing herself in Syria.

The events of the period from 1920 to 1922 reduced these schemes to much more modest dimensions. All that remained was the connection from Cairo and Haifa to Baghdad and Basra, which seemed to be menaced after 1921 by the rapidly rising power of Ibn Saud when he had subjugated the Emirate of Jebel Shammar and thus gained possession of the two chief roads leading northwards from Inner Arabia, the Wadi Rummah leading to Basra, and the Wadi Sirhan to Trans-Jordan. For the next four years British policy in Arabia was occupied in fixing the new frontiers. This was achieved in 1922 and 1923 in the direction of Wadi Rummah between south-western Iraq and north-eastern Nejd. In the district of Wadi Sirhan between Trans-Jordan and Nejd the frontier was so defined at the beginning of November, 1925, that a corridor was created about a hundred kilometres in width, joining Trans-Jordan and Iraq. By the two Treaties of Haddah and Bahrah, Nejd lost its common frontier with the French mandated territory of Syria, and Ibn Saud, who pointed out that the ancient, free trade-route from Damascus to Hail in the Jebel Shammar was economically necessary to his subjects, could only secure free transit across the corridor. The British imperial route from the Mediterranean to the Persian Gulf was established, and was further secured by the annexation of Aqaba, which added a third strategic point on the Red Sea to the two on the Mediterranean and the Persian Gulf.

MOTOR TRANSIT AND AIRCRAFT

But for the present the railway is of less importance in transcontinental communications between Europe, Asia, and Africa than motor transit and aircraft. Both have captured the East in recent years, set a new stamp upon desert traffic, and opened up new possibilities to administration and warfare in these regions. Motor transit has not the economic and strategic advantages of railway communication, but it is mobile and adaptable and cheap to install. Whereas in Europe railways formerly proved superior to road transit, which is only now recovering its importance, the East has been able largely to skip the era of the railway. Motor transit follows the ancient caravan routes which have determined the interchange of merchandise and culture between East and West for thousands of years. Even in everyday life in the remotest regions it is ousting the camel and the other traditional means of communication. Whereas aircraft has hitherto remained for the most part in the hands of European governments and companies—it was not till 1930 that the

Governments of Egypt and Iraq and Ibn Saud's administration began to make preparations for the developments of
their own air fleets—the motor-car has already thoroughly
established itself in the East. Since 1923 there has been a
regular motor service through the desert from Beirut and
Damascus via the Rutbah Oasis to Baghdad. Palestine,
Trans-Jordan, Syria, and Iraq, but chiefly the Hejaz and
Nejd, are being opened up on all sides by motor transit.
The desert motor service from Baghdad to Damascus is
used both for mails and passengers. In 1929 it carried 18,000
persons.[4] From Baghdad there are regular motor services
to Tehran. But as a regular means of transport the motor-car
is confined to relatively small areas. It is aircraft that connects
continents within a few days or hours. The great air lines of
the Old World which are already working or shortly to begin
working meet in the Egypto-Arabian region.

The pioneer in this field was the British air fleet, which
set up a regular postal service from Cairo to Baghdad in
1921, and so brought the Persian Gulf within a day's journey
of the Mediterranean. A few years later the military
administration handed over this line to Imperial Airways
to run. The future British transverse railway line from the
Mediterranean to India has already been anticipated by
aircraft. Until 1929 an air service went at first once a
fortnight, then once a week from Egypt via southern
Palestine, Trans-Jordan, and the Rutbah Oasis to Baghdad
and Basra. For several years this was the only air line from
the Mediterranean to the Persian Gulf. From April 1st, 1929,
this Hither Asian air service was extended from Egypt to
London, and from Basra along the southern shore of the
Persian Gulf to Karachi in north-western India. Thus the
plan of rapid communication between Europe and India,
pursued for decades, was realized.[5] The extension of the air
service from Iraq across southern Persia to India met with
opposition, due to the suspicions of the Persian Government.
The Persians demanded that the air route should pass over
the interior of the country, the English insisted on a route
along the shore of the Persian Gulf, which, in case of need,
could be defended from the sea by British ships. After
prolonged negotiations Persia consented upon conditions
for three years. Meanwhile Great Britain is endeavouring

to find the necessary bases on islands in the Persian Gulf in order to extend the route from Basra over the Persian Gulf to India. Thence it is to be continued actually next year (1932) to Singapore, and there to branch to Australia and Hong-Kong. The great air route across East Africa to Cape Town starts at Cairo. It, too, is almost entirely across British territory. Thus Imperial Airways will embrace almost the entire Old World in their system of air services. The vital centre of these air communications, the axis of transcontinental traffic, will be situated in the Egypto-Arabian region, in Cairo and Baghdad.

Baghdad is becoming the centre of air communications in Hither Asia. A French air route leads from Marseilles to Beirut, and thence to Baghdad, whence it has been extended since January, 1931, across India to Saigon in French Indo-China. In addition to this twofold connection of Baghdad with Europe by air, there is that provided by Junkers with Tehran, whence their aircraft connect with Europe via Baku and Moscow. The intense rivalry of the Powers interested in the Hither East before the World War in the field of railway construction is celebrating its resurrection in the air. It accentuates anew territorial political problems. Arabia and Egypt, on the geographical frontier of two worlds, acquire fresh importance. The land route from Europe to India, the air route from Europe to South Africa, have now been opened up for the first time by modern means of transport in such a way that the command of the seas is no longer enough. British Oriental policy, which has been determined for the past hundred and fifty years by care for the defence of India and its sea communications, has been confronted since the World War with the task of exploring new paths. Instead of the establishment and defence of coaling stations, the requirement of the near future will be the protection of the oil supply. This leads to the evocation of hitherto unknown subjects of dispute between the Powers. But not only have the new routes and means of communication raised new political problems, they have also begun to call forth a new cultural and social order.

II

FROM THE MIDDLE AGES TO THE MODERN ERA

THE NEW NATIONALISM

IN 1909 two European colonial governors, one an Englishman in British India, the other a Russian in Turkistan, called attention to the change beginning to take place in the social and cultural consciousness of the colonial races. Lord Ronaldshay at that time, speaking to the Central Asian Society in London—to men, that is, who had been engaged in political administration and scholarly research in the East, said : " Problems of far greater significance to the world as a whole, and to Great Britain in particular, are arising, which merit the most earnest thought and study on the part of members of our Society. I refer to the problems presented by the growing desire for self-assertion which is stirring the pulses of the Eastern races themselves. . . . This . . . is certain— that contact with Western thought and Western ideals has exercised a revivifying influence upon all the races of the East." *

That same year the Russian Governor-General of Turkistan wrote : " The wars, so astonishing in their consequences, and the social and economic questions which have recently come everywhere unexpectedly to the fore, have stirred even the Mohammedan world in its persistent inertia. A process of development has gone on within it : first the ideas of Pan-Islamism, then increasingly keen national ambitions, and of late openly revolutionary separatist ambitions have begun to reveal themselves. All that has stirred our hitherto inert Mohammedan masses to the depths of the social order and has roused in their midst a clear movement of ideas favouring national union and individual freedom, and indeed even Socialist ideas." [6]

Twenty years later India was involved in a struggle for

* Proceedings of the Central Asiatic Society Annual Meeting, June 29th, 1909, pp. 9, 10.

independence which fully occupied the attention of Great
Britain and the world, and in Turkistan the Russian province
under a Governor-General had been superseded by national
Socialist Republics. The words of those two statesmen had
been spoken at the parting of two epochs in the East. Ancient
ideas and conceptions were beginning to yield place to new.
Not the struggle for independence in Eastern countries, not
their resistance to foreign conquerors were new. What was
new were the forms assumed by that resistance and the ideas
lying at its roots. Whereas formerly resistance was dictated
by tradition and religion and took the form of the exclusion
of all that was alien and new, laying stress upon what was
stable and unchangeable, it now assumed the forms of a
nationalist movement and began to adopt European ways
of life and thought and to seek salvation precisely in change
and adaptation, since only so was there any hope of organizing
resistance successfully. Europe's superiority in the field of
technical science and organization, to which men had formerly
closed their eyes, was acknowledged, and people gradually
realized that Europe could be overcome only with its own
weapons. The national liberation movements in Europe in
the nineteenth century were taken as a model. Just as in
eastern Europe the nations without a history had been roused
in the nineteenth century to self-consciousness and the
endeavour to play an active part in history, so now the peoples
of the Orient were roused from a period of mediaeval feudalism
and religion to one instinct with the watchwords of
nationalism and middle-class capitalism. The conditions of
life in the East before the beginning of the present century,
which still prevail in its remoter parts, correspond to those of
mediaeval Europe, or of eastern Europe before the reforms of
Peter the Great. A traveller in the Middle Ages passing from
Europe through Asia did not find himself in a world differing
in its social order and its habits of thought, as was the case
in the nineteenth century. Even to-day we hear a similar
account of the conditions of life in Chinese Turkistan :
" At the present time conditions of life in Chinese Turkistan
are practically those that obtained all over Europe, and over
much of the East, in the days when Marco Polo found himself
so much at home in Central Asia. To anyone who has read
mediaeval history, it is sometimes almost uncanny to see how

life in Turkistan reproduces the distinctive features of life in Europe during the Middle Ages." [7]

The East, then, is entering upon an epoch in which nationalism is the highest and most vitally symbolic social and intellectual form and sets its stamp upon the whole era. A few years back religion was the determining factor in the East. Nationalism is not ousting religion, but more or less rapidly it is taking a place beside it, frequently fortifying it, beginning to transform and impair it. National symbols are acquiring religious authority and sacramental inviolability. The truth which men will defend with their lives is no longer exclusively religious, on occasion even it is no longer religious at all, but in increasing measure national. This process has been carried through with tempestuous speed in Turkey ; more cautiously it is going on in Arabia and Egypt. At the present day nationalism is in harmony with the newly arising social order. In the social order of Europe it had its significance and justification when there was need to supersede feudalism and tribal and local patriotism based upon agriculture, local markets, and small towns, and to rise to the larger territorial units required by the capitalist economic system. Nationalism was the intellectual form assumed by the needs of incipient capitalism and the youthful middle class. In the West to-day, when industry and social forces demand fields of activity which cross and shatter national frontiers, nationalism is in reality an outworn myth which, however, for that very reason clings obstinately to its place in men's thought, resorts to violence and, since it is no longer capable of mastering social and economic problems, throws off its early democratic guise and tends towards dictatorship. In the East nationalism still, or already—according to whether we regard the situation from the standpoint of Europe to-day or of the East in the recent past—meets social and economic needs. Capitalist forms of industry are making their way into the East, money economy and industrialization are taking their place beside barter and agriculture, and a youthful middle class is arising, becoming conscious of its mission and task, and entering upon a struggle against the feudal nobility. In so doing it feels itself to stand not for its own interests alone, but for the whole people, who are beginning to acquire national

consciousness. The forms assumed by this economic transformation and social upward trend are similar to those which
are familiar in European history ; here, too, the middle class
speaks the language of nationalism and democracy.

Countries like Egypt and Syria, in which this social process
is already in full swing, offer the spectacle of fully developed
nationalist movements in which nationalist habits of mind
have erased religious divisions from the consciousness of the
politically dominant sections of the population. In Nejd or
the Yemen, where the process of social and economic transformation has not yet begun, the people's aspirations towards
independence are still religious and mediaeval in character.
But the outstanding statesman of those territories, Ibn Saud,
is aware of the transitional nature of his political mission, and
Arabian youth in Syria and Palestine, even in the Christian
community, places its hopes largely in the strictly
Mohammedan desert Bedouin Ibn Saud. Even the Indian
Mohammedans have not been able to ignore the facts,
though they have resisted nationalist tendencies in a far
greater measure than the Turks, Egyptians, or Persians, and
have stressed a religious type of nationalism (characteristically
the Mohammedans in India have also offered a much more
vigorous and protracted resistance than the Hindus to the
penetration of a capitalist, middle-class economic system and
habit of mind). At the very time when the Turks in the first
article of their National Pact of January 28th, 1920, expressly
renounced the Arabian provinces of the Ottoman Empire
and, therefore, the Holy Cities of Islam, possession of which
was of the utmost importance to the religious Islamic State
of the Caliph, the Indian Caliphate delegation led by
Mohammed Ali declared on January 19th, 1920, to the Indian
Viceroy, and on March 19th to Lloyd George, that the Caliph
must retain his dominion over the three Holy Cities of Mecca,
Medina, and Jerusalem, since otherwise the peace treaty would
be inacceptable to every Mohammedan believer. " This is
the one governing consideration on which attention must be
focussed, and so potent is it that even if the Ottoman Turks
could be made to acquiesce in such a settlement, it would remain as unacceptable as ever to every believing Musalman." *

* Address of the Caliphate deputation to the Viceroy. *Times of
India*, January 20th, 1920.

Hardly a decade later one of the champions of Islam in India, S. Khuda Bukhsh, wrote in the leading Mohammedan periodical in India on the subject of the awakening of Islam : "The abolition of the Caliphate will, indeed, endure and permanently endure to the entire benefit of Islam. It will fashion for Islam a new sense of unity, founded not upon fiction but truth . . . With fullest consciousness has Islam realized that its future lies in its powers of cohesion and solidarity. It has further realized that that solidarity should draw its strength and sustenance from a scheme of things, real and vital, and that scheme is naught else save that of *Nationalism*, and Nationalism pure and undefiled. . . . That such is the trend of events is clear to all who seriously scan the political horizon."

And the Indian writer cites approvingly the words of the American, Wilson Cash : "The youth of Islam to-day is thinking in terms of politics more than religion. He is often far more interested in his nation's welfare than in the spread of Islam. The solidarity of Islam is not a question of the Caliphate, or the sheriah (religious law), but almost entirely a matter of political unity in the face of the West." *

NATIONALISM AND RELIGION

The difference between modern times and the Middle Ages may be expressed briefly by saying that the distinguishing mark of modern times is the notion of nationality and of all that it involves. *The Cambridge Modern History* begins with stating this fact.[8] Arabia and Egypt stand at the parting of two eras, the mediaeval and the modern, and the most concise symbolic expression of that fact is the statement that those regions have entered or are entering upon the age of nationalism. Intellectually and politically this takes effect primarily in two directions. As in earlier days in Europe, the nation is welded to a unit right across religious lines of cleavage ; religious differences lose their

---

* S. Khuda Bukhsh, "The Awakening of Islam " : *The Muslim Review* (Calcutta). Reprinted in *The Moslem World*, vol. xx, No. 1, p. 5 ff. The quotation from Wilson Cash is in *The Expansion of Islam* (Edinburgh House Press, 1928), p. 257. The word "nationalism " is printed in italics in the original.

importance. That is rendered possible not, indeed, by the disappearance of religion, not necessarily by any diminution of spiritual fervour, but by the fact that, whereas formerly it embraced the whole of men's personal and social life, it now abandons more and more of public life and the inner life of the soul to secularization. " It is amazing to observe how Islam is endeavouring to catch up in a few decades with a development that it has taken Christianity centuries to achieve, and how startlingly similar the ways and means adopted often are, thereby perhaps revealing once more the kindred origin and character of the two religions." This process is going on uniformly amongst all Mohammedan and Oriental peoples. " Only when we observe the uniform direction of progress—uniform, in spite of all minor differences, amongst all peoples and in all countries and similar in character in all fields of culture—only then do we discern its immense significance and are driven to the conviction that in very truth we are standing at the threshold of a new era in world history." This change has taken place not only within the pale of Islam but also in Oriental Christianity which, like Islam, did not share in the transformation that Europe underwent in the Renaissance and the age of rationalism.[9] The East is now making good the omission. A secular, rationalist, middle-class consciousness is arising. The world is losing much of the element of the miraculous to which men had no choice but to submit ; it is undergoing a process of rationalization ; because it is inherently subject to law its future can be calculated, and so it arouses man's initiative and sense of responsibility. As in Europe, it is the upper classes who are first seized with the spirit of rationalism. " What first appeared to be a difference between two eras, thus becomes a cleavage within a national community, a class distinction." The rational and enlightened form a separate class which has thus a historical mission to fulfil towards the whole social body.[10] And here it is not so much a question of ideas capable of definite formulation as of shifting emphasis and the transformation of values. Based upon the past and invariably linked with it, yet in perpetual, not always conscious, antagonism to it, a new life-sense grows up, not merely new intellectual concepts but something springing from the actual facts of life.

This process leads to a quantitative and qualitative transformation of religion, not to its dissolution. Religion ceases to be a decisive political factor, but remains in varying measure a life-force. Precisely from nationalism, from the consciousness of a bond with the past, from the new, critical spirit, it draws fresh vitality, finds itself confronted with fresh problems, is roused from its torpor, and puts forth a host of new shoots. What characterizes the transition period through which Mohammedan civilization is now passing is the tension in Islam in the conflict between change and inertia.

In 1928 the Turkish Republic proclaimed the definite severance of the State from Islam. Exactly twenty years earlier Turkey had been a theocracy based upon Islam. Religion had been the moulding, constitutive force in all fields of political, social, and personal life. Even at the time when Turkey was changing from a theocracy to a constitutional monarchy and later to a republic, nationalism was, indeed, superseding religion as the motive force in political and personal life, but the bond with Islam remained unaffected and gave a stay to the Republic in its youthful years throughout Islam. With a radical vigour that is characteristic of a transition period, the reformers in the Turkish Republic severed the bond that united them with Islam ; in the abolition of the Caliphate, which in itself meant the renunciation of the predominance willingly conceded to them in Islam, and in the secularization of their State, they have gone further than many European countries. Islam has become the private concern of the individual in Turkey. It has no longer the smallest connection with public life, with the Turkish nation, with the State. The President of the Republic no longer takes the oath of loyalty to the constitution in the name of God, but upon his individual, independent honour.

Turkey wishes no longer to stand at the parting of two eras ; she wishes to pass the boundary. Thus, whilst the Turks constitute the left wing of present-day Islam, nowise typical of it, the Wahabis and Yemenites constitute the right wing ; their conservatism and religious fanaticism are also no longer characteristic of Islam as a whole, and they have not yet reached the parting of two eras. Islam is endeavouring to reach a living adjustment and a historical solution of this tension, although it will gradually move in the direction of the Turkish reforms. To-day at the cultural boundary line, progressive adaptation to the West and the rationalization of economic and social life on the one hand, on the other the romantic affirmation of traditional ways of life and aspirations towards religious revival, hold the balance and are striving to remould an Islam conscious of its individual quality. Islam will continue to communicate to the peoples who profess it those vital forces of which it is capable and which have moulded their lives for so many centuries, but at the same time it will succeed in adapting itself to the demands of modern life and will not bar the road to that temper of mind which constitutes the greatness of Europe, with its dominance of natural forces and its achievements in the fields of organization and technical science.

In Egypt and Arabia Turkey's radical reforms were received with equanimity. Only twenty-five years ago the Turks, the Arabians, and the Egyptians described themselves first and foremost as Mohammedans. They were not yet conscious of ethnical designations, or only accorded them secondary consideration. To-day the Mohammedan is primarily a member of his nation or a citizen of his State, and only afterwards a Mohammedan.[11] What unites the Mohammedans is a common resistance to colonial penetration. The endeavours to revive the Caliphate can lead nowhere. The Caliphate is no longer in place in the present-day intellectual and political scheme of the Islamic world. For the Caliphate was not a spiritual or ecclesiastical institution, but a political and governmental one. It is not only in Turkey that this function of Islam is near its end. Probably the spiritual function of Islam has as long a future in Turkey as Christianity had with the coming of rationalism and secularization.

MODERN YOUTH

Directly after the World War, in the intoxicating experience of national unity which then first swept over the peoples of the East with exceptional vehemence, all religious differences seemed to vanish. Mohammedans and Copts in Egypt, Mohammedans and Christians in Palestine and Syria, Shi'ahs and Sunnis in Mesopotamia, Mohammedans and Hindus in India, fought side by side for a revolution in their political conditions. To-day the new national consciousness still persists, it is a factor in the history of these countries without which they can no longer be conceived, one which will mould their political history and their social and cultural development. In the home of Egypto-Arabian civilization religious differences will no longer play a part in politics. And this in spite of or, rather, just because of, the imperialist and reactionary policy of hindering the emergence and consolidation of united political consciousness by supporting and introducing religious or ethnical minorities. At the same time the religious and cultural bonds of Islam retain their vitality. Ancient forces are stirred to new life ; Islamic youth consciously and proudly seeks to link itself with tradition, to search out what it contains of value, to separate that from what is no longer in harmony with the times, and to create a rejuvenated Islam that takes over what is best in the Occident and vies with European cultures.

These young people combat the arrogance of Europe which confronts them as the bearer of civilization ; they repudiate missions and Christianity, though doubtless these have given them stimulus and guidance on their new path ; now, however, that they are advancing along their own path they believe that they have no further need of them. They find themselves faced by a number of fresh problems unknown to their fathers, with which the amazingly rapid change in the intellectual and social state of the East has confronted the young. New forces have entered into the lives of the young, and have created for the first time a Mohammedan Youth Movement. For centuries there had been no antagonism and no difference between fathers and sons in the East. Now men's relation to life, to the family, to Nature, is altogether changed. Sport, the love of rambling, the Pathfinders' movement, have captured the youth of the East, and the individual problems of love and marriage have entered into their emotional life. The education of girls, which is beginning on all hands, changes the relation of the sexes. Moreover, the young people aspire, though they have not yet the power, to make an end of the ancient, hereditary abuses of Oriental politics : dilatory methods and lack of initiative and energetic determination, the low standard of social responsibility, inability to sacrifice personal interests to the general good, and nepotism.

The Mohammedan Youth Societies were the focus of these aspirations. In the East the Young Men's Christian Associations had exercised an awakening influence both culturally and politically. It was often through them that the world of modern thought reached the youth of the East, and not Christian youth alone. In recent years Young Men's Mohammedan Associations have sprung up in Egypt, Syria, Palestine, and Iraq, and seek to provide similar intellectual and social centres for the youth of Islam. In the latter half of April, 1928, a conference of Mohammedan Youth Societies took place in Jaffa, with 120 delegates from Palestine. They resolved to issue a declaration in favour of the establishment of national Mohammedan schools and to ask the Government to open new schools and to modify the curricula of the foreign schools in a national spirit. They resolved on a badge, a song, and a banner for the confederation. Pathfinders' Clubs were to be started everywhere, to be affiliated to the Union of Mohammedan Pathfinders in Beirut, and their members were to be pledged to adhere to the faith. On the European model Friday was to be consecrated in a new spirit and to be kept as a weekly day of rest ; Mohammedan festivals were to be observed and new forms to be found for them. Amongst the remaining demands we may call attention particularly to the organization of evening classes for workers, the encouragement of the Arabic theatre, the establishment of Young Women's Mohammedan Associations, systematic child welfare, and the free treatment of the sick poor. These resolutions breathe a new spirit, unknown in Islam but a short time ago. They are influenced by Europe, but they seek to transplant such ideas to the soil of a rejuvenated Islam and to attain a synthesis within Islam. Moreover, the rising generation, both Mohammedan and Christian, is far more radical politically than the preceding one, thanks to the new school education and to European University training. Not only does it place national demands in the forefront with increasing rigour, but its mind is awake to the social problems and the necessity of new solutions in every sphere.

This mental change reveals itself in a multitude of forms which recall the corresponding stage in Europe's history. Just as once in Europe religion turned back to its origins across centuries that were felt to be a period of degeneration, and found in them the possibility of a purer doctrine, more in harmony with the spirit of the age, so to-day the reformers of Islam in Egypt, Turkey, and India turn back to primitive Islam and seek thence to renew the fresh creative force of free inquiry at the source. This tendency is taking the form of a rationalist cult of reason, for which the fundamental doctrines of Islam offer more support than those of mediaeval Christianity. It is not so much religious questions as the social decrees of Islam that are the centre of interest. Progressive Mohammedans reject scriptural proof in such questions as meaningless, and all reformers recognize that the social institutions prescribed or permitted in the Koran are historically conditioned and no longer justified at the present time.

THE NEW RELIGION

These aspirations are finding practical expression in the lives of the people in all Mohammedan countries, whilst it is primarily in Egypt that they find theoretical expression. Reformers and rationalizers in Islam have recently arisen there, and around them a struggle has ensued like that once fought in Europe. Efforts have been made there in several books to provide a scholarly basis for the general tendencies that are working themselves out in an unconscious process of gradual transition, and to interpret and explain to the public the process by which Islam is being transformed. They have not only met with antagonism among the conservatively minded clergy, but have played a part in political life and occupied the attention of Ministries and of Parliament.

The centre of religious conservatism, which here, too, feels itself closely akin to political conservatism, is the Mosque of El Azhar with its venerable theological University, which has hitherto borne the aspect of a mediaeval institution alike in the outward form of its teaching methods and in its

curriculum.   Nevertheless, Egypt's earliest reformers have
issued from its walls.   The greatest of them was Mohammed
Abdu, a disciple of Jemal ud Din el Afghani, who regarded
the purification of Islam and the revival of its early
philosophical greatness as the means whereby the Islamic
peoples would rise to their former political power and glory.
Jemal ud Din's influence was, perhaps, the strongest spiritual
ferment of the last century.   Mohammed Abdu was no stormy
petrel, but a Humanist of that tranquil yet forceful temper
that has characterized the first reformers in all religions,
men who have descried the light of a new era and have
advanced towards it with circumspection and deliberation.
He aspired to such a harmonious synthesis of knowledge
and faith as he believed to be discernible in the Islam of
earlier centuries.   To him religion was " a brake given to us
by God in order to avoid the excesses of the human reason
and diminish its errors, and to enable us to reach that state
for which divine wisdom has destined mankind.   If we understand religion in this sense it becomes the true friend of
learning, an incitement to absorb ourselves in the mysteries
of the universe, a call to respect well established truths ".
Mohammed Abdu was no politician.   To him what mattered
was quiet education in a new spirit.   Nevertheless, dying in
1905 as Grand Mufti of Egypt, he exercised a revolutionary
influence upon the traditional conception of religion, of
submission to the conditions of our life, and of the position
of the monarch.   " We teach that the sovereign, although we
owe him obedience, is only human like everybody else, is
subject to error and the prey of his passions, and that only
his people's counsel can enable him to avoid errors and bridle
his passions."

Modern reformers of Islam in Egypt go further than
Mohammed Abdu.   In the past decade two books have
given rise to animated discussion in the Egyptian Parliament
and among the people : Sheikh Ali Abdel Razek's *Islam and
the Principles of the State* and Taha Hussein's *On Pre-Islamic
Poetry*.   Both writers had sprung from the school of El Azhar.
Ali Abdel Razek had gone to Oxford after completing his
studies, and on his return home, as judge in an ecclesiastical
court, he wrote a learned book examining the principles of
Islam in the light of an intellectual rationalism in order to

disengage religion from the network of outworn tradition. Taha Hussein, who completed his studies at the Sorbonne, is a professor in the philosophical faculty of the Egyptian University.[12] He examined the pre-Islamic poetry of the Arabs and the traditions about their pre-Islamic civilization without regard to the legends consecrated by the Islamic religion. Certain things he declared to be apocryphal and legendary, and the Ulemas demanded the suppression of the book and the expulsion of the heretic from the University, since Islam was the State religion in Egypt, and it was the duty of the State to watch over the safety and purity of the faith. In 1926, and again in the spring of 1930, when a second edition of the book appeared in which the impugned passages had been suppressed, it was the subject of parliamentary discussion.

But it was precisely this dependence of the State upon the Church, the erection of religion into a State institution, which Ali Abdel Razek attacked in his book, and for this he was removed from his office as ecclesiastical judge by the unanimous vote of the Senate of El Azhar University. By citing the earliest sources he wished to prove that Islam was only a religion in the modern sense, not an institution embracing the whole of political and social life, not a State ; that Mohammed had been a religious prophet, not a king and ruler ; and that the Caliphate with its political authority was alien to primitive Islam. Islam had only a spiritual, universal mission, it appealed to the individual conscience, but originally it was in no way associated with political, governmental institutions, and what was needed was to detach it from them once more in order to restore its pristine purity.

By means of this reinterpretation which, however, like most reformers, he represents as a rediscovery of the original meaning, this modernist confesses an Islam in harmony with reason and science and permitting all progress in political and social life. Political institutions like monarchy and social institutions like polygamy are in no way parts of religion. That they have only become through a calamitous confusion of the essence of religion with social and political institutions. If a rejuvenated Islam is to hold up its head beside the European nations, it must probe its foundations, as they have been handed down unquestioned in recent centuries, by the methods of reason. Stripped of their learned garb and diluted, these perceptions have been penetrating the broad masses of the people and paving the way for the reforms which have set in throughout the intellectual and social life of the Hither East.

Latterly reforms have been effected even in the University of El Azhar, though political influences have obstructed the thorough reforms that have long been planned. Outward forms are to be modernized. The mosque is to be devoted solely to its proper purpose, and round about it modern buildings are to be erected to house the University and its students. The curriculum, which underwent its first reform in 1911, was to have been modernized after the autumn of 1929, together with the whole study of theology in Egypt. The University was to include a Faculty of Mohammedan Theology, one of Canon Law, and one of Arabic Language and Literature. In all faculties European languages and modern subjects were to be taught. When these external and internal reforms are carried out in El Azhar, the new education of the Mohammedan intelligentsia will exercise an influence on the whole of Egyptian life and hasten the process of modernization even outside the cities. Simultaneously the tendency is at work to accord to the life of the spirit beyond the pale of religion the position which is due to it according to modern ideas. For instance, we see the establishment of the Egyptian University in 1925, which provides a new basis for the existing institutions for higher education in Egypt; the endeavours to found an Arabic Academy and to produce a new Arabic Encyclopædia and an all-inclusive dictionary; the encouragement of the Arabic theatre, for which translations are to supply, with the help of the Ministry of Education, a programme of the best plays culled from the literature of the whole world; and the rise of modern plastic and pictorial art in Egypt. The solemn unveiling in Cairo on May 20th, 1928, of the allegorical group by the sculptor Mahmud Mukhtar, representing the liberation of Egypt, the intended erection of a mausoleum in the ancient Egyptian style, and a number of statues in which the nation pays honour to Saad Zaghlul Pasha, the encouragement of Schools of Art and Handicrafts, the establishment of Conservatoire to foster Oriental music, both improving Arabic stringed instruments by the introduction of other Oriental and Western instruments, and at the same time fostering the study of European music—these are innovations introduced into Egypt during the last decade.

These innovations are not confined to Egypt. They are imitated in the other progressive Arab countries. The fiftieth anniversary in 1926 of the oldest existing Arabic periodical, *El Moktataf*, in Cairo, founded by Syrian Christians, was a festal occasion for the whole Arab world. At the celebration in the great Opera House in Cairo all Arabic literature and art and the world of public affairs and politics in Egypt were represented. Deputations and greetings had come from all countries of Arabic speech and from distant continents where there are Arab emigrant settlements. The three greatest Arabic poets in Egypt, Ahmed Bey Shawki, Khalil Bey Mutran, and Hafiz Bey Ibrahim, also appear on public occasions and at public ceremonies as mouthpieces of the nation. The celebrations in honour of Ahmed Shawki at the end of April, 1927, in Cairo became a magnificent demonstration of Arab unity from Morocco to Iraq, from Lebanon to the Yemen, a rapturous festal week of national exaltation and memories of past greatness, giving sure promise for the future, an experience which is only granted to nations at the great turning-points in their destiny.[13]

THE MODERN WOMAN

The radical wing of Islam, Turkey and the Mohammedan peoples of the Soviet Union, have taken a decisive plunge into the modern era by emancipating their women and placing them on an equality with men in the eyes of the law and in public life. In this matter Egypt and Arabia are still at the parting of two epochs. In Egypt and in the more progressive Arabian countries the movement for women's emancipation has started in the past decade, and has already scored successes in the matter of the marriage law. But in 1930 the veil has not been dropped even in Egypt and Syria and woman is still far from being equal to man in her position. Politically women have played an active part since the World War in their people's national efforts for liberation. They have taken a leading part in demonstrations, have appeared in public, and have held congresses in order to urge the same national demands as their husbands. Zaghlul's wife, Safia, always stood beside him, and during his exile she represented him and was accorded the title of honour of " Mother of the Egyptians ". Gathered around her, a group of society ladies were active in the political support of Zaghlul.

It was in Egypt that the women's movement first assumed considerable dimensions, with Hoda Sharavi at the head, the widow of Sharavi Pasha who had accompanied Zaghlul in November, 1918, when he repaired to the British High Commissioner to present Egypt's demands. In March, 1923, a Union of Egyptian Women was founded which sent a delegation to the Congress of the International Alliance of Women in Rome in 1923. In her address there Hoda Sharavi referred to the false conceptions of women's position in Islam prevalent in the West. All that women needed in Islam was education and a reform of the marriage law in order fully to secure her due position. " It is particularly as a result of the great patriotic movement of 1919 that Egyptian women have been roused, at a moment when the whole nation needed all its forces in order to demand its independence. At that time women associated themselves with men and took active part in the struggle, writing in the papers and founding journals. With their own resources they set up handicraft schools for the poor, opened clinics for necessitous children, and organized literary and educational groups." [14]

The Bill dealing with the Mohammedan marriage law introduced in 1929 may be regarded as a success scored by the Egyptian women's movement. It makes divorce more difficult, whereas hitherto a husband has been able to repudiate his wife at any time without any formalities. The wife, too, acquires the right to sue for a divorce, if her husband puts himself so far in the wrong towards her that life together becomes unbearable. She can sue for a divorce before the Cadi, if her husband has deserted her for more than a year without adequate reason, or if he has been condemned to at least three years' imprisonment. The Bill also provides new regulations governing the husband's obligation to maintain his wife and cases of dispute about the dowry. If it is to the interest of the children, sons may be left with the mother till their ninth year, and daughters till their eleventh. Divorce declared by the husband is void if the formula is pronounced by him under compulsion or in a state of inebriation. Though these provisions, according to modern ideas, only represent obvious limitations in the interpretation of the previously existing law, the further stipulation that divorce pronounced by the husband without the intervention of the ecclesiastical judge is a punishable offence constitutes a change of far-reaching significance. The judge to whom the husband must appeal cannot refuse a divorce, but he must examine the reasons for it, and must endeavour to bring about a reconciliation. These reforms, whilst leaving the traditional foundations untouched, aim at adapting existing legal standards to the new social conditions. The provisions of the law are intended to prevent the hitherto frequent abuses. The Bill does not abolish polygamy, but it renders a second marriage more difficult by requiring the husband to prove before the ecclesiastical judge that he is in a position, financially and morally, to make full and adequate provision for his wives and for other persons who have valid claims upon him.

In the matter of women's emancipation Cairo is more progressive than Syria or Iraq. The programme of the Egyptian women's movement is primarily social ; it founds schools and training centres for women and girls who work for their living, instructs girls of the lower classes in schools of housewifery, so as to create a class of Egyptian female domestic servants, and trains nurses in the care of children, infants, and the sick. There is no active opposition to the veil either in Egypt or Syria. But an incident that occurred in Beirut in May, 1928, is significant of the gradual change in opinion. The number of Mohammedan women who appeared in public unveiled was increasing in that seaport with its large Christian population. A movement of protest was started, and leaflets called upon Mohammedans to take steps against unveiled women. The following Friday the Mohammedan clergy in the mosques spoke against this leaflet and demanded respect for individual freedom.

In Syria, Iraq, and Palestine also an organized women's movement has begun. In April, 1928, the first meeting of

Syrian women took place, dealing with questions of education and professional training for girls and the reform of the marriage law and marriage customs. The Mohammedan Women's League in Syria has suggested annual conferences of Arab women, to meet successively in Egypt, Syria, Palestine, and Iraq. In Palestine the Arab women's movement was first organized in the autumn of 1929, but for the present it pursues exclusively nationalist aims, the support of the struggle for Arab liberation. In Iraq, too, a Society to Raise the Position of Women has been called into existence in Baghdad after previous attempts that had been quickly abandoned. In Egypt and Syria there is a Press devoted to the interests of women and largely edited by women.[15]

The first congress of women of the Arab countries took place in Damascus in July, 1930, and was designed as a demonstration of Oriental unity. Delegations or greetings and reports were sent from the Hejaz, Iraq, Turkey, Persia, Afghanistan, and Mohammedan India. The International Alliance of Women had also sent a representative. For the first time a link was established between the Hither Asian and the general women's movements. Nur Hamadah, the president of the Congress, which was held in the building of the Arab University at Damascus, advocated confining the struggle for the present to the elevation of women culturally and socially, and not demanding their political rights. They must not, she said, antagonize by radical demands those whose help they needed in order to solve the educational problem. She warned them against publicly combating the veil. The Mohammedan woman's veil was contrary to nature, nor was it enjoined by religion. It would disappear of itself as the standard of women's education rose. A public campaign against it could only rouse stubborn opposition. Besides questions of education, the congress discussed reforms in the marriage law along similar lines as in Egypt and the problems of social welfare activities on behalf of working women. It demanded a reform of traditional marriage customs. Man and wife must know one another before marriage, and the importance attached to the purchase price amongst Mohammedans and the dowry amongst Christians must be combated. A unanimous resolution pledged the congress to devote itself to work for Arabic culture and to favour native Arab products and manufactures. The close association of the Mohammedan and Christian women of Arabia and Egypt in working to these ends, it declared, would render the women's movement an important factor of cultural and social progress in those countries.

It is only in a geographical sense that the Jewish women's movement in Palestine falls within this sphere. Amongst the Jewish population of Palestine the women in orthodox and Oriental Jewish circles are on a par with Arab women in their cultural and social organization. The Jewish women immigrants who have come to Palestine from Europe during the past five and twenty years, on the other hand, have brought with them the most progressive notions on the cultural, social, and political activities of women and have realized them in exemplary activities of organization. The girls, like the boys, all attend school, women's societies play a leading part in public health and social welfare, they devote themselves particularly to the training of girls and women for suitable professions, and lead the opposition to early marriage and the backwardness of Oriental Jewesses ; contrary to the ideas of orthodox and Oriental Judaism, moreover, women have secured complete political equality in Palestinian Jewry after prolonged struggles. Thanks to the efforts of Jewish women the Palestinian Government felt obliged to admit women to the Bar in 1930. But national and political considerations prevent any direct contact between the Jewish and Arab women's movements in Palestine.

Another instance of the fact that the nationalist movements in Arabia and Egypt still stand at a point of cultural transition is that they evince far less cultural than political enthusiasm and vigour. The masses of the people have already awakened to political and national consciousness. Their political interest, their political passion, and their active participation in political and national questions are remarkably intense. The cultural expression of their nationalist movement, on the other hand, is much feebler and has not yet reached the masses ; indeed, it has hitherto barely stirred the urban intelligentsia and roused them to a consciousness of active responsibility for the cultural education of the masses, for combating illiteracy, establishing popular libraries in towns and villages, building schools, and starting educational courses. True, political newspapers are amazingly widely read, and in the villages even those who cannot read hear their contents retailed and read aloud. Good books are far less widely read and are almost unknown to the masses, and most newspapers are poor in cultural value. There is, indeed, little to distinguish these people culturally from the masses in the Balkan countries before their political emancipation. When political, national aims are achieved, the energies of the movement will be able to turn to cultural ends in Egypt and Arabia as well.

III

CLASSES AND ESTATES

THE NEW MIDDLE CLASS

THE revolution in transit and economic conditions brought about by more lively and rapid communication with the outer world, and by the penetration of European capitalist undertakings, banks, and railways in the Hither East, necessarily affected social conditions and led to a regrouping of classes. So long as the foreign and home trade of the Hither East was quite inconsiderable, so long as it was not involved in the capitalist economic system of the West, its social structure, which had been stable for centuries, remained very simple. The dominant class was the wealthy landed nobility, which also supplied the higher posts in the bureaucracy. The country's economic structure rested upon land ownership and agriculture. As the new types of economic activity and transit penetrated, new classes necessarily arose. The habits of life and thought of the existing nobility had developed qualities, virtues, and characteristics which had ceased to meet the needs of the modern era. In their place, at first side by side with them, a new dominant class began to appear, the middle-class merchants and the urban intelligentsia.

This process went on in varying measure in the different countries of the Hither East. It has gone furthest in Egypt, where the political history of the twentieth century may be explained in the light of the struggle of the rising middle class against the nobility. From the social point of view, Zaghlul Pasha's importance was that he was the mouthpiece of this class rising from the ranks of the fellaheen. Nejd and the Yemen are still untouched by the process. Palestine and Iraq were drawn into the stream by the World War, although some beginning had been made in the seaports even before the War. Thus the Hither East stands socially at the parting of two eras. Everywhere we find in varying measure relics of the feudal period, which has not yet been left quite behind ; everywhere the approaching symptoms of the capitalist period, whose day has not yet quite dawned, show varying degrees of activity.

Social change in the Hither East is complicated by the racial and religious differences between the various classes. It was the Christians in Syria and Egypt who first introduced the new economic order and so became the protagonists of the rising social classes. That is true of the Copts in Egypt before the War, as likewise of the Christians in Lebanon and Beirut. On the other hand, the land-owning nobility in Egypt was a racially alien element. It was made up of the Turko-Circassian ruling class in a country conquered by the Turks. To-day the antagonism between Copts and Mohammedans in Egypt is entirely overcome. Thanks to the rapid penetration of the country by capitalist industry a large and now preponderant middle-class element has risen from the ranks of the fellaheen and the Copts have united with it in the struggle to assert national claims. The antagonism still counts in Syria. In the persistent hostility between Lebanon and the interior of Syria not only religious but also social differences play an important part.[16] Islam in its traditional structure is still more unfriendly to capitalism than was Catholicism originally. Thanks to their education in European mission schools and their emigration to countries with a highly developed capitalist system, whence they have returned after a period of years with capital and experience, the Lebanese Christians have evolved that spirit of individual initiative which is essential to capitalism. The inhabitants of Lebanon and the coastal region at its foot are descendants of the ancient Phœnicians. They became the natural allies and agents of European capital in its penetration. Beside the ancient wealth consisting of immovable property, a new wealth arose, consisting of movable property. The new links with the world economic system, the import of cheap corn from distant countries, people's newly enhanced wants, had all depressed the value of landed property even before the serious agricultural crisis which has gripped the Hither East more and more severely during recent years. Money economy replaced barter and a new, dynamic element broke in increasingly upon the traditional social and economic structure, formerly stable and now shaken to its foundations. In Islam, which was bound up with the dominant social structure of the political community, the convulsion was incomparably more violent than among Oriental Christians, who had no sense of obligation towards the dominant political and social order. This social and religious antagonism in Syria served, moreover, as the basis of the opposing policies pursued in that country by France and England even in the nineteenth century. Republican, capitalist France found support in the rising Christian middle class, and the secular Republic entered into an alliance with the Vatican solely on account of that policy. But in the ranks of the British colonial and diplomatic civil service the values and tastes of the landed, aristocratic gentleman prevailed, and Great Britain looked for support to the Mohammedan and Druze feudal nobility, whose dignified, traditional culture and chivalrous virtues appealed to her people more than the shrewd and pliant temper of the Levantines.

These social antagonisms still have their repercussions in the disinclination of many Lebanese Maronites for union with Syria. But they have lost importance. The Mohammedans, in accordance with the laws of economics, have developed a middle class of merchants and lawyers, and this has diminished the social and economic antagonism between the religious communities. Native Christian capital (it is a question of trading and banking capital and only in the earliest phases of industrial capital) saw a menace to itself in the competition of European capital enjoying the protection of capitulations and privileges (and in Palestine of Zionist capital), and so social and economic influences led it to that union with the Mohammedan element to which the inherent laws of national development were in any case driving it.

THE BEDOUINS

A line of cleavage peculiar to the Arab countries is that which divides the Bedouins from the settled population. Here, too, dynamic forces are shifting the boundary line. Ibn Saud's endeavours to settle the Bedouin population of Nejd have made him one of the great reformers of Inner

Arabia. In acting so he was pursuing political as well as
social aims. The settled Bedouin is more easily subjected to
a central authority than the nomad. Each tribe and each
group were allotted land in an oasis where they built villages
or towns and entered, with the cultivation of the soil, upon
a new life. These new towns are called *hijar* (places of
emigration ; the singular of the word is *hijrah*), for the
inhabitants have gone forth from the nomad state to a settled
life, or from a world of instability and ignorant banditry
to one of divinely ordered security. The first of these *hijar*,
of which there are now nearly a hundred, was Artawiya,
founded by the Mutair tribe in 1912 east of Boreida in the
province of Kasim. It became an important centre of
agriculture and trade. In the largest *hijar* the population is
estimated at 6,000 to 7,000 men capable of bearing arms.
But in the short time since these settlements were established
there has been no change in the war-like and fanatical spirit
of their inhabitants. Ibn Saud has still a great educational
task before him.[17]

Experience in other countries has proved that the
Bedouins are ready for the transition to a settled or semi-
settled peasant life. For they live a life of great poverty and
of perpetual want and danger. They are prevented from
changing to agricultural occupations by lack of land,
experience, capital, and organization. Nevertheless, the
transition is gradually taking place. Even the settled
Bedouins have not renounced their tribal organization and
tribal customs. The settlement of the Bedouins, not only in
Central Arabia, but on the edge of the fertile land, wherever
the population already settled leaves room for them, is one
of the most important tasks before the governments of the
Arab countries from the political as well as the social point
of view. In the days of Ottoman rule it proceeded but slowly
and without organization. Gertrude Bell has described it
among the agricultural tribes in Mesopotamia :—

" Some have been established in Mesopotamia from a
remote period, others have come in during the last two or
three hundred years, but all are originally nomads from the
interior wilderness. The unbroken drift of her peoples northwards is one of the most important factors in the history
of Arabia. The underlying causes were probably complex,

but chief among them must have been a gradual change in the climatic conditions of the peninsula, involving slow desiccation, together with the pressure of an increasing population on a soil growing steadily poorer. To the hunger-bitten nomad the rich pastures of the Syrian frontier, the inexhaustible fertility of Mesopotamia, offered irresistible attractions." This migration has been going on for centuries, and " it will not be arrested in the future, though the nature of the immigration may be altered . . . The surplus population of Arabia may find in a Mesopotamia reconstituted by good administration, not only abundant means of livelihood, but far-reaching possibilities of social and intellectual advance."[18]

The rapprochement between Bedouins and settled Arabs, between peasant and town-dweller, is the basic problem of the Arab nationalist movement, if ever it is to advance beyond separation into districts and countries to a union of the whole Arab people. To-day the Bedouins are separated from the settled Arabs not only by disposition, the inevitable result of different occupations, but by social organization. Whereas the other social antitheses in the Hither East are analogous in their rise, growth, and solution to the corresponding stages in European development, the problem of the nomadic population confronts the governments of the Hither East with new tasks which, however, are easier of fulfilment with the fuller resources of modern organization and technical science than was the case in the past.

THE LABOUR QUESTION

The penetration of capitalism in the Hither East is also leading to the gradual rise of an urban working class. Thanks to the growth of the towns, the mechanization of transport, the beginnings of industry, and the great distress of the poor peasantry, workers are gathering in the towns, are slowly loosening the ties which bind them to the village community, and are beginning to form a proletariat that is gradually awakening to the consciousness of its economic and social claims. The past decade, therefore, has witnessed the first beginnings of an organized Labour movement in Egypt and Syria. For the time being it is only a question of sporadic attempts which, as in the early capitalist period in Europe, have yet no disciplined organization or stability. Amongst the early champions of labour organization are the railway and tram employees and the printers. Immediately after the World War strikes broke out in Alexandria. In recent years attempts have been made alike in Alexandria and in Beirut to create a homogeneous Trade Union organization.

The Labour movement received its initial impetus from the nationalist movement. All nationalist movements are democratic at the outset ; they carry on a struggle against oppression and feudalism, and for that purpose they need the co-operation of the masses, who have to be roused to a consciousness of their national allegiance. Even though the nationalist movement has its origin in the middle-class intelligentsia, it finds support in the labouring masses, the peasants and workers. Alien rule over a nation is invariably the starting-point not merely of a national but also of a kindred social movement of liberation. The alien nation in the process of penetration often succeeds in assimilating the socially privileged classes and winning them by conferring honours and admitting them to a share in economic advantages. National resistance then depends upon the masses of peasants and workers, upon the fellaheen whose determination to win social freedom inevitably assumes the form of a national struggle and who, when their historical leaders, the nobility and the clergy, are alienated from their own people, produce a new middle class and new leaders from their own midst. " Wherever a nation lives under alien rule, the party of the oppressed classes, whether democratic or actually socialist, can only survive if it fights for the language of the oppressed people and for their national independence." [19] On the other hand, the socially dominant class in an oppressed nation can lead the struggle for national freedom, only if it is still conscious of its national allegiance, if it looks for support to the masses of the people and champions their claim to political freedom, a democratic suffrage, and social betterment. The existence or the danger of alien domination everywhere leads to common action of all classes. The movements of national liberation in Egypt, Palestine, Syria, and Iraq have, therefore, also adopted the slogans of democracy and mass welfare in their programmes. Not till national freedom has been won, at the stage of assured political independence, will social antitheses work themselves out in the Hither East. For the time being the social and national struggle for freedom go hand in hand, as is the case with all oppressed nations. It is just the national struggle for liberation that has set up a fermentation in the popular masses, roused them to a consciousness of their own quality and dignity, snatched them out of their dull lethargy, and enlarged their outlook so that they perceive new chains of association.

Such fermentation involves opportunities for Communist propaganda, which is active in Hither Asia as elsewhere. The Communists have thoroughly grasped the connection between national and social emancipation. That is their strength amongst oppressed peoples. In recent years the Soviet Union has turned its attention to Inner Arabia, and has concluded treaties with the Hejaz and the Yemen. At King Ibn Saud's court the ambassador of the Soviet Union is the doyen of the diplomatic corps. But it is only in non-independent countries that Communist propaganda is of real significance ; there Great Britain and France, supported by the fear of a social revolution among the dominant classes, carry on a bitter struggle against Communist propaganda, greatly over-estimating its true dimensions. Its prospect of a certain measure of success is due to the absence of national freedom in the peoples amongst whom it is carried on.

In Palestine, Syria, and Iraq we already find the first beginnings of modern labour legislation. The greatest advance is marked by the all-embracing Bill promulgated in Egypt in December, 1928, which mainly provides for the protection of juvenile labour and working women. Juveniles up to the age of sixteen may not work more than eight hours a day, they are forbidden to do night work in factories or to be employed in dangerous or unhealthy processes, and in shops and offices they may not be employed later than 10 o'clock at night. The employment of women and juveniles in mines is forbidden. A working woman has the right to six weeks' leave of absence at childbirth with full pay, and afterwards she is entitled to suckle her child during working hours. Children under twelve may be employed in factories only if they have received at least an elementary education and work under their parents' supervision. Employers and their representatives are required to behave with propriety towards the workers and their agents. Workers coming from a distance must be conveyed back to their homes with their families at the employer's cost when their work is at an end. If the place of employment is a long way from the nearest market, the employer must supply his workers with food at the market price, without including the cost of transport. If the work is interrupted for reasons for which the worker is not responsible, he receives half his wages.

Besides the provisions for health and the payment of wages punctually and in cash, there are clauses recognizing the workers' right of association. The law forbids employers to compel workers to withdraw from their union. Working hours are fixed at nine for day work and eight for night work. But three hours' overtime may be worked by mutual agreement, though they must be paid at a 20 per cent higher rate. The workers' right to a weekly day of rest is recognized. In places where there are no schools, if there are more than twenty-five children of school age, the employer is required to build a school. Where more than 200 workers are employed a doctor must be appointed at the charge of the factory. The law does not overlook nationalist claims. Employers must engage at least 80 per cent Egyptian workers, and all foreign directors of labour who come in contact with the workers must know Arabic.

Foreign workers in the seaports and the Jewish workers in Palestine have influenced the development of the Hither Eastern Labour movement. The Jewish Labour movement in Palestine is sharply divided from the Arab by national and political antagonism, by its higher cultural level and its Socialist training. The Jewish working class in Palestine is a very influential part of the Zionist movement, the most active and best organized within the country ; in so far as these workers come from Europe, they have brought with them the most advanced principles of Trade Union and Co-operative organization, and have carried them out in Palestine with great zeal and ability. The national liberation movement of the Jewish people which, as with other peoples, aims at territorial independence, provided favourable soil for the development of socially progressive ideas. The Jewish

General Labour Organization, which counts some 25,000 members in Palestine, is exceedingly active in the political, social, and educational fields, and nowise inferior to the best organized European federations. The organized Jewish workers in Palestine are affiliated to the Second International and the Amsterdam Confederation of Trade Unions ; they are pressing the Palestinian Government to introduce modern social and labour legislation. The Jewish workers have a Hebrew daily in Palestine and several periodicals. The nationalist struggle, the question of immigration and of securing new places to work in, and the markedly superior social and cultural standard of life of the Jewish workers, confront the Jewish Labour movement in Palestine with thorny problems. Isolated efforts on the part of small groups to raise class interests in Palestine above national interests have inevitably failed in view of the sociological and historical conditions of national struggles for freedom.

THE PEASANTRY

The general Jewish Labour organization in Palestine embraces alike town workers, agricultural labourers, and small peasants. The social structure of Palestine's Jewish population is based upon a far higher level of urban and capitalist economy than that of the Hither East. Of the 165,000 Jews in Palestine, only 34,000 live in villages, and of these a number have other than agricultural occupations, so that barely a fifth of the total number live by agriculture.

Totally different conditions obtain in Egypt and amongst the settled Arab population. There agriculturalists form 62 to 75 per cent of the whole population. The social problem in these countries is, therefore, as in all countries where capitalism is undeveloped, a peasant problem. Of these peasants or fellaheen some are tenants on large estates or State lands, paying part of the produce of the soil to their landlord, others are freeholders ; yet their economic position is very hard, thanks to the excessive burden of taxation which falls especially heavily upon land ownership and agricultural produce, and thanks also to heavy indebtedness at a high rate of interest and to primitive methods ; in recent years the burden has been further increased by the fall in the prices of agricultural produce and by international competition. According to a census of December 31st, 1928, the number of peasants with less than one feddan of land was 67·3 per cent of the total, whilst only 10·7 per cent of the land was in their possession. Only 25·3 per cent of the peasants possessed from one to five feddans, and to these 20·6 per cent of the land belonged. The great majority of the peasant population in Egypt has, therefore, less than five feddans or two hectares. Only 0·6 per cent of the population have more than fifty feddans, and to them 36·9 per cent of the land belongs. Amongst these large landowners there are more than 10 per cent foreigners, who own 30 per cent of the land.[21] This distribution of land-ownership explains the great importance of the Five Feddan Act, promulgated in 1912 by Lord Kitchener, in giving the fellaheen security and raising their status, for it protected the small peasants from the worst effects of bad harvests or a fall in prices. The Act exempted estates of less than five feddans from distraint for debt. At the same time the peasants could get loans from the Agricultural Bank at 8 per cent. This was to protect them from the usurers, mainly foreign, who then managed to gain possession of the encumbered land themselves at a low price.

Improvement in the condition of the fellaheen depends upon a number of government measures, of which the most important are the reform of taxation, the protection of the small peasantry from distraint and the enforced sale of their land, the protection of tenants from eviction, the establishment of cheap sources of credit, agricultural education, and encouragement to practice more intensive cultivation. In the field of research, of the prevention of locusts and diseases, and of agricultural education, some progress has been achieved. In 1926 agricultural credit banks began to function in Syria, if only on a small scale. In Palestine there is as yet no agricultural bank. Only in Egypt, when Makram Ebeid was Minister of Finance, a detailed scheme was worked out for the establishment of a large agricultural credit bank. Speaking generally, it is just the mandatory governments that have failed to devote adequate attention to this key problem. Everywhere there has been retrogression in comparison with the Turkish period, with its *Banque Agricole*

and the good Act of March 25th, 1916.* In Palestine it was
not till after the disorders of 1929 that the mandatory
Government began to turn its attention to questions of
protecting and raising the status of the fellaheen. The
extreme distress of the fellaheen and the fall in the price of
grain led the Governments of Syria, Palestine, and Egypt
to introduce import duties on grain in the summer of 1930.
In Syria and Palestine the tithe or tax on agricultural produce
was reformed. But it was not abolished, as it was in Turkey.

LAW AND PROGRESS

In the matter of law, too, the Turkish Republic can point
to far greater legislative achievements directed towards
the modernization of social life than those countries whose
development has been entrusted, for that very purpose, to
the guidance of a European Power. Whereas in Nejd, the
Hejaz, and the Yemen, Islamic canon law still holds
unrestricted sway and is not out of keeping with the still
stationary social conditions, Turkey, by sweeping away
altogether her only half-modernized mediaeval system of law
and by adopting the most up-to-date European codes, has
laid foundations upon which modern social development can
proceed. In Iraq, in Syria, and in Palestine, on the contrary,
the former Ottoman laws, now repealed even in Turkey,
still remain on the Statute Book, and are only adapted to
more advanced social conditions as each case arises, by single
Acts borrowed, in the case of Iraq and Palestine, from
English law, in that of Syria from French. This lack of
progress in legislation, which denotes so markedly the
transitional state of the countries, is most disastrous in its
effects in the province of personal, family, and succession
laws.† Any modernization of social life in these countries
pre-supposes the growth of a uniform manner of life and
thought amongst the various sections of the population.
Ottoman law and the Ottoman State, which was a mediaeval
religious State, were based upon the legal recognition of a

* See A. Ruppin, *Syrien als Wirtschaftsgebiet* (Kolonialwirtschaft-
liches Komittee, Berlin, 1917), p. 108.
   † See Hans Kohn, " Die Rechtstellung der Ausländer in Palestina " :
Archiv des öffentlichen Rechts (Tübingen, 1930-1).

juridical difference between the various religious communities which affected social life as a whole. There was no uniform law, and therefore no uniform type of social life. Each religious community determined those questions of personal and family law which are of decisive importance precisely in social life according to its own mediaeval canon law. All questions of personal status were withdrawn from the civil and transferred to the ecclesiastical courts.

Neither in Syria nor in Palestine has this weakness of Ottoman law yet been swept away. Such vital matters as marriage and divorce, wardship and inheritance, are removed from the jurisdiction of the State and determined by each religious community in accordance with its canon law. The social process of modernization which Eastern countries are now undergoing finds expression in a growing sense of community among the people of each particular country. The penetration of capitalism and the slogans of nationalism and democracy have led to a common national consciousness ousting the old religious and social divisions. Legal reform is needed to help this new consciousness, this new unity in practical life, to assert itself.

The fact that men's thoughts in the Hither East are mainly fixed upon the field of political activity exercises a retarding influence socially as well as culturally. The intelligentsia, who grasp the need of the times and the task before them, are too few in number to be able to fulfil all the demands of the times with equal zeal. In the struggle for emancipation which nationalism is carrying on against imperialism in the Hither East to-day, the political element is far more marked, far more in evidence, than the cultural and social. This political character may, indeed, mould the outward form of the struggle and inspire it with passion, but only when it attains a social and cultural character will it gain a profounder meaning.

IV

IMPERIALISM AND NATIONALISM

THE FUNCTION OF NATIONALISM

Iғ the nineteenth century has earned the name in history of the era of nationalism, the opening twentieth century may be designated the era of imperialism. The two concepts are hard to distinguish in their origin and essence. Both are phenomena in the struggle for the mastery of certain widening portions of the earth's surface. Similar forces are at work in both. Imperialism is for the most part a later phase in the process begun by nationalism. Nationalism strives to unite the members of one nation, politically and territorially, in a State organization. When that is accomplished the struggle for the possession of the earth proceeds further. The tendency towards political and economic expansion incites the nation to extend its political and economic domination to foreign peoples or fractions of peoples and the territory they inhabit, and in various ways to organize their government under the suzerainty of the expanding nation. This imperialism then inflames the nationalism of the oppressed peoples or fractions. Thus imperialism and nationalism are interlocked.

The century following the French Revolution was the era of nationalism in Europe, for it was then that the German and Italian peoples attained territorial unity and the nationalist movements of the Greeks, Magyars, Poles, and Czechs found expression. It was not till the twentieth century that the peoples of the Russian Empire and the East entered upon the nationalist era. Just as formerly French imperialism had roused German nationalism and Austrian imperialism Italian and Czech nationalism, so, too, in the Russian Empire and in the East imperialism acted as the awakener of nationalism. In the wider sense Czechoslovakia and Poland, where the dominant nationality in the State uses the power of the State organization in order to exercise political and economic control over alien races within the national boundaries, are likewise imperialist.

49

The hall-mark of imperialism in the narrower sense is association with economic penetration and the opening up of large areas, the domination of regions and populations, direct or indirect, political or merely economic, and the attempt to organize them so as to ensure permanent possession or influence. This type of imperialism, which has borne the name for barely half a century, only became possible with modern mechanical developments in communications and industry. But in principle this new, world-embracing imperialism is not different from the earlier types. It, like nationalism, is an expression of the collective egotism and love of domination of the social group which is the active political unit of the present day, namely, the nation. Ours is the age of highly developed nationalism and imperialism, of the clash between nationalism and imperialism. The voluntary limitation and rational self-discipline, which individual egotism imposes upon itself through social organization and self-control, have as yet no validity for national egotism.

In the Hither East nationalism is exercising the intellectual and economic function that it exercised in Europe a hundred years ago. There nationalism stands approved in its original character as a struggle for freedom, the dawning consciousness of the national individuality as a creative force. The masses are stirred out of their apathy, the new means of transit detach them from the soil and so from their limitations. The larger economic area of the national territorial unit, essential to development, is established, whilst identical moods and sentiments can sweep over the whole nation within a few hours. What Friedrich Liszt said of Germany a hundred years ago, extolling the railways, applies to-day to the Eastern peoples who are being welded to political, spiritual, and economic unity; the railways, he said, strengthened the national spirit, for they destroyed the evil of an outlook confined to the parish pump, of provincial self-sufficiency, and girt themselves like a strong belt around the loins of the German nation, binding its limbs together in a war-like, vigorous body. Here, at once, we perceive the twofold aspect of nationalism. " The prospect of a national advantage to be won by force immediately causes an outburst of collective egotism and subjects the individual in the highest degree to the general will ; thereby it actually develops moral forces which, if not of the loftiest quality, are yet intensely strong. This impulse and this capacity to refer every vital activity of the people and the individual to the touchstone of the national good, must lead to obedience to moral laws, springing from the realization that a degenerate people is incapable of performing national duties." [22]

Nationalism in Europe has already fulfilled that function. Whereas in the East we may still appraise it, morally and economically, as a positive and progressive force, in Europe it already belongs, morally and economically, to a past phase of development. Progress in Europe can come only from the supersession of political nationalism. Nationalism and State patriotism here have fulfilled their historical function and lost their ethical meaning. " The original principle of nationality now lives on," as Karl Renner forcibly declared during the World War, " in the awakening nations without a history, that is to say, in the nations of the Balkans and further east. There the process of building up national States is going on to-day ; already it has shattered European Turkey ; soon England will feel its force in Egypt and India." [23]

In the East Europe's imperialism is to-day coming into conflict with Eastern nationalism. The nation is a new political factor in the East. " The nation is not a concept belonging to natural history, to ethnology, or to sociology, but to politics. Simply as inert bodies the nations are exceedingly ancient, but as conscious, active units they have not existed very long. The science of politics regards the nations as organized masses of humanity or, at least, masses capable of organization, which detach themselves spatially from the whole body of mankind and mark themselves out by a unique history, language, and civilization, strive after power side by side and in conflict with one another, and exercise power ; and thus emerge as units that will and act. The common exercise of power is the fundamental and essential object of political activity." *   This awakening of

* Karl Renner, *Das Selbstbestimmungsrecht der Nationen in besonderer Anwendung auf Oesterreich* (Franz Deuticke, Vienna, 1908), p. 7.

national consciousness is rendering the swallowing of one people by another, denationalization or assimilation, impossible even in the East. In former centuries it was a frequent occurrence. In nineteenth century Europe, as soon as the nationalist era dawned, its success was at an end. In spite of every means of coercion in the hands of the State, and in spite of the great cultural and social difference in power and standard of life, Prussia failed in her effort to denationalize the Poles, the Magyars to denationalize the Slovaks, and the Russians to denationalize the Ukrainians or Lithuanians. " Experience has shown that in the struggle of nationalities one has never succeeded in swallowing another. That was successful only in periods when the antagonism of nationalities was unknown, but never after people had become conscious of that antagonism. Such endeavours have achieved the exact opposite of what they strove to effect ; they have not enhanced the national unity of the State, but have brought about an alienation hitherto unknown between the nationalities." *

THE EXAMPLE OF CYPRUS

Though imperialism in the modern sense is a new phenomenon, yet the methods it employs and the language it speaks are old and familiar from many historical instances beyond the limits of Hither East.[24] Nationalism in the East, too, has learnt its language in the school of nineteenth-century Europe. The statements made by the British Colonial Secretary and the Greeks of Cyprus in the second half of 1929 are characteristic examples of this situation in the Hither East, where imperialism and nationalism stand face to face.

The island of Cyprus in the eastern Mediterranean was handed over by Turkey to British administration in return for a promise to help Turkey in the defence of her Asiatic possessions against Russia. After the British occupation of the island a Legislative Council was created, consisting of six British officials and twelve elected representatives of the

* Waldemar Mitscherlich, *Nationalstaat und Nationalwirtschaft und ihre Zukunft* (Verlag C. L. Hirschfeld, Leipzig, 1916), pp. 42 ff.

population, nine from the Greek majority and three from the Turkish minority. In spite of the limited powers of the Council, this constitutional innovation represented an advance on the previous position. As the Turks, who constitute less than a quarter of the population, and the Greeks were hostile to one another in Cyprus, the three Turkish representatives in the Council voted with the six Englishmen, and so, with the help of the presiding British High Commissioner, swayed the balance against the nine Greeks. Great Britain, by looking for support to the racial and religious minority, facilitated the task of administration but hindered the growth of unity in the population.

When war broke out with Turkey, England annexed Cyprus, which had in 1921 a population of 310,000, only 19·4 per cent Mohammedans. Ever since the Balkan Wars the Greek inhabitants of the island have demanded union with the Greek motherland. During and after the War the British Labour Party declared for the fulfilment of this wish of an overwhelming majority of the population. But the British Government refused for strategical reasons and in 1925 the island was declared a British colony. The number of Greeks in the Legislative Council was raised to twelve, but at the same time the number of Englishmen was increased to nine, so that, with the three Turkish votes, they still balanced the Greeks. The Cypriot Turks feared union with Greece which, in view of the strength of nationalism in that country, would have rendered them powerless, whilst the English in Cyprus relied upon Turkish support even at a time when they were inciting the Greeks to war on the Turks in Asia Minor.

On July 20th, 1929, the Greek members of the Legislative Council presented a memorandum to the British Government demanding the union of the island with Greece. A delegation went to London to put forward the demand and in a letter, published on November 18th, 1929, they wrote : " We are convinced that, if a plebiscite were taken in the island to-day, the result would clearly demonstrate the strength of this natural sentiment of the historical section of the Cyprus population for their political union with their Mother Country. This desire is not prompted by any unfriendly feelings towards Great Britain, to whom the whole Hellenic world bears a lasting gratitude, coupled with that admiration

and respect which are due to the most liberal among the civilized nations of to-day. It is purely the outcome of the national aspiration of a civilized people to be united to, and form politically part of, that free nation with which, through strong ties of race, of blood, of language, of religion, and of tradition they in fact share one national conscience." *
The delegation further urged that union with Greece would involve no menace to the Turkish minority, whose rights should be safeguarded by special agreements. In case of a rejection of their claims, the Cypriots demanded the introduction of parliamentary government. The country's constitution, they said, had remained unchanged for the past fifty years, and the people had no share in the administration and very little in legislation. The autocratic administration was to blame for the retrograde condition of the country. The memorandum criticized England's economic and financial administration.[25]

At the end of 1929 the British Colonial Office made a detailed reply to the memorandum, indistinguishable in spirit and letter from the replies of Conservative Governments of the British Empire, although it was issued by a Labour Cabinet. England, it said, could only give the same answer as that already given by previous Colonial Secretaries, that the question of the union of Cyprus with Greece was " definitely closed ". Even more characteristic is the indication that the time had not yet come when it would be to the general advantage of the people of Cyprus to change the constitution in the direction of parliamentary government. The reason cited is that the institutions already functioning in Cyprus which are subject in varying measure to popular control have given insufficient proof of the people's capacity for government. In reply to the proposal to appoint a Commission to inquire into conditions on the island the British Government only replied with the traditional wisdom of all governments, saying that the people would do better to concern themselves with business and economic development than with high affairs of State. Finally the British reply compares conditions on the island with those of 1878, and emphasizes the progress made. Amongst the great advantages

* *The Near East and India*, November 21st, 1929.

reaped by Cyprus in consequence of British rule are the absence of all military service, internal order, and security, stable finance, and the sound administration of justice, advantages which might count for something in an era not dominated by nationalist ideology.

To this imperialist utterance the answer of the Cypriot delegation retorted with an expression of the nationalist spirit. They pointed out that the statements of the Colonial Office conflicted with the ideas of freedom and justice which should form the basis of every progressive government's policy. " Though it may be needless here to emphasize that, despite Lord Passfield's statements, the subject (i.e. of the union of Cyprus with Greece) will never close, so far as the people of Cyprus are concerned, until . . . the air of freedom breathes again on those historic and long-neglected shores, yet it should be made clear that such adverse statements, far from having a disheartening effect on the Cypriots, will only stimulate their inherent desire for freedom, which is inseparably bound with the honour of every self-respecting people." * Confronted with a refusal to concede a larger measure of self-government to the Cypriots, the reply of the Greek delegation points out the threadbare character of the reasons put forward. For peoples on no higher a level of culture than the Cypriots have been accorded self-government. If, however, the people really are not ripe for self-government, the reason is to be found in the method of government hitherto in force. " It cannot be denied that an autocratic system of administration which gives no real voice, no opportunities, and no responsibility to the people is not likely to educate them in the use of their own initiative and to promote their latent qualities, nor can it be conducive to high political standards. Only in liberty and in responsibility can the people effectively advance, become constructive, and politically mature. Deny them responsibility and you have the safest way of impeding their progress and of rendering them always destructive and inefficient, thus creating a vicious circle, which cannot be too strongly condemned." † The Cypriot delegation readily acknowledged

* *The Near East and India*, February 6th, 1930, p. 152.
† *Ibid.*

the progress to which the Colonial Office referred, but declared that it was hardly complimentary to the British administration to compare its achievements with those of the Turkish administration, and that half a century ago. If, however, instead of comparing the condition of Cyprus to-day with that of 1878, we compare it with that of other countries which have thrown off the Turkish yoke in the interval, we then see how little progress Cyprus had made. But all these questions are of minor importance compared with that of nationality. " Who would prefer the benefits of external security to the blessing of national liberty ? Who would have an imposed safety within four walls rather than the dangers incidental to the freedom of open space ? "

If Great Britain still keeps a firm hold upon Cyprus, it is hardly for the sake of economic advantages, although the island has an active trade balance and the British colonial government, here as elsewhere, has striven successfully to make the colony financially independent ; Cyprus is of strategic importance to Great Britain, and that importance may increase in the future. Originally the island was intended to protect the Suez Canal from the east by prolonging the Gibraltar–Malta line and providing a strategic point for the defence of the Dardanelles to the north. With the development of the transcontinental system of communications Cyprus acquired new importance on the south-east. It is only forty miles from Asia Minor and sixty from Syria, and it protects the land and air route to India leading across Hither Asia from the north. The ports of Alexandretta, Tripoli, Beirut, and Haifa are within reach of Cyprus, a fact which is the more important because the three first-named have come under French influence through the World War. The importance of Cyprus is still rather potential than actual. It is not at the present time a base for British forces.[28]

Herein it differs from Malta, which is of great present importance to Great Britain and can hardly increase in potential importance. Great Britain is endeavouring to keep both Cyprus and Malta under her sway. That is why she resists any extension of autonomy which might intensify irredentist feeling among the inhabitants. True, she granted a constitution to Malta in 1921, under which the island enjoys almost the same measure of self-government in domestic affairs as the Dominions, although all questions not only of strategical, but of any sort of imperial concern in Malta are decided arbitrarily by the Governor, and the population have no influence whatever in such matters. In Gibraltar the people enjoy even fewer rights than in Cyprus ; there the Governor is invested with all legislative and executive power, assisted only by a Council of four officials and three nominated members. Cyprus stands midway between Gibraltar and Malta, whilst in all but domestic affairs Malta is no better placed than Cyprus. Before 1921, under the constitution of June 3rd, 1903, Malta was actually the worse placed of the two. It was not till 1921 that Great Britain held it possible to grant the Maltese people autonomy in local affairs with a Ministry responsible to Parliament, for she had no irredenta to fear in Malta. And when such an irredenta did arise there in 1930, fostered by the Vatican, the island's constitution was suspended. In Cyprus, Great Britain feared from the outset that a far-reaching measure of autonomy might encourage the external demands of the Cypriots and so create difficulties for Britain's imperial position. That is why at the end of 1929 the British Government put an end to the cultural autonomy hitherto conceded in a liberal spirit to the Greeks, and placed all education in the island under government control.[29]

RECENT BRITISH IMPERIAL POLICY

The example of Cyprus shows that in regions which are of importance for world communications Great Britain exercises direct control, especially in relatively small areas where it can be done with comparatively small military expenditure, and opposes the rise of a national or irredentist spirit even to the extent of interfering with education, whilst in larger countries less susceptible of military control, like Egypt and Iraq, she has evolved a new and very loose relation of interdependence in foreign policy and strategical questions since the World War. Egypt was annexed to the British Empire at the same time as Cyprus, and even in 1919 the

Milner Mission to Egypt was enjoined to determine what form of constitution " under the Protectorate will be the best calculated to promote its peace and prosperity ". Hardly a year earlier the draft constitution of the British Adviser to the Egyptian Ministry of Justice had proposed the absolute restriction of the Legislative Assembly to advisory functions, the establishment of a Senate with a majority of nominated official and European members, and the Anglicizing of the judicial system. Originally the mandates designed for Iraq and for Syria were almost identical.

The agreement reached between Lord Milner and Zaghlul may serve as the starting-point of the new policy, which was then extended to Iraq. It was elaborated in the treaties between Great Britain of the one part and Egypt and Iraq of the other part. Its aim was to give Egypt and Iraq full self-government in domestic affairs, and even external sovereignty, and yet to keep them within the actual or potential sphere of imperial political power and to be able to use them as bases for operations undertaken in defence of the imperial routes. The Labour Government in their dealings with Malta, Cyprus, and Palestine simply took over the policy of their predecessors, just as they did in the case of Egypt and Iraq. All the essential decisions had already been taken by England's Conservative Ministries. Great Britain conceded full liberty to the Egyptians and the Iraqis, but she kept the external control of those places where the great arteries of world communication cross and which, therefore, have become centres of world interests. Great Britain, Egypt, and Iraq are now only allied " for the purpose of securing the defence of that vital artery of British imperial communications ". This military alliance restrains the youthful nationalism of the East from indulging in the enticing but risky game of international politics ; the Eastern peoples gain in return, along with external neutrality, security and opportunities for development at home which they could never win by their own efforts. Such inter-dependence in foreign policy requires vital co-operation between these States and, therefore, the development of an organization for determining their interests in common. It is precisely as a result of the policy adopted towards Egypt and Iraq that the problem of the British Empire as an organization of free, sovereign peoples and of the assurance of their co-operation arises. The transformation of the original colonial relation to a new and free one comes to act as a powerful stimulus to the development of an international order, of new, supernational forms of intercourse.[30]

In the field of political training and education British imperialism has always done pioneer work. So it was in the case of the youthful nationalist movement. It has played an important part in civilizing education, more than French imperialism, which has acted as a civilizing and politically stimulating force only where it had not entrenched itself, but wished to gain influence. England left her stamp less because of any missionary intention than because of the influence of her inherent nature, her ideas of freedom, citizenship, and the formation of character. In this sense she influenced Europe in the nineteenth century and the East in the twentieth. It was in her struggle with the selfish colonizing ambitions of whites, Englishmen and others, in Africa and other parts of the British Empire that England's striving after reform developed into a conscious mission, a great trusteeship, on behalf of backward nations. In that struggle England confronted colonists of her own and of alien race as the protector of the natives, opposing steps calculated to prejudice the natives' interests, especially in the matter of land ownership and their share in self-governing institutions, due to the greater intellectual and organizing ability and stronger economic position of the colonists. England's influence spread far beyond her political sphere of influence. The period following the first Russian revolution witnessed the awakening of Mohammedan peoples in the Tsarist Empire from their lethargy. Their leaders were often ecclesiastics who had received modern ideas from Egypt and Turkey, not from Russia. Even at that date a Russian observer remarked : " In Egypt, as in India, English liberty has stirred ideas in Islam which may yet be destined to transform the whole inner life of the Islamic world." *

* See L. Sternberg's valuable study (in Russian), " The Alien Nationalities " in the miscellany : *Formi Nacionalnavo dviženia v Sovremennich Gosudarstvach.* Edited by A. I. Kastelianski (Obščestvennaya Polza, Petrograd, 1910), pp. 558 and 553.

SOCIAL FORCES

The nationalism of the Eastern peoples has been organized under European influence, and the social changes caused by European penetration have supplied its new dominant class. The old dominant class, too, the feudal aristocracy, had acted faithfully as national leaders where there was a question of repulsing foreign domination. But even in the cases where they assumed the rôle of oppressors of their fellow-countrymen, it was they alone who fostered general national interests and stood in the eyes of the masses as the symbol of national unity. " The Kalmuks of Astrakhan, who were liberated in 1891 from the despotism of their feudal lords, have not yet (1909) ceased to look to them as their natural protectors. We must remember that even the most hated aristocratic fellow-countryman is more closely akin to the native than the Russian official, for he lives the same life, and national arrogance is unknown to him." *

But in course of time the aristocracy lose their influence, ancient systems become out of date and disintegrate, and the middle-class intelligentsia appear on the scene as the ferment that stirs people to fresh activity ; the pasha class is confronted with the class of effendis, merchants, government officials, lawyers, doctors, teachers, and journalists, who are soon thrust into the sphere of nationalist activities and impelled to propagate European social ideas among the masses. Educated partly in foreign languages they have had to use their native speech in order to influence the masses, and to revive and enrich it for that purpose. Whereas at first the language was a means to an end, they soon came to love the means and the people from whom it sprang, with their past, their sufferings, and their hopes, until at last all has culminated in the desire for self-determination. At such times nationalism acquires glory and power. The revolutionary instinct, the consciousness of entering upon a new era, of economic changes and social convulsions, all drive the masses to a naïve and unrestrained nationalism.[31]

Nationalism in this sense is hardly more than a decade old in Egypt, whilst it is only now coming into being in the

* *Ibid.*

Arab countries. Its first beginnings in Egypt go back to the last decade of the previous century, in Arabia to the first of the present century.[32] Here, as everywhere, the effect of nationalism was twofold : it welded the people together, reconciling the different classes and estates in the exaltation of the national struggle for liberation and of cultural self-discovery, and it led to the endeavour to unite all the various territories inhabited by the people in a single state organization, to unify the people and their country. It is here that imperialism began to combat nationalism by seeking to organize the various classes and sections of the people one against another, and to obstruct the union of several countries mainly inhabited by a single nationality. Both these elements appear in the example of Cyprus : the exploitation of the Turkish section of the population against the Greeks and the prevention of Cypriot union with Greece. We find such things in Arabia and Egypt, more varied in form and wider in scope. But they are nowise peculiar to modern colonial imperialism. They are the indispensable prerequisite of all forcible domination of one nation over other nations, of one class over other classes. The Tsarist Empire resorted to them against the non-Russian peoples, the Holy Alliance used them to hold down nationalist movements in Europe, they have been adopted alike against the Irish and the Poles, against the Magyars and later by the Magyars, in India and in South America. They fill the pages of the history of men's struggles for power and dominion. But what is peculiar to the present era is that more than ever those who apply such methods cloak their lust for power beneath a veil of morality, and that instead of pleading the instinct of self-preservation, the impulse to expand, and the extension of national power, they put forward the appeal, consciously or unconsciously untruthful, to justice and benefits to be conferred on the other party. It is the age of propaganda. It is characteristic that people refuse to concede to the other party those vital rights and the opportunity to assert them which they claim for themselves, yet refuse professedly in the interests of the other party. Perhaps, however, the very fact that they are forced to deceive their own conscience and the public opinion of the world is an indication that a new historical order is dawning.

THE CIVILIZING MISSION

The old type of imperialism is disintegrating because it has completed its civilizing task even in the East. Without doubt imperialism, especially British imperialism, was a bearer of civilization,[33] like Roman imperialism in past days, and derived thence not only the justification for but the possibility of its existence. " A gigantic state, a supernational commonwealth, arises thanks to the impression made by the experience of achievements above the average by one people on behalf of a multitude of peoples and countries. Almost without exception these are, in the first instance, the protection of a large civilized region against the mass irruption of less civilized intruders. A primarily defensive system like this necessarily acts offensively against the turbulent neighbours in order to render them as far as possible permanently harmless, and so incorporates their country as a geographical glacis in the superior State. It follows automatically that the subjected people gradually assimilate the superior civilization and that the task of bearers of civilization is accomplished by the rulers with all the consciousness of a cultural mission ; and whether from the point of view of the historian or the historical philosopher, we cannot but regard this as part of the universal process of the spread of civilization." * Inequality in the level of civilization and civilizing energy are of the very essence of imperialism.

This state of affairs has fundamentally changed in recent years. " In recent decades the world political system has become a homogeneous system interlocking in all its parts and functions. All countries have assumed the aspect of European States or have begun to assume it, the aspect, that is, of a national State with a written constitution, an elected popular representative body, an organized Ministry and bureaucracy, a State taking part in legally controlled international intercourse. . . . Together with the political structure of the State the forms of economic organization, transit, and culture characteristic of Western and Central European States have everywhere secured recognition and,

* See the profound dissertation by Richard Schmidt, " Die Zukunft des modernen Imperialismus ": in *Zeitschrift für Politik*, vol. xviii, pp. 357 ff., 364 ff.

as a basis for all this, a dawning consciousness has emerged of national unity amongst the people who form the mainstay of each country and State, of a united popular will to organize and govern themselves according to their own manners and disposition. A psychological change has begun to come over the peoples which may be briefly described as the transition from political passivity to political activity. On a vast scale the radically changed relation of Asia, in all the principal areas of its immense complex of countries, to Europe to-day illustrates these new ideas of the State and political aims." Hence " a new ideal, a new aim that cannot and will not be reconciled any longer with total or partial dependence upon European and American colonial empires. The idea of a civilizing mission, an exalted calling to protect, police, benefit, and rule the extra-European nations, is no longer conceded to European States, and with the loss of this prestige the ethical claim of the Great European Powers to incorporate those peoples by force in their great alien States is itself lost. Not till the present day has the ideal of the national constitutional State become absolutely universal. Cases hitherto localized, in which the national idea has asserted itself independently, have at any rate consolidated in the struggle against the great empires of Europe and North America in an objective of which the Asiatic and African peoples will never again lose sight ; and in so far as these latter feel increasingly their equality of rights with the European Powers and strive for the outward realization of such equality, the prerequisites for the assertion of cultural priority, which is the essence of the imperialist State structure, must inevitably collapse." *

Because traditional imperialism has raised these problems, the way is prepared for its transformation. The old imperialism is still powerful, it still makes use of old and new methods to retain its hold.[34] But the tendency of the colonial peoples to assert their national independence and equal rights is depriving imperialism first of its justification, and afterwards of the possibility of survival. The cultural mission of the West as a basis of its dominance is no longer recognized in the East, and even in the West it is called in question by an increasing number of people. In so far as the West has a cultural mission it can no longer be carried out through

* *Ibid.*

domination, but only through living together on a footing of equality and through community of interests. Because the nations and peoples of the earth are entering upon a more uniform order, imperialism is being replaced, even in the East, by the co-operation of peoples enjoying equal rights. Here, too, Great Britain has done admirable pioneer work, first in the relation of the Dominions, with their white populations, to the mother country, and now in the revision of her relations with Egypt, Iraq, and India. On the other hand, the Union of Soviet Republics has sought to shape the law of nationalities within its empire in a manner which points the way to future progress. Meanwhile, however, the old imperialism is striving to prolong its existence by its traditional methods.

THE METHODS OF IMPERIALISM

One of the chief means by which one nation seeks to dominate another is to play off one class in the nation which it wishes to oppress against another, to make itself the uninvited mouthpiece of one class against another, and to brand the national leaders as selfish agitators. Ancient as this method is, it is still very widely used in propaganda. " We hear it said of India, of Ireland, of the Negro, of the proletariat that they would be perfectly contented if it were not for the agitators who work up the people to demand a freedom of which they are incapable and which they do not really want. The peculiar fact is the recurrence of this phenomenon in every case where there is repression. It is not true, as is alleged, that the agitators are merely psychological or moral perverts who are actuated by self-interest. Their type is much the same in whichever of the groups they are found. They are symbols of the psychosis of the group, and are the stuff of which martyrs are made. Sometimes they are personally normal and eminent, and sometimes they are excitable and fanatical, but in either case they are the product of the condition under which they develop. They discover that, as members of the nationality or class to which they belong, there are limitations placed upon them of which they cannot help becoming conscious, and they react to that consciousness on behalf of the whole group. When the movement has gained some momentum, the leaders become identified with it in a peculiar way, so that the mass feels that any attack on the leader or agitator, according to the point of view, is an attack upon themselves. It is a customary procedure to try to suppress these leaders, and invariably the result is an increase in the solidarity of the group behind them, which it is the real object to suppress." * In the view of the reactionaries (and amongst ruling peoples reaction may easily be represented by Liberal and Labour parties), national (and also social) liberation movements are merely the agitation of a sectional intelligentsia that profits by them materially or politically, whilst the mass of the people is contented and aims at material well-being which is assured to them rather by the rule of the alien nation than by the agitators. Those who are called agitators to-day were called demagogues in Metternich's time, the aristocracy and intelligentsia of the Italians, Magyars, and other peoples struggling for freedom, and the visionaries in Germany who dreamed of a united German Republic.

To-day, as then, the methods of oppression are tried against the agitators and against the masses whom they lead or incite. Those methods have not stood the test of history. After the suppression of the Polish rising of 1863 Prince Cherkaski declared that "no power in the world could revive the Polish question". That same year the Russian Minister of the Interior proclaimed : " There is no Little Russian language, there is none and can be none." For years, perhaps, suppression was successfully carried out, but the Polish question and the Ukrainian language rose again to new and tempestuous life. Nor was it otherwise in Ireland, in India, and in the Arab countries. History shows that enslaved peoples and classes have won their freedom only through movements of violence and insurrection. So long as they remain quiet no attention is paid to their demands ; indeed, people often point to the calm prevailing in the colonies as proof that all is well. Peaceful protests are heard sometimes with sympathy, more often with indifference, for the most part with impatience and weary annoyance. It is only when bloodshed and riot occur that public opinion is

* Herbert A. Miller, *Races, Nations, and Classes* (J. B. Lippincott Co., Philadelphia, 1924), pp. 120 ff.

forced to pay attention and give ear to the grievances expressed by the riots. And these risings assume the character of cruel and sporadic deeds of violence amongst colonial peoples, who have frequently been wholly disarmed.

Even countries like Great Britain and Switzerland, which have preserved their independence for centuries, are no exception to this historical law that national and social liberation has hitherto been achieved by insurrection. At the threshold of Swiss independence stands an assassination glorified by legend and poetry, and England's peaceful development in recent centuries was rendered possible by decades of confusion in the revolution of the seventeenth century. Since that period compromise has been the peculiar and distinguishing mark of British policy, a readiness to adapt itself and yield, always, indeed, endeavouring to suppress by force efforts to secure social and national emancipation— we need only refer to the Chartist period and to Ireland— and yet prepared at last to meet them half-way. This policy is the property of all parties, and only the extreme Conservative wing regards it as inadmissibly weak and yielding, putting a premium on disorder and insurrection, an incitement to further violence. In this English policy of yielding, though late, to national and social insurrection lies the hope of a new ordering of national and social relations.

Imperialism has always tried to play off social, racial, or religious antagonisms in order to consolidate its rule. Politicians who will have nothing to do with bettering the lot of the lower classes or minorities at home become the champions of the lower classes or minorities in countries where they have to defend imperial interests. In the World War the various States took up the cause of national and social emancipation on behalf of classes and races in enemy States, yet concerned themselves but little with those of their own countries. The Tsarist Government was quite capable, where convenient, of opposing the large landownership of the nobility. " In its endeavour to de-Polonize Poland the Russian Government even resorted to such dangerous methods as intensifying the local antagonisms of classes and nationalities. To that end it abandoned its customary relation to the peasants and its benevolence towards the landowners in Poland and carried through measures of land reform there which emphasized its benevolence towards the Polish peasants and its hostility to the interests of the Polish land-owning nobility." *

European colonial administrations and European business men and colonists have conferred many benefits upon the East. That is true of every penetration of a more highly developed civilization, every stronger and more vital political force, in countries inhabited by backward or stationary peoples. These advantages were not only the blessings of orderly administration, impartial justice, security, and order. European administration and colonization have awakened a new spirit in the East, have endowed the East with new powers, have organized it for resistance. But over against these advantages there were disadvantages : the soul of the East suffered violation, human self-respect was killed in the subjugated peoples, racial arrogance had a demoralizing effect. To weigh advantages against disadvantages is impossible. We are considering a historical process which was, in fact, necessary in order that the East should win freedom, that Europe and the East should be brought together, and that the way should be paved towards the union of mankind. To-day the peoples of the East are no longer faced with a question of the advantages or disadvantages of European colonization, nor with the question whether it has enriched or plundered them. In so far as European colonists and administrators did benefit the East, they did it not for love of the East, but for their own advantage. From the point of view of the East, European penetration has now served its purpose. The East now wishes to choose its own instructors and counsellors, and to learn how and what it will. It is the peculiarity and the delusion of the age of nationalism that national freedom is valued more highly than good government or economic prosperity. Social antagonisms cannot come into play until national freedom is won. Till then every attempt to introduce the social struggle

* M. Slavinsky, "Russia's National Structure and the Great Russians " in the above-mentioned miscellany : *Formi Nationalnavo Dviženiya v Sovremennich Gosudarstvach* (Russian), pp. 288 ff. See, too, Lord Lloyd's speech to the British Empire Union, *The Times* (London), December 6th, 1929.

into the ranks of the oppressed people from without is doomed to failure. The Labour parties and peasant organizations that are formed will be strictly nationalist in character and will be no less radical in their nationalism than the other classes.

More disastrous than the playing off of social antagonisms has been that of national which, in the East, is often equivalent to religious antagonisms. It is the distinguishing mark of the age of nationalism in the East that men strive to attain national unity and to exclude or assimilate minorities. In the Ottoman Empire the Great Powers made use of the Armenians as a wedge to drive into the body politic of the Empire and to weaken it. The Armenians were the victim of that policy and, indeed, after the World War the Great Powers abandoned them to their fate, regardless of repeated and solemn promises.[35]   After the World War Lloyd George made use of Greek nationalism as a similar wedge to drive into the Turkish body politic, and likewise left it in the lurch afterwards. The Copts in Egypt were to be used in like fashion, but they did not lend themselves to the scheme.[36]   The racial and religious antagonisms in Syria and Palestine have a like significance for imperialist interests, and are used by France and England in order to consolidate their position in the country as long as possible as protectors of the minority.*

THE CAPITULATIONS

Another device for controlling the weaker States and nations is the establishment of economic and cultural institutions in their countries. These activities—the founding of trading companies and industries, the acquisition of land and its cultivation by modern methods, the establishment of schools and hospitals—may in themselves be actually beneficial to the country in which they are carried on. But political demands often result from the investment of economic and cultural positions ; the foreign colonists and

* See Arnold H. Toynbee, *The Islamic World since the Peace Settlement* (*Survey of International Affairs*, 1925, vol. i, Oxford University Press, 1927), pp. 21, 22.

missions and their property require protection and so lead to acts of intervention. Indeed, activities of this kind may give rise to a claim to the possession of the whole country, as happened in the case of France and Syria. The United States of North America have adopted such a policy towards Mexico and other Central American States [37] ; in the East we find it primarily in the former Ottoman Empire, China, and Egypt.

This predominance of the stronger States and the interests under their protection finds expression in the East in the system of capitulations. In all Oriental countries a struggle is going on for the abolition of the capitulations. Their history is a good example of the transformation of historical institutions, of the way in which their meaning changes. They are a relic of the mediaeval system of international law, and date from the time when the foreigner had as yet no claim to the protection of the law and no juridical status in an alien land. Later the foreigner was conceded protection on the basis of privileges or was dealt with abroad in accordance with his own laws, for in those days laws concerned personal rather than territorial units. The foreigner had no part in the legal rights of the race or religious community in whose midst he lived. He was considered unworthy of being treated on an equality with co-nationals or co-religionists. Since he could not lay claim to the social institutions of the race, he had to be dealt with in accordance with his own code and his own customs. Foreigners in the East, therefore, lived in their own quarters in the cities, under their own laws, with their own system of taxation and expenditure. This legal and fiscal autonomy was quite compatible with the loose political structure of the feudal period. In 1060 the Byzantine Emperor conceded to the Venetians the right to send judges to Constantinople to judge the Venetian residents there both in civil and criminal cases. So, too, the Italian merchants in France and the Low Countries in the thirteenth and fourteenth centuries possessed the right to have their disputes settled by their own fellow-citizens. The Ottoman Empire at the zenith of its power, for the first time in 1535, conceded freedom of settlement and legal and fiscal autonomy to French subjects, and later to those of other governments. These treaties, known as capitulations, were quite compatible with the Islamic State founded upon the principle of personal law.

Towards the end of the nineteenth century, when Eastern States began under European influence to transform themselves into modern States, the capitulations were felt to encroach upon complete sovereignty and to fetter the country in its legal and economic development. The authority of several foreign States upon the territory of another constantly gave opportunity for intervention in the sovereign prerogatives of the latter. The foreigners' privileged position, their distinctive treatment, and the fact that they were withdrawn from the authority of their country of residence, was a humiliation to the newly stirring national consciousness of the Eastern peoples. What had once been normal, on the basis of a bygone juridical order, and had been granted freely and by agreement, had changed into an abnormal right to exceptional treatment which could be maintained only by compulsion. The Eastern States, therefore, as soon as they were strong enough, aimed at the abolition of the capitulations. The European Powers likewise acknowledged that the capitulations were survivals of an outlived past, but they abolished them, in fact, only where they were compelled to do so. In Turkey, by Article 261 of the Treaty of Sèvres, the capitulations were to continue. Not till Turkey had defeated the Greeks were the Powers compelled, in Article 28 of the Treaty of Lausanne (July 24th, 1923) to agree to the total abolition of the capitulations. What Turkey won by force of arms Egypt, undoubtedly no less advanced juridically and economically, failed to win by means of negotiation. In the negotiations with Great Britain during the past decade the capitulations have played a central part. To-day their abolition is already accomplished or in process of accomplishment throughout the East. Characteristically, they survive only in Egypt and in the mandatory territories of Syria and Palestine which were detached from the Turkish Empire, although they were in force there only inasmuch as those countries formed part of the Turkish Empire.

The survival of the capitulations in Syria and Palestine casts a curious light on the nature of the mandatory system. In the mandates for Syria and Palestine the capitulations are not abolished, but abrogated for the period of the mandate. When the mandate expires they are to be revived in full force. Whilst Great Britain has agreed to their final abolition in Mesopotamia and has been willing to agree to their abolition in Palestine, France has insisted upon their continuance in Syria, and the United States of North America to their continuance in Palestine. In Egypt, too, Great Britain has been more willing to make concessions than the other Powers. Nevertheless, both in Syria and Palestine remnants of the capitulatory system remain in force even under the mandate, and concede a privileged position to foreigners in legal proceedings. Syrian public opinion has protested again and again. These regulations are contrary to the intention of the mandatory system, by which the mandatory Government is to train the inhabitants of the mandated territory to full political and juridical maturity. How can the capitulations be put in force again in a country raised to such a level, after the expiration of the mandate ? The privileges conceded to foreigners in Palestine and Syria during the mandate are based fundamentally upon mistrust of the ability and integrity of the native judges. Such a justification throws a strange light on the quality of British and French mandatory government. In Palestine the administration and control of justice and the courts rest exclusively in British hands. The appointment of the judges, their training and personal qualifications, fall entirely within the competence and under the direct responsibility of the British Administration. The mandatory Powers will fulfil their responsibility as mandatories only by the creation of a judiciary such as will render the privileges of the foreigners superfluous. In this matter Great Britain has already come forward to meet the demand in Iraq. There, too, under the Judicial Agreement of March 25th, 1924, foreigners enjoyed legal privileges. In the spring of 1929 Great Britain presented to the League of Nations Council a proposal for the cancellation of the Judicial Agreement, announcing that in future all the special rights of privileged foreigners in Iraq would be abolished, that all foreigners and natives in Iraq would receive equal treatment, and that a homogeneous method of procedure would be established for all. In the covering note to this proposal Great Britain pointed out that the privileges of certain foreigners in Iraq, as in all other Eastern States, being relics of the capitulations, were regarded as an insult not only by the native inhabitants, but also by such other foreigners, like the Persians or Turks, who did not enjoy them. In its session of March 9th, 1929, the League Council declared its agreement with the British arguments, and consented in principle to the abolition of special privileges for foreigners in Iraq. This procedure in Iraq should serve as an example for the other territories.

NEW METHODS IN THE ANCIENT DISPUTE

Iraq, moreover, is the only territory where the mandatory system created in Article 22 of the League of Nations Covenant has been carried out in the spirit of that article. The manner in which the mandates have been drafted and distributed in defiance of the plain text of Article 22, which prescribes consideration for the wishes of the inhabitants in the choice of the mandatory, has hardly conduced to raise the prestige of the League of Nations in the East. Great Britain and France have secured mandates within the territory of the Ottoman Empire in accordance with plans laid even before the World War. They only did so where it seemed to them desirable and not too difficult. Those parts of the Arabian Peninsula that were detached from the Ottoman Empire were not placed under mandatory rule, nor was Armenia or Kurdistan, both of which, but especially Armenia, really wished it. At the Conference of San Remo in April, 1920, where the Turkish Empire was dismembered and the Treaty of Sèvres drawn up—a Treaty which, indeed, proved its impracticability within a few years—the mandates for parts of the former Ottoman Empire, including Armenia, were distributed. Moreover, imperialism, seeking to realize its long-standing schemes in the Eastern question at the Conference of San Remo, there laid down detailed plans for the A mandates. True, the other decisions of this Conference were no more carried into effect than the Treaty of Sèvres. The mandate for Armenia was dropped, thus breaking the many solemn promises of the Powers ; the mandate for Iraq was never carried out in its original form ; and the other mandates were subjected to limiting interpretations of their texts.

The Arab population of the mandated territories never recognized these mandates and has struggled against them throughout the past decade. During the World War the Allied Powers [38] gave a number of assurances and concluded a number of treaties which are mutually contradictory, so that they could not be carried out in full, and in part were not intended to be fully capable of being carried out. As late as November 7th, 1918, the official proclamation of the English and French Governments upon their policy in the Arab districts of Turkey announced as their aim " the complete and definite emancipation of the peoples so long oppressed by the Turks, and the establishment of national governments and administrations deriving their authority from the initiative and free choice of the indigenous populations ". The failure to honour this undertaking led to great disappointment among the inhabitants ; no less was that of the Egyptians who were refused permission in 1918 to put forward their claims at the Peace Conference and were informed in 1919 in Paris that President Wilson had agreed to the British Protectorate in Egypt, and that the question was settled. The peoples of all these countries have struggled ceaselessly for their independence during the past decade. The Syrians summed up their demands as follows—first to the French High Commissioner, De Jouvenal, and then in the petition to the Mandates Commission of the League of Nations, dated February 11th, 1927 :—

" The Syrians demand, above all, their full and integral independence like all civilized countries. They also demand the full exercise of their national sovereignty. They therefore ask to be admitted to the League of Nations ; that is to say, that they mean to enjoy all the consequences of independence in fact and in law. . . . In recognition of the sacrifices made by France in Syria and Lebanon, the representatives of the Syrian and Lebanese people shall recognize her right to a certain number of economic advantages which may be summed up as follows : the issue of loans, the training of the Syrian Army, the eventual creation of a French naval base on the Syrian coast and, lastly, the conclusion of a mutual alliance in case of peril." *

* Permanent Mandates Commission. Minutes of the Eleventh Session (C. 348. M. 122.127.vi), p. 195.

The treaties between Great Britain and Iraq tended in the direction thus adumbrated by the Syrians. In its struggle with imperialism, nationalism in Egypt and the Arab countries has definitely advanced in the past decade. Such an advance is in harmony with the incipient remoulding of the political relations between East and West which progresses hand in hand with the reshaping process, embracing every expression of social and intellectual life, that has the whole East in its grip to-day, and has made itself felt with growing intensity since the World War.

Soon after the Conference of San Remo the Powers began to take this new situation in the East into account. The declaration of Egyptian independence of February 28th, 1922, the treaties with Iraq and Trans-Jordan, the constitutions of the Republics in Syria and Lebanon, the Peace Treaty of Lausanne with Turkey, the withdrawal of British troops from Persia, the concessions to the independence movements in China and India—all this represents a change not to be under-estimated in the attitude of the European colonial Powers towards the East, which would have seemed improbable before the World War.

Egypt and Arabia are not satisfied with the position attained. The yoke of dependence which the European Powers have fixed upon them, however light, is to them a fettering clog. Not only for the intelligentsia in these countries, but for all the inhabitants, the national State is at the present day the goal to be aimed at, and they feel European guardianship as alien domination just as much as a European nation would in a like case. Hence clashes between the European Powers and the native population are inevitable.

In Turkey, Persia, and Afghanistan the position is otherwise. There the political conflict between Europe and the East has ceased to be acute since 1923. There is no longer any Eastern question in the old sense. These States enjoy full internal and external independence. Difficult tasks lie before them : the modernization of their political structure, their penetration by European methods and thereby the preservation of their political and economic independence. These three countries are under the direction of statesmen strong in leadership and personality who have taken up the task of reorganization. They have secured external independence and their task is now to achieve reconstruction at home. The present political contest between Europe and the East is left in the Hither East to Egypt and Arabia.

The awakening to new historical life of peoples who have no history, of the fellaheen, of civilizations that have been petrified and undergoing dissolution for centuries, is an historical process which must be accepted alike in its good and evil aspects. The political emancipation of Egypt and Arabia will progress further in the next few years. When the peoples have won greater independence and their energies are released, it will be easier for them to prove creative in the cultural and social fields. At the present day Egyptian and Arabian society still suffers from weaknesses characteristic of the mediaeval way of life : lack of organizing power and wide vision and of sustained and systematic energy in achievement. These weaknesses likewise militate against success in the political struggle. The people do not attach enough importance to cultural and economic strategic positions and are too easily intoxicated with fine words and proclamations of natural rights which, however, they do not adequately sustain by a realization of the actual conditions of power. And so their nationalism tends to be a little wordy and superficial. Twenty-five years ago Martin Hartmann wrote : " The peoples of the East are still in the convulsions of nationalism ; with some these are just beginning. Few, indeed, realize that the formation of character, upon which the justification of their activities rests, means a serious effort of self-education. We who know how hard it is to create anything of real cultural value, and even to assimilate permanently existing cultural values and to save them from oblivion, we confront the aspirations of the awakening Eastern peoples with cool criticism. We are readily inclined, when we come upon immaturity and too blustering and hasty an advance, to judge harshly and exclaim against charlatanism, ambition, and humbug. We readily forget that, in order to advance one step, it is necessary to take two, and that without the too stormy temperaments the cautious would never leave their snail's shell." * Barely a decade after these words were written it turned out that the European

* " Beiträge zur Kenntnis des Orients " : *Jahrbuch der Münchner Orientalischen Gesellschaft*, 1904–5, vol. ii, p. 96.

peoples, too, are still in the convulsions of nationalism, except for a small advance guard in the ranks of each. The European peoples have passed through at least a century of evolution in nationalist politics, and individuals, at any rate in their midst, have learnt from it. The Arabic-speaking East is only at the beginning of that evolution. At the present day Arab nationalism is struggling for liberation and self-expression, for the opportunity to re-enter history as an active factor, whilst European imperialism is struggling to retain its predominance, to prolong its rule over alien peoples, conscious of its cultural mission and its superior creative potency. In the present phase of the battle Arab and Egyptian nationalism, in spite of its far inferior cultural creative energy, is the more progressive political force. Its ideal is the national State such as Europe has evolved.

But just as that ideal has failed in Europe, so it will fail in the East. World economic organization and world politics are driving us towards a planned union of the largest possible areas, in fact, of the whole earth. Political and cultural subjection has become as impossible in the East to-day as in the Russia or Austria-Hungary of the past. Those States were doomed to dissolution because they learned too late the necessity of allowing for the political and cultural independence of their nationalities. What has emerged in Central Europe and the Border States is hardly an advance upon the earlier condition from the point of view of general progress. The future of the East raises once more in its acutest form the same problem that arose in Europe after the idea of the national State had triumphed : that of remoulding the concepts of State and authority, and of the new organization of the nations, in such a way as to guard their freedom no less than to allow for world economic needs and plans to promote the welfare of the masses.

The evolution of the East during the past thirty years leaves mankind as a whole confronted with the same problems. The wide gulf which separated East and West only a few decades ago no longer exists. Countries and peoples are merging more and more in a common destiny. The problems of one continent cannot be solved without the co-operation of the rest. " He who knows himself and others will recognize here, too, that East and West can no longer be separated." [39]

V

EGYPT

THE WINNING OF INDEPENDENCE

FICTITIOUS INDEPENDENCE

On February 28th, 1922, the British Government recognized Egyptian independence, but in questions affecting the security of British imperial communications, the defence of Egypt against any external attack, and the protection of foreigners and minorities in Egypt and in the Sudan, the *status quo* was to be maintained until these points should be settled between Great Britain and Egypt. By this step the Protectorate in Egypt was abolished, and the country's independence was formally recognized. But Great Britain, through the medium of the reserved points, retained the right and possibility of perpetual intervention in Egypt's domestic affairs, especially since the interpretation of the reserved points lay in her own hands. At the same time a British Note to the Powers expressly declared that the ending of the British Protectorate in Egypt implied no change in the *status quo* as regards the position of the other Powers in that country. Lloyd George declared in the House of Commons that Great Britain would " never allow the progress which has been made (in the Sudan) and the greater promise of future years to be jeopardized ". No change must be made in the Sudan " which would in the slightest degree diminish the security of the many millions of British capital . . . already invested in its development ".

This declaration of independence, which was a unilateral act on the part of the British Government and has never been recognized by Egypt, involved, therefore, no real Egyptian independence either in domestic or foreign policy. It was a makeshift to maintain Britain's supremacy in Egypt. It sprang from no true understanding of the situation, but was the forced product of circumstances and, like all make-shifts, it proved futile.

The declaration of independence had been preceded by the

bloody revolution of March, 1919. For a short time Cairo and the provincial towns and villages were in the hands of revolutionary committees, communications were paralysed, and the fellaheen had killed a number of unarmed Englishmen and destroyed many houses. Ignorant of the true position, the British Government resolved on a policy of the strong hand. Lord Allenby was promptly sent to Egypt to suppress the disorders. The Milner Mission which was to follow the Field-Marshal in order to " inquire into the causes of the recent disorders and to report on . . . the form of constitution, which under the Protectorate will be best calculated to promote . . . peace and prosperity, the progressive development of self-governing institutions, and the protection of foreign interests ", was seriously hampered, not only by its terms of reference, which mentioned the Protectorate, the progressive development of self-governing institutions, and the protection of foreign interests, but also by its composition. It consisted exclusively of Englishmen. The weapon of non-coöperation, adopted by the Egyptians, was employed against the Milner Mission. Nevertheless, the proposals made by Lord Milner in 1920 represented an advance. He recognized Zaghlul as Egypt's true representative and his report contained the proposal, then made for the first time, to substitute for the Protectorate an alliance between two independent States, still conceived by him as permanent. Negotiations on this basis in 1921 between the then Prime Minister, Adli Yeghen Pasha, and Lord Curzon broke down because the Egyptians demanded the withdrawal of British troops to the Suez Canal zone, whilst the English insisted on liberty for the troops to occupy any part of Egyptian territory they chose.

After the breakdown of the negotiations Adli resigned. All this time disorders had not ceased in Egypt. A number of Egyptians had been condemned to death by courts martial and executed, and still more condemned to severe penalties. Martial law was in force throughout the land. Once more Zaghlul Pasha was deported, this time to Seychelles. Lord Allenby realized that it was impossible to uphold the Protectorate against the determined resistance of the Egyptians. At his suggestion the declaration of independence of February 28th, 1922, was promulgated. He wrung it from the Government in London. But this declaration, though it might satisfy the Sultan of Egypt, who had assumed the title of King of Egypt on March 15th, 1922, was repudiated by the Egyptian people, since it left all fundamental questions unaffected. The assassinations of English officials continued, martial law remained in force, and was only abolished on July 5th, 1923, after the Egyptian Government had promulgated an Act of Indemnity pardoning all illegal measures and actions on the part of the authorities during the state of siege.

After the declaration of independence was issued, Sarwat Pasha, who had conducted the negotiations with Lord Allenby, undertook to form a Ministry. In November, 1922, he was forced to resign. The Ministry's most important task had been to work out a Constitution. Precisely on that question differences had arisen with King Fuad, who rejected the idea of a parliamentary monarchy from the outset.[40] Here, already, it became apparent that in the immediate future the Egyptian people would have to carry on a twofold struggle, against Great Britain and against their own king. It was a struggle not only for independence and sovereignty, but also for parliamentary democracy, for the assertion of the popular will as the source and director of political life. A long struggle for both lay ahead, and even to-day it is not ended. A commission was charged with the duty of drafting the Constitution and not a National Constituent Assembly, as was widely demanded. England's declaration of Egyptian independence was an advance upon Lord Curzon's offer to Adli Pasha, since it did not make the abolition of the Protectorate dependent upon Egypt's acceptance of the reservations. None the less, an eminent historian who describes what happened from the British point of view, has called the designation of Egypt as an independent, sovereign State a " diplomatic fiction ", and declares : " While the sovereign independence which the declaration had conferred on Egypt might eventually be translated from shadow into substance if the agreements contemplated in the declaration itself were duly concluded, it was equally true that, if their conclusion were indefinitely postponed, some untoward event might take even the shadow of independence away from Egypt once again." [41]

The history of the succeeding years was the product of the conflicting views held by the British and Egyptian Governments of the relation between the two countries. Here, again, there was no difference between particular British Governments—Ramsay MacDonald confronted Zaghlul's demands with the same determined " No " as his Conservative predecessors—but neither was there any between Egyptian Governments. Zaghlul could not abate his demands, for he knew that he was speaking in the name of the whole people and that, if he had not done so, every Egyptian Parliament would have repudiated even him. That is why the inevitable consequence of the British view was not merely the removal of Zaghlul from his position as political leader, but the impossibility of any constitutional parliamentary life in the country, once the question was revived of a settlement of Anglo-Egyptian relations and the four reserved points ; and that was bound to happen again and again.

Egypt, therefore, lived in a state of perpetual crisis, which affected not only foreign but also domestic policy. Not only Egypt's independence but Egypt's democracy were in constant danger, and naturally the struggle for external independence and for internal democracy became merged into one in the Egyptians' minds. The survival of Parliament became at once the symbol of independence. It was a delusion on the part of the English to suppose that it would be possible by any means whatsoever to find any considerable section of the Egyptian people who would abandon the demands put forward by Zaghlul. Again and again the English allowed themselves to be deluded by the hope, encouraged by their newspaper correspondents in Egypt, that there must be Egyptian politicians to be found, who would not submit to be terrorized by the " extremist agitators " who were pictured as a mere handful. Again and again this hope was inevitably disappointed, and Great Britain was driven to have recourse to an autocratic régime in Egypt, for any consultation of the national will, in whatever form, was inevitably bound to return the one answer that England would not hear. The underlying reason for this crisis lay in the conflicting assumptions with which the two parties entered into the negotiations.   Great   Britain   regarded   the   Egyptian

independence that she had granted in 1922 as a gift to the
Egyptians, an act of grace, which gave her the right at all
times herself to determine the measure of that independence
and to harmonize it with her own interests, which took
precedence. For Great Britain, therefore, the principal
question was how far she could go in her concessions. The
Egyptians, on the other hand, regarded their independence
as their natural right, which nobody could confer upon them ;
any restriction, although possible as an act of force from
without, was out of the question as enshrined in a treaty
by their free consent. England, they held, had robbed Egypt
of her freedom for decades, contrary to law and justice, and
had herself always admitted as much formerly and declared
her willingness to evacuate Egypt. It was, therefore,
impossible to ask Egypt how far she could meet England in
restricting her own liberty. First of all Egypt's natural right
must be acknowledged and then Egypt, in complete freedom
and independence, could grant certain concessions, taking
account of the needs of British imperial strategic communications without prejudice to Egypt's national
sovereignty.

Thus there was no common basis of understanding
between Egypt and Great Britain ; but under an autocratic
régime in Egypt it could be replaced by a semblance when a
Ministry supported by England, and only maintaining its
authority thanks to the British army, appeared to represent
Egypt's will abroad. But as soon as an attempt was made,
even under the strictest control, to introduce the forms of
democracy once more and to proceed to elections, it
immediately became plain that the extra-parliamentary
Ministry represented nobody and that the popular will in
all classes and sections was almost unanimously behind the
" extremists ". Latterly, people began to realize these facts
even in Great Britain, so that an Anglo-Egyptian understanding began to appear possible.

Although the gulf separating the British and Egyptian
points of view was thus narrowed, the internal conflict on
the question of democracy was nowise abated. Originally
the Egyptian people's struggle for freedom, the struggle
against foreign and domestic autocracy, had been opposed
by a united front. As elsewhere in the East, the English had

supported the king whom they themselves had installed, in opposition to the national will and aims. This was in accordance with British policy in Egypt at the time of the occupation, when the English had protected the Khedive against the first stirrings of the national movement under Arabi Pasha. It was not till quite recently that the English began consciously to take into account the political and social changes in the East and to recognize that the only way to solve the crisis was to come to an understanding directly with the Egyptian people and their representatives. This widened the gulf between the king and people still further, and to the latter democracy and the Parliament acquired intrinsic worth, not merely as symbols of independence.

THE WAFD AND ITS ADVERSARIES

In the years immediately following the World War, the Egyptian people knew nothing of parties. The Wafd, the delegation which demanded independence of Great Britain in the name of the Egyptian people, represented the people. Its composition varied, partly because its members were arrested or deported, partly because a few members declared their opposition to the undisputed head of the Wafd, Saad Zaghlul Pasha, for personal reasons or because they disapproved of the methods adopted. The Wafd was not a party, but everywhere in Egypt it had set up district and local committees, and had at its disposal such a complete organization that it was able to direct the fortunes and demonstrations of the whole country from its local centre in the " People's House ", Zaghlul Pasha's residence in Egypt. At that time there was only one party in Egypt, the National Party or *Watanists*, founded long before the War by Mustafa Kemal Pasha, and it had but few members. This party was, according to its programme, far more extreme than the Wafd ; it was opposed to any negotiations with Great Britain, and demanded the absolute independence of the whole Nile Valley, its evacuation by the English, a declaration that all the decrees promulgated in Egypt since the imposition of martial law at the beginning of the World War were invalid, and the neutralization of the Suez Canal under Egyptian protection.

On October 29th, 1922, a new party was established, that of the Constitutional Liberals, under the presidency of Adli Yeghen Pasha. First and foremost the representatives of the aristocracy belonged to it. Its programme likewise demanded Egypt's absolute independence and sovereignty and that of the Sudan, the evacuation of the country, a constitutional democracy, and a number of progressive social and educational measures.

It was not till after the election of the first Egyptian Parliament in April, 1924, that the Wafd formed itself into a party and adopted the name of Parliamentary Wafd Party. Zaghlul Pasha had at first opposed this step, declaring : " We are not a party, we are the nation itself." But the requirements of parliamentary discipline rendered it desirable to form a regular party. It was not till January, 1925, that another new party arose in Egypt, the Union Party or *Ittihad*, seeking its support exclusively from the king and Court.[42] From the outset there were marked differences between the king and the Wafd, giving rise even in 1922 to rumours that the Wafd aimed at the deposition of the king and the establishment of a republic. It proved, indeed, that these differences subsisted not only with the Wafd, but soon with others who did not, so the king feared, share his views.

In spite of the declaration of Egyptian independence in February, 1922, hardly anything was changed in the internal state of the country until July 5th, 1923, the date upon which martial law was abolished. In the name of the foreign officials who were to be retired under the new régime, the British Government demanded compensation on a scale which even Englishmen criticized as excessive. In July, 1923, the British and Egyptian Governments agreed upon the compensation to be paid to such foreign officials as might wish to terminate their contracts. It amounted to as much as £8,500 for single officials in the higher ranks. In not a few cases the officials retired upon these terms, received compensation which amounted to a total of nearly £6,500,000, and were then re-engaged under a special contract. It was this question of the foreign officials which gave rise to a series of acrimonious debates in the Egyptian Parliament in 1926.

Article 23 of the Egyptian Constitution of April 21st, 1923,[43] drafted on the model of the Belgian Constitution, declares that " all power emanates from the nation ". Egypt is a parliamentary hereditary monarchy. The king has the right to refer back a Bill passed by Parliament within one month. If in such a case the Bill is passed in the same parliamentary session by a two-thirds majority, or in a succeeding session by a simple majority, it becomes law without the king's consent. The Ministers are responsible to the Chamber ; they must resign if the Chamber passes a vote of no confidence, and may be impeached by the Chamber. Article 68 provides for the promulgation of a special law dealing with cases of ministerial responsibility not coming under the Criminal Code. Parliament consists of a Senate and a Chamber of Deputies. Two-fifths of the Senators are appointed by the king, the other three-fifths elected by universal suffrage. The king has the right to dissolve the Chamber and to adjourn Parliament, but only for one month, and only once during the session. If the Chamber is dissolved on account of a particular question, the new Chamber cannot be dissolved for the same reason. The decree of dissolution must, moreover, include a writ for a new election within two months, and the new Chamber must assemble within ten days of the new election. The king must summon Parliament to its regular session before the third Saturday in November, otherwise Parliament is legally entitled to meet on its own initiative on that day. At the expiration of the life of Parliament fresh elections must be held within the sixty days before the expiry ; should fresh elections prove impossible, the old Chamber's life is prolonged until the new elections. Steps have been taken to make any alteration of the Constitution difficult. Those articles which concern Parliament and its rights cannot be altered at all. Article 155 expressly lays down that the assembly of Parliament as provided for in the Constitution may not under any circumstances be stopped.

Amedeo Giannino concludes his study of the Egyptian Constitution with the following words : " Indubbiamente l'Egitto sapra far vivere la sua nuova Costituzione con quella stessa energia e passione con cui ha tenacemente difeso la sua indipendenza e l'ha conseguita." This struggle the

Egyptian people have carried on, and it is not yet finished.
Seven years after the Constitution came into force the
Egyptians have not had a single Parliament that has survived
for its normal term. Thrice in that short space the king has
suspended the Constitution and ruled autocratically, four
times during those years elections have been held, and the
time during which the government has been carried on
unconstitutionally without Parliament has been longer than
that of parliamentary, constitutional government.

THE FIRST NATIONAL MINISTRY

On September 17th, 1923, Zaghlul returned for the second
time. For weeks previously Egypt had lived in expectation
of his return and had been making preparations. Zaghlul's
reception in Alexandria and Cairo was like a triumphal
procession. On September 27th the primary elections were
held. The Egyptian electoral law provided for a universal,
democratic, but indirect suffrage. Every thirty electors
chose one for the secondary elections. The Wafd had no
electoral programme except in so far as it was embodied
in the phrase *el istiklal et tamm*, absolute independence.
As regards foreign policy, all parties made essentially the
same demands. The Nationalists were bitterer in their
hostility to England, and more unyielding and abstract
in the conditions they laid down. They were in open
opposition to King Fuad and wanted the recall of the Khedive
Abbas Hilmi, who had been deposed by the English at the
outbreak of the War. They were strong Mohammedans.
The Wafd, on the contrary, had not tied its hands in any
doctrinaire manner on the question of negotiations with
England and included both Copts and Mohammedans. The
Copt Wissa Wassif Bey, the future President of the Egyptian
Chamber, had been nominated as a Wafd candidate in a purely
Mohammedan constituency. Zaghlul's election manifestos
contained no definite programme. They were typical of the
lyric nature of Eastern nationalism. They contained such
passages as this : " We shall meet with difficulties in our
path ; we shall remove them. The king of the country stands
with the people ; the people are united and resolute. We
have right on our side and God is on our side ; what, then,

is lacking to the attainment of our goal, to victory ?   Now my voice may cease. For in all your mouths are the songs of freedom and your hearts are overflowing with them and their echoes are sent back from within the walls of tombs and coming generations will rise up to their sound. You are the forgers of your own hopes, the builders of your own glory, you are the sons of immortal Egypt. I bow in homage to your national sentiment and to the nobility of your aims and with you I cry : Long live Egypt ! . . . The days that stand between you and the elections are numbered ; your most important duty is to understand the high nature of the action that is required of you, the significance of the task to which you are summoned. Before these elections the nation was rent into classes and parties, aristocracy and peasantry, handicraftsmen, labourers, and merchants. But with these elections you have all, without distinction, entered a new camp. It is needful now that the national will shall prevail and the country govern itself as it pleases."

The elections, which took place in January, 1924, gave an overwhelming victory to the Wafd. It obtained 188 seats as against 27 of the other parties. On January 28th Zaghlul Pasha undertook to form a Ministry. The British High Commissioner agreed to a complete political amnesty, to include everybody with the exception of those whom both the High Commissioner and the Egyptian Prime Minister considered a menace to the public safety. On March 15th the first Egyptian Parliament was opened. In the King's Speech Zaghlul assumed an exceedingly moderate tone. Neither was the question of the Sudan expressly raised, nor was there any protest against the four reserved points in the declaration of independence of 1922. The Opposition press and a number of deputies attacked Zaghlul for his moderation, but Zaghlul was able to restore the country's absolute confidence in himself.

THE SUDAN

On July 29th, 1924, a new electoral law was promulgated, which introduced direct election for the Chamber and the Senate. Every male Egyptian over 21 had a direct vote for the Chamber, and all over 25 for the Senate. Only those might be deputies who could read and write properly, but the regulation was abolished by which candidates could only stand for election in the provinces in which they were entitled to vote. This was the only considerable measure in the domestic sphere passed by the first Egyptian Parliament. For the most part it occupied itself with debates on the Sudan and on relations with Great Britain, a proof of the impatience that consumed the deputies. From the outset the question of the Sudan occupied much attention. All Egyptian parties were agreed in regarding the Sudan as an inseparable part of Egypt. Their reasons were identity of religion and speech (which, however, only held good as regards the more important northern part of the Sudan, not the equatorial part), the unity of the economic system based upon the Nile, and the fact that for a hundred years the Sudan had belonged to Egypt. In 1924, moreover, the Sudanese and the Egyptians in the Sudan sought repeatedly to give expression to their attachment to Egypt, but all their attempts were severely repressed by Great Britain. In actual fact Great Britain administered the Sudan as she thought good without rendering any account to Egypt, whilst Egypt bore a considerable part of the cost of the English administration in the Sudan,[44] supplying and paying a number of the officials of middle rank and the greater part of the occupying force. The English administration in the Sudan could point to the fact that it had done a great deal for the development and opening up of the country. Even after the declaration of Egyptian independence, British public opinion regarded the Sudan as part of the British Empire. This inevitably angered the Egyptians, who regarded the condominium, to which they contributed heavily, as a mere fiction. Thus all the material for a serious conflict was present.[45]

In Khartoum, the capital of the Sudan, a White Flag Society had been founded, on whose banner the whole Nile Valley was depicted in red on a white ground, united (under Egyptian sovereignty). The members of this Society were educated Sudanese, who had passed through the English Gordon College in Khartoum, and Egyptians resident in the Sudan. In June, 1924, an Egyptian who was to present a loyal address to King Fuad in the name of this Society was stopped at the frontier and sent back by the English, which led to prolonged demonstrations and disorders in the Sudan. The reply of the British Government, contained in Lord Parmoor's statement, was as follows : " Now I want to say, in absolutely definite language, that His Majesty's Government is not going to abandon the Sudan in any sense whatever. It recognizes the obligations which have been taken towards the Sudanese and . . . it regards those obligations as of a character which this Government could not abandon without a very serious loss of prestige.* This declaration, however, did not restore calm in the Sudan, but increased the excitement. In August there was a serious revolt of the cadets in the Military College at Khartoum.

These incidents deprived the negotiations to be conducted in London between MacDonald and Zaghlul, at the former's invitation, of any great prospect of success. Zaghlul had to defend himself against continual accusations on the part of the Egyptians that he was prepared for compromises. Lord Parmoor's declaration on the subject of the Sudan caused Zaghlul to offer his resignation to the King who, however, did not accept it. On July 12th an Egyptian student attempted to assassinate Zaghlul because he suspected him of meditating a betrayal in the coming negotiations with England. The negotiations, which took place in London at the end of September, proved futile. Following the advice of the Committee of Imperial Defence, England insisted upon the continuation of the British occupation in Egypt. On his return thither Zaghlul was received with enthusiasm. When the Egyptian Parliament reassembled he once more offered his resignation, which was not accepted. Meanwhile, a Conservative Government had come into office in England. The continuance of a parliamentary régime and of the Wafd Ministry, which had tried to restore Egypt's autonomy in domestic affairs, seemed intolerable to England. The murder of the British Sirdar of the Egyptian army and Governor-General of the Sudan, Sir Lee Stack, on November 19th, brought about a solution in this impasse, and was the occasion of a turn of events which met English desires.[46]

In his Note of October 7th, 1924, MacDonald had told

* *Hansard*, House of Lords, June 25th, 1924, col. 986.

the British High Commissioner that England would take steps for the maintenance of order in the Sudan, that she had obligations to the Sudanese that she could not abandon, and that she would not tolerate a continuance of the existing state of affairs. England, he said, certainly recognized Egypt's rights in the Sudan, but they were exclusively economic, and concerned her share in the water of the Nile and her financial claims. Such a definition of Egyptian claims to the Sudan made nonsense of the condominium, and was inevitably felt by the Egyptians to be an open threat, which did, in fact, materialize soon after the murder of Sir Lee Stack.

The assassination of the Sirdar enabled Great Britain to accomplish two aims : the removal of Zaghlul, and with him of Parliament, and the annexation, unrestricted in fact, of the Sudan. On November 22nd Lord Allenby handed Zaghlul two Notes from the British Government, stating that the Government was of opinion " that this murder, which holds up Egypt as at present governed to the contempt of civilized peoples, is the natural outcome of a campaign of hostility to British rights . . . in Egypt, and the Sudan, founded upon a heedless ingratitude for benefits conferred by Great Britain ". Besides various demands, such as an apology, the punishment of the assassins, and the payment of an indemnity of half a million pounds, the Note took the opportunity to realize all England's aims by means of an ultimatum ; the withdrawal of all Egyptian troops from the Sudan, the total abolition of the last practical traces of the condominium, a revision of the compensation paid to foreign officials in Egyptian service in accordance with English wishes, the restoration to the English Financial and Judicial Advisers of all their rights and, first and foremost, the unlimited extension of the irrigation area in the Sudan.[47] Zaghlul Pasha sent a conciliatory and dignified reply, but Great Britain insisted upon the demands contained in the ultimatum and resorted to military measures, so that Zaghlul resigned on November 24th. The King entrusted the President of the Senate, Ahmed Ziwar Pasha,.with the formation of the new Ministry.

Great Britain's demands, especially her claim to the unlimited use of the Nile water for the Sudan, roused opposition even in England. For this involved a menace to the very existence of the Egyptian fellaheen, and a breach of England's solemn assurances that she would always respect Egypt's claim to the Nile water, and would never extend the irrigation area in the Sudan except with Egypt's consent. And, indeed, England found occasion later to withdraw this demand. But the Sudan passed to a purely English administration and the revolts of the Egyptian troops there at the end of November were suppressed with sanguinary severity. This meant, in fact, that the Anglo-Egyptian treaty of 1899 concerning the Sudan was set aside. The Sudan had become a purely British colony, whence at any moment Egypt could be menaced and destroyed by the disposition of the Nile water.

A series of trials followed the murder of Sir Lee Stack, and the police endeavoured to clear up the earlier assassinations as well. An *agent provocateur* helped the accusing counsel. In the first trial in June, 1925, eight persons were condemned to death, mainly students and young officials. A second trial in February, 1926, brought seven persons to the bar, including such members of the Wafd Ministry as Mahmud Nukrashi and Ahmed Mahir. But only one of the accused was condemned to death in May, 1926 ; the rest were acquitted, whereupon the English President of the Court announced publicly that he had been outvoted by his two Egyptian colleagues, and resigned his post.

THE FIRST DICTATORSHIP

Ziwar's was a Ministry of the aristocracy, composed originally of members of the Constitutional Liberal party and of the Court party, formed shortly afterwards round the person of the king's favourite, Nashaat Pasha. The real anti-Wafd leader and the strong man in the Cabinet was Ismail Sidky Pasha, well known as a clever financier and energetic politician ; he had accompanied Zaghlul in his first exile, had then soon afterwards broken with him, and thenceforward his aim was the destruction of the Wafd.

The new Ministry dissolved Parliament in November, 1924. The fresh elections that were to be held in January were postponed till March, and the whole pressure of the administrative machine was brought to bear in order to assemble a Parliament complaisant to the new policy. The election was held in accordance with the original law in two stages, not under the Act passed by the new Parliament. At the end of March Parliament met. The very first sitting was decisive. When the President of the Chamber was elected Zaghlul Pasha obtained 125 votes, and Sarwat Pasha, the candidate of the Government, only 85. That same day the newly elected Parliament was dissolved, the date of the fresh elections fixed, according to the constitution, within the next two months, but then immediately postponed indefinitely, " in view of the necessity and urgency of a change in the electoral system, so as to ensure better representation of the country," as the official text declared. A Government Commission was appointed to devise this electoral law, and continued its labours till the end of November, 1925. For that whole year Egypt was ruled autocratically in defiance of the Constitution and without Parliament. The experiment, which the English forced upon the country, and were to repeat again later, seemed successful. The British Government and the British press believed that a triumph had been scored and that conditions in Egypt had been restored to normal. At the beginning of September there was a split in the Ziwar Ministry. The immediate occasion was the conviction of Sheikh Ali Abdel Razek for heresy, contained in a book he had written on Islamic principles of government. But the real reason was to be found in the king's hostility to the Constitutional Liberals and their progressive tendencies. The king wanted to gather round him only his own immediate followers, and to have a Ministry that would be compliant to his wishes. The Constitutional Liberals, led by Abdel Asis Fahmi, resigned. This happened whilst Ziwar Pasha was in Europe. Ismail Sidky Pasha, who was also in Europe at the time, communicated with his colleagues by telegraph and joined them in resigning. The split led to a fresh loss of prestige on the part of the dictatorship. In spite of the severe measures adopted, unrest increased all over the country.

Under these circumstances the new British High Commissioner, Lord Lloyd, arrived in Egypt. He was confronted with the growing determination of the Egyptian people to bring their country back into constitutional paths, and to put forward the demand for national independence. The mature political wisdom of Egyptian statesmen and Zaghlul's ability as a leader united all the Egyptian parties once more in 1925 in a national coalition against the Court and the English, unassailable so long as Zaghlul lived. Only a few weeks earlier people would have regarded such union as impossible.

According to the Egyptian Constitution, Parliament must meet on the third Saturday in November every year. Ignoring the Government's prohibition, and the fact that the Parliament House was occupied by troops, the Deputies and Senators of the three parties met on November 21st, 1925 ; the meeting, under the presidency of Zaghlul, became a great demonstration of national unity and the resolve to restore constitutional conditions in the country. Without outward demonstrations a revolution had taken place. Once more, as in 1919, the whole people formed a united front, under the leadership of Zaghlul. He was supported by the Constitutional Liberals under Mohammed Mahmud Pasha [48] and the Nationalists. Later on, as had happened after 1919, this coalition again fell a victim to the endeavours of the English to make play with social and personal antitheses in Egypt.

On December 10th, to everybody's delight, King Fuad dismissed Nashaat Pasha from his post as Director of the Royal Cabinet, and appointed him to the foreign diplomatic service. This was done at the instance of Lord Lloyd, who hoped thereby to win in particular Ismail Sidky Pasha for the Ministry again, and thus to enable the weak Ziwar Cabinet to hold its own against the Wafd. Lord Lloyd's hope proved vain.

On December 8th, 1925, the Government promulgated the intended new electoral law. This electoral law, which served as a model to later would-be dictatorships, made 30 the minimum age for the active franchise, whilst the Commission under Abdel Asis Fahmi had originally even demanded 40 ; electors who could show that they had reached a certain level either in education or as taxpayers were to enjoy the active franchise at 25. Indirect election was reintroduced. The elections to the third Egyptian Parliament were to be held under this law. The national coalition threatened to boycott the elections. The Ministry hoped that the boycott would fail, for Deputies whose re-election was certain would surely be tempted by the sweets of office. The Government deceived itself. The electors were too well disciplined. The hope of splitting the Opposition parties was disappointed. The three Opposition parties had summoned a national Congress in Cairo for February 19th. Probably more than 95 per cent of all persons who played a part in Egyptian public and political life were present. The demonstration was perfectly orderly, and might claim to voice the sentiments of the whole nation. Even before the Congress met, it had scored its first great triumph. On the previous evening the Ministerial Council resolved to set aside the new electoral law and to hold the elections in May under the Act of 1924, passed by Parliament. Again the elections showed an overwhelming majority for the Wafd, which had come to a prior agreement with the other parties on the seats due to it.

Zaghlul, the chief of the majority party and the coalition, the unquestioned leader of the people, ought to have been Prime Minister. This Lord Lloyd opposed. His intention of humiliating the Wafd led to an essentially unsound compromise. Adli Yeghen Pasha undertook to form a Cabinet, in which the Zaghlulists were to have the majority of portfolios. Lord Lloyd addressed a letter of thanks in the name of the British Government to Ziwar Pasha, expressing gratitude for the valuable services he had rendered to Great Britain during his term of office. Nothing could have damaged Ziwar's prestige in the country so much as this letter, which gave proof of Lord Lloyd's conception of his own position in Egypt, and Egypt's relation to England.

SAAD ZAGHLUL

In its first session the new Egyptian Parliament devoted its attention solely to domestic questions. Valuable progress was made in education under the Minister Ali Shamsi,[49] in public works under Osman Moharram, and in agriculture under Mohammed Fathallah Barakat Pasha. It was not till the second session that mention was made in the King's Speech, on November 18th, 1926, of the question which was of supreme importance to Egypt, that of a settlement of relations with England. Mention was made of the good relations between the two Powers, whose understanding became daily more cordial, and Chamberlain responded in the same spirit in England. But beyond these diplomatic courtesies relations remained fundamentally unchanged. On the contrary, Lord Lloyd evinced a growing tendency to restrict the liberty hitherto enjoyed by Egypt in domestic administration. As is always the case when the relation between Great Britain and Eastern countries is in question, the tone adopted by the correspondents of London papers in Cairo might be regarded as the best barometer of the true relations between the countries. In these a number of internal measures adopted by the Egyptian Government were criticized with a degree of acrimony which the British Press only uses towards colonial countries. The most moderate Constitutional Liberals, like Ismail Sidky Pasha, repeatedly pointed out in the Egyptian Chamber that, whilst Egypt was working for a good understanding with England, the English Press was conducting an unjustifiable campaign against the Egyptians which was a violation of the most elementary laws of decorum. Lord Lloyd wanted to govern Egypt as Lord Cromer had done forty years earlier. He overlooked the fact that that day was past in Egypt, and not only in Egypt. His autocratic ways offended the Egyptians, and afterwards even the Court and the foreign settlements. He behaved as if Egypt were still a province of the British Empire, and he the proconsul whose part it was to dazzle the people by the power and brilliance of his state and so to convince them of England's greatness.

It is comprehensible, therefore, that irritation began slowly to find expression among the Egyptians, leading to a ministerial crisis. In April, 1927, Ali Yeghen Pasha resigned. Hopes of a breach in the national coalition were disappointed. The new Ministry under Sarwat Pasha was just like its predecessor. Sarwat was a statesman of exceedingly moderate views, although he no more lost sight of the goal of national independence than any other Egyptian. A conflict soon arose under the new Ministry. The immediate occasion was the question of the British Sirdar's position and the reorganization of the Egyptian army, especially the substitution of modern equipment for what was absolutely useless, and the reduction of the period of service from five years to three. Lord Lloyd retorted by a sharp Note and the dispatch of warships.[50] In this Note, also, reference to the inadequate security of foreigners in Egypt was not omitted. The Egyptians replied that few peoples were so hospitable as they, and that before the British occupation foreigners had always lived in perfect safety in Egypt. If anything could menace the security of foreigners in Egypt, it was the British policy of occupation and the system of capitulations.

The crisis was settled by Egypt giving way. In the summer of 1927 King Fuad visited the capitals of Western Europe, and was everywhere received with the highest honours, especially in London. Sarwat Pasha took the opportunity to open negotiations in London with the British Foreign Secretary, Sir Austen Chamberlain, for an Anglo-Egyptian treaty. At this vital juncture in Egypt's history, on August 23rd, 1927, Saad Zaghlul died, Egypt's leader and one of the great statesmen that have been granted to mankind in recent years.

Zaghlul's name is inextricably linked with the critical period in modern Egyptian history. He was the leader of the Egyptian independence movement since its first flickering rise under Arabi Pasha, more than forty-five years ago, and remained so till his old age. Both as a young and an old man he suffered persecution in consequence. Abroad he was the accredited representative of his people and at home a sacred symbol to the broad masses, embodying all the dim political consciousness of the peasantry and the political aims of the intelligentsia. He was far and away the ablest man that modern Egypt has produced, and of an integrity rare not only in Eastern countries. He stood, as no other politician could, for years the unquestioned head of his people, who trusted him to an extent perhaps unique in modern history the world over. In the eyes of the English during his life-time he was an extremist and an agitator ; it was only after his death that they knew better. He alone among his people held their fate in the hollow of his hand for ten years.

By descent Zaghlul was a fellah who made his way up into the newly rising middle-class intelligentsia in accordance with the sociological process that has dominated Egyptian

life for the past fifty years. Zaghlul was through and through
a representative of the fellaheen, an Egyptian of the purest
water, only in him all the negative qualities of the Egyptian
peasant emerged in an ennobled form. Instinctively the
people recognized and loved in him their representative and
hero. His name is associated not only with the rise and
triumph of Egyptian nationalism, but also with that of the
Egyptian middle class in their struggle against the hitherto
dominant land-owning nobility. For a long time the
aristocracy could not forgive Zaghlul, who was an upstart
in their eyes, for helping to introduce in Egypt a new order
which first disputed and finally overthrew the exclusive
authority that they had hitherto exercised. But Zaghlul's
personality succeeded in 1919 and 1925 in overcoming all
these antipathies and bringing even the aristocracy under
his leadership and thus achieving for years a degree of
national unity hardly ever attained elsewhere. His undisputed
position and the continuity of Egyptian policy guaranteed
by his person for so many years stand alone in modern
history, and more than ever mark his greatness. Its influence
did not cease with his life.

In forty-five years of struggle Zaghlul had succeeded in
training his people to use the machinery of democratic and
parliamentary government and in forcing European politicians
to recognize their ambitions. Once more, in July, 1927, it
was granted to him to point with pride to the high standard
of the Egyptian Parliament in his farewell speech on the
adjournment ; he was then seventy-six, and in poor health,
but he had presided over the long and exhausting session
from November, 1926, on into the height of summer.

On his death many European observers expected the
decline of Egyptian nationalism and the dissolution of the
national coalition. It was plain that Zaghlul's death could
not bring about the breakdown of Egyptian nationalism, for
the rise of the national movement in Egypt was no more the
work of individual agitators and demagogues than in Italy
or Serbia, but rather an inevitable sociological and historical
process that will not halt till it has reached its goal. Yet
even discerning observers might believe in the danger of
the Wafd, Zaghlul's party and his own creation, falling to
pieces. For neither sociologically nor temperamentally was

the Wafd homogeneous. But Zaghlul's heritage and the political maturity which the Egyptian people owed to him were strong enough to maintain not only the Wafd, but even the national coalition, in spite of the fact that in Eastern countries personal forces and jealousies exercise a greater influence than in Europe. Zaghlul's wife Safia, the daughter of a well-known anglophile Turkish Pasha, continued to be the adviser of the Wafd, the mother of the people.[52]

THE SARWAT-CHAMBERLAIN NEGOTIATIONS

Zaghlul was succeeded as leader of the Wafd and President of the Chamber of Deputies by Mustafa Nahas Pasha ; even his outward appearance was different from Zaghlul's, he lacked the dead leader's intellectual adaptability, but he was elected unanimously by the Wafd as their leader for his uprightness, his incorruptibility, and his devotion.[53] On November 17th Parliament met in a new session. In his Speech from the Throne the King made two hopeful announcements. The first concerned relations with England, the second the abolition of the capitulations. The Egyptian Government was going to appoint Commissions in order to make legal preparations for the modification and subsequent abolition of the capitulations. In the spring of 1928 a conference of all the capitulatory Powers was to be called in Egypt, in order to resolve upon a modification of the system of capitulations. At the end of December the Egyptian Government addressed a Note to the capitulatory Powers, proposing certain quite minor changes in the existing system, and asking the Governments to communicate their acceptance or their views, if possible by January 31st, 1928, so that a conference might meet in February to determine the question of the changes. Very few Governments sent any answer at all. Neither the limited conference nor the wider one ever took place. Egypt's hope of a rapid and peaceful solution of the question of the capitulations was not fulfilled. True, Great Britain repeatedly declared her readiness to meet Egypt in the matter, but the influential foreign settlements and the holders of European capital invested in Egypt would hear nothing of the abolition of the capitulations.

At the beginning of 1928 Egyptian public opinion became increasingly interested in the negotiations between Great Britain and Egypt, begun in the summer of 1927. There were three main subjects of discussion : the Sudan ; the defence of British imperial communications, and hence the question of the British occupation of Egypt ; and thirdly the protection of foreign interests in Egypt, and hence the question of the capitulations. Everybody in Egypt was convinced that two other matters could be settled without difficulty : Egypt's complete domestic autonomy and her entry into the League of Nations, which could only benefit by the entry of the first Sunni and Arab State member. Moderate Egyptian opinion, as represented by Sarwat Pasha, regarded the first three problems, which seemed the thorniest, somewhat in this light : it was realized that for the time being the problem of the Sudan was insoluble. What was desired was a reversion to the formal condominium, as it existed before 1924. For the rest, the final solution of the question must be left to future developments. Egypt resisted any attempt to treat the Sudan as British colonial territory, for strategic and economic considerations make it essential to her. The Sudan controls the Upper Nile and therefore Egypt's water supply, upon which the country is wholly dependent. The Power that controls the Sudan controls Egypt, indirectly but absolutely. The cotton growing promoted by British companies in the Sudan threatens the Egyptian fellaheen, whose livelihood depends mainly on cotton, with crushing competition. For the same reasons that Egypt desires to possess the Sudan, Great Britain also desires it. If, therefore, this question seemed insoluble, the others seemed all the easier of solution. It was unnecessary to provide for the protection of foreigners ; such measures could only serve as an excuse for perpetual intervention in Egypt's internal affairs. In a free and independent Egypt foreigners would be just as safe as in any other country. For the defence of British imperial communications Egypt was prepared to conclude a military alliance and a treaty of friendship with Great Britain, which would have given her the right to protect Egypt from all external attacks and to count, in case of war, on Egypt's full support. A continuation of the British occupation would have been unnecessary. In

case of need English troops could have reached the Suez
Canal from Malta within a few hours. Egyptian friendship
would be the best defence for British imperial communications. But if the continued presence of British troops
in Egypt were necessary, they might perhaps remain a few
years longer in the Canal zone. The existing state of affairs,
with British troops quartered in the citadel of Cairo and in
all the important points in the chief cities of the land, and
constantly marching through the streets, not only implied
a perpetual humiliation to Egyptian national sentiment, but
also the possibility and menace of continual intervention in
Egypt's domestic affairs.

Such were the ideas current in moderate Egyptian circles
concerning the future relations of Great Britain and Egypt.
It is, therefore, easy to understand that the draft Anglo-
Egyptian treaty presented to the Government and to
Parliament at the end of February, 1928, was unanimously
rejected by the Egyptians. The Conservative Government
in Great Britain never dreamed of interpreting the four
reserved points in the declaration of 1922 in a sense
favourable to Egypt's desire for independence. Sarwat
Pasha conducted the negotiations with unwearying readiness
to meet Great Britain half-way and with a genuine effort to
win her friendship.[54] But even this most moderate of
statesmen was amazed at the British draft treaty and gave
frank expression to his amazement in his Note to
Chamberlain : " The British drafts in places lack precision,
employing certain vague formulæ which in practice would
not fail to give rise to the same difficulties which we are now
endeavouring to dispose of. Where the drafts are precise,
they tend to subordinate the action of the Egyptian
Government to a preventive control which on more than one
point would actually be in conflict with the liberty which
that Government have enjoyed in recent years. Egypt,
therefore, does not have the consolation of reflecting that by
accepting, under a Treaty of Alliance, certain limitations
to her sovereignty, she would ensure the disappearance of
certain others. The draft does not create for her a more
favourable situation than if she had remained under the vague
régime resulting from the four reserved points. Interference
in the country's affairs could not go further, under the

last-named régime, than it would under the régime of the draft." * Sarwat Pasha showed in detail how the British draft meant less favourable conditions than those at present obtaining, and that its system of strict control implied nothing less than a protectorate such as Egypt had never recognized, even many years earlier.

Sarwat Pasha did, indeed, succeed by his representations in securing certain changes in the draft treaty. But it was plain to him, as he explained to Lord Lloyd at the beginning of February, that " the last word of His Majesty's Government would not satisfy Egyptian public opinion, and he could, in consequence, see no prospect of the treaty's acceptance either by his colleagues or Parliament. The discussion in London showed that the whole difficulty lay in the maintenance of the British army on Egyptian soil. Egypt could only be convinced of the necessity of this if it should be shown that the advantages of the treaty were such as to outweigh this disadvantage. How, he asked, could he point to Egypt's complete liberty in her internal administration when the treaty laid obligations on her in the matter of the Egyptian army and the police, as well as of the Judicial and Financial Advisers ? " † Sarwat Pasha demanded further modifications, but Chamberlain declared that Great Britain had spoken her last word, and urged him to lay the treaty, which had hitherto been kept strictly secret, before the Egyptian Ministry. And so what Sarwat Pasha had foreseen inevitably happened. The treaty which could not, as it then was, satisfy even the most moderate Egyptians, and which continued the Protectorate under another name, was unanimously rejected by Egyptian public opinion. On March 4th, 1928, Sarwat Pasha presented Lord Lloyd with the official answer of the Egyptian Ministry, and handed in his resignation. Six months later he was dead.

A PARLIAMENTARY INTERMEZZO

Chamberlain, in his communiqué to Lord Lloyd of March 1st, 1928, had instructed him to tell Sarwat Pasha

* Egypt No. 1. Cmd. 3050, 1928. *Papers Regarding Negotiations for a Treaty of Alliance with Egypt.*
† *Ibid.*

that the British Government could not continue indefinitely to hold out the hand of friendship. In case of a rejection of the treaty, he immediately added a threat. Under Sarwat Pasha the Egyptian Parliament had discussed a number of Bills to secure the democratization of the public services and civic liberties. Lord Lloyd was instructed to protest against these Bills on the ground that they would make it more difficult for England to fulfil her obligations in the matter of the four reserved points. Lord Lloyd had tolerated the Egyptian Parliament because he had hoped that it would ratify the treaty with Great Britain and thus legalize the English occupation and intervention in domestic affairs. He had hoped to be able to attribute this success to his policy and, having accomplished this one imperial task, to be called to greater ones. That hope proved deceptive. Thenceforward the fate of the Egyptian Parliament was sealed. As in 1924, England saw no way out of the impasse but to suspend the parliamentary constitution in league with the king. The coalition, indeed, held together, and on March 15th the king was forced to form a Ministry under the premiership of Mustafa Nahas Pasha. This, too, was a coalition Ministry including, like its predecessor, Mohammed Mahmud Pasha as the representative of the Constitutional Liberals. The programme put forward by Mustafa Nahas, Egypt's absolute independence together with genuine friendship with England and readiness to form an alliance, was universally supported by Parliament and the nation.

But the new Ministry was destined to survive no longer than three months. The threats adumbrated in Chamberlain's communiqué to Lord Lloyd were carried out. As early as 1924 the Egyptian Parliament had begun to reform the laws, dating from the period of martial law, concerning local government, freedom of assembly, and the possession of arms, in harmony with the spirit of the democratic constitution. Ever since England had imposed martial law during the War, Egyptians had been forbidden to carry arms, whilst Europeans were allowed to do so. As the circumstances that had given rise to martial law were past and gone, the legal rights of the Egyptians were to be assimilated to those of the Europeans, and they were to be allowed to carry arms if they obtained a special licence. In reply to England's protest Nahas Pasha answered that legislation was Egypt's internal affair, a right guaranteed in the constitution, and she would allow no foreign State to intervene. Even the English weekly, *The Near East and India*, which is in close touch with British colonial circles, counselled that these Bills should be allowed to pass, and that intervention should only be undertaken if it proved later that there was a real menace under the new laws to the safety of foreigners. Lord Lloyd chose a different course. At the end of April he sent a short-term ultimatum, the third within the bare two years of Egypt's existence as a parliamentary State since the fall of Ziwar Pasha; again he summoned warships from Malta to Egypt and demanded the immediate withdrawal of the Bills. Mustafa Nahas reiterated that Egyptian legislation was the affair of an independent State, and refused to admit English intervention. Nevertheless, he offered to postpone the Egyptian Senate's discussion of the Bills till the following parliamentary session in November, 1928. This satisfied Lord Lloyd.* There was to be no session of the Egyptian Parliament in November, 1928. The third Egyptian Parliament, after a life of barely two years, was done away with, thanks to the alliance between Great Britain and the king, supported by the Constitutional Liberals.

In spite of all efforts to maintain the coalition, it broke up in the spring of 1928. The Constitutional Liberal Ministers, in the first instance Mohammed Mahmud Pasha, resigned, and three of the Wafd joined them. In the midst of this already confused situation came the accusation put forward by the Opposition Press that the Prime Minister and the President of the Chamber, Wissa Wassif Bey, a leading Wafd Copt, had abused their position in order to win a lawsuit concerning the estates of Prince Seif ed Din, whose counsel they were, and thus to secure high legal fees. The most important evidence was a stolen letter from a Wafd Deputy, which was never sent and which he declared to be a forgery. These accusations, which were later proved to be wholly unfounded, were very welcome to the English and the king. In June, 1928, the king carried out a *coup d'état*.

* See the British White Book, Cmd. 3047, 1928, on the Anglo-Egyptian crisis arising from the Bill for the regulation of public meetings.

He called upon Mustafa Nahas to resign, saying that his
Ministry had originally been based on a coalition and had
no claim to continue when the coalition ceased.   When
Mustafa Nahas refused to resign, pointing out that the
Ministry represented by far the strongest party in Parliament
and possessed the full confidence of Parliament and the
country, the king dismissed him, identifying himself with the
accusations scattered abroad by the Opposition Press.   He
entrusted Mohammed Mahmud Pasha with the task of forming
a Ministry.   It was clear from the outset, that though
Mohammed Mahmud Pasha's Government had the confidence
of the king, and particularly of Lord Lloyd and the English
Press, it by no means had that of the Egyptian people.   Thus
the mere formation of this Government foreshadowed the
king's resolve, taken in agreement with Lord Lloyd, to make
an end of the Egyptian Parliament and the Egyptian people's
constitutional liberties.

THE SECOND DICTATORSHIP

The new Prime Minister, who sprang from the richest
land-owning family in Upper Egypt, was the first Egyptian
Prime Minister who had received his education in England.
This was why Lord Lloyd's choice fell upon him, and for this
reason the English Press gave him a warm welcome and
delighted to extol him as the greatest man in Egypt.   Like
other dictators, Mohammed Mahmud's chief desire was to
restore law and order, though it was only his coup that
endangered them, and to carry out a number of economic
and social reforms which, as it turned out, had all been
previously introduced and discussed in Parliament ;   but
under the dictatorship precisely that atmosphere of political
calm was lacking that is essential to the cultural and social
labours of which Egypt has need.
The monotony of Egyptian history from 1922 to 1930
is staggering.   It is the necessary consequence of the
disposition of forces struggling for mastery in Egypt.   It is
just because the newly won constitutional popular rights are
in constant danger that the mass of the people prize them.
Those rights have still the sacred character of a treasure
long desired, and hardly yet enjoyed.   Zaghlul again and

again gave his mind to the question of the constitution; he had taught the fellaheen to love the constitution. Zaghlul knew well enough that he must carry on a struggle with England for Egypt's independence and with the European foreign settlements for the abolition of the capitulations, but that the constitution, the sovereign, democratic Parliament, must also be defended against the king's autocratic inclinations, supported by England and the foreign settlements, and against the feudal nobility; for the feudal nobility, accustomed to domination and of alien blood, regarded the rise of the new middle class to political power and the awakening of the fellaheen with anxiety, and were no more able than the English and Europeans in Egypt to accept the idea that times change.

On July 19th, 1928, the king and his Ministry carried out the *coup d'état* rendered necessary by the appointment of Mohammed Mahmud Pasha; it was a revolution from above under the banner of autocratic reaction. A royal rescript altered the democratic constitution and suspended it for an indefinite period, at least three years. The articles dealing with the assembly, re-election, and legislative powers of Parliament and with alterations in the constitution were suppressed, and freedom of the Press abolished. The Prime Minister proclaimed a dictatorship, benevolent if possible, but relentless against all opposition, and announced a number of reforms for the protection of the fellaheen and the workers and the improvement of their lot. He also promised a thorough reform of the administration, good government. Parliament, he said, was discredited by party strife. As if party strife were not the essence of Parliament, and as if the Egyptian Parliament in particular had not been free from that strife for the greater part of its life, thanks to the coalition, and would not have been further spared any paralysing strife thanks to its large Wafd majority. But it was precisely the power of the Wafd that was to be broken.

This time the reaction proceeded further than three years earlier under Ziwar Pasha, who had left the constitution theoretically intact and allowed the Senate to continue its sessions. The English Press and Europeans in Egypt welcomed the *coup d'état*. It was, they said, in the interests of the fellaheen, who were tired of politics and

Parliament. As in the days of Lord Cromer, so now
Lord Lloyd, with the help of Mohammed Mahmud, would
extend his protection to the fellaheen. Considering this
anxious care for the fellaheen, who according to the
dictatorship were hostile to the Wafd, it was strange that
the Government did not hold fresh elections in which the
fellaheen, protected and encouraged by Mohammed Mahmud
Pasha's administration, could give expression to their dislike
of the Wafd ; and it was strange that the Government
announced its intention of creating a new electoral system
which would exclude the mass of the people from the
franchise.

The dictator's Ministry consisted of abler and more
distinguished men than Ziwar Pasha's had done. It could
count upon Lord Lloyd's support. It had announced a good
programme of reforms. But it bore within itself the seeds of
dissolution and was doomed to bring disorder and internal
strife instead of contributing to Egypt's consolidation and
elevation. The dictatorship installed its own supporters in
all administrative posts, whether in the central ministries
or in the provinces. Whether this led to good government is
a question ; what is certain is that the people preferred
self-government.

The Wafd opposed the dissolution of Parliament, and
adhered to the thesis that the suspension of the constitution
was illegal and that, therefore, Parliament was still in being.
On July 28th the Deputies and Senators held sessions which
could not be in the Parliament House, for that was occupied
by troops and all the entrances barred, but in a private
house close by. The session declared that the Government
was illegal, and that any treaties it might conclude were
invalid. According to the constitution the next meeting of
Parliament was to fall on the third Saturday in November.
Meanwhile a lawsuit was in process to investigate Nahas
Pasha's alleged abuse of his office. The suit was conducted
under pressure from the Government, and Nahas Pasha's
bitter enemies. Nevertheless, the Bench was obliged, after
a lengthy inquiry, to acquit Mustafa Nahas of all suspicion.
The Government forbade reports of the judgment in the
Press. None the less, the news spread like wildfire throughout
Egypt. The whole nation exulted and this decisive victory

for the Wafd could not be ignored even by the English High Commissioner.

The seeds of dissolution which the Ministry bore within itself began to grow and bear fruit. The dictatorship embodied the will of Lord Lloyd and Mohammed Mahmud, not, as the king had expected, his own. Mohammed Mahmud soon lost favour with the king. The old conflict between the Constitutional Liberals and the Court party revived. The attempt of the dictatorship to break the Wafd by censorship and terror, by organized demonstrations and large expenditure, did not succeed.

Mohammed Mahmud did not proceed to carry out the reforms. Egypt's domestic politics were involved in the question of the dam at Jebel Auliya above Khartoum.[55] The whole energies of the Ministry were occupied in securing its own existence. The Press was forbidden to report the great demonstrations of representatives from all parts of the country, of Egyptian ladies, of lawyers who went on strike for a week. In defiance of all the Government's threats, Mustafa Nahas was also acquitted of having asked too high a fee by the Disciplinary Senate of the Chamber of Advocates, consisting of the judges of the Court of Appeal in Cairo. In giving its reasons for the judgment the Court actually laid stress on the improper methods adopted by the prosecution. Mustafa Nahas received great ovations. The Government suppressed all expressions of the popular will, and even annulled the elections to the Chamber of Advocates, which showed an overwhelming majority for the Wafd candidates.

When the new Labour Government came into office in England a new situation arose for Egypt. The new English Foreign Secretary, Henderson, took the opportunity of Mohammed Mahmud Pasha's visit to London to submit a new draft treaty to him which differed fundamentally from the previous one.[56] It made an end of the veiled Protectorate, and its first article proclaimed that the military occupation of Egypt by British troops should cease. Whilst former draft treaties had recognized only one-sided obligations on Egypt's part, the new treaty of August 3rd, 1929, was based upon the principle of absolute equality of rights. The preamble to the treaty provided for its submission to the Egyptian

Parliament. This gave a new turn to Egyptian politics, and to Egypt's relations with Great Britain. Still more important, perhaps, was Henderson's recall of Lord Lloyd on July 24th, and his appointment in August of Sir Percy Loraine as High Commissioner in his place. Henderson pointed out that Lord Lloyd, in his autocratic policy in Egypt, had even acted contrary to the wishes of the Conservative Foreign Secretary, Chamberlain.* Even the Constitutional Liberal Press in Egypt and King Fuad welcomed Lord Lloyd's recall.

PARLIAMENT AND PEACE

On October 2nd Mohammed Mahmud Pasha's Ministry resigned, and a temporary Ministry was formed under Adli Yeghen Pasha to carry out fresh elections. The fourth Egyptian Parliament was to meet eighteen months after the dissolution of the third. The Constitutional Liberals declared that they would take no part in the elections. The leader of the Wafd and his party refrained from all comment on the draft treaty. They would wait for Parliament to pronounce on it. But it was plain that Henderson's draft treaty appeared as an acceptable basis of agreement to the Wafd. It ended the English occupation of the land, which MacDonald had still been unable to concede in 1924, and which Chamberlain would have been willing under no circumstances to grant in 1927. It was under Henderson that the English first made up their minds to give precedence to diplomatic over strategic considerations that were out of date in the age of air fleets.

The elections took place on December 21st, and produced the anticipated result. The Egyptian Parliament that met on January 11th, 1930, was almost exclusively Wafd. Mustafa Nahas Pasha undertook to form the new Cabinet. The negotiations took place in a wholly new atmosphere. Sincere friendship for Great Britain, and confidence that the period of five years' struggle for their independence was nearing its end, inspired the Egyptian people. The new British High Commissioner made a speech in December to the British colony in Alexandria, which had expressed fears

* For the reasons for Lord Lloyd's recall see Henderson's speech in *The Times*, London, July 27th, 1929.

of the results if the Anglo-Egyptian treaty were concluded ;
he said that England was now approaching the settlement
of her relation to Egypt in a spirit which sought confidence
where hitherto there had been only doubt and suspicion,
friendship in place of hatred, and a sincere desire for
understanding.

The new Parliament was confronted with great tasks.
On February 17th the new customs came into force, which
represented for the first time Egypt's tariff autonomy.
Whilst the customs hitherto in force had been fixed not in
the country's own interest but in that of European import
trade, and were based upon long past economic conditions,
the new tariff was primarily designed to protect agriculture
and the industries that were to be developed by lowering
the import duties on necessary raw materials and machinery.
At the same time the new tariff was to bring the State
increased receipts in order to provide for the growing social
expenditure in the Budget. The capitulations forbid Egypt
to tax the trading and banking capital of foreigners in Egypt
in order to cover national expenditure. Great schemes of
reform fail for lack of money, and that is why the abolition
of the capitulations is an essential prerequisite of all social
and cultural progress in Egypt. Pending that, Parliament's
reforming activities must be obstructed.   Nevertheless, it
had before it a number of schemes for the establishment of
Agricultural Banks,[57] for cheap agricultural credit and the
protection of the small peasantry, and for the introduction of
new crops and the increase of the area under cultivation by
large-scale irrigation and the construction of railways and
roads, thus providing opportunity for more intensive
cultivation and improved marketing facilities. Bills had been
drafted for the protection of the workers and for infant
and child welfare. A scheme of reorganization of Egypt's
educational system, which had grossly neglected elementary
instruction under English control, provided for the practical
realization of universal compulsory education, already
decreed, in 1935, and for the special promotion of trade and
craft teaching.

Egypt hoped that now Parliament would be able to
develop its full activity. The conclusion of the treaty with
Great Britain seemed imminent.   Parliament chose a

delegation to go to London and conclude the treaty, consisting of Mustafa Nahas Pasha, the Minister of Public
Works Osman Moharram Pasha, the Finance Minister
Makram Ebeid, and the Foreign Minister Wassif Ghali
Pasha. The two last-named are Copts. Makram Ebeid, who
studied in Oxford and afterwards in Paris and was Professor
at the School of Law in Cairo, is regarded as one of the most
distinguished of the young Wafd leaders. The delegation
could count on the unanimous support of the Chamber in
its negotiations. The negotiations were conducted in London
in April and May, 1930, in a hitherto unaccustomed spirit
of friendliness and accommodation.[58] Although they broke
down over the question of the Sudan, nevertheless both
parties regarded the rupture as a merely temporary
interruption, and both Henderson and Mustafa Nahas
Pasha's declarations gave assurance of undiminished
friendship.

If the treaty had been concluded, Egypt would have
secured complete independence in all her domestic affairs
and in the formal conduct of her foreign policy. In her internal
administration she would still have had to carry on the
struggle for the total abolition of the capitulations, but that
would not have been a struggle with Great Britain, and she
could have counted upon Great Britain's support in it. In
her foreign policy she would have been bound by consideration
for her alliance with Great Britain, but not more than other
States are bound in their foreign policy by alliances, and the
support of the British Empire in all questions of external
security would have guarded Egypt from many a danger.
Great Britain had conceded to Egypt in the treaty complete
domestic autonomy and emancipation from English control,
and had only stipulated for Egypt's inclusion in the strategic
communication system of the British Empire. The remaining
traces of Great Britain's former predominance in Egypt,
still embodied in Henderson's original draft treaty, had been
removed after the negotiations with Mustafa Nahas Pasha.

Thus the Egyptian problem presented itself to England
very much like the Irish problem, which is equally of vital
strategic importance in the defence of the British Empire,
because of Ireland's position immediately to the west of the
island of Britain. It was possible to solve the Irish problem

by copying the model of Dominion status, which gives the country absolute independence and sovereignty in all its domestic affairs and yet keeps it within the sphere of influence of the British Empire in matters of foreign policy. The failure of British colonial statesmen to learn to extend the Dominion system to non-European races before it was too late has brought much trouble upon them. But the more Great Britain conceded absolute freedom to Egypt in all domestic matters, the more was it necessary for her to take steps to secure guarantees for her foreign policy in the bordering countries east of the Suez Canal and on the Upper Nile. Yet Egyptian and English interests were irreconcilably opposed in the question of the Sudan, so that no formula could bridge the difference. The Sudan is of importance to the English, not only strategically in relation to Egypt and the Red Sea, but also as the first of the uninterrupted series of East African possessions and for economic reasons. The English have done much to open up the Sudan, even if it was done in their own interest. For the Egyptians expansion in the direction of the Sudan is a question of the future. The only way now open is to leave the problem of the Sudan unsolved. In the three other reserved points of the 1922 declaration the Egyptian nationalist movement won an absolute victory in 1930. Mustafa Nahas Pasha was able to return to Egypt after the rupture of the negotiations with the knowledge that he had won the last round in his country's struggle for independence. Both Nahas and Henderson declared that the door was open for fresh negotiations, that these fresh negotiations would soon begin, and that the friendship between the two peoples had been consolidated by the way in which the negotiations had been conducted, and by mutual elucidation of the views held on both sides. There was, therefore, every reason to hope that Egypt would win her independence in 1930 and that one problem of British imperial policy would be solved after the lapse of fifty years.

THE THIRD DICTATORSHIP

But for the time being that consummation was to be delayed. The opponents of the Wafd in Egypt, especially

the foreign settlements, hardly concealed their displeasure
at this success scored by the Wafd. The idea that a time was
soon to come when foreigners living in Egypt would have to
pay taxes in the country where they lived and made money,
to share in the financial burden of developing the country, and
to submit to its jurisdiction alarmed the foreigners. Perhaps
it must be reckoned particularly to Henderson's credit that
he did not allow himself to be frightened by the repeated
protests of the British foreign settlements in Egypt and
prevented from placing the relation between Great Britain
and Egypt, and further, the relation between East and West,
on a new basis, more in harmony with the spirit of the times.

The Wafd had a foreboding of the menace to the country's
parliamentary system. It sought, therefore, to render the
revival of a dictatorship impossible. Article 68 of the Egyptian
constitution provided for the passage of a law governing
ministerial responsibility. When the new Parliament was
opened the King's Speech announced the introduction of
this Bill. And so the Ministry now introduced a Bill making
any suspension or alteration of the constitution without the
consent of Parliament high treason, for which the responsible
Ministers could be condemned to penal servitude for life and
a fine of £10,000. Any violation of the constitution as regards
the parliamentary régime was to amount to high treason,
even if there were no formal alteration of the constitution.
If this Bill had been passed, it would have put an end once
for all to the repeated attempts to introduce a dictatorship,
for the king would hardly have found Ministers ready to
expose themselves to such severe penalties. The king refused
his assent to the Bill, and had already made known his
unconcealed opposition to the Wafd in a number of questions.
The resignation of Nahas Pasha's Ministry on June 17th,
1930, was accepted. Ismail Sidky Pasha, already regarded as
a vigorous enemy of the Wafd and of democracy and a great
favourite in European financial circles in Egypt, was entrusted
with the formation of the new Ministry.

The new dictatorship followed in its predecessors' foot-
steps. Parliament was first prorogued for a month on
June 21st, then dissolved. The Wafd newspapers were
suspended and the supporters of the dictatorship installed
in all administrative and judicial posts. This time the English

remained neutral. Parliament stood unanimously behind Mustafa Nahas. When the decree of prorogation was read the Deputies and Senators forced their way into the Parliament House on June 23rd in defiance of the Government. After it had been read the assembly swore to be faithful to the constitution and defend it with all their might. Three days later a National Congress was held in Cairo, in which not only the Senators and Deputies took part, but also the members of the Provincial Councils, over 800 representatives of the people in all.

The opposition between the king and the Wafd, which has governed the course of Egyptian history for the last ten years, reached its climax in this conflict. That is why the struggle was carried on with such bitterness on both sides. During July, in spite of the Government's military precautions, there were sanguinary encounters between Egyptian troops and demonstrators, especially in El Mansuriya on July 8th and in Alexandria on July 15th. In the autumn of 1930 a new constitution was promulgated by decree, greatly restricting the rights of Parliament and enlarging the king's power. Elections for the new Parliament were to be held under a law which raised the age for the franchise and restricted the suffrage. Not only the Wafd, but also the Constitutional Liberals protested against the new Constitution, and the latter renewed their co-operation with the Wafd. It is significant that the two men who had headed former attempts at dictatorship in Egypt, Ziwar Pasha and Mohammed Mahmud Pasha, were both strongly opposed to Sidky Pasha's anti-parliamentary Government.

TREATY AND FREEDOM

Sidky Pasha at first placed his hopes in the fall of the Labour Government in England. But even a Conservative Government, if it wants to secure a treaty with Egypt, can adopt no other method than Henderson. The Court, Sidky Pasha, and the influential foreign settlements in Egypt, whose views are mirrored in the English Conservative Press, refuse to believe that a new Egypt has arisen. In their eyes it is not to the historical process of social evolution in the East that the new conditions are to be attributed—a process which the War and the new economic and political situation have vastly accelerated—but to the agitation of the Wafd leaders. This simple-minded conception of historical processes is so convenient partly because it appears to offer so simple a remedy. It is only necessary to put the leaders of the agitation out of action, to govern with a strong hand, and the evil will be cured. It is not only among foreigners in Egypt that this conception is found ; it is characteristic of imperialist circles and reactionaries in all Eastern countries. And we must not forget that foreigners in the East for the most part live entirely cut off from their neighbours and are thus totally unaware of new tendencies among the people.

In the struggle now going on in Egypt between the Wafd and the autocracy the Wafd will undoubtedly prevail and Parliament be restored to its rights. After a century of parliamentary government Europeans regard Parliament with more scepticism than Orientals. In the present phase of historical evolution in the East, Parliament has the same emotional value as in Europe a hundred years ago. Parliament is the great hope for the consolidation and free development of the awakening popular forces. It not only means liberation from ancient despotism and feudalism, but it stands, too, as the symbol of emancipation from petrified tradition and centuries of corruption. It embodies a new confidence of the nation in itself. And it has in the East a second mission, in addition to this spiritual enfranchise- ment. In Europe the parliamentary system in its heroic phase had to wage fierce war against the ancient, dominant powers in the State. In the East, Parliament, at once the standard-bearer and the offspring of nationalism, is still confronted by the foreign adversary. In Egypt it has won that adversary's recognition. Great Britain knows that no treaty and no peace with Egypt is possible, unless it is approved by a democratic Parliament. And no future English Government can depart from the basis of Egypt's independence and equal rights, as laid down in the negotiations between Henderson and Mustafa Nahas.

But independence is of no value in itself. In the present phase of historical evolution in the East it is only the essential prerequisite of any further development. The question arises, what is to be done with this independence. Sooner or later the Wafd will attain its object of safeguarding national freedom and democracy. Then it will be faced with the difficult task of giving vital content to what it has won. Enemies within and without have prevented it hitherto from realizing its aims in full. Once independence is secured the struggle, already begun, against the ignorance of the masses, against their low standard of life, against backward sanitary and social conditions in the villages, must be carried on with greater energy than ever. The end of the nationalist revolution must be the beginning of a more far-reaching cultural and social movement to raise the people and breathe new life into them, affecting more powerfully than ever their traditions and habits.

THE MANDATES

INTRODUCTORY REMARKS

The Arabian nationalist movement in those territories which, in the words of Clause 4 of Article 22 of the League of Nations Covenant " have reached a stage of development where their existence as independent nations can be provisionally recognized subject to the rendering of administrative advice and assistance by a mandatory until such time as they are able to stand alone ", does not evince that solidarity which has been such a remarkable feature of the Egyptian nationalist movement since 1919. True, the Arabian nationalist movement in the mandated territories has advanced in recent years beyond the phase in which the Egyptian nationalist movement stood before the World War under the leadership of Mustafa Kemal and Mohammed Farid ; it has spread beyond the intelligentsia to the mass of the people, but it has not consolidated into that unity and precision which characterized the Egyptian movement as led by the Wafd. It had no great leader, and territories in question were too small and too poor, thanks to the policy of partition pursued by the European Powers. Moreover, capitalism was less developed in these territories than in Egypt. The nationalist movement certainly did succeed almost everywhere in bridging religious differences, but the old feuds of the leading families and groups continued to exercise an influence, though often less powerful and combated by the younger generation. It was only at times of the most violent disturbance, when the nationalist movements concentrated in armed revolts, in Iraq in 1920; in Syria in 1925, and in Palestine after the August riots of 1929, that a powerful, united front was created, and the agitation penetrated far into the masses and long continued to operate. But the lack of strong organization and persistent effort in the pursuit of an aim, weaknesses still characteristic of the country's Oriental, mediaeval phase of development, and only slowly to be overcome, made themselves felt again

115

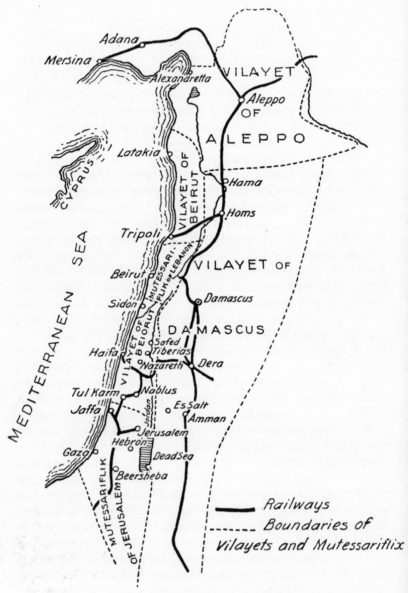

Adana
Mersina
Alexandretta
VILAYET
Aleppo
OF
ALEPPO
Latakia
CYPRUS
VILAYET OF BEIRUT
Hama
Homs
Tripoli
MEDITERRANEAN SEA
Beirut
MUTESSARI-
FLIK OF LEBANON
VILAYET OF
DAMASCUS
Sidon
VILAYET OF BEIRUT
Damascus
Haifa
Safed
Tiberias
Nazareth
Dera
Tul Karm
Nablus
Jaffa
Jordan
Es Salt
Amman
Jerusalem
Gaza
Hebron
Dead Sea
MUTESSARIFLIK OF JERUSALEM
Beersheba

―――― Railways
------- Boundaries of
Vilayets and Mutessariflix

SYRIA AND PALESTINE IN 1917.

Page 116]

and again. It was a significant omen that the Syrian rising brought about close co-operation between the Druzes, hitherto rigorously isolated and never moving outside their own religious, tribal bounds, and the Syrian intellectuals of Damascus. At any rate, during periods of profound national excitement the nationalist movement in Arabia united the intellectuals, the peasantry, the primitive feudal chieftains, and the Bedouins. Professor Toynbee has compared the co-operation between the Druze chieftain, Sultan el Atrashi, and Dr. Abdul Rahman Shahbander, the leader of the People's party in Damascus, with the co-operation between chieftains of primitive mountain tribes, like Petros Mavromichalis, robber chiefs like Kolokotronis, and Europeanized intellectuals, like Prince Mavrogordato, at the beginning of the Greek struggle for independence in 1821.

In its political form the Arab national movement was younger than the Egyptian, in its cultural form older. The renaissance of the Arab language and literature had emanated from Syria in the sixties of the last century, and thence had been carried to Egypt. Syria's poverty and backwardness at that time and Abdul Hamid's suspicion of any cultural activity contributed to transfer the centre of the Arab renaissance to Cairo, where its leaders were at first mainly Syrians. When in the first decade of the twentieth century the Arab national movement assumed a political form and Abdul Hamid's fall allowed greater freedom in the Ottoman Empire, the aim of uniting all Arab territories and restoring the Caliphate to its original bearers, the Arabs, was proclaimed from the first. The Syrian Arabs, alike Mohammedans and Christians (at that time Syria embraced Palestine and Trans-Jordan),[59] the Iraqi town-dwellers in Baghdad and Basra, and the Bedouins of the Hejaz and Inner Arabia, were at one in this aim.

The negotiations with Great Britain, which were begun even before the War with this end in view, assumed definite form during the World War, barely ten years after the foundation of the first Arab League for the independence and unity of all Arab territories. England promised the Sherif Hussein of Mecca her support in establishing a Great Arab empire and regaining the Caliphate. It appears from the negotiations of 1915 and 1916, the details of which are still not known with absolute certainty because of the English Government's refusal to publish the documents, that the Arab State, which was conceived as a Federal State or federation of States, was to embrace all Arabia except Aden, though Great Britain excluded the coastal strip west of the districts of Damascus, Homs, Hama, and Aleppo. This doubtless meant the coastal region between those four cities and the Mediterranean, to which France had long laid claim. According to the English view, Palestine was also included in the reserved area, whilst the interior of Syria and Trans-Jordan were to belong to the Arab Empire. Sherif Hussein refused to recognize these reservations, but declared his readiness to postpone negotiations on the subject till after the War.

For a short time it seemed as if this Arab Federation was really to come into being within certain limits. In 1919 and in the first half of 1920 Hussein ruled as King of the Hejaz, his son Feisal ruled the adjacent Inner Syria (the vilayets of Aleppo and Damascus, of which Trans-Jordan formed part) ; and Iraq, also adjacent and occupied by the English, was intended for a prince of the same house. Thus a single dynastic unit stretched from the Red Sea to the Persian Gulf. The Syrians, alike Mohammedans and Christians, had supported Hussein in his negotiations during the World War.[60] When their activities were discovered by the Turkish authorities, their leaders were executed for holding intercourse with the enemy. The day of the execution, May 6th, is still celebrated as a day sacred to the national martyrs in Syria and Lebanon. Syria's second day of national mourning, the anniversary of the Battle of Khan Meisalun, on July 24th, 1920, when King Feisal's Syrian army was defeated by the French, marks the end of the first attempt to establish an Arab Federation. For, in the meantime, the Allies had determined the fate of the Arab territories in a different sense.

In a secret agreement, concluded by Sir Mark Sykes and Georges Picot in the name of Great Britain and France, and confirmed in a correspondence between Sir Edward Grey and Cambon in May, 1916, an effort had been made to do justice alike to Great Britain's promises to Sherif Hussein, to France's traditional wish for a foothold in Syria, and to Britain's imperial interests. In this agreement France and Great Britain had reserved spheres of influence and control for themselves in the proposed Great Arab State. The southern portion, Iraq with Basra and Baghdad, was to be placed under direct British administration ; the Syrian coast, from Acre to Alexandretta and Cilicia, adjoining it on the north, under direct French administration. France had wished at first to assert her claim to the whole of Syria, *la Syrie intégrale*. This would have involved, especially in view of the sharp opposition at the time between English and French Oriental policy, the danger to Great Britain of seeing another Great Power established on the eastern bank of the Suez Canal. In view of the Egyptian desire for independence it was of greater importance than ever to Great Britain to defend the Suez Canal from the east, as was proved by the Turko-German attack, and also to secure the long-sought land route to India from the Suez Canal to the Persian Gulf.[61] For this reason the secret agreement provided for the separation of Palestine from Syria and Trans-Jordan. Therewith Palestine's character as a Holy Land was to be recognized, and the territory between Gaza, Hebron, and Jericho in the south, and Acre and Tiberias in the north, was to be entrusted to an international governing body, regard being paid to the claims of the Sherif of Mecca and to those of Russia, which had acquired great power before the World War by supporting the Orthodox Church in Palestine. Great Britain only reserved for herself the ports of Haifa and Acre, and the right to build a railway from thence to Mesopotamia. Thus the realization of old colonial ambitions and the future configuration of the Arab territories, in particular the partition of Syria, were already marked out in this secret agreement.

The situation was further modified by the secession of Russia and therefore the disappearance of the Orthodox Church as a political factor in Palestine after the Russian Revolution,[62] and by the direct incorporation of Palestine in the English area of control through the proclamation known as the Balfour Declaration, issued on November 2nd, 1917, by the British Government ; according to this Declaration a Jewish National Home was to be established in Palestine. Just as France based her schemes in Lebanon on a protectorate over the Maronites, so Great Britain found a basis for her claims in Palestine in her protection of Zionist aims. The Conference of San Remo in April, 1920, enabled the Allied Powers to go beyond the provisions of the secret agreement of 1916. France extended her mandate over all Syria, Great Britain over the whole of Iraq, Trans-Jordan, and Palestine. This partition of Arab territories, the installation of different Governments, and the favour shown to certain minorities in the various areas, were a serious blow to the Arab demand for unity. The separate territories allotted to the European Powers, especially those attributed to France, were still further partitioned.[63]

Arab nationalist sentiment regarded all these partitions as merely transitory,[64] and the effect of partition was rather to strengthen the sense of unity. Arabia feared that English and French policy would mean the loss of her fertile coastal region, her most promising ports, and her access to the Mediterranean and therefore to Europe. Economically and politically the Mediterranean coast was to be a key position in the hold of the two Great Powers. France's creation of the State of Great Lebanon inevitably enhanced the disunity in Syria, and started a conflict not to be settled by peaceful means so long as the Maronites, profiting by the creation of Great Lebanon, could count upon French support ; and this, again, was designed to render France's presence in Syria necessary as mediator and guarantor of peace. This step, therefore, was in direct conflict with the intention and hope of the mandatory ideal, that it might soon be possible to grant Syria full independence.

A similar situation arose in Palestine. There, too, disposal of the country against the wishes of a majority of the population inevitably created a focus of political animosity which, again, required the presence of Great Britain as mediator and guarantor of peace. Moreover, the Balfour Declaration contained more peculiar seeds of discord than the creation of Great Lebanon or of the Alawi State, established for a like purpose ; for whilst the latter only consolidated and exacerbated existing antipathies and thus tended to check national development, the former involved the aim of altering the existing ratio of nationalities in

Palestine to the detriment of the majority; indeed, it was hoped or feared in certain circles that it would actually lead to the subjection of the majority to a minority constantly increasing by means of immigration from abroad. Thus it came about that in Syria and Palestine the mandates were repudiated from the outset by a majority of the population, and had to be imposed upon them from without.[65]

Only in Iraq developments assumed a wholly different aspect. The relatively large size of the country, its extensive frontiers which would be difficult to defend, and the proximity of aspiring and warlike States, suggested to Great Britain the undesirability of assuming too strict a responsibility for Iraq and undertaking the considerable expense of its military occupation and subjection. Fairly soon, therefore, Iraq was enabled by Great Britain to carry on an independent existence, which accorded with the people's wishes and the intention of the mandatory system. Palestine, on the other hand, very much smaller and with easily defended frontiers, its defence rendered easier still by the creation of the Trans-Jordan Marches, was to remain under Great Britain's direct rule. In some respects, therefore, a situation arose in Palestine similar to that of Cyprus, only rendered peculiarly complex and more dangerous by the dynamic element of a constant shifting in the relative power of the nationalities. Professor Toynbee attributes the fact that in general the Palestinian Government was long able to develop its activities in a calmer atmosphere than the Syrian to the British administration in Palestine being better, abler, and more impartial than that of the French in Syria,[66] although the Palestinian Arabs were more dissatisfied with the policy of the mandatory Government than the Syrian Arabs. Moreover, the British Government issued repeated and official interpretations in which it sought to explain the Balfour Declaration and the terms of the mandate based upon it in such a way as to assuage the fears of the Arab population. But in so doing it necessarily came into conflict with Zionist hopes, just as the French administration in Syria came into conflict with the Maronites by dropping isolated hints of the reunion of parts of Great Lebanon with the rest of Syria. The tragic situation which thus arose from imperialist ambitions, dating from pre-War days yet still operating, from

War promises and the decisions of the Peace Conferences, from conflicting nationalist movements and separatist traditions, and from the sense of injustice and the memory of sufferings and wrongs—this tragic situation persisted through the succeeding decade. Nevertheless, unsolved problems have been brought nearer to elucidation during the course of those years.

VI

PALESTINE

JEWS AND ARABS

ZIONISM

PALESTINE was detached politically from the united group of adjoining countries for three reasons : because of its position as a bridge-head on the Suez Canal and the land route to India, because it was the Holy Land of Christendom, and most of all because it was the historic territory where the Jews had celebrated their great religious achievements, a land with which the Jews had felt themselves to be inextricably bound up in thought and sentiment for two thousand years of dispersion, and which they had never ceased to regard as their home. It was not only in their own consciousness, but in that of the Christian peoples that the Jews remained closely linked with Palestine. That consciousness was particularly strong in Anglo-Saxon countries where the Bible, especially the Old Testament, had until quite recently formed the basis of mental and spiritual life. Right on into the nineteenth century the association with the land of their fathers, daily proclaimed in their prayers, was a living spiritual reality to all Jews. In the seventeenth century Safed had been the spiritual centre of all Jewry. Thence new life-giving streams had flowed to the countries of the Diaspora, whilst teachers and schools that carried on their labours there were the last in all Jewry, alike in the East and the West, to enjoy undisputed authority.

Emancipation in the beginning of the nineteenth century started to break up Jewish unity. The Jews in Western and Central Europe grew one with the cultural communities in which they lived, playing a full and often fruitful part in their life. But amongst the Jewish masses in Eastern Europe and the Orient the ancient yearning for Zion survived undiminished. Economic distress and political oppression intensified their desire to find a land where the Jewish masses could live in security, enjoying perfect freedom and forming part of an economic organization that should embrace all branches of social life. Even if individual Jews had found their home, yet Jewry had no home where it could develop its own creative genius freely like other peoples and discover the institutions that suited it best. So long as the peoples round about had lived under a mediaeval, religious system, the situation of Jewry could not appear altogether strange and exceptional, for as Heine expressed it, Jewry had found a movable home in the Bible. But the dawn of the age of political nationalism changed all that. All peoples began to strive for territorial unification, for a cultural expression of their individual character in a framework of political security. Each people wanted to form a State in order to place the resources of the State at the disposal of their economic and cultural development and, by the widest possible extension of the area under their control, to secure that development from attack and enrich its vitality. As nationalism penetrated to Eastern Europe, the longing of Jewry for emancipation began to assume the form of a modern nationalist movement. At first Jewish nationalism was a movement confined to a small section of middle-class intellectuals, from whose midst the renaissance of the Hebrew language and literature emanated. Hebrew, hitherto the language of religion and of scholastic theology, underwent a process of rejuvenation ; thanks to the efforts of thinkers and poets, it developed into a flexible literary language, well suited to modern literature and the needs of scholarship and daily life, embodying memories of the beauty of a former free homeland and of the nation's great history, and therefore for the first time bringing home the ideas of modern nationalism and present-day Europe, associated with the " love of Zion ", to the students in the traditional theological seminaries of Eastern Jewry. At the same time Yiddish, the popular tongue of the masses in Eastern Jewry, was raised to the level of a literary language. A new attitude towards Judaism has emerged in the last thirty years in all sections and classes of the Jewish people, things imagined to be long dead have returned to life, and a new epoch has dawned in Jewish history. The most marked expression of this change is the Zionist movement.

Under its inspiration the Jews began to re-colonize Palestine in the eighties of the last century. Amidst indescribable hardships the first Jewish villages sprang up in what was then an exceedingly backward country Baron Edmund Rothschild saved them from the economic collapse that threatened them, and by introducing new and improved crops established them on a firmer basis. But this colonizing groundwork would have had no vital significance for Judaism as a whole if Zionism had not succeeded in making the colonization of Palestine a political ideal, the object of endeavours on the part of all Jewry and of general sympathy. The outward organization of Zionism was the work of Theodor Herzl, at the first Zionist Congress at Basle in 1897. There the goal of the movement was proclaimed as the creation of a legally assured home for the Jewish people in Palestine. For the first time after a long period the various sections of Jewry were summoned and united for common action. The Zionist movement everywhere strengthened Jewish sentiment, created new intellectual and social values, roused a new consciousness of unity in the separate sections of Jewry, revived associations with the heritage of the Jewish past, and carried on the traditional activities of Jewish social welfare work in a new spirit. Emanating from the Zionist movement, though often apart from it and not seldom in conflict with it, Jewry experienced a new wave of consciousness of its historic mission. It was precisely in its youthful phase that Zionism operated as a fructifying and awakening force, as is the case with all nationalist movements at that stage ; it burst the bonds of mediaeval petrifaction, imparted the happy consciousness of inner unity, protection, and creative vigour, and liberated mighty idealist forces of enthusiasm and self-sacrifice.

Even before the World War the Jewish population of Palestine had grown to about a hundred thousand souls. By their own efforts, against the opposition of the Ottoman Government, and supported by a relatively small section of the Jewish race, they had built up their own cultural and social national life, in which Hebrew was more and more becoming the language of public life as a whole, of education, and of youth. Side by side with the idea of a return to their own country, that of Jewish independent peasant labour had emerged. At a time when the flight from the land and immigration to the large towns was a universal phenomenon, Jewish students and town-dwellers declared for a return to agriculture, to Nature, a radical occupational change, and absolute self-devotion to the Jewish soil; and they began to put these ideals into practice. The political goal of the movement was the creation of a Jewish State, but its leaders were wise enough to adapt their pronouncements to the existing political situation.[67] The majority in the movement were concerned in Palestine with the solution of the Jewish question in its cosmopolitan political and economic aspect. The masses of Eastern Jewry, who carried on a miserable and oppressed existence in the countries of their birth, were to be transferred to healthy economic conditions in Palestine, and were to find a land there where they could not only attain prosperity and happiness, but could live in perfect freedom, a nation amongst other nations, masters of their own fate, an independent people. Such was Theodor Herzl's idea. The great idea of human freedom was the spirit that breathed in Zionism and made men's hearts beat high with happiness.

Other sections of the movement regarded a mass immigration of Jews into Palestine on an economic basis as Utopian. Achad Haam,[68] whose influence was growing in the years immediately preceding the World War, when the struggle for the political goal seemed hopeless, was regarded as their intellectual leader. To them there was no question of a political, but rather of a colonizing, movement; it was a matter of establishing a Jewish centre in Palestine important mainly because of its quality, a microcosm of the Jewish people, to be a bond of union to Jewry in the Diaspora, strengthening its will to live and enriching it culturally. The problem of the economic and political distress of the Jews in the various countries, it was held, could be solved only in those countries themselves; Palestine could do nothing to help; but what it could do was to create a Jewish community in Palestine which should move Jewish hearts in all countries to loving and practical sympathy, a community which should endow Judaism with new spiritual values. Achad Haam evolved his teaching in sharp opposition to political Zionism. Although his national cultural demands,

as contrasted with Herzl's belief in cultural assimilation, had
become the common property of the Zionist movement, the
majority in the movement adhered to Herzl's political ideals.
In their inmost hearts the Jewish masses and those who
spoke for them always craved for something other than a
cultural centre. They wanted a country that would be their
own country in the same sense in which Russia is the country
of the Russians, and Germany that of the Germans. They
craved a complete and normal national life.

The World War, which fulfilled, or seemed to fulfil, the
national political desires of so many peoples, brought the
Zionists also the recognition of their aims as the fruit of
twenty years of devoted propaganda. It came from England,
where even before the World War leading statesmen had
evinced sympathy and understanding towards the movement.
Herzl had placed his hopes in England from the outset.
At the fourth Zionist Congress in 1900 he declared that
England, great, free England, whose view encompassed the
earth, would understand them and their aspirations. With
England as their base they might rest assured that the
Zionist ideal would rise higher and mightier than ever before.

Seventeen years later that prophecy was destined to be
fulfilled. The Balfour Declaration proclaimed, in agreement
with the Basle programme adopted twenty years earlier,
that the British Government regarded with sympathy the
establishment of a National Home for the Jewish people in
Palestine. This Declaration was supported by other
Governments and was made the basis of the League of
Nations mandate for Palestine. The Jewish masses welcomed
the Balfour Declaration with enthusiasm as the first step
in the realization of their dream of liberty and their desire
for a national State. Jewish circles which had hitherto held
aloof from the Zionist movement and had regarded its aims
as Utopian turned with sympathy or active support to the
labours of the Zionist Organization in Palestine. The Palestine
idea penetrated far and wide amidst the Jewish people.
Many Zionists, and especially those sections of the masses
in whom a fervent religious sense of oneness with Palestine
survived in its unbroken, pristine simplicity, waited
impatiently for the foundation of the Jewish State.

As soon as this Zionist ideal came in contact with the

realities of Palestine, and the actual political conditions, the inevitable result was disappointment and a tragic situation. To the Jews, especially the popular masses from Eastern Europe, Palestine was the Jewish country, " Erez Israel," a phantasm of their dreams and longings, the refuge of their souls for two thousand years, a land, therefore, where history had stood still. Now the Diaspora was to end, the curse to be removed from the Jewish people, the salvation awaited by so many generations to begin.[69] The tidings that the country was not altogether a barren desert, that Arabs had been living there for thirteen centuries—a period as long, perhaps, as that of the Jewish occupation of the land—and that these Arabs formed a single nation with the surrounding peoples, had hardly penetrated Jewish consciousness. And suddenly, to their genuine amazement and comprehensible indignation, these Jews found their country, at whose gates they stood at last after two thousand years' migration, occupied by aliens who disputed their right to it. Some of the Zionist leaders themselves had no idea of the changed realities in the East of to-day. Theodor Herzl had demanded an unpeopled land for a landless people. And now, at the very moment of its supreme success, when its boldest hopes seemed about to be realized, the Zionist movement was confronted with the fact that Palestine was not an unpeopled land. Further, it was just at that time that the Arabian people, like Jewry and the peoples of Eastern Europe a few decades earlier, had awakened to national consciousness ; like the whole East they were undergoing a process of profound change ; the World War had stirred them to the depths, and to them as to the Zionists, the promises of the Great Powers had offered the vision of a new and glorious life, a revival of their national culture and political greatness.[70] They, too, were rejoiced by the breath of a new freedom.

THE BALFOUR DECLARATION AND THE MANDATE

Palestine's history since the World War has been determined by the Balfour Declaration. It was an act born of the War and its character was determined by its origin. Like so many war-time proclamations, it stirred great hopes and equally great fears. The political realism of the English

clothed it from the outset in an elastic form, which left room
for adaptation to the post-War situation. The Balfour
Declaration was itself even a considerable attenuation of
Zionist demands. In July, 1917, the Zionist Organization had
submitted a formula which recognized the whole of Palestine
as a Jewish National Home. The Balfour Declaration, on
the other hand, only spoke of a Jewish National Home *in*
Palestine and expressly emphasized the protection of the
Arab population's rights. It read as follows : " H.M. Government view with favour the establishment in Palestine of a
National Home for the Jewish people, and will use their
best endeavours to facilitate the achievement of this object,
it being clearly understood that nothing shall be done which
may prejudice the civil and religious rights of existing non-
Jewish communities in Palestine . . ." When this formula
was submitted to them, the Zionist Organization had wanted
the words " the *reconstitution of* Palestine as *the* National
Home " to be substituted for " the establishment *in* Palestine
of *a* National Home ", but the British Government rejected
their formula. Thereby the dual character of the Balfour
Declaration, and the course of development towards a community made up of two nationalities in Palestine, was
determined. During the decade from 1920 to 1930 the
Balfour Declaration was interpreted in harmony with a
consistent policy of setting bounds to Zionist hopes, originally
so great.[71]

The Zionists regarded the Balfour Declaration as the
promise of a Jewish State. But difficulties arose immediately
after the military conquest of Palestine. For two years the
military administration there did not dare, out of regard for
the Arab population, to proclaim the Balfour Declaration in
Palestine. It was not till 1920 that it was mentioned publicly
in a speech by the British representative there. Under these
circumstances the Zionists began to doubt Great Britain's
intention to abide by the establishment of a Jewish National
Home in Palestine. The speech by Dr. Chaim Weizmann,
the leader of the Zionist movement, made in London on
August 20th, 1919, is characteristic of the point of view held
at that time. He pointed to the universal unrest in the East.
Palestine's economic and racial conditions, he said, linked it
with Syria and to some extent with Egypt, and all events

in Syria and Egypt had their echo in Palestine. The Pan-Arabian movement had penetrated into Palestine and had inevitably created great difficulties in a country where there were some ten Arabs to every one Jew. The Pan-Arabian movement was hostile to Zionism and made the position in Palestine very difficult for England. The situation was complicated by the promise given to the Zionists. Under these circumstances it was impossible to demand the immediate establishment of a Jewish State. When the expression " Jewish National Home " was first used in the Balfour Declaration, "it had an enormous effect, and everyone read into it all that he pleased. Many understood it as equivalent to a Jewish State. A state was a political organization in a definite territory, which embraced all the activities of a given human society; it consisted of men, institutions, and things. A state existed only when there existed a group of men conscious of naturally cohering, when the land, the schools, and all other kinds of institutions had been developed. It could not be made unless these things were in existence. Would the opportunity be given them that would enable them to build a Jewish State ? " Dr. Wiezmann said that the answer he would give to this question was " Yes ". A Jewish people speaking its own language, and having its own institutions, would ultimately, perhaps in a generation, be developed, and would constitute a Jewish State.[72] In the Zionist claims of that period Herzl's notions of political Zionism re-emerged, of a Jewish Colonization Chartered Company to acquire public concessions and rights in the land, which should be withdrawn from private purchase. Dr. Weizmann pointed out again and again how small was Palestine's economic capacity for absorption ; thus in his speech of August 20th, 1919, he said : " Every chance must be afforded that would enable as many Jews as possible to be absorbed in the country in a reasonable time. The present power of absorption of Palestine is extremely limited. But, given right conditions, the power of absorption could be increased." But large numbers of Zionists, opposing his statesmanlike wisdom in urging moderation, demanded unrestricted Jewish immigration into Palestine, and the transference of great multitudes from Eastern Europe. Just then Palestine appeared more than ever a rock of salvation.

The World War had intensified the misery of the Jewish masses in Eastern Europe in an unprecedented degree, sanguinary pogroms in the Ukraine and Poland threatened the very lives of the Jewish population, the national aspirations of other peoples had been realized in an astonishing manner, small nations of minor historical importance were witnessing the revival of their own existence as States ; and were not the fifteen million Jews, with their great and unique past, their outstanding abilities in many fields, a people to whom Western civilization owed its religion, to be restored to their rights after two thousand years of unparalleled sufferings in this hour of the birth of a new world order and the redress of so many historical wrongs, were they not to live freely in their historic homeland like other nations ? It is comprehensible, therefore, that in those years and often later the Zionists demanded a Jewish State in Palestine as their goal or, as it was called in the official reports, a Jewish Commonwealth, a country inhabited by a Jewish majority, with institutions predominantly Jewish in character. Dr. Weizmann declared before the Versailles Conference on February 27th, 1919, in the name of the Zionist Organization, that the establishment of a Jewish National Home implied the creation of such conditions in Palestine that it would be possible to settle fifty to sixty thousand Jews there annually on the land, besides developing Jewish institutions and schools and the Hebrew language, so that in the end Palestine should be as Jewish as America is American and England English. The general opinion of the Zionist Conference, to whom he reported, was that Dr. Weizmann's demands had not gone far enough.[73] Prolonged negotiations followed between the Zionist Organization and the British Government about the text of the mandate. The Zionists succeeded in imposing their view on many points, but in the essential questions of the interpretation of the Balfour Declaration and of the aim to be pursued the difference remained unbridged. The Zionist wish for the declaration of a Jewish Commonwealth as the ultimate goal of the mandate was not granted. Apparently the British Government was very decided in its categorical refusal. The official Zionist report states : " As to the reference to a ' Jewish Commonwealth ', it had already been intimated to Dr. Weizmann that the British Government might not be prepared to accept the Mandate at all if this point were insisted upon." [74] Similarly the Zionist demand for the inclusion of Trans-Jordan, Hauran, Hermon, and the southernmost portion of Lebanon in the area of the Jewish National Home was refused by England and also by the League of Nations, as being contrary to Great Britain's obligations in those territories.

The British Government adhered to its restrictive interpretation of the Balfour Declaration. The first British High Commissioner in Palestine, Sir Herbert Samuel, who was appointed to the office on account of his active sympathy with Zionism, said in his speech of June 3rd, 1921 :—

" Let me, in the first instance, refer once more to the unhappy misunderstanding that has existed with reference to the phrase in the Balfour Declaration ' the establishment in Palestine of a National Home for the Jewish people '. I hear it said in many quarters that the Arab population of Palestine will never agree to their country, their Holy Places, and their lands being taken from them and given to strangers : that they will never agree to a Jewish Government being set up to rule over the Moslem and Christian majority. People say that they cannot understand how it is that the British Government, which is famous throughout the world for its justice, could ever have consented to such a policy. I answer that the British Government, which does, indeed, care for justice above all things, has never consented and will never consent to such a policy. That is not the meaning of the Balfour Declaration. . . . They (the words) mean that the Jews, a people who are scattered throughout the world, but whose hearts are always turned to Palestine, should be enabled to find their home, and that some among them, within the limits that are fixed by the numbers and interests of the present population, should come to Palestine in order to help by their resources and efforts to develop the country to the advantage of all its inhabitants. If any measures are needed to convince the Moslem and Christian population . . . that their rights are really safe, such measures will be taken. For the British Government, the trustee under the Mandate for the happiness of the people of Palestine, would never impose upon them a policy which that people had reason to think was contrary to their religious, their political, and their economic interests." *

Sir Herbert Samuel's statement, that the extent of Jewish immigration must be limited by the number and interests of the existing population, was confirmed by Churchill, at that time Colonial Secretary, in the House of Commons on June 14th, 1921, and repeated once again in a letter of the Colonial Office to the Arab Delegation dated March 1st, 1922. Thenceforward all English Governments, whatever their party, declared that they would adhere absolutely to the Balfour Declaration and the establishment of the Jewish National Home in Palestine, which had become, through the mandate, an international obligation, but that the National Home must be interpreted in such a limited sense that the interests of the indigenous population should not suffer. The British Government considers itself bound by a twofold obligation, alike to the Jews and to the Arab population of Palestine. If it opened to the Jews the possibility of immigration, settlement, and cultural and social development, it held itself equally bound to protect the Arabs against the dangers they dreaded of excessive Jewish immigration and, as the Arabs feared, the consequent lowering of the existing political and economic status of the Arab population. In this spirit the first *Report on the Civil Administration of Palestine* states :—

" The policy of H.M. Government contemplated the satisfaction of the legitimate aspirations of the Jewish race throughout the world in relation to Palestine, combined with a full protection of the rights of the existing population. The Zionism that is practicable is the Zionism that fulfils this essential condition. The measures to foster the well-being of the Arabs should be precisely those which we should adopt in Palestine if there were no Zionist question and if there had been no Balfour Declaration. There is in this policy nothing incompatible with reasonable Zionist aspirations. On the contrary, if the growth of Jewish influence were accompanied by Arab degradation, or even by a neglect to promote Arab advancement, it would fail in one of its essential purposes. Simultaneously there must be satisfaction of that sentiment regarding Palestine—a worthy and

* *Zionist Review,* July, 1921, p. 53.

ennobling sentiment—which, in increasing degree, animates the Jewries of the world. The aspirations of these fourteen millions of people also have a right to be considered. . . . The degree to which Jewish national aspirations can be fulfilled in Palestine is conditioned by the rights of the present inhabitants."

This point of view was again emphasized in the correspondence of the British Colonial Office with the Arabs and the Zionist Organization in 1922. There stress was laid on the fact that the British Government was bound by the Balfour Declaration whilst at the same time Sir Herbert Samuel's statement of June 3rd, 1921, about the meaning of the Declaration was repeated, and the readiness of the British Government announced to give the Arab population adequate guarantees that this policy would be upheld. A statement of British policy dated June 3rd, 1922, proclaimed :—

" The tension which has prevailed from time to time in Palestine is mainly due to apprehensions, which are entertained both by sections of the Arab and by sections of the Jewish population. These apprehensions, so far as the Arabs are concerned, are partly based upon exaggerated interpretations of the meaning of the Declaration favouring the establishment of a Jewish National Home in Palestine made on behalf of His Majesty's Government on November 2nd, 1917 (the Balfour Declaration). Unauthorized statements have been made to the effect that the purpose in view is to create a wholly Jewish Palestine. Phrases have been used such as that Palestine is to become ' as Jewish as England is English '. His Majesty's Government regard any such expectation as impracticable and have no such aim in view. Nor have they at any time contemplated, as appears to be feared by the Arab Delegation, the disappearance or the subordination of the Arabic population, language, or culture in Palestine. They would draw attention to the fact that the terms of the Declaration referred to do not contemplate that Palestine as a whole should be converted into a Jewish National Home, but that such a Home should be founded *in Palestine*. . . . So far as the Jewish population of Palestine are concerned, it appears that some of them are apprehensive that His Majesty's Government may depart from the policy embodied in the Declaration of 1917. It is necessary, therefore, once more to affirm that these fears are unfounded. . . . When it is asked what is meant by the development of the Jewish National Home in Palestine, it may be answered that it is not the imposition of a Jewish nationality upon the inhabitants of Palestine as a whole, but the further development of the existing Jewish community, with the assistance of Jews in other parts of the world, in order that it may become a centre in which the Jewish people as a whole may take, on grounds of religion and race, an interest and a pride. But in order that this community should have the best prospect of free development and provide a full opportunity for the Jewish people to display its capacities, it is essential that it should know that it is in Palestine as of right and not on sufference. That is the reason why it is necessary that the existence of a Jewish National Home in Palestine should be internationally guaranteed, and that it should be formally recognized to rest upon ancient historic connection." *

The Executive of the Zionist Organization stated that they had taken note of this declaration of British policy in Palestine and would carry on their activities in accordance with it. This declaration of British policy, which became known as the " Churchill White Book ", preceded the final confirmation of the Palestine mandate by the League of Nations Council, and may be regarded as the official British interpretation of the terms of the mandate. A second official interpretation by the British Government, embodied in a letter addressed to the Secretary-General of the League of Nations, and dated July 1st, 1922, served the same purpose ; in it the British Cabinet communicated to the League of Nations the correspondence of the Colonial Office with the Palestine Arab Delegation and the declaration of British policy in Palestine of June 3rd, 1922, and presented to the League an answer to Cardinal Gasparri's Note of May 15th, 1922. Here once again the British conception of the Balfour Declaration and the mandate is stated. The following passage occurs : " His Majesty's Government fully share the opinion expressed by Cardinal Gasparri that Article 22 of the Covenant

---

* *Correspondence with the Palestine Arab Delegation and the Zionist Organization*, June, 1922, Cmd. 1700, p. 18.

of the League of Nations would be incompatible with a mandate that proved to be an instrument for the subjection of the native populations for the benefit of another nationality." This Note expressly states that the " civil rights " of the population—the Balfour Declaration had already promised that these should not be infringed—included political rights.

This attitude of the British Government has been stressed again and again in the succeeding ten years, in which the policy laid down by Sir Herbert Samuel and Churchill has been maintained.[73] It satisfied neither Arabs nor Jews. To the vast majority of Zionists the Balfour Declaration appeared meaningless, unless it was to lead to a Jewish majority in Palestine. A Jewish minority would not involve conditions fundamentally different from those prevailing in the other countries of the Diaspora. British Zionist policy would have no meaning unless the Jews were to be in the normal position of a majority race in Palestine alone of all countries. The Arab population was not to be oppressed but was to enjoy all the rights of a minority in progressive States. The Arab nation possessed in Syria, in Iraq, and also in Inner Arabia, countries where they could satisfy their full national claims as an undisputed majority, and could develop their abilities and aptitudes without restriction, as the wielders of power in the State ; the Jewish people, whose millions were scattered over the earth and were everywhere a minority, could become a majority only in Palestine, their historic homeland, for which so many Jewish hearts beat high, and thus determine their own fate and develop their capacities unhampered in the political and social fields. What drew such numbers of Jews to Palestine was not only political and economic distress, but the yearning of many generations and a love which found expression in selfless devotion and joyful labour. For these reasons the objective of the British Government, which was primarily concerned with maintaining the rights of the Arab population, did not appear to the Zionists to do justice to Zionist aspirations.

Thus while the Zionists pointed out the unique situation and the ties of destiny and sentiment which bound the Jewish people to Palestine, the Arabs, on the other hand, declared that they would resist, as every other people would, being turned into a minority in their own country by immigration from without. They pointed out that in the Balfour Declaration England had promised something to the Zionists that did not belong to her, and that no nation on earth would allow themselves and their country to be given away without resisting to the utmost. The Arab population of Palestine demanded that self-determination which the Allies had proclaimed as one of their War aims, the introduction of a democratic constitution, and the right to determine how far Jewish immigration was compatible with Arab rights. The country was too small to admit large multitudes of immigrants without ousting the Arab population, especially the peasantry. The land must remain Arab in character and culture, and must be united with Syria, with which it formed a natural unit and had always been one, and with the rest of Arabia, from which it had been detached solely in the interests of imperialist policy. Zionism had been an accomplice of British imperialism ; responsible Zionist leaders had constantly urged what an advantage a strong Jewish National Home would be to the English in guarding the road to India, just because it was a counteracting force to Arab national aspirations. Zionism introduced an element of unrest and strife into the Middle East, for the Arabs could never rest content with the deprivation of Palestine. English assurances about the safeguarding of Arab political and economic rights did not offer an adequate guarantee, for the Arabs were powerless against the wealth, the superior organization and education, and the brilliant advocacy and propaganda of Zionist interests throughout the world. Their poverty compelled them to sell their land, and under English protection Jewish immigration, in spite of all England's assurances, would lead to a Jewish majority and so to the Jewish Commonwealth in Palestine.[74] The Arab inhabitants of Palestine, both Mohammedans and Christians, were united in their opposition, and were supported by the Arabs of the surrounding countries, and sometimes by their other Mohammedan or Christian co-religionists.[75] It seemed to them that the objective of the British Government, which was primarily concerned with establishing a Jewish National Home without drawing clear and definite limits to its extension, threatened ruin to Arab aspirations towards freedom.

Thus the British Government in Palestine found itself confronted with conditions which must inevitably bring about political tension. Alike Zionists and Arabs were concerned the one with the creation, the other with the preservation of basic conditions which they regarded as vital to the very existence of their peoples. It was a struggle for land and nation in which the points of view originally adopted by the two peoples have not changed during the decade. It was precisely to the example of the Jewish nationalist movement and the resistance to Zionist efforts at expansion that the Arab movement owed its growth. Whilst the Zionists demanded the more active support of the British mandatory Government in their constructive labours in Palestine, an acceleration and constant extension of Jewish immigration into Palestine, and the settlement of the immigrants in accordance with the terms of the mandate, so that the percentage of the Jewish population and its share of the land should increase continually and lead to a Jewish majority in Palestine within measurable time, the Arabs, appealing to the right of self-determination of the peoples and to the sense and text of Article 22 of the League of Nations Covenant, demanded the creation of a national government of the inhabitants of Palestine in accordance with democratic principles, the annulment of the Balfour Declaration, and the union of Palestine with the other Arab countries.

THE ARAB MOVEMENT

The history of the Arab nationalist movement in Palestine in the past decade falls into two periods. The first extends to 1925. Its guiding principle was non-co-operation with the English Government so long as the latter adhered to the Balfour Declaration. The second began with the seventh Arab National Congress, and its guiding principle was the demand for democratic popular representation, and later for laws to protect the fellaheen against dispossession and against the crushing burden of taxation and debt. Although the programme of the second period retained the unaltered aim of combating Zionist aspirations, yet it may be regarded as an advance on the mere negation that preceded it. The protagonists of the Arab nationalist movement had at first been the Mohammedan-Christian associations which sprang up in Jerusalem immediately after the British conquest of the country ; they were led by the Husseini, a Mohammedan noble house, and were intended to demonstrate the unity of the Arab people. The first Congress of Palestine Arabs, which was held at the beginning of 1919, marked the rise of these associations to the zenith of their activity ; they had sprung up in all the towns and in the larger villages. The second Congress was held for political reasons in Damascus, the capital of the Arab Syrian kingdom, and was summoned by the League for Palestine's Rebirth in February, 1920.

These two first Congresses both demanded the union of Palestine with Syria. The third Congress in Haifa in 1921 was the first to take the separation of Palestine into account and, by electing an Executive Committee, to lay the foundations of a permanent organization. The fourth Palestine Arab Congress, which was held in Jerusalem in May, 1921, elected a delegation of six, four Mohammedans and two Christians, with Musa Kasim Pasha el Husseini as its leader and Shibli Jemal Husseini as secretary, in order to go to London and promote the Arab cause in the negotiations on the Palestine mandate, which were nearing their conclusion, and to urge the revocation of the Balfour Declaration. Their mission ended in complete failure.

Meanwhile, on July 1st, 1920, the military administration in Palestine had been replaced by a civil administration under Sir Herbert Samuel. In October, 1920, he nominated an Advisory Council consisting of ten British officials and ten Palestinians, of whom seven were Arabs and three Jews. All Bills were submitted to it, and it was empowered to discuss questions of public interest. In his report Sir Herbert Samuel pointed out that this Advisory Council had rendered valuable service and that the Government had always been in a position to pay heed to the criticisms of its non-official members. But it was not of a nature to relax the tension in the country and assuage Arab fears.

At the beginning of May, 1921, attacks were made by the Arabs on the Jews in Jaffa, and in the Jewish settlements of

Pethah Tiqva and Chederah. The Government appointed
a Commission of Inquiry under the chairmanship of the Chief
Justice of Palestine, Sir Thomas Haycraft. This Commission's
report, which was published, has much in common with the
report later drawn up on the August disturbances of 1929.
The two commissions reached similar conclusions both on
the nature of the occurrences and on their underlying causes.
In 1921 likewise we find the non-Jewish communities in
Palestine united in their hostility to the Jews. The Arab
and non-Arab witnesses, Mohammedans, Orthodox Christians,
Catholics, Maronites, and Anglicans, gave consistent evidence
on the reason for the agitation against the Jews. Even at
that date, moreover, the Arabs no longer drew the distinction,
formerly recognized, between different classes of Jews.
The old colonists and the new immigrants, strictly orthodox
Jews and Jewish Socialists, Oriental and Russian Jews, all
were equally regarded as one and the same. Even then the
fears expressed by the Arabs included the acquisition of
Arab land by the Jews and the supersession of Arab labour.
The report closed with these words : " Much, we feel, might
be done to allay the existing hostility between the races if
responsible persons on both sides could agree to discuss the
questions arising between them in a reasonable spirit, on the
basis that the Arabs should accept implicitly the declared
policy of the Government on the subject of the Jewish
National Home, and that the Zionist leaders should abandon
and repudiate all pretensions that go beyond it." The
suggested discussion never took place.

The negotiations of the Arab Delegation in London broke
down over the demand for a Palestinian constitution to
provide for a democratic national government and guarantees
for the civil, political, and economic interests of the people
and for minority rights. The constitution proposed by the
English Government did not come near satisfying these
demands, for the Colonial Office replied that the establishment
of a democratic Government in Palestine would make it
impossible for the British Government to carry out its
accepted policy of the Balfour Declaration. The policy of
the Jewish National Home represented an international
obligation of the British Government and must, therefore,
form the basis of any constitution for Palestine. In the course

of these negotiations the British Government issued the statement of policy of June 3rd, 1922, cited above. The Arab Delegation was unable to accept this statement. In its detailed reply of June 17th, 1922, it wrote : " We can find no reason for this delay (i.e. in introducing democratic Government) but in the eagerness of the Government to allow time to elapse during which the Jews will have increased in numbers and the powers of Zionism become more established in the land. . . . We are to understand, then, that self-government will be granted as soon as the Jewish people in Palestine are sufficiently able through numbers and powers to benefit to the full by self-government, and not before. . . . The hope is finally expressed in the Memorandum (on British policy) that ' a policy upon these lines cannot but commend itself to the various sections of the Population '. We would heartily wish this were so. But what do we see as the result of this policy ? Discontent of 93 per cent of the population, dislike of the Zionist policy, a strong feeling against those who enter Palestine through the sheer might of England . . . against the will of the people who are convinced that these have come to strangle them. . . . The fact is that His Majesty's Government has placed itself in the position of a partisan in Palestine of a certain policy which the Arab cannot accept because it means his extinction sooner or later."

On July 24th, 1922, the Palestine mandate was confirmed by the League of Nations Council. In spite of the fact that this was an A mandate, it resembled a B mandate in the provision that all powers of legislation and administration were to be invested in the mandatory Power.[76] It differed from the mandates for Syria and Iraq in placing Palestine on the level of a British colony. The whole Executive and all the higher official positions were exclusively in British hands, and Great Britain only conceded so much share in legislation to the population as falls to their lot in many British colonies, leaving all the real power in the hands of the British Representative. The terms of the mandate were framed with a view to the wishes of the Zionist Organization. It was recognized as the Jewish Agency in order to advise the Palestine Administration and to co-operate with it in all matters affecting the establishment

of the Jewish National Home.   Provision was made, subject
to guarantees for the rights and position of the rest of the
population, for assistance to Jewish immigration and the
promotion of Jewish settlement.   The acquisition of
Palestinian citizenship was to be facilitated for Jews, and
Hebrew to be recognized, together with English and Arabic,
as an official language.   As the mandatory Power did not
wish altogether to forego the people's co-operation in
legislation, the Palestine constitution of August 10th, 1922,
provided for a Legislative Council.   This Council was to
consist of ten officials and twelve members elected by the
people of Palestine, ten Arabs (eight Mohammedans and two
Christians), and two Jews ; the High Commissioner was its
President.   These twelve members were to be indirectly
elected under the Ottoman electoral law.   The franchise was
to be democratic, equal, and universal. The suffrage depended
upon no kind of means or educational test.   The High
Commissioner had the right to veto all the Council's decisions,
and was bound to exercise the veto if these decisions conflicted
with the mandate.   Moreover, the English king retained the
right to annul all decisions within a year and himself to
promulgate laws on all Palestinian affairs.   Protection for the
provisions of the mandate was thereby ensured that, as in
Cyprus, the British officials and the two Jewish representatives always formed a majority against the Arabs.   Only
in controlling immigration was more power conceded to the
popular representatives.   On this question the High
Commissioner was to consult a committee consisting of not
less than half the elected members of the Legislative Council,
and thus having an Arab majority.   In case of differences of
opinion between the High Commissioner and the committee,
the British Secretary of State in London was to decide
the issue.

When news came that the mandate was about to be
confirmed the Palestinian Arabs organized a two-days'
protest strike, and recalled the Arab Delegation from
London.   On August 22nd, 1922, the fifth Palestine Arab
Congress met in Nablus.   It resolved to boycott the elections
to the Legislative Assembly, to carry on propaganda against
the sale of land, and to protest against the Rutenberg
Concession, which gave the monopoly in exploiting all

Palestine's chief water power for the generation of electricity and for irrigation to a Zionist company for seventy-five years. The Congress appointed committees to consider economic questions, the establishment of a national bank, and the spread of education inspired by a national spirit. At the beginning of February, 1923, the first Palestine Arab Economic Congress met in Jerusalem. Among other things it demanded the protection of the small peasantry, on the model of the Egyptian Five Feddan Law, in case of the forced sale of their land, the establishment of an Agricultural Institute and agricultural colleges, the abolition of tithes, and the re-establishment of the Agricultural Bank.

The elections to the Legislative Council in February and March, 1923, were boycotted by the overwhelming majority of the Arab population. Thereupon a supplementary statute to the constitution, dated May 4th, 1923, declared the elections void and temporarily suspended the articles relating to the Legislative Council. During 1923 the Government made two more efforts to induce the Arab population to co-operate with it, first by proposing to set up an Advisory Council constituted exactly like the proposed Legislative Council, and then by attempting to form an Arab Agency with functions similar to those laid down in Article 4 of the mandate for the Jewish Agency. Both suggestions were rejected by the Arabs in accordance with the resolutions of the sixth Arab Congress held in Jaffa in June, 1923. On November 9th the British Colonial Secretary announced that until further notice Palestinian legislation would rest with the High Commissioner and an Advisory Council, consisting solely of British officials. Thenceforward for seven and a half years Palestine was governed in a purely bureaucratic manner. The people had no share either in legislation or administration. This was certainly detrimental in a number of important questions of popular concern, such as education, public health, the encouragement of agriculture, and the modernization of taxation. Even a beneficent governing autocracy could not carry out the reforms necessary for the people's cultural and social betterment without contact with the people and their needs, especially in those important matters.[77]

To some Arabs the implacable policy of non-co-operation

pursued by the Arab Executive did not seem to produce the desired results. Under the leadership of the Mayor of Jerusalem, Ragheb Nashashibi, a new Arab party arose, doubtless not without encouragement from the Government. This was the National party, and its programme was nowise different from that of the Mohammedan-Christian associations. It, too, demanded the full independence of Arab Palestine as one of the Arabian countries, the revocation of the Balfour Declaration, the formation of a democratic national Government, the recognition of Arabic as the sole official language, and measures to improve the position of the fellaheen and of Arab industry. But the new party showed readiness to co-operate with the Government and to accept from it all that could be obtained at the moment, without abandoning its final aim. At the same time the first Arab Peasant Congress put forward the demand for the abolition of tithes, the establishment of an Agricultural Bank and of Agricultural District Councils, and the encouragement of cultivation by irrigation.

But even these parties never really managed to develop any true vitality. Its exertions between 1919 and 1924 seemed to have exhausted the energies of the Arab nationalist movement in Palestine for a time. The various endeavours to summon the seventh Arab Congress and to unite all parties around it had no success until 1928. This was partly due to the fact that from the end of 1925 Zionist immigration, after a sudden great spurt, had been steadily decreasing, that the Jews had begun to emigrate in large numbers, so that in 1927 the emigrants greatly exceeded the immigrants, that there was widespread unemployment among the new immigrants, and that many Arabs already believed that Zionist colonizing activities would never recover from the crisis. But of greater importance was the change that had taken place in the Arab camp between 1923 and 1928. A new generation, educated in contact with Europe and full of the spirit of radical nationalism, was elbowing its way to leadership. These younger people realized the necessity of constructive social activities, of educating the Arab masses and consolidating the economic structure. The memorandum presented to the League of Nations by the Executive Committee of the sixth Palestine Arab Congress on October 6th, 1924, contained, besides complaints of the refusal of constitutional liberties, a detailed criticism of the Government's economic and financial policy. The Executive reproached the Government with having so impaired the condition of Arab agriculture by various legislative measures, and especially by closing the Ottoman Agricultural Bank, that Arab farmers were compelled to sell large tracts of land to the Zionists.

In the summer of 1925 Sir Herbert Samuel left Palestine. In his report on his five years of office he was able to point out that the peaceful condition of the country had rendered possible a continual diminution of the British garrison. His successor, Lord Plumer, was able to carry on this policy of dispensing altogether with the military garrison in Palestine. Lord Plumer continued the British policy hitherto pursued of steering a middle course between the demands of the Arabs and Jews. He was chiefly concerned with the country's financial and administrative consolidation : financially Palestine became entirely self-supporting and ceased to burden the British Treasury ; a government loan was issued, the *gendarmerie* reorganized in accordance with strategic considerations, the construction of the port of Haifa begun, and the road system improved. On the other hand, no attempt was made during Lord Plumer's period of office to conciliate Arab-Jewish differences, which still persisted. Lord Plumer seemed chiefly concerned to secure the financial and strategic position of the British Empire in Palestine, not in order to solve the country's own problems, but from the far wider point of view of British imperial communications.

In a memorandum addressed to the Permanent Mandates Commission in 1927, the Arab Executive protested against Palestine alone among the territories under an A mandate having no popular representative body and against the solution of problems of vital importance to the country altogether without the participation of the inhabitants, such, for instance, as the loan and the grant of what probably constituted Palestine's chief natural wealth, the concession for exploiting the mineral resources of the Dead Sea, to a British Zionist consortium. Only a minute portion of the revenue was applied to the promotion of agriculture, of education, and of public health. During the preceding years the Government had accumulated a surplus of £1,500,000. But it had not been used to raise Palestinian industry and develop the railway system, originally planned for strategic purposes, nor to serve and open up fertile agricultural regions, but to pay back old debts to England dating from the World War. Thus it was again economic questions which led the seventh Arab Congress to place the question of a Parliament in Palestine in the centre of its deliberations when it met in Jerusalem on June 20th, 1928.

The Congress marked the beginning of a new epoch in the Arab nationalist movement in Palestine. It had assembled after prolonged efforts and negotiations between the Husseinis, who had played a leading part in previous Congresses and in the Supreme Moslem Council,[78] the Mohammedan Opposition, consisting of groups in the north and Nashashibi's party in Jerusalem, and the Liberal party which was principally an association of Jaffa Christians. Three hundred delegates took part, and the Congress was the first to represent the restored unity of the Arab people in Palestine. It put forward its claims, as had been done in the memorandum of 1926 addressed to the League of Nations, in a very moderate tone. Its economic and cultural resolutions dealt with the abolition of tithes, the reform of taxation, increased public expenditure on education, and the social welfare of Arab workers. But its chief demand was for the introduction of a democratic representative body. This resolution was as follows :—

" By a unanimous resolution taken by the Palestine Arab Moslem-Christian Congress held to-day, June 20th, 1928, at Jerusalem representing all Arab parties now amalgamated in Congress we hereby demand as of right the establishment of a democratic parliamentary system of Government. It is the duty of the League of Nations to see after ten years of absolute colonial rule in Palestine that such system of Government be granted in accordance with the Covenant of the League of Nations and pledges and declarations made to the Arabs by the Allies. Palestine stands on equal basis with the neighbouring Arab countries which now enjoy parliamentary Government in different forms. The people of Palestine cannot and will not tolerate the present absolute colonial system of Government, and urgently insist upon and demand the establishment of a representative body to lay its own Constitution and guarantee the formation of a democratic parliamentary Government." *

An Executive Committee was elected with forty-eight members, twelve of them Christians. It submitted the wishes of the Congress to Lord Plumer and to his successor, Sir John Robert Chancellor, appointed in the summer of 1928. The new High Commissioner showed sympathy with these demands, and promised to discuss them with the Colonial Office in London in the summer of 1929. But by that time the disturbances of August, 1929, had created a new situation.

THE BUILDING UP OF THE JEWISH NATIONAL HOME

Like the history of the Arab nationalist movement in Palestine, that of Jewish colonization there since the World War falls into three divisions, of which the first reached its climax in the summer of 1925, and the second includes the crisis and transitional period till the summer of 1928 ; there followed a period of renewed ascent, a process of economic consolidation, and the enlargement of the Jewish Agency by the entry of non-Zionists. These years witnessed an amazing experiment and one of the greatest of colonizing feats achieved under exceptionally difficult conditions : human material little fitted for purposes of colonization, coming from utterly different countries and civilizations where wholly different languages were spoken, bringing with them from their homelands the most varied customs and ideas and having to accustom themselves to a new climate and new occupations ; an undeveloped, poor, infertile land, almost devoid of natural wealth, from which only hard labour and the most devoted self-sacrifice could extract crops ; a population who were just awakening to historical activity and national consciousness and were naturally hostile to the stream of immigrant settlers. In spite of these difficulties, the degree of success attained was astonishing. It was least in the political sphere, where no serious attempt was ever

* *Permanent Mandates Commission, Minutes of the Fourteenth Session*, October 26th to November 13th, 1928. Annex 9 (C.P.M. 767), p. 246.

made to come to an understanding with the indigenous population ; indeed, that was probably impossible in consequence of conflicting aspirations, in spite of the honest goodwill to which repeated resolutions of the official Zionist bodies gave expression.

It was in the social and cultural sphere that the achievements were greatest, being often of an exemplary nature. In the economic sphere much was achieved, especially when we compare the failure of many similar efforts at colonization under incomparably more favourable circumstances, for instance, the simultaneous attempts to settle British peasants in Australia, generously supported by the financial wealth of the State and promoted by all its resources. At the beginning of the decade the various sections of the Jewish population were still complete strangers to one another. There was the orthodox, religious element in the old quarters of Jerusalem, Tiberias, Hebron, and Safed ; Jewish communities originating in the most various Eastern countries, often more retrograde than the Eastern peoples themselves in their manner of life and their superstitions ; the colonists from the settlements supported by Baron Rothschild, who had been there before the War and attained to comparative prosperity ; the representatives of the Russian Jewish middle-class intelligentsia in the newly founded Tel Aviv ; and the Jewish workers, reinforced after the World War by an idealist and enthusiastic youthful generation who came in search not only of their ancient homeland, but of a new way of life ; these workers had begun to immigrate into Palestine after the first Russian Revolution in 1905, and many of them were inspired by the ideals of the Russian Socialist parties at that date. Thanks to a uniform education of the young, all these elements began in the course of the decade to make surprisingly rapid progress towards unity. The Zionist ideal began to inspire them all ; many it captured gradually thanks to the impressive progress and the exemplary devotion of the labour pioneers, the Chaluzim.

Immediately before the World War the Hebrew tongue had still a struggle to assert its claims in the ranks of Judaism in Palestine. Now it had not only become one of the official languages, it had also won an undisputed place as the only language of Jewish public life, of the schools, the Press, and all cultural institutions, and it was becoming to a greater and greater extent, not only the language of the younger generation, but also that in common use in Jewish family life. In spite of the small number of Jews in Palestine— they increased from about 60,000 in 1918 to about 170,000 in 1930—cultural and literary activity in Hebrew was remarkably brisk. Palestine became the centre of the Hebrew publishing world and the Hebrew Press, likewise for all countries of the Diaspora. What was needed was to create a literature for the rising generation, principally by means of translations. Hebrew dramatic and operatic companies sprang up. As regards culture, Jewish Palestine was the centre of all that was modern in the national life. The educational committee of the Jewish workers' organization and other societies arranged for lectures, courses, and adult education both in the towns and the country.

Economically the Jewish National Home was to be based on agriculture ; only a people rooted in the soil could really assure a national renaissance. But many immigrants were attracted to agriculture by social as well as national enthusiasm. They wanted at once to till the soil and to introduce new and better social institutions. Jewish agriculturalists introduced modern methods and machinery into Palestine, and strove to assimilate all the experience and discoveries of recent years. Large tracts of land were acquired after the War, especially in the fertile plains along the coast and in the low-lying strip between Haifa on the one hand and the Jordan and Lake Tiberias on the other. Besides the older settlements with their individualist owner-ship and economy, and the new ones of a similar type which sprang up around them, new kinds of settlements appeared. Some were communist settlements, built up on the principle of communal life and production, others were settlements of small peasantry, where property and cultivation is individual, but where there is a large measure of co-operation in a number of branches of cultivation and in marketing, and where the principle of family labour has been introduced and the employment of wage labour on the farm is forbidden by statute. An agricultural experimental station provides for the introduction and diffusion of new methods of cultivation and for the rationalization of industry. Co-operation has made magnificent progress in Palestine.

All this has been rendered possible by the support of Jews all over the world ; in the past decade the Jews have spent nearly £10,000,000 on agricultural settlement alone in Palestine, about half through national societies. The economic results were not, indeed, quantitatively equal to expectation. With the help of that sum only 2,700 new farms were started, and a number of them were not yet established and economically stable at the end of seven years. This applies in particular to a number of settlements in Emek Jesreel, the plain between Haifa and the Jordan. According to the census of 1927 the total population of the Jewish villages was 30,500. Of these 4,297 were farmers and 3,644 agricultural labourers. Since then the number of labourers has considerably increased. The rest of the population followed non-agricultural occupations, or were dependents and persons without occupation.[79] But incomparably greater than the numerical and economic importance of Jewish settlement in Palestine was its symbolic and spiritual significance. This company of some 10,000 Jewish agriculturalists in Palestine, men and women, farmers and labourers, meant far more morally to Judaism than the numerically and economically incomparably stronger Jewries of other countries.

A separate Jewish urban industry hardly existed in Palestine before the War. That was the creation of the post-War era. Tel Aviv, which in 1918 was a small residential suburb of Jaffa, with a population of 3,000, rapidly grew to a city of 40,000 inhabitants thanks to immigration. Modern Jewish quarters sprang up round Jerusalem, Haifa, and Tiberias. In Haifa and Tel Aviv, moreover, modern Jewish industry arose. That and the building trade account for the development of a Jewish urban working class.

With the help of resources contributed to the Zionist fund by Jews in all countries the public health and educational services of the Palestinian Jews have been raised to an exemplary level, hitherto unknown in the East. Malaria, trachoma, and infant mortality have been successfully combated. Universal school attendance, unknown in other Eastern countries, has been made a reality amongst the Jewish population of Palestine. The complete

educational ladder starts from the kindergarten and leads up
to the University. In all towns with a Jewish population
there are hospitals and in all villages out-patients' departments. Special attention is devoted to children and young
people. In them is the hope of the future, they give assurance
that the great labour and devotion of the people will bear
lasting fruit. A visitor to the Jewish settlements will be
repeatedly struck by the handsome and well-cared-for
appearance of the children. Trained nurses and kindergarten
teachers take charge of the children from the first. In many
of the village schools the most modern principles of pedagogy
are applied and special care is taken to attract the children
early to agriculture and manual work. All Jewish workers
are insured with the Jewish workers' organization. Jewish
constructive activities have changed the face of the country.
The inflow of Jewish capital on a large scale since the World
War and the introduction of modern European methods in
industry and modern European habits in daily life have
benefited the rest of the inhabitants in many ways.

The Government has done nothing material to promote
all these developments. The Jews met the cost of colonization
from their own resources, partly from donations collected
all over the world, partly from private investment. The
inflow of Jewish capital during this decade is estimated at
about £30,000,000. The Government, with a Budget showing
a considerable surplus thanks to the increased revenue due
to Jewish immigration, used the money to repay old war
debts to the British Treasury and that part of the Ottoman
National Debt for which Palestine was made responsible.
The Jews made vehement attacks on this financial policy
of the Government ; they reproached the mandatory Power
with doing nothing by an appropriate economic and financial
policy to increase the country's power of absorbing further
immigrants, and with even leaving it to the Jews to meet the
cost of their own educational and public health services. The
Jews received the impression that the Palestinian
Administration in particular was indifferent, if not hostile,
to the task of building up the Jewish National Home, as
promised in the mandate.

In the years 1924–5 Jewish immigration reached its
maximum. It seems that it exceeded the country's economic

power of absorption at the time, as was stated even by an expert commission of the Jewish Agency (Joint Palestine Survey Commission). The number of Jewish unemployed rose for a time to 8,000. Among the immigrants were a number of the Polish middle class, who possessed too little capital to form the basis of a stable livelihood or who failed to adapt themselves to the conditions obtaining in the country. For nearly two years immigration stagnated. But this very circumstance proved an advantage in consolidating the Jewish economic structure ; for it was now possible to prove that for the most part it was firmly established in the country. Whereas the immigration years resembled inflation, and many undertakings founded upon hopes incapable of fulfilment had to be liquidated, the urban and rural enterprises that proved sound actually entered upon a new period of prosperity. The economic structure found its natural equilibrium. The inflow of Jewish private capital began again, and it was particularly profitably invested in the cultivation of oranges in the plain round Jaffa. Preparations were begun to exploit the mineral wealth of the Dead Sea, the construction of the port of Haifa promised to benefit all economic activities, and the moment approached for the construction of the great central power station of the Rutenberg Company on the Jordan and the Yarmuk. In 1929 the crisis that had begun in the autumn of 1925 was entirely overcome. At a Congress in Zurich in August, 1929, the Zionist Organization united with the representatives of non-Zionist opinion in a common Jewish Agency to promote the development of the Jewish National Home in Palestine. The Jewish community in Palestine showed all the features of the Jewish National Home : a working society, economically and socially fully organized on all sides, with its own national and religious institutions, its own autonomous culture and language, rejoicing in the consciousness of freedom founded upon its own achievements. Since the Diaspora the Jewish people had nowhere formed such a community. That is the secret of the significance to Judaism of this centre established in Palestine, in spite of the smallness of its numbers. That, also, is the secret of the happiness that so many Jews feel in Palestine ; they know that they are living, free and active, in new conditions which confront them with constructive tasks ; the Jewish peasant and worker have reached a high cultural standard, they have plentiful intellectual interests, they live in grand country full of historical memories and are conscious of being pioneers of Judaism as a whole, and in some cases of a new social order.

Even now therefore Palestine, economically a relatively poor country, with an Arab population undergoing a process of national and social awakening and beginning to stir to activity in all spheres, offers all the prerequisite conditions for the establishment of productive Jewish settlements, economically and socially united and independent, which might be an object of love and pride to all Jewry, an intellectual, national, and religious focus whence new streams of Jewish vitality might flow to the remotest corners of the Diaspora. But to the overwhelming majority of the Zionist Organization this goal appears inadequate. Their aim is rather by unceasing constructive labours during a transition period before they attain their ideal, continually to establish new political, economic, and cultural bases in the country, and at the same time to increase the number of Jews as rapidly as possible by a maximum of immigration, so that Palestine may become a land with a Jewish majority. Without a Jewish majority Jewish settlement in Palestine would offer no remedy for the mass misery of Eastern Jewry, nor would it have that element of security that is necessary for its autonomous development. The same problem that is to-day the universal political problem, that of security and the fear that springs from it, likewise dominates the situation in Palestine. The Arabs, too, are anxious about their political and economic position in the country, and believe that a Palestine with a Jewish majority would thrust itself like a wedge into the framework of Arab territories at a vital point, and might thus prove an obstacle to the united and independent Arabia of their desires.

POLITICAL AND ECONOMIC CONFLICTS

These fears were the underlying causes of the rising of August, 1929. The attacks by Arabs on the Jewish quarters of Jerusalem, Hebron, and Safed, and on a few isolated villages, were hardly the outcome of a systematically

organized insurrection, which would then have assumed other
and far more serious dimensions, although they consolidated
within a few days into a rising against British mandatory
policy in Palestine. As in 1921, they were the outcome of
excitement of which the underlying causes were to be found
in the political and economic state of Palestine ; its proximate
cause, however, was the growing intensity of religious and
national sentiment due to the propaganda of some of the
Arab leaders, and its immediate occasion was to be found
in false and exaggerated rumours, so characteristic of the
East and of the tension in Palestine, rumours aggravated
by propagandist agitation, and in the feelings of fear and
insecurity thus produced. A year of heated religious agitation
had preceded the riots ; the bone of contention was the
Wailing Wall which, as a remnant of the wall surrounding
Herod's Temple, had been to the Jews for centuries the last
monument of their great past, and which was the scene of
impassioned religious devotions. Now, however, it forms
part of the western wall of a Mohammedan sanctuary, the
Mosque of El Aqsar, and it stands upon Mohammedan soil.
The Jews were unwilling to allow their ancient prescriptive
right to pray before the wall to be infringed by the inter-
ference, which they felt as a provocation, of the
Mohammedans led by Haji Emin el Husseini, the Mufti of
Jerusalem and President of the Supreme Moslem Council.
The Arabs feared that the Jews would claim rights in the
Wailing Wall and that, once those rights were acknowledged,
Jewish claims might extend on historical grounds to the site
of the Temple, where stands to-day the third most important
Mohammedan sanctuary in the world. This holy place,
interwoven with ancient legends and superstitions, became
a symbol of the political struggle of two peoples. Thus it was
that incidents beside the Wailing Wall had power to inflame
the religious passions of Mohammedans in the poor mountain
villages of Palestine.

The Arab attacks on the Jewish quarters in the cities
were accompanied by acts of great savagery. According
to the proclamation of the British High Commissioner, who
returned a few days later and condemned these cruelties
severely, the riots, from which hitherto the Palestinian
Christians and a section of the Mohammedans had held

aloof, developed into a new impetus to the Arab nationalist movement, which gathered fresh vigour. All sections of Mohammedans and Christians united and the Mufti of Jerusalem, whose popularity had been considerably impaired before these events, and who had been confronted by a number of opponents even within the Mohammedan camp, became the undisputed leader of the Arab nationalist movement, at least for a time.

The actual riots were quickly suppressed by the British military arm and outward order was assured by a considerable increase of British troops in Palestine and the establishment of a British police force. But the excitement consequent on the riots had penetrated to the masses of the people and into the villages, and so the tension remained. The struggle was transferred from the field of open violence to that of political and economic organization and propaganda, and gained in bitterness in the process. The protagonists of the movement were the Executive of the Arab National Congress. The Government, moreover, recognized the Executive as representatives of the Arab people in Palestine, and admitted them as such to the proceedings of the Commission of Inquiry which the British Government dispatched to Palestine under the chairmanship of Sir Walter Shaw to investigate the riots and their causes. Whilst the Zionist representatives before the Commission of Inquiry attacked the Palestine Government principally for its vacillating policy and its failure to prevent the riots, the Arab representatives took the opportunity to put forward their national grievances, especially the question of Jewish immigration, Jewish land purchase, and the lack of a democratic representative body.

The Arab nationalist movement had managed to sink religious differences in a common national sentiment. Some of the Arab Christians played a leading part in the movement. At the Arab National Assembly, where nearly 600 delegates met in Jerusalem on October 27th, more than a quarter of the delegates were Christians, including priests and monks. At the first meeting the Christian Deputy Mayor of Jerusalem took the chair, and at the second the Mufti of Safed. The great protest strikes which the Arabs repeatedly organized during the course of the year demonstrated the solidarity of the Mohammedans and all Christian

elements. For the first time, moreover, Palestinian Arab
women took part. On October 25th the first women's congress
was held, representing both Mohammedan and Christian
women. The eager participation of young people attending
school was likewise typical, and tended more and more to
give the movement a radical character. A congress of Arab
agriculturalists which met in Jaffa at the beginning of
November, 1929, repeated the demand made years before
by Arab leaders for measures to improve the lot of the
fellaheen, economically and culturally; they asked for a
modernization of the system of taxation, which falls
particularly heavily on the small peasantry in Palestine, for
the establishment of an agricultural bank to lighten the
excessive burden of debt on the fellaheen, for more village
schools and better sanitation in the villages, and for the
introduction of a Bill to secure a minimum livelihood for a
peasant who sold his land and to protect the tenant farmer
from eviction when the owner sold the land. At the end of
November a conference of Arab merchants and tradesmen
met in Haifa. All Arab demands culminated in the introduction of a democratic representative body in Palestine.

These same demands were put forward by the Arab
Delegation, which was again headed by Musa Kasim Pasha
and went to London in March, 1930. Meanwhile, the report
of the British Commission of Inquiry had been published;
its conclusions were sharply repudiated by the Zionists.
The report found the underlying causes of the Arab
disturbances in Arab opposition to the policy of the Balfour
Declaration, and in their fear that Jewish immigration and
Jewish land purchase would mean the eviction of Arab
tenant farmers, and that the Jews might come to form a
majority in the country. The majority of the Commission
held that the causes of this hostility and tension were rooted
in the very nature of the Palestine mandate and the Balfour
Declaration. One of its members, Harry Snell, however,
adhered to the Zionist view that Arab hostility was rather the
consequence of propaganda, but he proceeded: "The
greatest danger at the present time is that Arab resentment
may become permanent. . . . The most essential need in this
direction is that the Arabs should be convinced that their
fears for the future of their race in Palestine are greatly

exaggerated, and that there is no intention on the part either
of the Jews or the Government to make them landless or to
subordinate their interests as a people." * The Commission's
recommendations concerned the questions of immigration
and land purchase. The tables subjoined to the report showed
that the immigration of 20,000 Jews annually would give
them a majority in Palestine in 1956, whereas 10,000 annually,
a very considerable number decidedly exceeding the present
figure, would render Arab fears of a Jewish majority baseless,
for the natural increase of the Arabs would still be greater
than that of the Jews including immigrants. Under those
circumstances Palestine would have about 1,700,000 Arab,
and about 1,100,000 Jewish, inhabitants in 1975.

The official census taken by the Palestinian Government
in the autumn of 1931 has confirmed the extraordinary
growth of both sections of the population, Arab and Jewish.
According to this census the Jewish population numbered
175,006, as compared with 83,794 at the last official census
(1922), the Mohammedans 759,952, as compared with
590,890, and the Christians 90,607, as compared with 73,024
in 1922. The Arabs (Mohammedans and Christians), with
their 850,559 souls, forming about 83 per cent of the population, have increased since 1922 by 185,645, or about 20,000
yearly. The Jews, now forming 17 per cent of the population,
have by immigration and natural increase raised their
numbers during these nine years by 91,212, or about 10,000
yearly.

Linked with that of immigration is the question how far
there is still unoccupied land available in Palestine. On the
basis of statements which can be tested only by future
scientific investigation, the Commission reached the conclusion that there was a danger of a large number of Arab
tenant farmers and agricultural labourers, for whom no other
was available, being deprived of their land. The members of
the Commission hold that Palestine cannot support an
increased agricultural population until the present methods
of cultivation are radically changed. Moreover, any land
policy must take into consideration the rapid natural growth
of the existing peasant population. The tendency to evict
the peasant cultivators and tenant farmers when the land is

* *Shaw Report* (Cmd. 3530), p. 182.

purchased must be checked and the need of the fellaheen for credit must be satisfied.

In general the British Government accepted the conclusions of the Commission of Inquiry. The Arab Delegation in London, supported by the Commission's recommendations, demanded the cessation of Jewish immigration into Palestine, legal protection for the Arab peasants and tenant farmers, and the introduction of a democratic régime in Palestine embracing the whole population. These demands were unacceptable to the British Government, since their satisfaction would make it impossible to carry out those clauses of the mandate which provide for the establishment of a Jewish National Home. But they promised, within the terms of the mandate, to pay heed to the recommendations of the Commission of Inquiry, and the wishes of the Arab population, and to remove Arab fears for their political and economic future in Palestine. In a new British White Book issued in May, 1930, the dual character of the mandate was emphasized afresh, but it contained no pronouncements favourable to the Arabs that at all went beyond the aim of British policy repeatedly and long since proclaimed. The Arab Delegation, therefore, returned to Jerusalem without having accomplished its purpose. But at this juncture Jewish immigration in the category of wage-earners was suspended. The League of Nations Mandates Commission, which considered the situation in Palestine at a special meeting in June, 1930, criticized the English Administration severely as having failed to prevent the disturbances of August, 1929, and having in general displayed too little resolution and zeal in fulfilling its mandatory duties. The Mandates Commission contested important points put forward by the Shaw Commission.

The suspension of the immigration of workers and the mandatory Government's announcement of intended legislation on land purchase and agriculture, together with fears of new constitutional developments, excited vehement protest on the part of Jewish public opinion, and the Jews organized stormy meetings of protest against the British Government all over the world. Though the attitude of the British Government, therefore, satisfied neither of the two peoples, yet the disturbances and the report of the Commission of Inquiry moved it to turn its attention for the first time to the question of improving the economic position of the fellaheen, reforming taxation, and providing agricultural credits. The report of Sir John Hope Simpson, the expert sent to Palestine to investigate the problems of land and immigration, reached conclusions which, in spite of full recognition of the remarkable achievements of Zionist colonization, were unfavourable to its rapid or wide extension. " It has emerged quite definitely," he wrote, " that there is at the present time and with the present method of Arab cultivation no margin of land available for agricultural settlement by new immigration." Simpson, likewise, primarily stressed the necessity of helping the fellaheen. On the strength of his report the British Government issued a new White Book on Palestinian policy on October 20th, 1930, which was violently attacked by many as contrary to the terms of the mandate, on account of its anti-Zionist tone and the announcement of measures that would make the development of a strong and extensive Jewish National Home impossible. Zionist public opinion unanimously rejected this White Book as the basis of co-operation with England. It had, moreover, announced the establishment of the Legislative Council already conceded in 1922, and rejected at that time by the Arabs. The pressure of public opinion in Zionist circles and those friendly to Zionism caused the Government to issue an interpretation of the White Book in February, 1931, that was markedly more favourable to Zionist aspirations.

The problems raised by the Balfour Declaration have not yet reached their solution. The British Government, in keeping with its character, will not commit itself to any unequivocal goal for Palestine's political future. Its policy seems to aim at securing a firm foothold in Palestine and for that purpose encouraging the increase of the Jewish minority, thereby promoting the country's economic prosperity; but it will not, apparently, endanger the numerical superiority of the Arabs. Perhaps it hopes in this way to meet the wishes of both sides and yet to obstruct both, by imposing upon the Arabs a strong Jewish minority whose cultural and economic superiority will far outweigh their superiority in numbers, and at the same time failing to take steps to enable the Zionists to achieve their aim of a Jewish majority. In actual fact, the British Government will thereby do justice to neither party. For hope and fear are stronger forces than actual facts in moulding the lives of the nations. Great Britain can neither afford to rouse the hostility of the Arab and Mohammedan world nor wholly to disappoint the Zionist hopes confirmed by international engagements, and so in addition to actual, present complications are added psychological complications far more disastrous to peace and to the cultural and social development of the land.

The political situation in the Holy Land, the national aspirations finding expression there, and the passion with which men are struggling to realize them, present one of the most tragic and pathetic spectacles of our time. This little country, which has yet attracted the attention of mankind more than any other, makes an impassioned appeal to our feelings and sympathies, and because of that appeal its problems are echoed far and wide and agitate men's minds. Two movements confront one another, both inspired by national ideals, both the outcome of love for the same soil. Although experience hitherto makes it appear unlikely that a Jewish majority can be attained in Palestine,[80] the Zionists hope for it and the Arabs fear it. They point out that within the brief space of one decade all the economic strategic points in the country by which its future will be determined have passed into Zionist hands : a very large proportion of the orange-growing land and of the fertile plains, the land round about the Bay of Acre which gains vastly in importance through the construction of the port, the monopoly for the exploitation of water power for electrical generation and irrigation, and the Dead Sea concession. The Zionists, they urge, have not only the world-wide support of Jewish wealth and power, but also that of the League of Nations and the British imperial power ; Britain, it is true, does not fulfil all their wishes, but she maintains them in Palestine by her power, and allows them to gain steadily in strength.

The Zionists, on the other hand, point to the right to live of a people with so high a civilization and such creative cultural potentialities. They desire the preservation and national development of Judaism, and are convinced that its existence and growth depend upon the establishment of a Jewish Palestine. The buoyant idealism and joyful devotion which that conviction confers upon the movement augments its vigour. To the Zionists the loss of any prospect of a Commonwealth with a Jewish majority in Palestine means the continuance of a base and miserable existence in exile, which must lead to the total decay of Judaism. A Jewish Commonwealth in Palestine appears to them the only hope of salvation from persecution and humiliation that have continued for centuries, and still continue, the only hope of carrying on a great past to which mankind owes much, and developing the Jewish national character on new and creative lines.

Thus both groups are guided by motives of self-preservation and self-development. That is why in all their words there is an impassioned appeal to the heart. Perhaps it was necessary for the Zionist movement to set itself an impossible goal in order to attain the maximum possible, perhaps it had to rouse a determined and ardent craving for freedom and a tempestuous yearning, in order to enable its followers to bring their weary sacrifice of arduous labour. But in their opponents, who are so much poorer and more backward and yet know that they are part of a rising movement and aspire to freedom, that very appeal roused not only resistance, but sentiments of fear amounting to terror, as unique as the whole situation in the Holy Land.[81] Unique like this country, like the nation that was moulded in it and is now returning to it, mysterious and disquieting, deeply moving and instinct with promise and doom, is the destiny that is being determined in it, with a symbolic significance, at the cross-roads where two worlds meet, that radiates far beyond this narrow strip of Canaanite soil.

VII

TRANS-JORDAN

THE ANCIENT FRONTIER LAND

A STATE COMES INTO BEING

THE collapse in the summer of 1920 of the Arab Federation promised by Great Britain led to her establishing an Arab administration in Trans-Jordan in fulfilment of her promises. Thus a new State was erected with a dual function : it formed a march bordering the desert, a buffer State between the fertile land along the coast and the Bedouins who were a constant menace to this fertile strip, breaking forth from the desert again and again ; such had already been its function in Roman days, as witness the magnificent ruins and military roads ; at the same time it was an important part of the new British route to India, the passage to Iraq. It was to be so organized that it could carry on its existence with a minimum expenditure on the part of Great Britain, free from all avoidable domestic friction, and at the same time be stable enough to guarantee the security of that essential section of the land and air route to Central Asia.

Trans-Jordan lay within the region which was to be placed under an Arab national government according to Great Britain's promises to King Hussein in 1915 and the agreements of May, 1916, between England and France. At first, therefore, it formed part of the Arab Syrian kingdom of Damascus. When that kingdom collapsed in the summer of 1920, the British High Commissioner in Palestine, Sir Herbert Samuel, visited Trans-Jordan and helped the people in setting up local representative bodies. A treaty was concluded between Trans-Jordan notables and the British Major Smith at Umm Qeis on September 1st, 1920, declaring the country's independence. The occasion offered for Great Britain to give form to that independence in February, 1921, when Emir Abdullah, the eldest son of King Hussein of the Hejaz, originally selected for the throne of Iraq, came to Trans-Jordan to attempt the recapture of Damascus from the

162

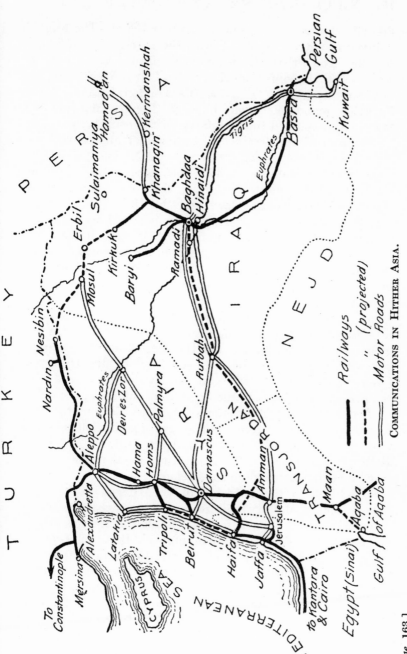

COMMUNICATIONS IN HITHER ASIA.

Railways
   ,, (projected)
Motor Roads

Page 163.]

French, who had driven out his brother Feisal. The English resolved to entrust Abdullah with the government of Trans-Jordan. The British Government confirmed these arrangements—first the conference that met in Cairo under Churchill's direction and later, in 1922, the London Cabinet. The Palestine mandate which, like the French mandate for Syria, was extended to the interior of the country, provided for separate administrative institutions in Trans-Jordan, and on September 16th, 1922, the League of Nations Council, at Lord Balfour's instance, decided that none of the articles of the Palestine mandate regarding the establishment of a National Home for the Jews and the Holy Places should apply to Trans-Jordan. Thereby a juridical position was established totally different from that of Palestine and rendered possible the gradual growth in the course of a decade of a stable and normal State. Trans-Jordan, still without organization or an assured future in 1920, had become a State in 1930.

In contrast to Palestine, Trans-Jordan was to be organized as a State in the spirit of the A mandates. Great Britain was guided by the Iraq model. For this reason, also, the general terms of the Palestine mandate could not be directly transferred to Trans-Jordan in so far as they did not accord with the general provisions of the other A mandates in the spirit of Article 22 of the League of Nations Covenant. The foundation of Trans-Jordan's political organization was laid in a statement made in Amman in April, 1923, by the British High Commissioner for Palestine in the name of the British Government. This statement declared :—

" Subject to the approval of the League of Nations, His Britannic Majesty will recognize the existence of an independent Government in Trans-Jordan under the rule of His Highness the Amir Abdullah, provided that such Government is constitutional and places His Britannic Majesty in a position to fulfil his international obligations in respect of the territory by means of an Agreement to be concluded with His Highness." * Thus the independence of the State of Trans-Jordan was recognized. At the eleventh session of

---

* Harry Charles Luke and Edward Keith-Roach, *The Handbook of Palestine and Trans-Jordan* (Macmillan, 1930), p. 421.

the Permanent Mandates Commission the British representative made the following statement about Trans-Jordan's
position : " It is not part of Palestine, but it is part of the
area administered by the British Government as Mandatory
under the authority of the Palestine Mandate." * [82] Since
1924 the reports of the British Mandatory Government to
the League of Nations have contained separate accounts of
Palestine and Trans-Jordan, and the latter's independence
is indicated in the title of the report. Trans-Jordan's
independence was solemnly proclaimed on May 25th, 1923.
After the treaty between England and Trans-Jordan had
been signed, the office of High Commissioner of Trans-Jordan
was separated from that of Palestine, although the two are
still combined in a personal union. [83] Nevertheless, a considerable measure of unity was maintained between Palestine
and Trans-Jordan in customs and currency.

Trans-Jordan developed very slowly. Emir Abdullah had
as his Prime Minister Ali Riza Pasha Rikabi, who had
formerly been Prime Minister to Feisal in Damascus.
St. John Philby acted as British representative in Trans-
Jordan. Emir Abdullah had difficulty in winning the
confidence of the people. On October 14th, 1922, at the
invitation of the British Government, he came to England
with Rikabi Pasha and Philby, and preparatory steps were
taken to establish the country's future independence. Rikabi
Pasha resigned at the beginning of January, 1923. For a short
time he was succeeded by Muzhir Bey Raslan ; he, however,
was replaced in September of that same year by Hassan
Khalid Pasha Abdul Huda, who enjoyed the Emir's confidence
but was little loved by the people from the first. The country's
peace was disturbed by a series of Bedouin risings, such as
that of the Adwan tribe under Sultan Ibn Adwan, and of
inroads by the Wahabis, with whom several Trans-Jordan
Bedouin tribes were in sympathy. In these early years Great
Britain had to make a fairly large contribution to the Trans-
Jordan Budget. It was not till 1924 that matters began
to mend.

In the spring C. H. F. Cox was appointed British

* *Minutes of the Eleventh Session of the Permanent Mandates
Commission, p. 111.*

representative and Rikabi Pasha again assumed the office of Prime Minister. Severe economies and strict control restored order to the country's finances. In recent years Trans-Jordan's Budget has amounted on the revenue side to an average of £250,000, on the side of expenditure to about £300,000, the deficit being covered by grants from the British Treasury. A number of good motor roads were built, public order was so firmly established in the country that it may pass for complete, modern administrative methods were introduced, and Amman, the capital, was transformed from a quiet village to an active little town with brisk commercial intercourse. Within the very narrow limits of the country's budgetary resources measures were also taken to promote public health and education.[84] The number of students who go to foreign Universities after passing their examinations at the Universities of Trans-Jordan is continually increasing. The population of Trans-Jordan was slowly welded to political unity. Of the 300,000 inhabitants or thereabouts, some 130,000 are settled in towns and villages. A further 120,000 are settled Bedouins who, however, still live under tribal law, and about 50,000 are nomad Bedouins. Except for about 10,000 Mohammedan Circassians, who were established in Trans-Jordan by the Ottoman Government after the Russo-Turkish war of 1878, all the inhabitants are Arabs, and of these some 20,000 are Greek Orthodox and Catholic Christians. In all towns and larger villages elected councils were set up, and the country was divided into four administrative districts with a District Administrative Council in each, consisting of the Provincial Governor (Mutessarif), the Finance Member, the Mohammedan ecclesiastical judge, and two elected members, one Mohammedan and one Christian.

Trans-Jordan frontiers were extended, first by the annexation of the districts of Maan and Aqaba; these had belonged to the kingdom of the Hejaz, which never agreed to their annexation; then in the autumn of 1925 the Haddah Agreement with the Sultan of Nejd established a corridor about a hundred kilometers wide between Nejd and Syria, by which Trans-Jordan and Iraq acquired a common frontier. By the former frontier demarcation Trans-Jordan gained access to the sea and a port of its own in Aqaba which, though it is now an insignificant fishing village, may acquire importance by the construction of a branch line of the Hejaz Railway and the development of a harbour. By the second, although Trans-Jordan lost almost the whole Wadi Sirhan except for its north-western extremity, and in particular the disputed oasis of Qaf or Quryat el Milh, the headquarters of the Ruvalla Bedouins under Nuri Sha'lan, it gained the undisputed possession of a fairly long common frontier with Iraq. The two Arab countries ruled by princes of the same house thus adjoined one another. The intended railway from Iraq to Haifa, which is to run through this corridor and Trans-Jordan, is to link them still more closely.

Emir Abdullah always stressed the close connection between Trans-Jordan, the Kingdom of the Hejaz where his father ruled, and Iraq where his brother Feisal was king. The negotiations which King Hussein conducted with Great Britain in 1923 and 1924 concerned the conclusion of a close alliance between the three States. When King Feisal first visited Amman, the capital of Trans-Jordan, in July, 1923, he made a speech at a banquet at which the British deputy High Commissioner, Sir Gilbert Clayton, and a delegation from Palestine headed by the Mufti Emin el Husseini were present ; he said :—

" The people of Iraq, who love you as themselves and feel all that touches your feelings as their own concern, rejoice at the rise of your country to prosperity, the accomplishment of the aim for which its noble sons have striven. Iraq will not rest content until it is united with all Arab countries, which form an indivisible unit. I have dedicated myself to Arabia's cause, and have sworn to devote myself to that aim until it is achieved. I am fully convinced that the Arabs, in spite of their great and rapid progress, have not yet attained their chief goal. But I am not the man to be discouraged when I see that much remains to be done. The present conditions in all Arab countries are unnatural and it is unlikely that they will persist. I am, therefore, firm in my confidence that within measurable time these conditions will make way for the permanent order for which the Arabs passionately long, and I am convinced that the Arabs will accept nothing less than the unity of all Arab countries." *

* See *Oriento Moderno*, 3rd Year, pp. 227 ff.

Emir Abdullah, moreover, was the first to urge his father publicly to assume the title of Caliph even before the abolition of the Caliphate in Turkey. On January 18th, 1924, King Hussein arrived in Trans-Jordan. He stood then at the height of his power. He received a number of delegations, especially from Palestine, the first being the Latin Patriarch of Jerusalem as the Pope's representative. And there King Hussein was proclaimed Caliph on March 14th. But the scheme failed. King Hussein's and Emir Abdullah's ambition had set just such an aim before them as was bound to endanger King Hussein's very kingdom. In the autumn of 1924 the Wahabis, after invading Trans-Jordan, made an end of this dream of the Caliphate by their attack on the Hejaz.

THE CONSOLIDATION OF THE STATE

The succeeding years were occupied with preparations to fulfil the conditions set forth in Trans-Jordan's declaration of independence. In May, 1924, Hassan Khalid Pasha had again assumed the office of Prime Minister. The delay of four years before the treaty was concluded between Great Britain and Trans-Jordan roused protests by the people against such procrastination. In 1927 the People's party was founded, the first recognized party in Trans-Jordan's public life. At first it conducted a bitter agitation against the concession to the Zionist electrical company in Palestine, which received permission to erect its central power station in Trans-Jordan domains, east of the Jordan. The new party wanted to exercise control over the negotiations for the Anglo-Trans-Jordan treaty in Amman and London, and demanded the immediate establishment of a Parliament and a responsible Ministry. The newly organized movement also undertook responsibility for the publication of the first newspapers in Trans-Jordan, where hitherto there had only been an official journal. The Government tried to enlist the people's co-operation, and had summoned a conference of notables with two representatives of each district in Trans-Jordan to draft a constitution. Without awaiting the result of their deliberations, the Government itself put forward a draft treaty and constitution, but this the conference of notables refused to approve. They opposed the creation of a Legislative Council with limited powers instead of a Parliament, and demanded that the Deputies should be elected by the whole population, instead of setting aside certain seats for minority representatives. As it proved impossible to reach an agreement, the Government dissolved the conference of notables. Negotiations about the draft treaty and constitution were conducted solely between the Governments in London and Amman. But the agitation did not cease, and when the treaty was published in the spring of 1928 the opposition increased in violence.

The treaty was signed on February 20th, 1928, in Jerusalem. It provided for ratification by the National Legislative Assembly which was to be elected on the basis of the Trans-Jordan constitution, promulgated in Amman on April 16th, 1928, and the Electoral Law promulgated in Amman at the end of June, 1928.* As with Iraq, the treaty and its ratification formally regulated relations between Trans-Jordan and Great Britain by a bilateral agreement instead of, as hitherto, their being imposed on the mandated territory by a unilateral document. But although the treaty, therefore, implied a great advance as compared with the state of affairs in the other territories under A mandates, and proved a step towards the fulfilment of the purpose of the mandatory system, it was yet far less progressive than the Iraq treaty. It did not replace the mandate, but supplemented and interpreted it. Trans-Jordan was not recognized as a sovereign State, but as an independent territory, although that territory bore all the outward marks [85] of a fully developed State which had only abandoned some of its sovereign rights by treaty obligations. Whereas in the constitutions of Iraq, Syria, and Lebanon legislative power emanates from the people, in Trans-Jordan legislative and executive power resides in the Emir, who is constitutionally restricted in its exercise by the rights of the Legislative Assembly. In all foreign relations and important financial affairs Trans-Jordan is under Great Britain's tutelage. England has the right to maintain military forces

* For the text of the treaty see Cmd. 3069, 1928, and of the constitution Harry Charles Luke and Edward Keith-Roach, *The Handbook of Palestine and Trans-Jordan* (Macmillan, 1930).

in Trans-Jordan and to raise, organize, and control such armed forces in the country as she considers necessary for its defence and for the maintenance of order ; in principle the cost of the forces necessary for Trans-Jordan's defence are to be borne by the country's own revenues. The imposition and enforcement of martial law are also under British control. Trans-Jordan engages to facilitate the movements of British troops in every way, and to be guided by Great Britain's advice in all matters relating to the grant of concessions, the construction and administration of railways, and the raising of loans. No time limit is placed to the treaty, but there is express provision for its adaptation from time to time to changing conditions. The treaty determines Trans-Jordan's political status on a basis fundamentally different from that of Iraq. England's advice to Iraq was to be given without prejudice to her national sovereignty, and Iraq really has become a provisionally independent State in the sense of Article 22 of the League of Nations Covenant, whilst her full independence was anticipated from the first at no very distant date. So, too, the military clauses in the Iraq treaty are milder, whilst in the Trans-Jordan treaty they make the country strategically an actual part of the British Empire. It is, therefore, easy to understand that the treaty caused great disappointment in Trans-Jordan and called forth bitter opposition.

The constitution, on the other hand, which resembled that of an independent State in its general outline and its provisions, called forth little opposition. It declared Islam to be the State religion and Arabic the sole official language. The Emir is assisted by an Executive Council, consisting of a chief Minister and five members. The Legislative Assembly, which is re-elected every three years, meets annually in regular session on November 1st. The Prime Minister presides at its sessions. The Ministry is not responsible to the Assembly. The Legislative Assembly numbers sixteen Deputies, of whom thirteen are Mohammedans and three Christians ; two of the Mohammedans are Circassians. Every male citizen of Trans-Jordan over eighteen exercises the active franchise. The elections are indirect, each 200 electors choosing one of the second class. Members of the Executive Council, if they should not be chosen from the

Assembly, belong to it *ex officio*. Originally it was intended that the Legislative Assembly should meet in 1928, but that was rendered impossible by the agitation against the treaty. Protests were directed less against the Emir than the Prime Minister. At first the Government tried to suppress the movement of protest. The Trans-Jordan Press was placed under censorship and papers which supported the opposition were forbidden. The leaders of the nationalist movement were harassed and, if they were not Trans-Jordan citizens, expelled. In recent years Trans-Jordan had become a centre of the Arab nationalist movement in consequence of the Syrian insurrection. The town-dwellers in Amman, El Kerak, and Irbid had not only laid the foundations of a strong national organization, but had succeeded in enlisting the interest of the Bedouin tribes in the nationalist movement. The Government could not, therefore, subdue the protest movement. On July 25th, 1928, a National Congress met in Amman, representing the towns, villages, and Bedouin tribes with Hussein Pasha el Tarvana as its leader. The Congress appealed to the Arab alliance with the English during the World War, to England's promises to the Arabs, to Article 22 of the League of Nations Covenant, and to Wilson's Fourteen Points, and adopted a National Pact in which the fourth clause, a protest against the Balfour Declaration, refers to Palestine. The other clauses are as follows :—

" The Emirate of Trans-Jordan is an independent Arab State and is sovereign within its own frontiers. It is ruled by a constitutional, independent, Arab Government under the guidance of Emir Abdullah and his successors. It does not recognize the mandatory principle, except in the form of technical assistance to be defined in a treaty which shall determine mutual rights and interests without prejudice to national sovereignty. No elections to a representative body in Trans-Jordan can be regarded as the expression of the popular will unless they are held in such a way as to give true popular representation, together with ministerial responsibility. The decisions of a representative body which violates Trans-Jordan's fundamental rights must be regarded as the arbitrary acts of the mandatory Government exercising its own despotic power. The financial grants of the British Government are merely a necessary outlay on the security of the British Empire's communications and do not give England the right to control the country's finances."

In accordance with these resolutions, an overwhelming majority of the people boycotted the attempt to make an electoral register in the second half of 1928, and in the district of Maan it proved altogether impossible. It was not till February, 1929, that the elections were held. Great Britain had agreed that when the Trans-Jordan Assembly had ratified the treaty she would start negotiations for its modification in a sense favourable to Trans-Jordan. In spite of this a large section of the people protested against the elections. In these circumstances the Government managed to assemble in Parliament principally supporters of its own policy and of the ratification of the treaty. Characteristically enough, the bitterest opposition to the treaty and the Government came from the Christian and Circassian Deputies.

On April 2nd, 1929, Emir Abdullah solemnly opened the first session of the Trans-Jordan Legislative Assembly. In his Speech from the Throne he pointed to the independence that Trans-Jordan had now finally won and recommended the acceptance of the treaty. It was accepted on June 4th. In the course of the year the Ministry was democratized by the inclusion of two members of the representative Chamber, one Christian and one Circassian. The Ministry consists solely of Trans-Jordan citizens. There are only twelve British officials in Trans-Jordan's service, one as Adviser to the Ministry of Justice, and one in the Ministry of Finance. Among these twelve, who are all Trans-Jordan officials, including the Advisers in the Ministry, and are appointed by the Emir, there are three officers of the Arabian Legion and two directors of the Archæological Department. In view of the shortage of competent men, a number of official posts in Trans-Jordan are filled by Palestinians or Syrians.

On October 31st, 1929, the British High Commissioner for Trans-Jordan left Jerusalem and came to Amman, where he announced that the King of England had ratified the treaty between Great Britain and Trans-Jordan, so that it had now come into force. The people of Trans-Jordan took advantage of the High Commissioner's presence to hold great demonstrations against British policy in Palestine and the Balfour Declaration. On November 2nd the Emir opened the first regular session of the Trans-Jordan Parliament. For the first time the Emirate's Budget for the coming year was submitted to the representative Assembly to be discussed and voted upon. In his Speech from the Throne, which sketched the Emirate's future policy, the Emir laid stress upon the intimate ties of friendship and confidence which bound Great Britain and Trans-Jordan, and emphasized with pleasure the fact that King George V had recognized his right to a salute of twenty-one guns, such as is the due of the heads of States. The Emir promised to strive to realize Trans-Jordan's hopes and aspirations and to win full national independence. He then spoke in detail of relations with Palestine and Iraq. He read a letter that he had addressed to the British High Commissioner, giving expression to his anxiety for the lot of the Arabs in Palestine. He emphasized the fact that the High Commissioner had replied in a very satisfactory manner, and had stated that the forcible suppression of the disturbances was not enough, that other measures were necessary in order to reassure the Mohammedans that their rights would be safeguarded and to banish their fears. Emir Abdullah had passed the second half of October with his brother Feisal, King of Iraq. He spoke with satisfaction of the cordial and brotherly relations subsisting between the two countries, and of the prospect that a close treaty of friendship would soon be concluded between Iraq and Trans-Jordan. After his speech the sitting was concluded out of sympathy with the Arabs of Palestine, November 2nd being the anniversary of the Balfour Declaration.

Emir Abdullah succeeded as the years passed in mitigating the dislike of the Trans-Jordan people for his person. His country has surmounted the precarious preparatory phase of political consolidation. After almost ten preliminary years, its political independence is recognized and firmly based on foundations which give hope to the people that it will advance steadily towards fuller liberties and union with other Arab territories. The country derives its strategic importance from its situation between the cultivated land along the Mediterranean coast and the desert : it is destined to be a bulwark of defence against the desert. Thence, too, it may derive its cultural significance as the transmittor of a settled civilization and of superior organization to the nomad sons of the desert. The fertile seeds of such possible development lie in the co-operation between the Trans-Jordan Government and Great Britain's colonial experience.

The constitution selected has proved in harmony with Great Britain's interests. It is an instrument that serves the ends of British policy in the important matters of strategy and communications, and yet releases Great Britain from a large part of the laborious work of government involved by responsibility for the details of internal administration, work which can only be carried on in opposition to the population. The native Government intercepts many of the attacks which would inevitably be directed against Great Britain, if she were to attempt to administer the country directly, and greatly mitigates their vehemence. Just because of the large measure of sovereignty and freedom of action left to the native Government, it learns to estimate realistically political limitations which only admit of a more gradual satisfaction of certain ambitions than the nationalists desire. The installation of a native Government and the recognition of the mandated territory as an independent State are not only in keeping with the letter and spirit of the League of Nations mandate, they have also proved their worth from the British point of view. Trans-Jordan hopes soon by negotiations with Great Britain to secure a modification of the treaty between the two countries which will concede to her a further measure of independence. The country needs union with larger and more advanced neighbours, and this has been Great Britain's intention from the first. Trans-Jordan was to form part of an Arab Federation. And the intention was realized from 1918 to 1920, and was to be realized in the treaty between King Hussein of the Hejaz and Great Britain that was being negotiated in 1923 and 1924. In the meantime the situation has changed. For the time being, at any rate, Syria and the Hejaz do not come into consideration. Of the territories which the Federation originally contemplated by Great Britain was to unite, only Iraq remains. Iraq is linked with Trans-Jordan by a common dynasty. Article 8 of the Anglo-Trans-Jordan treaty anticipates a treaty of alliance between Trans-Jordan and neighbouring Arab States. The

Emir's Speech from the Throne announced such a treaty with Iraq. Another mark of the close ties which are to bind the two countries is the dispatch of two commissions from Trans-Jordan to gather information at the Military Academy and the Police College in Iraq. The new railway that is to connect Baghdad and Haifa and to pass through Trans-Jordan will render closer economic bonds between Iraq and Trans-Jordan possible. It will form a basis in the field of transport and communications for the alliance between King Feisal's and Emir Abdullah's kingdoms.

VIII

SYRIA

THE POLITICAL PROBLEMS OF NATIONALISM

LEBANON : THE APPLE OF DISCORD

SYRIA is the most advanced of Arab countries ; this is due
to the contrasting elements upon which a higher unity is
based. The country embraces the Mediterranean coast, the
ancient Phœnicia, with its face always turned westward,
and likewise the great centres of the interior like Damascus,
situated on the edge of the desert and therefore constituting
from the earliest times meeting-places for economic and
cultural exchange. Damascus was the capital of the Arabian
Empire in the early days of its rise to power. Syrian territory
covers the passage from the fertile Mediterranean coast to
the desert, and many mountain ranges preserving ancient
traditions in valleys difficult of access and offering a refuge
to persecuted sects ; and the land presents many contrasts
in culture, customs, and religious traditions. A past filled
with embittered religious strife, often inflamed by the
interested intervention of European Powers, still influences
the present. Modern national sentiment, which has transformed Turkey and Persia in the last decade and is the
motive power of political development in the East in the
present historical phase, has not yet advanced so far in Syria
as to overcome the ancient religious, local, and tribal
antipathies and particular interests. Ever since the beginning
of the twentieth century there has been a growing tendency
in that direction. The demand for a unified State
organization in Syria and therewith for its union with other
Arab countries was universally adopted as a political
programme, but the time has been too short for it everywhere
to penetrate the consciousness of the broad masses and prove
stronger than inherited sentiments and antipathies. If the
mandate was to have any meaning it could only be justified

by the influence of a Western national State encouraging
and accelerating this process of Syria's development towards
modern Statehood. France's activities as mandatory may
be described as having obstructed that development from the
first. She justified her policy by the third paragraph of the
first article of the mandate which runs : " The mandatory
Power shall encourage local autonomy wherever circumstances are favourable." But she forgot that such
encouragement prejudiced development towards political
independence which it is the prime object of the mandate
to assist.

The very first measures which France adopted in Syria
were bound to call forth the bitterest opposition from the
first among the Syrian people and to constitute their resistance
as a struggle not for freedom alone, but for unity. On
November 22nd, 1919, General Gouraud arrived at Beirut
as French High Commissioner. He succeeded Georges
Picot in the post, who had negotiated the agreement with
Great Britain in 1916 by which the interior of Syria with
Damascus, Homs, Hama, and Aleppo were to constitute an
independent Arab State, or part of such a State. In
accordance with this agreement and with Great Britain's
and France's promises to the Arabs, an Arab Government
had been set up at Damascus under Emir Feisal, the son of
the King of the Hejaz. It was the wish of the vast majority
of the Syrian people that placed Feisal on the Syrian throne
on March 11th, 1920, and on July 3rd the Syrian National
Congress unanimously adopted a democratic constitution,
which proclaimed a united Syria on a basis of decentralization.
But General Gouraud, after a distinguished record in the
World War, could not accept the mission of organizing and
administering a narrow coastal strip in the Levant. The
Conference of San Remo in April, 1920, had allotted
the mandate of all Syria to France. On July 19th
General Gouraud sent an ultimatum to King Feisal. On
July 24th an Arab army, rapidly mustered under the
command of the Minister for War, Yussuf el Azmi, tried
to check the French advance at Khan Meisalun. The attempt
proved vain. The Arab commander fell at the head of his
troops. The first act in the drama of Syrian independence
was at an end. The French entered Damascus. But until

1924 hot-beds of disaffection were continually blazing up in various parts of the country, and in 1924 it required heavy military expenditure and an army of 60,000 to maintain peace in 1924. Hardly had the army been reduced in 1925, in consequence of events in Morocco, when a general insurrection broke out in Syria.

But Syria's political subjugation was followed by a heavy blow to the political sentiment of the Syrian people : the partition of the country. On September 1st, 1920, General Henri Gouraud solemnly proclaimed the creation of the State of Great Lebanon in Beirut :—

" At the foot of these majestic mountains which have been the strength of your country and remain the impregnable stronghold of its faith and freedom, on the shore of this sea of many legends that has seen the triremes of Phœnicia, Greece, and Rome and now, by a happy fate, brings you the confirmation of a great and ancient friendship and the blessings of French peace. . . . I solemnly salute Great Lebanon in its glory and prosperity in the name of the Government of the French Republic. . . ."

With the creation of the new State, French policy in Syrian mandated territory assumed a form which was the outcome of France's historical relations with the Levant, and was destined to determine the character of French policy in Syria in the years immediately following. Thus a long-standing French desire was accomplished ; remembering the heritage of the Crusaders, France had long endeavoured to gain a foothold in the Levant by means of systematic cultural propaganda, and a protectorate over the united Christian Churches in the East, and so to extend the colonial empire that she had established in the western Mediterranean also to the east. She was unaware of the difficulties that would confront her. Her politicians imagined that the Syrian Arabs resembled the Arabic-speaking population that they knew in Algeria and Morocco. The French governing classes had no inkling of the profound transformation of Eastern political and social life. They believed, moreover, that they would find in the Maronites of the Lebanon mountains a Christian population attached to the Roman Church, though retaining their native liturgy, with a priesthood educated for the most part by French Jesuits. France looked for support in Syria to these Maronites, and wanted to use them as a counterpoise to the Mohammedans who resisted alien rule.

In 1860, after a struggle between Maronites and Druzes, the mountain range of Lebanon, inhabited by an overwhelming majority of Maronites, had been granted a wide measure of autonomy within the Ottoman Empire at the instance of the Powers. In this struggle between Druzes and Maronites the French had assumed the rôle of protectors of the Maronites, as in the past. During the World War the Turks had abolished Lebanese autonomy, and the Maronite priesthood, known to be pro-French, suffered much persecution. This confirmed them in their opposition to union with Mohammedan Syria. They wanted a Great Lebanon to be set up within its " historical and natural frontiers ", which should be predominantly Catholic and might turn its face away from the East and towards the West. Some of the Maronite intelligentsia had received their education in France, and had identified themselves completely with French culture ; naturally they would not hear of Lebanon forming part of an Arabia that included the desert. On the other hand, a not inconsiderable number of Maronites and the overwhelming majority of non-Catholic Christians stood for the ideal of Arab unity and the Arab cultural renaissance. For had it not been just Maronites and other Syrian Christians who laid the foundations of a new Arab literature in the nineteenth century, and contributed most in Egypt and America to spread it and inspire it with greater profundity ? This school of thought feared that a radical process of Europeanization would mean uprooting from their native soil, and regarded the memory of Arab greatness and Arab history, and the hope of a free and culturally creative future, as the common bond that was to unite all the various religious communities and provinces of Syria. It was precisely these Syrian Christians who were pioneers in the endeavour to emerge from the mediaeval *régime communautaire*, inherited from Turkey and still encouraged by France, and to attain to a Pan-Syrian, Pan-Arab national consciousness.[86]

After the subjugation of the interior of Syria at the end of July, 1920, the French decided considerably to enlarge Lebanon, which they regarded as the base of their power against the Mohammedans, to unite with it districts of

economic and strategic importance principally inhabited by
Mohammedans, and so to give it just such a degree of
saturation with Mohammedans as was yet compatible with
the predominance of the Christians in the new State. For
such a State existence was, from the outset, only possible
if the strength and rights of the several religious communities
were balanced with the utmost care. Beneath the threadbare
pretence of modern democracy it inevitably presented the
mediaeval spectacle of perpetual feuds between sects and
clans for their own political claims. Such a State could not
flourish and necessarily depended for its power and security
solely on the support of the French mandatory Power. For
that reason alone it seemed to justify the permanent presence
of France in Syria. Not only Beirut, the chief seaport in the
country, was given to the mountain State of Lebanon ; this
admitted of geographical justification, because Beirut,
in which the Mohammedan and Christian population is
about equal, forms an enclave in Lebanon. What called forth
bitter opposition among the Syrians was the addition of
the fertile plains east of Lebanon with Baalbek, of the districts
south of Lebanon with Sidon and Hasbeya, and those north
of Lebanon with Tripoli. These regions were principally
inhabited by Mohammedans. The new State had a population
estimated in 1925 at about 600,000, in 1929 at about 800,000.
The Maronites were now a minority, but with the addition
of the other Christians they commanded a slight majority
over the Mohammedans.[87] The creation of Great Lebanon
was resisted by its Mohammedan inhabitants, who steadily
demanded union with the rest of Syria, and opposed by the
Syrians beyond its borders. By Great Lebanon Syria was
not only deprived of its most fertile districts and its access
to the sea, but became predominantly a State with its face
turned to the desert.

But France was not content with the creation of Great
Lebanon. At the same time, on August 31st, 1920, the coastal
region north of Lebanon was proclaimed an independent
territory of the Alawis, and in July, 1922, promoted to be
the State of the Alawis. Once more the French Government
profited by the traditional hostility of a mountain people,
the Nuseiri or Alawis, to the Mohammedans ; this timid and
secret sect had been much persecuted by the Turks. The new

State included a considerable number of Syrians besides the
Alawis, and amongst these the Mohammedans have never
ceased to demand union with the rest of Syria.[88] In this
way Syria was deprived of its whole sea-coast, and even the
small remaining strip in the north was constituted a separate,
autonomous Sanjak of Alexandretta on September 12th,
1921, in view of the large Turkish-speaking population there ;
Turkish was recognized as well as Arabic as an official
language.

But all these attempts provided no basis for a solution
of the Syrian problem. The question of Syrian unity has
never ceased to be discussed and still obstructs all the efforts
of French policy in Syria. The measures adopted by France
were designed to counteract the Arab nationalist movement,
to counteract the growing sentiment of national union by
the traditional religious cleavages that have involved social
differences in the East until quite recently, and so to
perpetuate them. In spite of their Christian faith and the
adhesion of their Church to the great Latin Church of the
West, the Maronites are thorough-going Orientals in their
social and cultural organization, like other Eastern Christians,
with the exception of a small, Westernized upper class. French
policy had gained nothing but the thanks or the Alawis, a
primitive, persecuted, mountain people making no claim
whatever to advanced political freedom or cultural progress,
who breathed a sigh of relief when French colonial and
economic rule freed and protected them from long-continued
oppression. The Maronites, on the contrary, were bitterly
disappointed with French policy, for they had confidently
expected that their State would rise to great prosperity and
attain genuine independence by French aid. The Maronites'
first enthusism soon, therefore, evaporated. Only their
dislike of union with the rest of Syria restrained them from
open hostility to the French mandate. French policy, to
which Great Lebanon owed its existence, proved doubly
misguided : it did not solve the Syrian problem, but charged
it with a new mass of explosive material, and it endeavoured
to counteract those historical processes which are more and
more gaining the upper hand in the East.

But even the interior of Syria did not escape the French
policy of partition, at least for a time. France took advantage

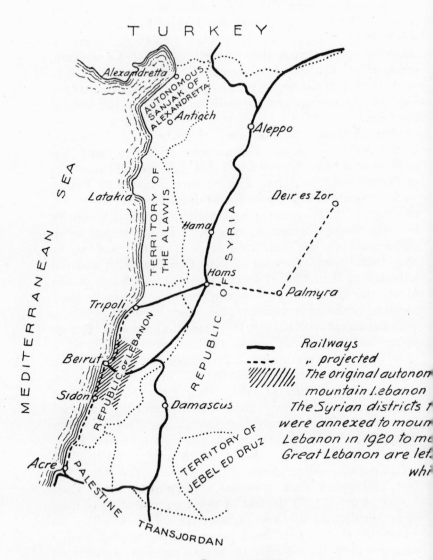

TURKEY

Alexandretta

AUTONOMOUS
SANJAK OF
ALEXANDRETTA
Antioch

Aleppo

MEDITERRANEAN SEA

Latakia

TERRITORY OF THE ALAWIS

Deir es Zor

Hama

REPUBLIC OF SYRIA

Homs

Palmyra

Tripoli

REPUBLIC OF LEBANON

Beirut

Sidon

REPUBLIC OF LEBANON

Damascus

Railways
„ projected
The original autonom
mountain Lebanon
The Syrian districts
were annexed to moun
Lebanon in 1920 to m
Great Lebanon are let.
whi

TERRITORY OF JEBEL ED DRUZ

Acre

PALESTINE

TRANSJORDAN

SYRIA IN 1930.

of the rivalry of the two largest cities in Syria, Damascus and Aleppo, each of which had been the capital of a vilayet till 1918. Besides these two States of Damascus and Aleppo, an autonomous State of Jebel ed Druz was created on March 4th, 1921, by a treaty with the Druzes, and its independence proclaimed on April 5th, 1922. But the peoples in the States of Damascus and Aleppo were too keenly desirous of union for the French Government to be able to resist them. So a Federation was first set up, embracing Damascus, Aleppo, and the Alawis, until at last in the summer of 1924 General Weygand, the new French High Commissioner, dissolved the Federation and united Damascus and Aleppo in a single Syrian State, whilst the State of the Alawis resumed its former independence. Thereafter Syria was composed of five different States, if we include the autonomous Sanjak of Alexandretta. But all these partitions are of far less importance than the hostility between the Mohammedans, especially the Sunnis, and the Maronites. It was exacerbated by the French choice of Beirut instead of Damascus as the headquarters of the High Commissioner, and by the fact that the first French High Commissioners were clerical generals who were believed to favour the Christians at the expense of the Mohammedans. Without Syrian unity there can be no question of freedom, and so none of realizing the mandatory ideal. Unless religious differences are bridged over in political life and in the administration, there can be no question of modernizing the clumsy and expensive machinery of the State, nor of unifying and raising cultural and social life. Nor have these fundamental errors of French policy in Syria been corrected during the past decade, although the insurrection of 1925 induced France to meet the wishes of the Syrian people in some respects and to turn to a more liberal policy by summoning a National Constituent Assembly and adopting a democratic constitution for Syria.

CONSTITUTIONAL EXPERIMENTS

Until 1922 there were no popular representative bodies in the several Syrian States. In Lebanon the Governing Commission was retained, consisting of fifteen members appointed by the High Commissioner and having only advisory functions. It was not till March 8th, 1922, that Lebanon was granted a provisional constitution by which executive power was vested in a Governor appointed by the High Commissioner ; the initiative in legislation was also his right alone. He was assisted by a Representative Council elected by universal suffrage with power to discuss the legislation proposed by the Governor, and to adopt or reject those items of the Budget that were not compulsory, besides certain measures relating to public works and social welfare. This Council, with its exceedingly limited powers, consisted of thirty Deputies indirectly elected on a democratic franchise ; it was the Governor's duty to see that the various religious communities were represented in proportion to their numbers. In order to avoid friction between the different religious communities, the nominated Governor of Lebanon was always a Frenchman. The Representative Council comprised sixteen Christians (ten Maronites, four Greek Orthodox, and two Greek Catholics), thirteen Mohammedans (six Sunnis, five Shi'ahs, and two Druzes), and one representative of the minorities in Beirut, where of the five Deputies two were allotted to the Sunnis, one each to the Maronites and Greek Orthodox, and one in common to the remaining religions (Shi'ahs, Druzes, Greek Catholics, Jews, and Protestants). The installation of this Council called forth a flood of vehement protest from the people of Lebanon, for the new Council's powers were far narrower than those of the Council in Turkish days. Popular discontent repeatedly found expression in the Assembly itself, and in the Press. In the spring of 1924, the Deputy Fuad Arslan stated emphatically in the Council that the mandatory Power's reports to the League of Nations nowise depicted the true state of affairs. He protested against the statement of Robert de Caix, the French representative, before the Mandates Commission, describing the position in the mandated territories as satisfactory. The question of creating a unified Lebanese nation without regard to traditional religious groups was seriously discussed in the Council and in the country ; this was put forward as an alternative to the retention of the religious communities as legally recognized public corporations in the country's political life. In the spring of 1924 when the electoral regulations for the Beirut

Town Council provided for proportional representation of the several religions, various Deputies opposed them, including Emil Eddé, Fuad Arslan, and Dr. Thabet. The unity to which the Lebanese people aspired, he said, was incompatible with these confessional divisions, and it was an unworthy act to lay down any such principle. The most fitting candidates should be freely chosen for Lebanon's elected bodies; they must not become a mirror to reflect religious fanaticism. But only six votes supported this progressive motion, whilst another attempt to grant the franchise to women only received three votes.

Similar Representative Councils were set up in the other States. There, however, the opposition often assumed more violent forms than in Lebanon. On April 1st, 1922, Charles Crane had come to Damascus, he who had visited Syria and Palestine in 1919 together with H. C. King on behalf of the United States, and recorded the people's opposition to the mandatory system. Advantage was taken of his presence to hold great demonstrations in which Arab women made public speeches and took a leading part. The Government condemned several national leaders to severe penalties; thus Dr. Abdul Rahman Shahbander, who had been Foreign Minister under King Feisal, was condemned to twenty years' penal servitude. The retort was a seven days' protest strike and disturbances continuing for weeks and spreading to other parts of Syria.

Representative Councils were set up in the several States like that in Lebanon, and also a Federal Council for matters of common concern. It was not till November 12th, 1923, that the Council could be opened in the city of Damascus by the Governor of the State of Damascus, Hakki Bey el Azm; for in Damascus as in Aleppo, unlike Lebanon, the Governor was a Syrian. Subhi Bey Barakat of Antioch, a Turk, was President of the Federation; indeed, the French generally preferred to look for support to the old Turkish section of the population, who were more accustomed to subordination from pre-War days and more aloof from Arab nationalist aspirations. The Syrian Federation, moreover, was given its own green and white flag, with the colours of the French Republic in the upper corner; whilst Lebanon had adopted the French tricolour for its flag, with a Lebanese cedar in the centre. The mere choice of these emblems reflects Lebanon's closer tie with France. Syria, indeed, had to wait for eight years after the grant of this flag, chosen by France and bearing a French emblem, before she was allowed to fly the national Arab colours without any mark of the bond with France, colours which, instead of emanating from French choice and French instructions, expressed her unity with the other Arab countries.

The real power of all these representative bodies was exceedingly small. Until 1923 the Federal Council consisted wholly of nominated members. It was not till the autumn of 1923 that elected Councillors were introduced and a number of political prisoners released. Among these was Dr. Shahbander, who declared in a speech at Damascus on November 6th :—

" Every nation has its own, unchanging characteristics which cannot be suppressed. Ireland has retained its characteristic national traits unimpaired in spite of four centuries of oppression. The same is true of the Syrian Arab people. The Syrians are an Arab people with their own sharply defined religious ideas and moral traditions which no power and no obstruction can destroy, unless the nation itself is annihilated. Henceforth every heart knows its duty, its great responsibility towards the Syrian community ; a new movement has begun that will raise the Arabs to their true historic position."

In its first session the Damascus State Council unanimously demanded Syrian unity, the convocation of common Constituent Assembly for all Syrian States, and the establishment of a single Government responsible to Parliament. At one of the earlier sessions the foreign mission schools had been fiercely attacked. The representative of the Greek Orthodox Christians had described the foreign schools as the root of all evil and demanded, amidst general agreement, that all schools should be placed under the direction of the State. Later the constitution of January, 1930, fulfilled this demand. But before that the country had to pass through the ordeal of the great Syrian revolution. What that meant, and how much the Syrian revolution did to compel the French to adopt a different attitude towards the Syrians, may be seen if we compare the

decree of December 5th, 1924, on the constitution of the
Syrian State with the constitution of May, 1930. True,
the decree of December, 1924, provided for a State with an
elected President, a Ministry appointed by him, and an
elected Council, but the Council had only the same exceedingly
limited functions as its predecessor, and every act of the
President and Ministers required confirmation by the French
High Commissioner and his officials. Nor did the constitution
provide for the protection of political and civil liberties,
which simply did not exist in Syria at that time. As in
Lebanon so in Syria, the directly French character of the
administration was barely disguised, and the elected representatives of the people hardly exercised even a formal
influence upon it.

The year 1925 brought the crisis in the history of the
Syrian mandate. On January 2nd the new French High
Commissioner, General Sarrail, arrived in Beirut. Politically
he was a Liberal and anti-clerical, and he tried to break with
the existing French tradition in Syria, which had looked for
support to the Catholic Churches. He wanted to make an
end of the state of siege that had continued uninterruptedly
in the country since the World War, to introduce freedom of
the Press, of assembly, and of speech, and to lead the country
along the path of freedom and liberal thought. Education,
which had hitherto been left entirely to the private care of
the religious communities in Lebanon, was to be encouraged
by the State, and the rising generation was to be trained in
common non-sectarian schools to realize their civic duties
as children of a common motherland. In Lebanon this
attempt met with determined resistance from the Christian
priesthood.

On the day of his arrival, Sarrail had proposed to the
Representative Council the election of a Lebanese instead of a
French Governor. But when the Council failed to reach
agreement he himself appointed Leon Cayla Governor, and
dissolved the Council. The dissolution was generally welcomed
in Lebanon, for in its three years of activity the Council had
proved its incompetence and its scanty interest in reform,
but Cayla immediately earned the hostility of ecclesiastical
circles by saying that it was undesirable for Lebanon to have
no national but only sectarian religious schools. " We mean

to create truly national schools based upon the principle of lay control, schools which do not favour one religion rather than another, but imbue all scholars with the conviction that they belong to a single family." The government schools were to be an instrument of concord between the various sections of the population. The Jesuit organs attacked Cayla's policy violently. Most of the progressive organs of Arab opinion, especially *Ahrar*, the chief Beirut daily, defended it vigorously. At any rate, credit is due to Sarrail for having raised one of Lebanon's and Syria's basic problems, that of surmounting religious cleavages in politics and education. It is still unsolved, like the second basic problem, that of Lebanon's relation with the rest of Syria. Cayla had devised a new electoral law for the election of the new Council in March, 1925, which was a considerable advance on the existing law, for it replaced indirect election in two stages by direct election, and abolished all religious distinctions between the candidates. Article 1 of this draft, which never became law but is nevertheless of historical importance, ran as follows :—

" In future no account shall be taken of the division into various religious communities in assigning seats in the Representative Council to the several sections of the Lebanese population. The members of the Representative Council shall be elected directly and by the list system of proportional representation."

The elections for the new Council were, however, held on the basis of the original electoral law of 1922, only slightly modified, as the French Foreign Minister thought the new draft electoral law premature and had suspended its application. On July 16th, 1925, the new Representative Council met.

THE STRUGGLE FOR INDEPENDENCE

Meanwhile in Jebel ed Druz, an ancient hotbed of unrest in Syria, a local insurrection had broken out led by Sultan Pasha el Atrashi,[90] which was destined to develop rapidly into a general national rising. The immediate occasion was offered by tactical mistakes on General Sarrail's part ; the rising, however, was not directed against him and his régime, which was far the most liberal that Syria had yet known under France, but against the system that France had introduced from the first. The causes of Syrian discontent, which burst forth in the insurrection, were not rooted solely in political conditions, though these were of prime importance, nor in the destruction of Syrian hopes of unity and freedom, but in the very nature of French administration and in the suppression of all personal and political liberties [91]; and this was what gave the actual final impulse to the outbreak. French officials were not very capable, they were seldom acquainted with the language and customs of the country, and their bearing often wounded the people's sensitive pride. Especially the reorganization of the courts of justice met with opposition ; particularly in Lebanon they were placed altogether under French control, and French judges who were unacquainted with the country's laws and ignorant of Arabic, the language of most of the litigants, were given the dominant voice. In the matter of personal and political liberties France had introduced a régime of the strong hand, which not only necessitated a large army,[92] but proved a double-edged weapon in the long run, as always happens. In this respect French rule in Syria compared unfavourably with British rule in the other mandated territories. In particular the French policy of the strong hand was based upon military or administrative proceedings against political offences and a widespread network of detective agents and spies. The Syrian officials whom the French selected and appointed in the central and district administration and the elected representative bodies, consisting mainly of pro-French notables, had not the smallest influence upon the actual administration, in spite of a moderation that was above suspicion ; in every official act they were subordinated to French advisers and officers of the French secret service. The French pointed out that it was their duty to educate the Syrians to political maturity and independence. The Syrians replied that the right to independence was as much a natural right for Syrians as for Serbians, Albanians, or Persians, and that it could not in Syria's case be withheld until the Syrian people had proved their fitness to the satisfaction of their teachers under peculiarly cramping conditions and by means of small experiments permitted from time to time by those teachers. They accused the French of colonial ambitions in Syria, saying that at best they wished to set up a protectorate like that in Tunis. The proceedings of the Permanent Mandates Commission showed that the number of cases of flagrant abuse of their power by the French officers and bureaucracy was by no means small. Besides these complaints of political and legal oppression, there were others of France's omission to encourage economic progress. The influx of some 100,000 Armenian refugees from Asia Minor had introduced into Lebanon and Syria a population of exceptionally industrious, frugal, and skilful handicraftsmen and workers who proved keen competitors with the native townspeople. The universal depression in agriculture affected Syria, the country's trade suffered severely during the disturbances, and France, whose own currency was not then stabilized, was not in a position to invest large sums in Syria. The people of the mandated territory protested especially against the introduction of the French paper franc, whose value was steadily falling at that time, as the basis of the Syrian currency, and against the grant of all important public works and concessions to French firms. Thus the causes of the great Syrian insurrection of 1925 were to be found in all departments of public life.

The insurrection began in the Druz mountains near the south-eastern frontier of Syria. There lived some 50,000 Druzes [93] under their old feudal system in mountains difficult of access. Amongst these primitive votaries of a secret cult who, like all mountaineers, were proud, well trained in arms, and lovers of freedom, the ancient tribal sentiment persisted in undiminished strength, uniting the feudal lord and his vassals by a firm bond. The separate clans and feudal lords were often divided by feuds and tribal hostility. The treaty of March 4th, 1921, between the Druzes and the French mandatory Government had confirmed the privileges of the Druzes and the inviolability of their customs and had conceded their organization under a native, elected Governor. Shortly afterwards Salim Pasha el Atrashi was elected Governor. After his death the Druze chieftains could not agree upon a successor, and the French Adviser, Captain Carbillet, was elected Governor. He was a man of energy, devoted to the public weal, who took his task seriously and worked indefatigably to raise the economic and cultural level of Jebel ed Druz, to modernize it, and to free the peasants from the often oppressive domination of the feudal lords. But he failed to take the proud and strange character of the Druzes into account; his methods were rough and harsh, and he not only made enemies of the feudal lords, but also estranged the peasants. He was a well-meaning despot, but his great severity and lack of psychological finesse prevented the Druzes from recognizing his good intentions. General Sarrail refused to give ear to complaints against Carbillet and to recall him. He was deaf to the many warnings which reached him even from French officials. He did not receive Druze delegations and finally he invited several Druze leaders only in order to make them prisoners, though they had come to him on trust, and to retain them as hostages.

Sultan Pasha el Atrashi had not accepted the invitation. In the middle of July, 1925, the revolt in Syria broke out under his leadership.[94] It was the beginning of a national rising, in which the whole people were involved. It is, nevertheless, remarkable that the banner of national insurrection was first raised by the Druzes, who only a few years before had been at enmity with all other Syrians and, granted their own independence, had been indifferent to Syria's fate. Their first successes brought them rapid popularity. Within a few days they occupied Salkhad, the second largest town in their territory, annihilated a French column, captured Es Suweida, the capital, and besieged the French troops in the citadel there. A French detachment of 3,000 men advancing to the relief of Es Suweida under General Michaud was wiped out at the beginning of August, and rich booty fell into the hands of the Druzes. On August 24th Sultan el Atrashi made his first attack on Damascus. There he found in the People's party a group of Syrian nationalists ready to take active part in the rising. The People's party had been founded on February 9th, 1925, with General Sarrail's permission as the first party organization in Syria. It included some 350 intellectuals,[95] and Faris Bey el Khury had declared at its inaugural ceremony: "If the party's programme is not carried out, that means that Syria has lost the hopes which blossomed on the graves of her executed martyrs, and that her national aspirations are trampled underfoot by a triumphant imperialism." The programme of the People's party included the recognition of Syria's sovereignty and her absolute right to a democratic régime, the union of Syria within her national boundaries, guarantees for the freedom of person, of the Press, and of assembly, the education of the people in the spirit of democratic, civic, and social unity, a unified educational system with compulsory elementary schooling, and the protection of national industry. The constitution of 1930 was to fulfil all these demands on form, except that of Syrian unity.

If the whole Syrian people had been organized for insurrection at that time, in August, 1925, and if a few of the notables had not hesitated, still hoping that the French would fulfil their wishes, the Syrian rising might easily have led rapidly to the establishment of a national government for the whole country. As it was, there only followed months of serious unrest and general insecurity. In August the French arrested the leaders of the People's party. But Dr. Shahbander succeeded in fleeing to Jebel ed Druz with other nationalists. There a Provisional Government was set up and the Arabian national flag, that had flown above Damascus under King Feisal and was not restored to its rightful place till the new constitution came into force in 1930, was raised in Jebel ed Druz. The Provisional Government called upon the people to fight and win "the complete independence of Syria, one and indivisible, both the coastal region and the interior, the establishment of a national government, and the free election of a Constituent Assembly to draft the constitution, the withdrawal of the foreign army of occupation, and the creation of a national army to guarantee security and apply the principles of the French Revolution and the rights of man."

The Syrian war of independence was destined to continue for many months. The theatre of war was principally Damascus and the fertile and thickly populated Ghuta Oasis that surrounded it, further Jebel ed Druz and southern Lebanon, whither an army had pushed on under Said, Sultan el Atrashi's brother, in order to reach the coast from thence. But there were also hotbeds of long-drawn-out disturbance in and near Aleppo, Homs, and Hama. The insurrection dragged on for two years and, in spite of the very large French forces and their complete technical equipment, they did not succeed in subduing it till June, 1927. Not till that month was the Druze resistance completely broken so that Sultan el Atrashi with a number of his followers was forced to flee first to Trans-Jordan and later to Nejd ; then only were the last engagements fought round Damascus and the disturbances in Homs and Hama flickered out.

Widespread interest was roused in the Syrian insurrection by the bombardment of Damascus ; from October 18th to 20th, 1925, the town was bombarded by artillery and aircraft and much of it reduced to ruins. This bombardment caused very great excitement throughout the Arab world.[97] In the two succeeding years the Syrian insurrection was the centre of interest in the Arab world. From the outset the French tried to crush it as quickly as possible by systematic terror. On the slightest suspicion whole villages were burnt and the inhabitants decimated. The Armenian and Circassian auxiliary troops employed by the French proved a double-edged weapon. Their conduct excited great indignation amongst the Mohammedan population. The French, who always asserted that they were in Syria to keep the peace between the several religions, resorted to the dangerous method of arming the Christian population of southern Lebanon against the Druzes and Mohammedans, and thus profited by the traditional hatred which they did not shrink from stirring up anew. Maronite peasants were to undertake the difficult task of intercepting the first onset of the Druzes in southern Lebanon, instead of French troops. The Syrians and Druzes, on the contrary, always declared that theirs was not a religious struggle but purely national, and they invited the co-operation of the Christians. Said el Atrashi, who commanded the Druze army in Lebanon, dismissed Hamzah ed Dervish, who was the only Druze to lay stress upon the religious motive in the struggle. Said did his best to protect the Christians. just as during the bombardment of Damascus Mohammedan notables had risked their lives to protect the Christian quarters which the French abandoned and exposed.[97] The harsh conduct of the French nowise contributed to end the war quickly. Towards the end of 1925 their position became increasingly difficult. They only managed to maintain their hold in the large towns, and even there the constant depredations by small gangs were surprisingly frequent and bold. The small towns and the open country were in the hands of the rebels. The eighteen months during which the war dragged on—months which witnessed profound embitterment, savage cruelties, and reckless courage on both sides—convinced the French that this was no affair of robber gangs, but a people's struggle for national freedom. At the end of 1925 General Sarrail was recalled and Henri de Jouvenal came in his place, the first civilian politician and parliamentarian whom France sent to Syria. He quitted his post in July, 1926, without having succeeded in restoring peace to the country. Till late in 1927 Syria and Damascus resembled a military camp.

A TURN IN EVENTS : THE NEGOTIATIONS

De Jouvenal came to Beirut intending to negotiate with the nationalists. He did, indeed, make a number of speeches during the months that he passed in the mandated territory, and made liberal promises to the Syrians, but the equivocal wording of his declarations and his contradictory actions only increased the suspicions of the Syrians. In his first months of office De Jouvenal failed to recognize the true strength of nationalism in Syria, and official opinion in France was persuaded that it was only a question of agitators' activities and a mob incited to rebellion. It was only after De Jouvenal had left Syria in the summer of 1926 that he came to see the situation more truly, and the negotiations that he conducted with Syria's representatives in Paris might have led to an immediate peace, if the French Government had not caused their breakdown. But in the winter and spring of 1926 matters had not advanced so far. In his negotiations at that time with the Executive Committee of the Syro-Palestinian Congress in Cairo and with the rebel leaders in Syria the same demands were submitted again and again : the substitution of a treaty of limited duration between Syria and France for the mandate, complete internal autonomy, a freely elected National Assembly to draft a constitution, and the union of all Syria with the exception of the original mountain Lebanon. At that time the negotiations were fruitless, for De Jouvenal was prepared for no unequivocal concessions and the nationalists declared that they did not trust French promises. But the negotiations enabled De Jouvenal to call attention to them and to the hope of early agreement, and so to secure further credits and reinforcements and money, at a critical moment when opposition to the mandatory policy was growing in the parties of the Left in the French Chamber.

In order to prove the sincerity of his desire for constitutional reforms, De Jouvenal promised to introduce a constitution in Lebanon, which had remained quiet. The Syrian insurrection had offered the Lebanese a chance to state their political wishes. Large numbers of them lived abroad on account of the great flow of emigration, and the National Lebanese League in Egypt had addressed a memorandum to the Sixth Assembly of the League of Nations in September, 1925, signed exclusively by Christian Lebanese, who insisted on retaining the separation of Lebanon from Syria. They demanded that a freely elected Lebanese National Assembly should draft a Lebanese constitution in accordance with the country's natural and legitimate rights, and that Lebanon should be admitted to the League of Nations as an independent and sovereign State. These wishes were only fulfilled in a very limited measure in 1926. De Jouvenal submitted a ready-made draft constitution to the Lebanese Council which it discussed from May 19th to 22nd. The new constitution, which laid the foundation for a new State, the Republic of Lebanon, was brought into being in breathless haste. When the draft constitution was discussed, establishing a parliamentary Republic with two Chambers, all the Mohammedan members of the Council made a pronouncement in their own name and that of the Mohammedan population, protesting against the existence of Great Lebanon and against the annexation of Syrian territory in 1920, and demanding that their protest should be recorded in the proceedings in respect for their rights. The discussion brought only slight alterations in the draft constitution. The original draft had provided that Arabic and French should equally be official languages in Lebanon. The final text laid down that the official language in all

State departments should be Arabic, and that a special law should determine the cases where French might be used as an official language. On May 23rd, 1926, the constitution was promulgated, with transitional clauses which left the existing Representative Council to take the place of the Chamber of Deputies for its remaining life-time, that is till 1929. On May 24th the Senate for which the constitution makes provision was nominated by the High Commissioner; on May 26th the two Chambers united in congress elected the first President of the Lebanese Republic, Charles Debbas, a Greek Orthodox; and on May 31st the first Lebanese Ministry responsible to Parliament was chosen. In little more than a week the Lebanese Republic with all its organs— President, Senate, Chamber of Deputies, and Ministry— had come into being. Seats in the Senate as in the Chamber were divided among the religious communities. Of the sixteen Senators nine were elected and seven nominated; the Christians obtained eight seats, the Mohammedans seven, and the religious minorities one.

The Lebanese constitution did, indeed, recognize Lebanon as an independent State. But the word " sovereign " is eschewed, and independence is restricted in the constitution itself by the terms of the mandate, which is to be regarded as an integral part of the constitution. Moreover, by an addendum to the constitution the legislative and executive powers of the French High Commissioner continue in force. Foreign relations and military questions are wholly within the competence of the High Commissioner. He has the right of veto and can annul all the decisions of the Lebanese authorities, if he holds that they conflict with the requirements of the mandate, the country's security, the preservation of order, or international obligations. It is not surprising that there was no enthusiasm for the constitution in Lebanon. The Syrian constitution of 1930, which recognizes not only the independence but the sovereignty of the Syrian Republic, never mentions the mandate, and may actually stand as the constitution of a sovereign State, shows what utterly different treatment revolutionary Syria has won by force of arms as compared with loyal Lebanon.

De Jouvenal tried to introduce constitutional reforms in Syria too. The Syrian President, Subhi Bey, resigned and

De Jouvenal negotiated with Sheikh Taj ed Din, the Cadi of Damascus, who was in sympathy with the nationalists, inviting him to accept the Presidency of Syria. The arrested members of the People's party were released, but De Jouvenal did not concede their demands of a general amnesty, the substitution of a treaty for the mandate, the recognition of Syria's sovereignty and her admission to the League of Nations, and the union of all Syria except mountain Lebanon. After this Syria was governed directly for a time by French bureaucrats and officers until, on April 28th, Ahmed Nami Bey was appointed head of the Syrian State ; although he was of Turkish descent and a son-in-law of Sultan Abdul Hamid, De Jouvenal hoped that he might serve as a mediator with the Syrian nationalists. But what proved the chief obstacle to any peace was De Jouvenal's equivocal attitude on the question of an amnesty, and his failure to concede the unanimous demand of all Syrians for the country's unification, with the possible exception of the original mountain Lebanon. The French nominee, Ahmed Nami Bey, had also worked out a programme in which he asked for the union of all parts of Syria, the election of a National Constituent Assembly, the conclusion of a thirty years' treaty with France on the model of the Anglo-Iraq treaty, and the gradual replacement of the French troops in the mandated territory by a national army. A few nationalist leaders declared their willingness to enter the new Cabinet, but shortly afterwards, seeing no change in the French attitude, they resigned and were arrested. The Syrian leaders' mistrust of the sincerity of the French administration in its desire for peace and of its impartiality was increased by the creation of the Republic of Lebanon against the will of the Syrian people, by the prohibition in Great Lebanon of all discussion and appeal for union with Syria, and by the refusal of a plebiscite, which would undoubtedly have demonstrated the desire for union with Syria among the people of the territories annexed to Lebanon.

But the unanimity of all sections of the population in Syria had convinced De Jouvenal, after a sojourn of six months in the mandated territory, that the solution of the Syrian problem was only to be found on the lines of Great Britain's successful attempt to solve the problem of Iraq. On June 17th,

1926, he stated before the Permanent Mandates Commission that lasting peace could be attained in the mandated territory only by the conclusion of a treaty between France and Syria on the model of the Anglo-Iraq treaty. In the summer of 1926 he conducted negotiations in Paris with the representatives of the Syro-Palestinian Congress, Emir Shakib Arslan, Ikhsan el Jabry, and Emir Michael Lutfallah, for the conclusion of a treaty. These negotiations had nearly reached a favourable conclusion, and peace seemed assured in Syria, when the French Government broke them off. De Jouvenal resigned, and Henri Ponsot was appointed to succeed him ; Ponsot was an administrative official of long standing in the Foreign Office ; he reached Beirut in October, 1926.

ON THE ROAD TO FREEDOM

Ponsot, unlike De Jouvenal, proved a silent politician who waited and watched. In the middle of 1927 the armed insurrection died down. The superior strength of the French army and its technical equipment and the economic distress consequent on the annihilation of so many villages, on the devastation of fields and harvests, and on the obstruction of trade, had caused many people to weary of the struggle. The first programme issued by Ponsot on July 26th, 1927, nowise satisfied the Syrians. Their demands remained unchanged. The Syrian nationalists were not conscious of defeat. The armed struggle was over, after two years of embittered warfare the French military had emerged victorious ; nevertheless, the Syrians believed that the revolution had achieved its aim. True, it had been beaten on the field of battle, but in men's minds it had triumphed. The national ideal, which had been confined only a few years before to the relatively small class of urban intelligentsia, had spread everywhere and won the masses during the months of fighting and had, in particular, penetrated amongst the peasantry. From the towns it had captured the countryside. A new sense of unity, a new consciousness of self, a new feeling of responsibility inspired the masses. The French had learnt to respect the Syrians and Druzes rather in Syria than in Paris, and to understand their national claims. New hope animated the Syrian people, new vistas opened to the lethargic masses.

The second half of 1927 did not, indeed, seem to fulfil these hopes. The Press censorship continued in all its rigour, the French courts martial carried on their activities, personal and civic liberties were annulled. Discontent was no less in Lebanon than in Syria. Even the Maronite Patriarch, France's most faithful adherent, had complained bitterly of French policy and the incompetence and corruption of French officials in a conversation with the deputy High Commissioner in the spring of 1927. He accused the French administration of having encouraged religious cleavages and disappointed even those Lebanese who were most devoted to France. The Lebanese regarded the reform of their constitution of October 17th, 1927, as a menace to their freedom ; it sought to increase the power of the Executive and united the Senate and Chamber of Deputies in a single Chamber, with one-third of its membership appointed by the President of the Republic and its power restricted.

This state of affairs was better known to the French mandatory administration in Syria than to the Government in Paris. In the autumn of 1927 the mandatory administration obtained permission from Paris for decided concessions to the Syrian nationalists. On October 25th, 1927, there was a conference of moderate Syrian nationalists in Beirut and a memorandum was presented to the High Commissioner containing a reply to Ponsot's July declaration. It emphasized the readiness of the Syrian people to forget the past and hold out the hand of brotherhood to the French people. The Syrians regarded the abrogation of all liberties and the maintenance of martial law as the most serious obstacle to an understanding. Mutual understanding could only be attained by the precise definition of rights and duties on either side, and on the basis of a constitution emanating from the people themselves. The memorandum also complained of the neglect of Syria's economic interests.

In February, 1928, Ahmed Nami Bey's Ministry resigned and Taj ed Din undertook to form a Cabinet in his stead, with the support of a few eminent nationalists of the moderate school. Martial law and the Press censorship were abolished, an amnesty was proclaimed which did not, however, extend to the chief nationalist leaders, and on March 10th, 1928, the writ was issued for the election of the National Constituent

Assembly. The elections were to be held under the old law of 1923, which restricted the candidates in each district to men resident in the district, thus preventing the political leaders, who live in the large towns, from offering themselves for election in rural constituencies. In spite of this, and in spite of the fact that the leaders to whom the amnesty did not extend were excluded from taking part in the election, the nationalists resolved to take part, and in April, 1928, they scored a thorough-going victory, although the Government had tried to influence the elections. Since the electoral law provided for the representation of religious communities in Syria, too, the leader of the nationalists, Faris el Khury, who was a Protestant, could not be elected in Damascus, for Damascus is represented by ten Mohammedans and one member each for the Greek Orthodox, Greek Catholics, and Jews. The Mohammedans professed their willingness to be content with nine seats, if a Protestant representative might be allowed. But the High Commissioner refused.

On June 9th the Syrian National Constituent Assembly was opened in Damascus. Hashim el Atassi was elected President; he had been Syrian Prime Minister under King Feisal in March, 1920, and together with Ibrahim Hanano was leader of the nationalists in the Assembly. A committee was chosen to draft the constitution and reported on August 2nd. This draft constitution was that of an independent and sovereign State. There was no reference to the mandate, Syria was made a strictly parliamentary Republic in which all authority emanated from the people. When the High Commissioner was informed of the substance of the constitution, he protested against six articles at the session of August 9th and demanded their modification. These articles dealt with Syrian unity (Article 2: The Syrian territories separated from the Ottoman Empire constitute an indivisible political unit; the acts of partition to which they have been subjected since the end of the War shall be ignored), with the President's right to grant an amnesty, to conclude international treaties, to appoint the Prime Minister and diplomatic representatives, and to declare martial law, and with the organization of the army. The Syrian Premier, Taj ed Din, tried to induce the Assembly to accept the High Commissioner's proposals. But only nine voted for his motion, and the rest refused any modification. Thereupon Ponsot adjourned the Assembly for three months on August 11th, in order to find a solution in the interval. The Assembly resolved that Hashim Bey el Atassi and the Vice-Presidents should continue to represent it. The negotiations between this Presidential Committee and the High Commissioner came to nothing, and on November 5th, 1928, the National Constituent Assembly was adjourned for another three months, and on February 5th, 1929, indefinitely. The High Commissioner proposed to the Syrians to leave the constitution unchanged and only to add a transitional clause to the effect that during the continuance of the mandate no article in the constitution might be applied in such a way as to conflict with France's mandatory obligations. When all negotiations proved vain the National Constituent Assembly was dissolved on May 14th, 1930, and at the same time the Syrian constitution was promulgated as drafted by the Assembly, with the addition of the transitional clause that the French desired.

THE POLITICAL IDEA EMBODIED IN LEBANON

At that time the Lebanese constitution had been in force for four years. Probably it failed really to satisfy any section of the population. The French mandatory administration had most cause to be satisfied. The constitution respected outwardly the independence granted to the Republic of Lebanon in the sense of Article 22 of the League of Nations Covenant. The political energies of the Lebanese found a field in Parliament and the Government and were thus diverted from disputes with the mandatory Power. Lebanese independence was not a mere form but, within definite limits, a fact. Nevertheless, the Parliament proved somewhat barren. It is explicable that it should have failed to solve the two great political problems of the Lebanese State, that of union with Syria and the bridging of religious differences. They were beyond its powers and in part beyond the reach of any influence of the Lebanese State. The Lebanese constitution differs from other Eastern constitutions in that it acknowledges no State religion. The inference, however, is not the separation of State and Church, but the recognition of all the religions in the State as political and juridical factors. The canon law of the several religions is the valid law of the land, on the personal principle, in matters concerning marriage, the family, and inheritance. Even more disastrous for the State is the fact that each religious community is rigidly set upon securing for its members their proportional share of official posts. Article 95 of the constitution actually enjoins this, if only as a temporary measure. It provides that the religious communities are to be represented both in the public service and in the composition of the Ministry, "but without prejudice to the weal of the State." The Lebanese Ministry is not, therefore, a party Ministry, for there are no parties in Lebanon, but a permanent coalition of all the religious bodies in the State. It is plain that such a system cannot lead to the appointment of the ablest men to the public service, but rather to nepotism and the rank growth of the bureaucracy. This small State, backward in its economic development, where a considerable annual emigration presents a serious problem, was obliged to maintain a numerous, badly paid, incompetent and inefficient bureaucracy. To merge religious differences in the consciousness of national unity is not for Lebanon a merely theoretical problem of the ideology now dominant in the East, but a pre-eminently practical task. Progressive circles in Lebanon have striven for a solution and have also worked for a modern codification of the laws to replace the several canon codes of personal and family law. But the problem of merging religious differences in a sense of national unity immediately raises the question of Lebanon's union with Syria as a single Arab State and part of the Arab Federation. The Lebanese Mohammedans have not ceased to press for this, and have had the support of a section of the Christians. At the beginning of 1926 the Unions of Advocates, of Ulemas, and of Merchants in the town and district of Tripoli, the representatives of the Guilds of Sidon, and the Town Council of Baalbek demanded the union of their districts with Syria. In March, 1926, a conference of one hundred notables was held in Beirut under the chairmanship of Negib Bey Sursuk, a Greek Orthodox notable, with the participation of all religions. All except the Maronites declared either for the return of those parts of Great Lebanon that were detached from Syria in 1920 or for the union of Lebanon as a whole with Syria. The prohibition of public discussion in the intervening years has not brought the question any nearer solution.

The Ministry of Emil Eddé, which took office on October 11th, 1929, made serious efforts to reduce the bureaucracy, to economize in public expenditure, and to raise the productivity of Lebanese industry. On May 8th, 1929, the Lebanese constitution had once more been emended so as to increase the powers of the President of the Republic, and Charles Debbas had been elected President for the second time. Eddé, a pupil of the French Jesuit schools and brought up exclusively under the influence of French culture, had already been an active protagonist of the French mandate during the World War. He took office with a declared programme of reorganization of the whole administrative and judicial system. On November 22nd, 1929, the Ministry laid its programme before Parliament in an elaborate statement and asked for authority to carry out the intended reforms in the first half of 1930 by way of decree, without parliamentary sanction, abolishing and combining official positions and revising the Budget accordingly. After some initial hesitation Parliament granted this authority. At the beginning of February, 1930, the Government issued the decree in question. The closing of State schools and hospitals called forth keen opposition from the Mohammedans, who were principally affected, since the educational needs of the Christian communities in Lebanon are provided by private, largely mission, schools. The Ministry stated that the closing of the schools was only a temporary measure, rendered necessary by their poor quality and the lack of suitable teachers. But the real cause of the Mohammedan opposition to the Eddé Ministry lay deeper and was rooted in hostility to the principle of the Lebanese State, as embodied in Eddé.

The Eddé Ministry planned a number of constructive measures, the modernization of Lebanese justice, the execution of great schemes of irrigation, the raising of a loan on the French Bourse to enlarge the harbour of Beirut and lay out a marine air-port at Tripoli. The Prime Minister gave expression to his ideas about the future of Lebanon in a speech on February 9th, the festival of St. Maron, the patron saint of the Maronites. He prayed the saint " to safeguard our ancient independence, so that Lebanon in the near future may behold all her religious communities perfectly united by the thought of their Motherland, and no question of rites and sects may arise in the service of the commonweal, but only of a united nation joining all classes ". In him, therefore, the religious particularism of the Maronite was superseded by a modern sentiment of Lebanese patriotism, though that, it is true, is in its essence a Maronite sentiment. His aim is in accord with the intentions of the French mandatory administration. But it is more than doubtful whether it will ever be realized. Detached from its Maronite basis, Lebanese nationalism is a fiction.

After a vote of no confidence in Parliament in March, 1930, the Eddé Ministry was obliged to resign without having executed its programme. The new Ministry put forward a policy as colourless as those of its predecessors. But in the session of April 5th, 1930, when the new Ministry expounded its policy, Emir Khaled Shehab demanded the supersession of the French mandate by a treaty between France and Lebanon, and Lebanon's admission to the League of Nations. This was the first occasion upon which a demand similar to that put forward in Syria and Iraq was raised in the Lebanese Parliament, which numbered chiefly supporters of the French mandate amongst its members. Alike in Parliament and the Press, the proposal met with general approval. Even the anti-Arab and pro-French daily *L'Orient* in Beirut advocated such a course. The treaty, it said, should be concluded for five, ten, or twenty years. After eleven years France must now be in a position to judge how long the treaty must continue in force in order to give Lebanon the necessary support on its road to independence. " All the misunderstandings created in recent years by uncertainty about the future will be dispelled by the conclusion of the treaty and on the very day of its conclusion. As time passes events prove more and more that a policy of co-operation, which is a fundamental condition of the mandate, can only be inaugurated by such a treaty. Then there could no longer be any question of imperialism and a colonial policy."

FREEDOM OR UNITY ?

On May 22nd, 1930, the constitution of the Republic of Syria was promulgated. At the same time the constitutions for the other French mandated territories were made known.* Thus it was intended to make an end of the uncertainty that had prevailed in Syria for years. Syria to-day is somewhat in the position of Iraq in 1922. But the constitution itself in inspired by a still more progressive spirit than that of Iraq, and the direction of future development is clearly marked out to follow Iraq's example. By that constitution Syria is an independent and sovereign State, a parliamentary Republic whose President must be a Mohammedan. The Arab national flag is the State flag, and every indication of association with France has been removed. " The nation is the source of all power. Legislative power is exercised by the Chamber of Deputies." Judgment in the courts is pronounced and executed in the name of the Syrian people. Syria decided in favour of the one chamber system. Every male citizen over twenty exercises the active franchise. The Chamber meets of its own right in spring and autumn on the days laid down in the constitution. The Deputies enjoy parliamentary immunity. The President of the Republic is elected by the Chamber for five years. His influence on legislation is slight. The Ministry is responsible to the Chamber. All public loans and all concessions and monopolies, which must have a time limit, require the sanction of the Chamber in the form of a law. Economic legislation is to foster the development of local industries.[98] " The aim of education is to raise the people's moral and intellectual standard in a national spirit and to establish concord and brotherly goodwill between all citizens. Primary education is compulsory for all Syrians of both sexes and is free in the public schools. Curricula are to be laid down in a law ensuring a uniform system of education. All schools are subject to government control." [99]

This represents a marked advance on the Lebanese constitution of 1926. Moreover, France never expressed willingness to conclude a treaty with Lebanon. The elections

* See the text of the constitutions in *Oriento Moderno*, X Year, No. 8.

for the Syrian Parliament will shortly be held and the Government emanating from them will then enter into negotiations with France. The Syrian constitution was not, indeed, introduced in quite the liberal manner intended by the French mandatory administration when it convened the National Constituent Assembly in the spring of 1928. The liberal policy then inaugurated by the Secretary-General of the mandatory administration, Gaston Maugras, was a decided step in advance of the mandate. It confided the task of drafting the constitution to the Syrian people themselves, whilst according to the mandate the mandatory Power was to undertake that duty, consulting the Syrian authorities. Contrasted with this, the manner in which the constitution was promulgated was a retrograde step ; but the Right wing French Government could justify itself by the practice of the Mandates Commission itself, which had grown more conservative since 1925, and was satisfied with a restrictive interpretation of the mandates, not basing its pronouncements upon Article 22 of the League of Nations Covenant or the original intention of the mandatory system. Great Britain in Iraq followed a policy in harmony with the liberal interpretation of the mandatory system, and the example of this British policy has already influenced Syrian affairs and will doubtless continue to do so.

If, then, the constitution and the intended treaty satisfy the wishes of the Syrian nationalists in essentials, who further demand the dismissal of the unpopular Taj ed Din Ministry as a guarantee of the freedom of the coming elections, and an amnesty extending to all the nationalist leaders, yet the one important alteration made by France in the constitution adopted by the Syrian National Assembly raises the question of Syrian unity in all its acuteness. Article 2 of the draft constitution had declared that the acts of partition in Syria since its separation from the Ottoman Empire would not be recognized. It was now replaced by the colourless formula that Syria was an indivisible political unit. The constitution of the Lebanese Republic was promulgated anew at the same time as Syria's, and submitted to the League of Nations, and together with these the constitutions of the autonomous Sanjak of Alexandretta, of the autonomous Government of Latakia (formerly the State of the Alawis), and of the autonomous Government of Jebel ed Druz. These latter constitutions were fundamentally different from those of Syria or Lebanon. Both the territory of the Alawis and that of the Druzes were organized as French colonies, with very little participation by the people in legislation. Both are ruled by a Governor appointed by the French High Commissioner and responsible to him. No important legislative acts are promulgated until they have received the High Commissioner's sanction. Legislative power is vested in the Governor, who is assisted by a Representative Council with, for the most part, only advisory functions. Whilst the Council in the Alawi territory has two-thirds elected members, that in the Druze territory has only nominated members. The separation of these territories and their organization on a level suited to the primitive nature of the population retards Syria's general advance towards independence.

Simultaneously with the various constitutions a decree of the High Commissioner was issued introducing a " Conference for Common Interests ". For economically and financially the various States within French mandated territory constitute an indivisible unit. All such matters, which are yet of vital importance to the development and independence of these territories, are wholly within the competence of the French High Commissioner. On such questions he receives advice from the Conference for Common Interests which consists of delegates from the several Governments. In spite of the liberal nature of the Syrian and Lebanese constitutions, France has succeeded, by partitioning the mandated territory, in maintaining her permanent influence there and postponing the date of expiration of the mandate. That is why the question of Syrian unity involves not merely a theoretical nationalist demand, but the practical prerequisite of independence.

In the decade beginning with 1920 Syria, too, has made considerable progress. France has gone further than could have been foreseen half a decade ago, at the beginning of the Syrian insurrection. Even France herself does not regard the juridical position created by the present constitutions as final. She hopes that the task of solving problems yet unsolved can be carried on upon the basis of those constitutions. The solution must be sought along the lines upon which all the countries of the Hither East are evolving, where religious minorities who lived barely twenty years ago totally cut off from the broad stream of the national life have begun in an increasing measure to merge in the majority to whom they are bound by a kindred speech and culture. The traditions of centuries prevent the Maronites from moving rapidly in this direction, and so render the problem of Syrian unity difficult of solution in the immediate future. A far-seeing and rational policy on the part of the French and Syrians, taking account both of the requirements of unity and of the claims of particularity, will enable the Maronites, like the other Syrian Christians, to follow the path of unity with the whole Arab community ; just because of their traditional tendency to turn their eyes westward they are essential to the Arab community and will play such a leading part in its ranks as they have in the Arab literary renaissance since the middle of the last century. An understanding between the Mohammedans and the Maronites in Syria would be of symbolic significance for the growth of lasting Arab unity far beyond the borders of that country.

IX

IRAQ

A MODEL OF MANDATORY POLICY

THE establishment of the Kingdom of Iraq once more created an independent State in the most ancient centre of civilization, in Mesopotamia, after an interval of over two thousand years. It is true that there are no connecting links between the new kingdom and the civilization of the Babylonians and Assyrians ; the Mesopotamians of to-day are conscious of the past only as far back as the time when Baghdad under the Abbasside Caliphs was the centre of Islam. It is the ambition of the present-day inhabitants to make it once more at least the centre of the newly rising Arab nation. Baghdad's destined place in the great network of transcontinental communications between Europe and Asia is favourable to such a development.[100]

The Kingdom of Iraq is one of the States founded after the War under the slogan of the self-determination of the peoples and the liberation of Arab territories from Turkish dominion, and one of those to which the mandatory system was applied. But the fundamental idea of the mandates has been put into practice in Iraq alone, where the mandate was entrusted to Great Britain and where it is soon to expire with the declaration of full independence.

After the British troops had conquered Mesopotamia a military administration was at first installed. In March, 1920, an insurrection broke out in the north-west, which gradually spread to the whole country. This revolution broke out at the moment when Emir Feisal, son of King Hussein of the Hejaz, was proclaimed King of Syria in Damascus. Amongst his chief officials in Damascus were a number of Mesopotamians, who were members of a revolutionary organization and aimed at proclaiming the Emir Abdullah, Feisal's brother, King of Iraq. The disturbances in Mesopotamia coincided with like movements in Egypt,

Palestine, Syria, Turkey, Persia, and India. They were part of a universal movement in the East. Sir Arnold Talbot Wilson pointed to Arab national sentiment as their particular cause.* The revolution was a protest against Great Britain's decision to exercise mandatory authority in Iraq. Sir Arnold Wilson, at that time Civil Commissioner, had said to a deputation which came to him with a protest against the mandate :—

" His Majesty's Government having been entrusted with the mandate for Mesopotamia anticipate that the mandate will constitute Mesopotamia an independent State under the guarantee of the League of Nations and subject to the mandate to Great Britain ; that it will lay on them the responsibility for the maintenance of internal peace and external security, and will require them to formulate an organic law to be framed in consultation with the people of Mesopotamia, and with due regard to the rights, wishes, and interests of all the communities of the country. The mandate will contain provisions to facilitate the development of Mesopotamia as a self-governing State until such time as it can stand by itself, when the mandate will come to an end. The inception of this task His Majesty's Government had decided to entrust to Sir Percy Cox, who will accordingly return to Baghdad in the autumn and will resume his position on the termination of the existing military administration as chief British Representative in Mesopotamia. Sir Percy Cox will be authorized to call into being, as provisional bodies, a Council of State under an Arab President, and a General Elective Assembly representative of and freely elected by the population of Mesopotamia, and it will be his duty to prepare, in consultation with the General Elective Assembly, the permanent organic law." †

This statement already indicated Great Britain's future policy in Iraq. But it failed to lay the unrest. It was not till considerable reinforcements came from India and news arrived of the collapse of the Syrian kingdom that the

---

* *Encyclopædia Britannica*, 12th edition, 1922, vol. xxxi, p. 919. Wilson had been British Resident on the Persian Gulf for years and during the War he was British Civil Commissioner in Mesopotamia.

† Cmd. 1061. *Review of the Civil Administration of Mesopotamia*, 1920, p. 142.

insurrection began to wane. When Sir Percy Cox arrived in
Baghdad in October, 1920, the process of pacification was
far advanced. In his proclamation of October 17th, Sir Percy
Cox stressed the fact that he had come in order to carry out
England's settled policy of helping the leaders of the
Mesopotamian people to form a national government. The
new State's history in the succeeding decade proved Great
Britain's sincerity in making this promise. Iraq's entry into
the League of Nations in 1932 will not be the result of a chance
chain of events, nor the product of the policy of the last British
High Commissioner in Mesopotamia, but the course mapped
out by British policy from the beginning.* As early as
October 12th, 1922, Winston Churchill, then Secretary of
State for the Colonies, announced that when Iraq's frontiers
were finally settled and a stable government had been set
up she was to be admitted to the League of Nations ; thereby
a mandated territory becomes for the first time an
independent State in fulfilment of the intention of the
mandatory system, an event of import to the League of
Nations and international law far beyond the scope of its
own territory and foreign relations.

THE GROWTH OF THE STATE

As a first step in carrying out the programme announced
by the British Government, Sir Percy Cox decided to
establish a provisional national Government with the Naqib
of Baghdad at its head. The Naqib or hereditary marshal
is the head of the family of highest standing amongst the
city nobility. The Naqib at that time, Abd er Rahman,
was an aged man, greatly revered alike in religious and
secular circles. Most distinguished amongst the Ministers
for his Western culture, his vigour, and his experience, was
the Minister of the Interior, Syid Talib Pasha, the son of the
Naqib of Basra, and a former Deputy in the Turkish
Parliament. Not without justice, he laid claim among the
Iraqis to the leading position in the State. The Minister of
War was the former Turkish General Jafar Pasha el Askari,

---

* See the important article by the former British High Commissioner in Iraq, Sir Henry Dobbs, " Relations between Great Britain
and Iraq," in *The Empire Review* (London, September, 1929).

who had been Minister of Defence under King Feisal in Damascus. This Ministry, which was entitled a Council of State and came into office on November 11th, 1920, had the duty of preparing for the convocation of the promised National Assembly and drafting the constitution. The foundations of a native administration were laid. An Arab official was placed at the head of each district, with a British adviser at his side ; the Ministers also each had a British adviser. By the end of March the Town Council elections had been held throughout the country and preparations made for the creation of a native army.

The Conference held in Cairo at the end of March, 1921, which discussed the re-partition of Arab territories, and in which Churchill, the Colonial Secretary, took part, altered the course of British policy in Mesopotamia. Its practical aim was to reduce English military and administrative expenditure by making more of the independence and the self-government of the Arab territories, so that a British air force alone would be enough to maintain security and order. King Hussein's elder son, Emir Abdullah, was destined for Emir of Trans-Jordan, and his younger son, Feisal, for King of Iraq. Feisal had been the friend of T. E. Lawrence during the War as Commander-in-Chief of the Arab troops, and since he had been expelled from Damascus by the French in the summer of 1920 he had lived under British protection. Before all this could be accomplished it was necessary to get rid of Syid Talib Pasha. In April, 1921, he was arrested and exiled. At the end of June Emir Feisal arrived in Mesopotamia. His political tact and his universally known championship of Arab nationalism favoured British plans. On July 11th the Council of State resolved that Feisal should be King of Iraq on condition that his government should be constitutional, parliamentary, and democratic. By the wish of the High Commissioner a plebiscite of notables was held, in which they were to vote for or against the Council of State's decision. As was to be anticipated, 96 per cent of the notables consulted voted in favour of the proposal. On August 23rd, 1921, Emir Feisal was proclaimed King of Iraq. The Provisional Government resigned, the Council of State was dissolved, and on September 10th, 1921, the first Ministry was formed with the Naqib as Premier.

Therewith the foundation was laid for the structure of the new State. But the relation between Great Britain and Iraq was not yet clear. According to the Peace Treaty, Iraq was a mandated territory, but the League of Nations had not yet issued a mandate, so that no basis existed upon which mutual rights and duties could be defined. For Iraq, as for the other mandated territories, mandates were drawn up and promulgated.* But the opposition to any mandatory relation was so strong in Iraq that the British plenipotentiary told the League of Nations Council on November 17th, 1921, that in the opinion of the British Government, British obligations to Iraq could best be fulfilled by a treaty of alliance embodying the most important terms of the mandate, thus fulfilling its purpose and at the same time representing an important advance along the road to complete independence. Those opposed to the mandate were the whole urban intelligentsia, including the civil service, the Shi'ah clergy, and a section of the tribes. This opposition was also directed against the treaty intended to replace the mandate. The negotiations between the Mesopotamian Ministry and Great Britain dragged on for months, for the Ministry insisted that the treaty could not be ratified until a National Constituent Assembly had accepted it. They therefore demanded an immediate writ for elections and the drafting of a constitution to be submitted to the National Assembly at the same time. King Feisal emphasized the necessity of providing in the treaty for the possibility that, at the request of both contracting parties, the League of Nations should declare the mandate at an end. Sir Percy Cox, the British High Commissioner, urged these requests with the British Government. But before the treaty could be signed the country was destined to pass through another serious crisis which gave Sir Percy Cox an opportunity of interposing with a strong hand, of asserting Great Britain's authority, but afterwards of making an immediate and far-reaching concession to the ambitions of Iraqi politicians, and so bringing about the happy solution of a difficult problem ; when, therefore, in May, 1923, after nine years' activity in Iraq, he left the country and handed over the office of High

* For the text of the mandate see Cmd. 1500, 1921.

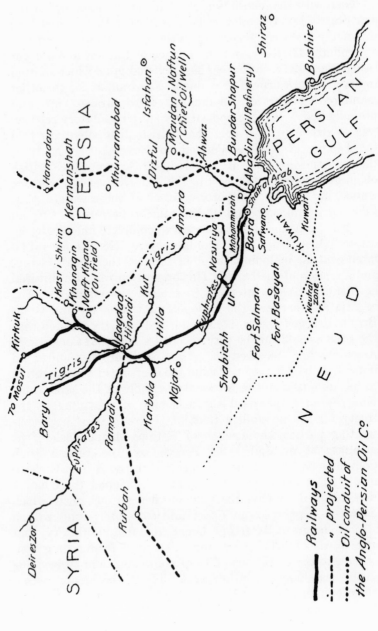

SOUTHERN IRAQ.

Railways
" projected
Oil conduit of
the Anglo-Persian Oil Cº

Commissioner to Sir Henry Dobbs, he was assured that Iraq was on the road to peaceful progress.

The political crisis reached its climax on the anniversary of King Feisal's accession, on August 23rd, 1922. Previous to this political parties had been formed and leading Shi'ah scholars had issued a fetwa, a decree backed by religious authority, excommunicating from the company of the faithful those who failed to defend the country's independence from alien influence.[101] The first success scored by those who were agitating for a wider measure of national independence was the resignation of the Ministry. The king's sympathies were with the nationalists, which contributed to bring about the Ministry's fall. On the anniversary of King Feisal's accession, when the British High Commissioner came to offer his congratulations, he was greeted at the palace gates by a hostile demonstration and cries of protest against the mandate ; and the king's gentlemen-in-waiting had had a hand in organizing the demonstration. That night the king was seized with an attack of appendicitis. The country was without a government, the king lay sick, the Ministry had resigned. On August 26th, Sir Percy Cox took over the government ; in a proclamation he declared that it was the earnest wish of the British Government to go as far as possible to meet the wishes of the Iraqi Government and people, but that the serious situation in Mesopotamia called for prompt measures, if peace and order were to be maintained, and that until the treaty was concluded the Iraqi Government and the High Commissioner would be jointly responsible for such measures. The nationalist newspapers were suspended, the parties dissolved, and a few leaders exiled. Leading Shi'ah clergy left Iraq and went to Persia. The disturbances in the provinces were suppressed, partly with the help of the British Air Force. In September the king recovered and a new Government was formed under the Naqib's premiership, with Abdel Muhsin Beg es Sadun, who had represented Basra in the Turkish Parliament, as Minister of the Interior.

On October 10th, 1922, the treaty between Great Britain and Iraq was signed, after Great Britain had given assurances that she would propose Iraq's admission to the League of Nations at the earliest possible moment, thereby terminating the mandate at the same time. This stipulation, contained in Article 6 of the treaty, was further confirmed by a statement of the British Colonial Secretary on October 12th to the effect that negotiations should begin on the application for admission to the League of Nations as soon as the new State's frontiers were defined and a stable, constitutional government was set up. By the treaty * Great Britain engages to give Iraq advice and help at her request and without prejudice to her sovereignty. Iraq undertakes to employ only British advisers or such as Great Britain approves. Article 3 of the treaty runs :—

" His Majesty the King of Iraq agrees to frame an Organic Law for presentation to the Constituent Assembly of Iraq and to give effect to the said law, which shall contain nothing contrary to the provisions of the present Treaty, and shall take account of the rights, wishes, and interests of all populations inhabiting Iraq."

By Article 18 the treaty must be ratified by the Iraq Constituent Assembly and is to remain in force for twenty years. Provision is made for its revision as occasion arises from time to time. In its outward form the treaty, which was drawn up in both languages, is a treaty between two independent States. It anticipated the conclusion of supplementary agreements, but these were not concluded until March 25th, 1924, in Baghdad. They dealt with the employment of British officials in the public service of the Kingdom of Iraq, with military questions and the co-operation of the two armies, with the execution of justice in cases involving foreigners, and lastly there was a financial agreement.

But although this was a further step towards the erection of the Kingdom of Iraq as a State, the agitation was by no means at an end. On October 21st writs were issued by royal decree for the election of the National Constituent Assembly. All male citizens of twenty-one and over enjoyed the active franchise. Election was indirect in two stages. To be eligible a man must have reached the age of thirty and, except for representatives of the tribes, must be able to read and write. Hardly had the work of registration begun when the Shi'ah leaders issued fetwas forbidding participation in the election. Naqib Abd er Rahman resigned and Abdel Muhsin Beg

* For the text see Cmd. 1757, 1922. Also *The Times*, London, October 12th, 1922, and *Oriento Moderno*, Anno II, pp. 299–401.

undertook to form a new Ministry. Jafar Pasha el Askari
went to London as plenipotentiary for Iraq. The Ministry
had been strengthened by the acquisition in his stead of
Yassin Pasha el Hashimi, an officer of tried merit in the
Turkish army, who had later been chief of staff under Feisal
and who constituted the nationalist element in the Cabinet.

Meanwhile, opposition to the treaty had not abated.
Especially the duration of twenty years was criticized. As
it is expressed in the British *Report on the Administration of
Iraq for the period April,* 1923–*December,* 1924, Great Britain
was accused of designing " to rule behind an Arab façade. . . .
The cry of the extremists was that the real masters of the
country were still the British officials, and that the Arab
Government was a sham." * The disturbances in the country
made it difficult to collect the taxes and led to a considerable
deficit. The northern frontier was unsettled. People suspected
Great Britain of wishing to erect a Kurdish buffer State
which, dominating the plains of Mesopotamia from the
mountains, would provide her with a permanent strategic
base from which she might control Iraq.[102]   The National
Constituent Assembly, which was to have met at the beginning
of 1923, could not be summoned on account of the boycott
of the elections. Sir Percy Cox, who had been to London,
returned in April, and on April 30th, 1923, a supplementary
protocol to the treaty was signed shortening its duration to
four years. In spite of the favourable impression created by
this protocol, it was only by the banishment of the leading
Shi'ah clergy, who opposed the elections and publicly
proclaimed their pro-Turkish sympathies, that the resistance
was subdued. A number of other Shi'ah leaders quitted the
country and went to Persia as a protest. Towards the end of
1923 it was possible to begin holding the elections and they
were completed in the following spring.

Meanwhile, Abdel Muhsin's Ministry had been succeeded
by one under Jafar Pasha. On March 27th, 1924, the
Constituent Assembly was opened by the king. There was
great opposition to the acceptance of the treaty. The debate
dragged on for weeks, and the opposition was most vehement
both in the Chamber and outside. It was only under pressure
from the British Government that the treaty was forced

* Colonial No. 13, 1925.

through by 37 votes to 24 at a night session on June
10th, when only 69 of the 100 Deputies were present.
Acceptance was on the express stipulation that negotiations
should begin immediately after ratification on a number of
points, especially those embodied in the financial agreement,
and that the British Government should respect fully Iraq's
right to Mosul. During the summer months the National
Constituent Assembly also adopted the constitution and
electoral law, and then dissolved.

The constitution, which came into force on March 21st,
1925,[103] declares Iraq to be a sovereign, independent, free
State, a constitutional hereditary monarchy with a parliamentary form of government. Islam is the State religion,
Arabic the official language. Parliament consists of a Senate
of twenty nominated by the king, and an elected Chamber of
Deputies with eighty-eight members, one Deputy for every
20,000 male inhabitants. The electoral law of October 22nd,
1924, resembles the earlier law in essentials. Parliament
meets annually in regular session on November 1st.

Therewith the foundation was laid for Iraq's existence
as a State. According to the protocol the Anglo-Iraq treaty
was to remain in force for four years after the conclusion of
the Turkish peace treaty on August 6th, 1924, so that it
continued until August 6th, 1928.

The first Mesopotamian Parliament assembled on
July 16th, 1925. It was soon faced with the new situation
that arose out of the League of Nations' discussions about
Mosul, and the decision of the League Council in December,
1925, by which the province of Mosul was to be allotted to
Iraq on condition that Great Britain concluded a fresh treaty
with that country prolonging the mandate for twenty-five
years, unless Iraq were admitted sooner to membership of
the League. Accordingly the treaty of January 13th, 1926,
prolonged the duration to twenty-five years, but Article 3
bound Great Britain to examine the question of Iraq's
admission to the League of Nations every four years, and to
consider it for the first time in August, 1928. The British
High Commissioner in Mesopotamia said that Great Britain
hoped the time would soon come when she could recommend
Iraq's admission. Iraq was uneasy at this prolongation of
the treaty, especially after the treaty between Turkey,

Great Britain, and Iraq signed at Angora on June 5th, 1926, had defined the frontiers of the new kingdom ; for this event, together with the adoption of the constitution and the introduction of parliamentary government, seemed to fulfil the conditions referred to by the British Colonial Secretary in 1922 as prerequisites for Iraq's admission to the League of Nations. Iraqi statesmen were certainly aware that the youthful State needed the help of European advisers in administration, finance, and technical science and, moreover, that for military purposes Iraq could not stand alone. But they wished for advice and assistance voluntarily accepted, as in Persia or Siam, and wished that military support should take the form of an alliance against external attack which the country was unable to repulse alone.

A further step on the road to independence was the formation of a Ministry of Foreign Affairs, and later the establishment of Iraqi agencies in London, Turkey, Egypt, and Persia. In Parliament two parties were formed, the Progressive party under Abdel Muhsin and Jafar Pasha, which was usually in office, and the National party under Yassin Pasha el Hashimi. Parliament was largely occupied with the question of introducing universal military service. Some politicians held that Iraq could attain full independence only if, by introducing universal military service, she so enlarged her army without increased costs as to be able to undertake the defence of her frontiers without external help. A part of the population was hostile to the proposed measure, which was supported primarily by the intelligentsia of the large cities. The British High Commissioner declared on behalf of his Government that his attitude was neutral, but that British troops could not help to force the introduction of compulsory military service against the will of large sections of the population.

During the past five years Parliament has functioned without a hitch, and a number of important laws have been passed. Great Britain's report to the League of Nations for 1927 states : " The work of Parliament is conducted entirely by Iraqis, and no British or other foreign officials are in any way engaged in the direction of the business of either of the two Houses. The efficiency with which parliamentary business is conducted is, therefore, evidence of the ability of the educated classes of the country to understand and adapt themselves to the spirit and practice of democratic government." *

In the spring of 1927 negotiations began between the Mesopotamian Government and the British High Commissioner for the modification of the treaty of 1922 and Iraq's admission to the League of Nations in 1928. It is of no small interest to hear that Sir Henry Dobbs, as has now been revealed, already advocated Iraq's admission to the League at that time. He himself has written on the subject, and his words deserve to be quoted because they indicate that change in the nature of British rule in the East which began to find expression even before the measures adopted by the British Labour Government in 1929 :—

" I . . . was myself inclined to think that there would be little danger either to Iraq or to British interests if a revised treaty could be entered into under which all formal control by Great Britain would be eliminated. From the first I had found the Iraq Government genuinely friendly and grateful for advice when not offered in authoritative guise, and I felt no doubt that, if they found themselves free of all treaty obligations to accept advice, they would be all the more ready to act upon it and that the loosening of apparent bonds would be the tightening of real ones. In short, I believed that the early entry of Iraq into the League of Nations and the making of a new treaty of alliance, with relaxation of formal British control, would be found the most effective and rapid method of attaining that end which the British Government had officially set for themselves in Iraq : ' The establishment of an independent Government of Iraq, friendly to and bound by gratitude and obligation to His Britannic Majesty's Government.' " †

At that time the British Government were unable to adopt his opinion. They declared their intention of discussing with Iraq the question of her admission to the League of Nations in 1932, on condition that in the meantime her peaceful development had continued and that the present rate of progress was maintained. This conditional assurance by no

* *Report to the Council of the League of Nations on the Administration of Iraq for the Year 1927*, Colonial No. 35, London, 1928, p. 14.
† *The Empire Review*, London, September, 1929, p. 181.

means satisfied the expectations of Iraqi politicians. But apart from the question of membership of the League, Great Britain declared her willingness to revise the treaty of 1922. Sir Henry Dobbs, King Feisal, and Jafar Pasha el Askari came to London in order that the new treaty might be drafted. The negotiations lasted for two months, and the treaty † was signed in London on December 14th, 1927. Article 8 of this treaty gave the above-mentioned conditional promise of admission to the League of Nations. In outward form it was a marked advance on the previous treaty. The preamble expressly emphasizes the fact that this new treaty is concluded " on terms of equality ", and Article 1 states that " His Britannic Majesty recognizes Iraq as an independent sovereign State ". But in substance the new treaty, which did not modify the existing supplementary agreement, marked no real advance on Iraq's road to independence. The Mesopotamian representatives did manage to secure that the new treaty should not be ratified until fresh supplementary agreements had been concluded on financial and military questions.

These supplementary agreements never materialized, and the treaty of December, 1927, was not ratified. Before Jafar Pasha's return it was made public by an indiscretion and universally repudiated in Iraq. The two nationalist Ministers in the Cabinet, Yassin Pasha el Hashimi and Rashid Ali Beg el Gilani, resigned, and this led to the resignation of the whole Ministry. Abdel Muhsin Beg es Sadun undertook to form a new Ministry composed entirely of members of the Progressive party. On January 19th, 1928. Parliament was dissolved and writs issued for the election of the second Mesopotamian Parliament. In spite of the fact that all the newspapers in the capital were against the new Government, the Progressive party won sixty-six of the eighty-eight seats. The official British report to the League of Nations for 1928 says of the Mesopotamian parliamentary system :—

" The elections may not produce a strictly representative Chamber, and until public opinion becomes more active and

---

* For the text of the treaty see Cmd. 2998, 1927. It is also to be found in *The Near East and India*, London, December 22nd, 1927, and in *Oriento Moderno*, Anno VIII, p. 3.

coherent it is scarcely to be expected that they should ; but they produce a body of men capable of criticizing the proposals of the Executive and of effectively resisting unwise legislation which might otherwise be put through by a small Executive not too closely in touch with rural feeling. The Chamber has its undoubted use, both as a brake and as a safety valve." *

On May 19th, 1928, the second Mesopotamian Parliament was opened. Its eighty-eight Deputies comprised twenty-six Shi'ahs, sixteen Kurds, sixteen Bedouin sheikhs, four Christians, and four Jews. The negotiations between the British and Mesopotamian Government on the supplementary agreements led nowhere. At this juncture Sir Henry Dobbs was succeeded as British High Commissioner by Sir Gilbert Clayton who had not, like his predecessor, been trained in the political and administrative services on the Persian Gulf, but in the Egyptian-Arabic service, and had represented British interests after the World War in Palestine and in successful negotiations with King Ibn Saud. Like his predecessor, perhaps even more than him, Sir Gilbert was regarded as a friend of the Arabs, who sympathized with their national ambitions and tried to bring them into harmony with the interests of the British Empire. On May 15th Sir Gilbert Clayton made a speech in Baghdad in which he said that he trusted, before the end of his period of office as High Commissioner, to see Iraq take the seat that was her due in the League of Nations Assembly. Normally Sir Gilbert's period of office as High Commissioner would not have ended till 1932. His statement was generally interpreted as meaning that he counted confidently on Iraq's admission to the League in 1932. But in the summer of 1929 an early death cut short his career. Before his death he had recommended that Great Britain should advocate Iraq's definite and unconditional admission to the League in 1932.

In one important matter Great Britain had already given ear to Mesopotamia's demands, in that of legal proceedings involving foreigners as litigants. Great Britain's willingness to annul the 1924 Judicial Agreement between herself and Iraq was largely due to her wish to improve Iraq's relations

* Colonial No. 44, London, 1929, p. 10.

with Persia and Turkey ; for these two States, and especially Persia, protested against a régime under which their nationals did not enjoy the same privileges as the nationals of European and American States. On February 16th, 1929, Great Britain presented a Note to the League of Nations concerning the privileges accorded in Iraq's judicial system to the nationals of the former capitulatory Powers, saying :—

" The system prescribed by the Judicial Agreements has . . . led to one serious anomaly. Under the present arrangements, the nationals of certain foreign States receive treatment more favourable than that accorded to the nationals of other foreign States. . . . This anomalous state of affairs has given rise to considerable resentment, which is not confined to the foreign States which are excluded from the special judicial privileges, but is felt generally by Iraqis, who resent the more favourable judicial treatment accorded to certain foreigners and the reflection upon their own judicial administration which that treatment implies. The feeling against the existing arrangement has become more marked in recent years as a result of the general tendency on the part of other Oriental nations to discard all forms of capitulatory and extra-territorial privilege. For example, within a comparatively short period, the special judicial privileges hitherto enjoyed by foreigners have been abolished in Turkey and Persia and replaced by an equal system of justice for all."

The Note then proceeds to state that the existing system has proved a hindrance to normal diplomatic relations between Persia and Iraq. These difficulties, it said, could not be overcome by granting the privileges to all foreigners.

" Not only would such a course be extremely distasteful to Iraqis themselves as perpetuating and extending an institution which they regard as anachronous and derogatory, it would involve such an increase of the British Judiciary as would seriously tax the financial resources of the country and hamper its economic development." *

Great Britain, therefore, proposed the introduction of a uniform judicial system for everybody in Iraq. In the League Council it was especially the Persian delegate who supported the British proposal. This British proposal is of interest not

* *League of Nations Official Journal*, April, 1929, C. 55, 1929, vi, p. 777.

only because it is expressly contrary to one of the stipulations of the draft treaty of December, 1927, by which the Judicial Agreement was to remain in force, but because it was a step in the direction of placing Great Britain's relations with Eastern States on a new basis and acknowledging the changes which the past decade has brought about in the political and social evolution of the East.

This step on Great Britain's part was soon to be overshadowed by one of even greater importance. When Sir Gilbert Clayton drew up the report for 1928 he had devoted a special section to pointing out the abnormal situation in which the mandate places Mesopotamia.

" The idea is growing that the Treaty of Alliance concluded with Great Britain in 1922 set up a state of affairs which, if continued, will not only impede the realization of the country's political aspirations, but will also prove inimical to the economic and social development of the country." *

Sir Gilbert, therefore, recommended that the British Government should substitute an unconditional promise to admit Iraq to the League of Nations in 1932 for the conditional promise previously given. In September, 1929, the British Government addressed itself to the League accordingly. Abdel Muhsin now undertook to form a Cabinet which, however, was not destined to survive long. Great Britain promised to inform the League Council at its next meeting that she would not implement the treaty of 1927 and that, in accordance with Article 3 of the Anglo-Iraq treaty of 1926, she would advocate Iraq's admission to the League in 1932.[104]

On June 30th, 1930, a treaty of alliance was concluded between the British High Commissioner, Sir Francis H. Humphrys, and the Prime Minister of Iraq, Nuri Pasha es Said, on the model of the Anglo-Egyptian draft treaty, annulling all previous agreements between the countries, and recognizing Iraq's full independence, alike in foreign and home affairs. In order to safeguard the route to India Great Britain obtains two bases for aircraft in Iraq, near Basra and west of the Euphrates, for the period of the treaty,

* Report to the Council of the League of Nations on the Administration of Iraq for the Year 1928, Colonial No. 44, 1929, p. 27.

which is fixed at twenty-five years. For the next five years, until an adequate Iraqi army has been created, Great Britain may also maintain troops at Hinaidi, Baghdad's air-port, and in Mosul. Financial questions were likewise settled between the two States on August 9th, 1930. The treaty was approved by the Iraq Parliament in November of 1930. Thereby the foundations of the independent State of Iraq were laid after a decade.

Meanwhile, Iraq's three great foreign and domestic problems, namely, relations with the Kurds, the only national minority in the land, with Turkey, its former overlord, and with Nejd, its rival for the hegemony of Arabia, were moving towards a satisfactory settlement.

THE KURDISH QUESTION

The dispute that broke out between Great Britain and Turkey after the end of the World War for the possession of the vilayet of Mosul brought the Kurdish question to the fore, since the Kurds are the predominant race there. After the end of the War a local Kurdish Government was set up in the north-east of the vilayet in Sulaimaniya ; at its head was Sheikh Mahmud Barzanji, chief of the most influential family in the land ; his father, Said Barzanji, had been killed in Mosul in 1908, which had strengthened Kurdish sympathies with the family. At first Sheikh Mahmud recognized a British protectorate, but on May 20th, 1919, he proclaimed his independence and opened hostilities with the English. On June 18th he was captured and deported to India. Direct British administration was set up, but Kurdish officials were appointed and the Kurdish character of the population was respected. After King Feisal's accession the district of Sulaimaniya was not placed under Iraqi rule, but remained in the hands of British authorities, who endeavoured to set up a Kurdish administration. On September 12th, 1922, Sheikh Mahmud was recalled to Iraq. In November, 1921, the British administration had installed a District Council of twelve in Sulaimaniya, eight elected members and the remaining four consisting of three Kurdish officials and the British Political Officer. Turkish influences had created unrest throughout the Kurdish districts. The British

Government attempted to establish an orderly administration there by the restoration of Sheikh Mahmud at the end of September, 1922. But Sheikh Mahmud was not content with the measure of authority conceded to him. In October he proclaimed himself Hukumdar, and a month later King of Kurdistan, and tried to create an independent administration and a Ministry. Meanwhile, the general political situation, as it affected the Kurds, had changed. It was clear that the Peace Treaty of Sèvres, which provided for a Kurdish State, was not going to be ratified. The peace negotiations had begun at Lausanne. There could, therefore, be no question of uniting the Kurds of Iraq and Turkey, especially as the Turks had no intention of granting the Kurds in their country autonomy or freedom to develop their national culture. The British-Iraqi administration tried to win the Kurds in the Mosul district by granting them opportunities of national development and so to counteract Sheikh Mahmud's schemes. At the end of December, 1922, the British and Iraqi Governments issued a joint proclamation saying :—

" His Britannic Majesty's Government and the Government of the Kingdom of Iraq recognize the rights of the Kurds living within the boundaries of the Iraq to set up a Kurdish Government within these boundaries, and hope that the different Kurdish elements will, as soon as possible, arrive at an agreement between themselves as to the form which they wish that Government should take, and the boundaries within which they wish it to extend." *

The British report to the League of Nations on Iraq administration says of King Feisal's attitude on this question : " Himself too far-seeing a nationalist not to recognize and respect the sentiment in others, he was ready to extend to the Kurdish provinces within the Kingdom of Iraq a full measure of local autonomy." † Sheikh Mahmud did not respond to these offers, and prepared an attack with the support of the Kemalist Turks. British troops drove him from Sulaimaniya in March, 1923, and forced him to withdraw to the mountains. When the British troops evacuated the town again Sheikh Mahmud once more occupied it for

* *Report on Iraq Administration*, April, 1922–March, 1923, Colonial No. 4, 1924.
  † *Ibid.*, p. 38.

a year. Thenceforward the district of Sulaimaniya was administered as part of Iraq. Sheikh Mahmud waged guerilla warfare from the Persian frontier for a long time, until he surrendered in the summer of 1927.

The League of Nations Commission of Inquiry which visited the district in 1925 with a view to the settlement of the Mosul question, reported on the Sulaimaniya province :—

" In this province we found a Kurdish national feeling which, though yet young, was reasonable enough ; for, though the people stated that their supreme desire was for complete independence, they recognized the advantages of an enlightened and intelligent trusteeship." *

The Kemalist endeavours to assimilate non-Turkish nationalities provoked a national Kurdish rising in Turkey in the spring of 1925, led by Sheikh Said. It ended with the execution of Sheikh Said, Dr. Fuad, and forty-six other national leaders. The Turks declared that the insurrection was an orthodox religious movement of protest against the Angora Government's attempted modernization and secularization. Although such motives played a part, yet the insurrection was mainly nationalist.[105] Iraq, on the contrary, did not pursue a policy of denationalizing the Kurds. From the outset the Deputies in the Iraq Parliament for Erbil, Kirkuk, and Sulaimaniya were exclusively Kurds. The administration in the Kurdish districts was in accordance with the wish expressed by the League of Nations Council when it decided, in December, 1925, that the vilayet of Mosul should be included in the Kingdom of Iraq. On January 21st, 1926, the Iraqi Prime Minister stated in Parliament :—

" This country cannot survive, unless all the elements that make up the Iraqi State enjoy their rights. We shall concede their rights to the Kurds. Their officials shall be chosen from among themselves, their official language shall be their own language, and their children shall be taught in the schools in their mother tongue."

The majority of officials in the Kurdish districts are Kurds, and the official language for local business is Kurdish. Kurdish national sentiment is very strong in the districts of

* Report submitted to the Council by the Commission Instituted by the Council Resolution of September 30th, 1924. League of Nations Document, C. 400, M. 147, 1925, vii, p. 76.

Erbil, Kirkuk, and Sulaimaniya. " There is a real enthusiasm for the use and development of the Kurdish language. . . . There is a hunger, too, for Kurdish education and a genuine love of Kurdish poetry and literature." * National sentiment is less keen on the northern frontier of the Mosul vilayet. It is significant that in the elections to the Iraqi Parliament in 1928 the Kurdish Deputies for the Sulaimaniya district in the previous Parliament were the only ones who carried on modern electoral propaganda, making declarations of policy and proclamations on the Western model. There were sixteen Kurds among the eighty-eight Deputies in the new Parliament.[106]

The solution of the Kurdish question in Iraq is the sole example in Eastern States of an attempt to solve the minorities problem, in contrast to the efforts of Turkey or Persia to denationalize their minorities. The Kurds of Iraq still have visions of a national union of the Kurdish populations across the frontiers of the three neighbouring countries which to-day have partitioned Kurdistan. For the present, however, it is only in Iraq that there is any opportunity for Kurdish national sentiment and literature to develop. But a memorandum drawn up in April, 1929, by six Kurdish Deputies in the Mesopotamian Parliament proves that even in Iraq a section of the Kurds wish for something more ; its asks for an autonomous Kurdish vilayet. Similar wishes were expressed in various petitions to the League of Nations in 1930 from the Kurds of Sulaimaniya.†

The Shi'ah question is not a national question in Iraq. With the exception of a few Persian leaders, the Shi'ahs in Iraq are Arabs. In the years following the World War they stood side by side with the Sunnis for Iraq's national claims, and were often in the foremost ranks of the opponents of the mandate. As compared with the Sunnis, the Shi'ahs represent the less Europeanized element, more strongly bound by religious tradition. But they, too, bow to the universal sociological law that rules the East to-day and implies the transition from mediaeval to modern forms of organization :

* *Report on the Administration of Iraq for 1927*, Colonial No. 35, 1928, p. 26.
† See *Oriento Moderno*, ix, 1929, p. 218 ; also p. 182. And *The Near East and India*, August 7th, 1930.

religious groupings lose power when confronted with the
consciousness of a common nationality and speech. Moreover, common participation in the elections and common
labours in the legislative bodies are building up a sense of
Iraqi nationality. In recent years it has been noticeable that
the Ulemas, who had hitherto dominated Shi'ah circles,
have been losing influence, with the result that the Shi'ahs
are striving more and more to gain a foothold in public life,
to extend their influence and to assert their interests through
the rich and influential members of their community. This
has brought them into conflict with the dominant, indeed
almost exclusive, influence of the Sunnis in public life. From
the moment when the first Iraqi Parliament met in 1925,
individual Shi'ah leaders have tried to form a party which,
without excluding Sunnis from its membership, would
principally serve to promote Shi'ah interests. It was not till
1927 that the plan succeeded, when the Shi'ah agitation
reached its climax. The occasion of the agitation is
characteristic. In 1927 a teacher of Syrian birth in a Baghdad
secondary school published a book on the history of the
Ommiades, in which he defended the founder of the Ommiade
dynasty against Caliph Ali, whom the Shi'ahs revere. The
Shi'ahs demanded the author's dismissal. There were
demonstrations by the scholars against his dismissal, the
dispute swelled to a general party conflict between the leaders
of the two sects, and this finally led to the foundation of the
desired Shi'ah party. A demand was put forward for a
decentralized administration in the Shi'ah Euphrates
province. The tension reached its climax in July, which
coincided with the month of Muharram in the Mohammedan
calendar, a month of religious excitement and mourning
among the Shi'ahs for their Caliph Hussein's martyrdom.
These days always revive the memory of the decisive battles
and hostilities between Sunnis and Shi'ahs. It was not till
the end of the year, when the great political questions of the
treaty with Great Britain came to the fore, that the tension
was relaxed, and in his report for 1928 Sir Gilbert Clayton
was able to point to the fact that the Shi'ah party was
dissolved and the excitement had died down. " For this
notable decrease of sectarian feeling and for the strengthening
of the common national consciousness which is beginning to

displace it, credit is due to the constant efforts of a number of men of influence among both communities." * [107]

RELATIONS WITH TURKEY

Iraq's relations with Turkey in the first half of the past decade were dominated by the dispute about the possession of the vilayet of Mosul, that is the definition of the frontier between Iraq and Turkey. The question was raised at the very beginning of the first Peace Conference of Lausanne in 1923. It was finally settled only in the tripartite Treaty of Angora of June 5th, 1926, between Great Britain, Iraq, and Turkey.[108]

This long-drawn-out contest between the two Powers, which twice led to hostile incursions of Turkish troops into the disputed territory under Iraqi rule, was not due to rivalry for the possession of the oilfields, but to strategic considerations and motives of domestic policy. On the north Mosul is surrounded by high, impassable mountains which offer a natural strategic base. If Turkey held these mountains and the plains adjoining them on the south, which are the most fertile district and the granary of Iraq, thanks to the constant rainfall, she would always have dominated Iraq strategically from that vantage ground. Besides, it is economically important, for the rivers upon which the Baghdad and Basra districts depend for irrigation have their origin in Mosul. The strategic importance of the Mosul mountains to Great Britain is due to their domination of Turkey and Persia, the Caucasus and Russia. They represent the second line of defence in the cordon by which Great Britain has striven to secure herself against Russia, and acquired vital significance when the first line, that was to be erected in the Caucasus in 1919, was rendered untenable by events in Russia, Turkey, and Persia. To the south this strategic position covers the great route to India, the importance of which is increased by the development of land and air in addition to sea communications. It is the natural crown of a policy pursued by Britain for over a hundred years and aiming at the assured control of the Persian Gulf and the

* *Report to the Council of the League of Nations on the Administration of Iraq for the Year 1928*, Colonial No. 44, 1929, p. 25.

mouth of Shatt al Arab and its harbour at Basra. From the outset the Mesopotamian campaign in the World War was designed to secure Great Britain's position on the Persian Gulf against all attacks from the north, a security which can only be made effective by holding the strategic mountain positions north of Mosul.

The vilayet of Mosul is of ethnographical as well as strategic significance. Whereas it was the policy of the Turkish Republic to get rid of the Christian minorities in the land, since they seemed impossible of assimilation and always prone to seek foreign support, Turkey hoped to be able to assimilate the Mohammedan Kurds, the more so because their national sentiment was barely awakened, their civilization of a very low type, and their literature still non-existent. Her hopes of accomplishing this purpose would be all the greater if all sections of the Kurdish people were, as far as possible, united within her frontiers, and if there were no other sections outside Turkey with opportunities for national development who might later on provoke the rise of a Kurdish irredentist movement in Turkey.

Such were the considerations of strategy and domestic policy which inspired the obstinate struggle for the possession of the Mosul vilayet for three and a half years. In the Treaty of Lausanne of July 24th, 1923, Article 3 leaves the frontier between Turkey and Iraq to be drawn by friendly agreement between Great Britain and Turkey. If this were not accomplished within nine months, the dispute was to be laid before the League of Nations Council. Lord Curzon, the British plenipotentiary at the Conference of Lausanne, gave an assurance that it must be a unanimous decision of the League Council and that Turkey would be represented with full and equal rights. The Turko-British Conference on the Mosul question ended without achieving its purpose on June 5th, 1924, in consequence of Great Britain's new and additional demands. England then brought the matter before the League Council on August 6th, 1924, and a Commission was appointed to report on conditions in the Mosul vilayet. Until then the *status quo* was to be maintained. A dispute as to how the *status quo* frontier was to be understood, which seemed for a time to threaten war, led to an extraordinary meeting of the League Council in Brussels at the end of October, 1924, and a provisional frontier line was drawn, the so-called Brussels line; the subsequent final frontier followed this line with only slight modifications. The League of Nations Commission came to the conclusion that the territory south of the Brussels line should be assigned to Iraq, if the League mandate for Iraq were prolonged for twenty-five years and Kurdish wishes for national autonomy were respected. The Commission's report was presented to the League on July 16th, 1925, and debated by the Council in September, 1925. As the Turkish and British Delegations adopted different views on the binding force of the League's decision, the Council determined to ask the Permanent Court of International Justice for its opinion whether the decision of the League Council was an arbitral award or a mere recommendation, whether it must be unanimous, and whether the representatives of both parties should vote. On November 21st, 1925, the Permanent Court ruled that the decision of the League Council should be binding and final, that it must be unanimous, that the representatives of the two parties should vote, but that their votes should not be counted for the purpose of establishing unanimity. At the Council's session in December, 1925, the Turkish delegate declared, in accordance with the view he had already expressed and with Lord Curzon's statement in 1923, that he would recognize the League decision as binding only if it were unanimous, including the two disputants. On December 16th, 1925, in the absence of the Turkish Delegation, the League Council decided to draw the frontier between Iraq and Turkey along the Brussels line, and the British Government was called upon to submit a new treaty with Iraq to the League Council within six months. This treaty was to assure the continuance of the mandate, defined in the treaty of alliance, for twenty-five years, unless Iraq were admitted to membership of the League of Nations before that period had elapsed. The British Government was also asked to report on the measures adopted to ensure local autonomy for the Kurdish population.

But this juridical decision did not dispose of the conflict. Turkey adhered to her protest. She retorted to the League's decision by concluding the Russo-Turkish treaty of December 17th, 1925. But the danger of an Italian attack upon Turkey, of which much was heard just then, induced her to conclude the treaty of June 5th, 1926, at Angora between Turkey, Great Britain, and Iraq, in which the Brussels line is established in a general way as the frontier. The treaty enjoined that for twenty-five years the Government of Iraq should pay to the Turkish Government 10 per cent of all dues to be received from the Turkish Petroleum Company or other companies for the exploitation of the Mosul oilfields. At the same time Turkey was given the option, to be exercised within a year, of capitalizing these dues at a sum of £500,000. In order to strengthen good and neighbourly relations, the Treaty of Angora established a permanent Turco-Iraqi Frontier Commission, which met in October, 1926. Thus for the first time direct neighbourly relations were restored between the two States.

CONFLICTS WITH NEJD

On the south and west the Arabian desert borders Iraq. The past decade has witnessed the rise in that region of a new power, uniting the various principalities, the Wahabi Kingdom of Abdul Asis Ibn Saud. There were two reasons why this Wahabi kingdom's relations with Iraq were disturbed by conflicts : it is exceedingly difficult to draw a definite frontier in the desert regions, where the tribes have been accustomed for generations to move from one well to another and to shift their pastures. No less powerful a factor was the enmity between King Ibn Saud and the house of the Sherif of Mecca, to which King Feisal of Iraq belongs. King Ibn Saud regarded King Hussein of the Hejaz, the former Sherif of Mecca, as a rival for the hegemony of Arabia, but also as the representative of an idolatrous corruption of pure Islam. He felt himself encircled and his expansion blocked by the erection of the two principalities of Iraq and Trans-Jordan under King Hussein's sons.

The problem of the relations between Iraq and Nejd became more actual and pressing when in 1921 Ibn Saud annexed Jebel Shammar to his kingdom by the conquest of Hail, and so acquired a common frontier with British mandated territory in the Syrian desert. It thus became necessary to define the frontier between Ibn Saud and the territories under British protection, the more so as Ibn Saud evinced a tendency to regard all nomad tribes on the borders of his kingdom as coming under his jurisdiction. The frontier problem did not concern Iraq alone, but also the Sultanate of Kuwait adjoining it to the south-west, which had played an important part in the dispute about the terminus of the Baghdad railway before the World War.[109]

During the struggle for Jebel Shammar a number of the Shammar tribes had fled from Ibn Saud to Iraq, and had found refuge there, some with the tribe of the Amarat Anizah west of the Euphrates, some beyond the Euphrates. Ibn Saud regarded the Shammar tribes as rebel subjects and demanded that the Amarat Anizah should acknowledge his overlordship.

After the fall of Hail, Ibn Saud and the British High Commissioner for Iraq agreed to define the frontier. Great Britain, however, made it a condition that the Amarat Anizah, the Dhafir, and the Muntafik should remain under Iraq's dominion. The Ikhwan (Brotherhoods) developed a lively propaganda amongst these tribes and in March, 1922, there were serious hostile encounters between the Wahabis, led by Feisal ed Dawish, and Iraqi tribes and camel detachments, so that the British Air Force was obliged to intervene. In view of the serious situation arising from these encounters, Ibn Saud declared that Feisal ed Dawish had acted without his sanction. On May 1st, 1922, the delegates of King Feisal of Iraq, Sultan Abdul Asis Ibn Saud of Nejd, and the British High Commissioner for Iraq met at Mohammerah and on May 5th they concluded a treaty which attributed the Muntafik, Dhafir, and Amarat tribes to Iraq and bound both Governments to prevent their tribes from attacking the other contracting party. The Shammar tribes were recognized as belonging to Nejd, and a commission was appointed to trace the frontier between the traditional wells and pastures of these tribes. On December 2nd, 1922, the treaty was supplemented by two frontier protocols of El Uqair.* These protocols defined a zone that was to remain neutral and common to both Governments with equal rights, both engaging not to

---

* The treaty and the two protocols are given in English in the *Report on Iraq Administration, April, 1922–March, 1923*, Colonial No. 4, 1924, Appendix II, pp. 183–6.

use the wells near the frontiers for military purposes, to erect no fortifications there, and to concentrate no troops.

But relations between Iraq and Nejd long continued unsatisfactory. Ibn Saud demanded the extradition of the Shammar tribes that had withdrawn to Iraq territory. The situation was rendered more serious because these tribes frequently attacked the Wahabis from their safe refuge in Iraq. These attacks of the Shammar tribes on Nejd caravans reached their climax in June, 1923. In addition to these not unreasonable complaints of Ibn Saud against the Government of Iraq, there was a second and deeper cause of conflict. The desert knows no territorial frontiers, but only the personal relation of the vassal tribes to their leader. That relation remains even when the tribes move their tents from one well to another in search of new pastures or on their customary annual migrations, a thing which happens as a matter of course among nomads. The Wahabi administration, which had not yet adapted itself to the needs of modern territorial organization, could not reconcile itself to fixed frontiers, which restricted its sovereignty over Wahabi tribes when they migrated. The difficulty of guarding the frontier line over a wide area made it harder for the Iraqi Government to control the fugitive Shammar tribes and to prevent them from attacking Nejd subjects. The endeavours of the British Government to summon a conference in Kuwait under the chairmanship of the British Resident on the Persian Gulf, S. G. Knox, in order to discuss and clear up relations between Nejd and the three Sherifian States of the Hejaz, Iraq, and Trans-Jordan, proved fruitless, partly because of the excessive claims of King Hussein of the Hejaz, partly because King Ibn Saud refused to attend in person. At last the conference did meet in Kuwait on December 17th, 1923, without the participation of the Hejaz. It was adjourned on January 26th, 1924, and its resumption was rendered impossible by a serious attack of the Ikhwan under Feisal ed Dawish on Iraqi tribes in March, 1924, in which 186 persons were killed and over 26,000 sheep, with other livestock, were seized. In the course of 1924 there were further encounters, although Ibn Saud himself was occupied with his war against the Hejaz from the autumn onwards. When the Wahabis' attention was concentrated on their western frontier, a noticeable relaxation of tension resulted on the east. On November 1st, 1925, Sir Gilbert Clayton succeeded in concluding a treaty with Ibn Saud at Bahrah, defining the frontiers of Nejd and Mesopotamia.* This treaty was supplementary to those of Mohammerah and El Uqair, and was designed to prevent frontier attacks in future. A Court was to be established to inquire into frontier disputes and fix responsibility and judge claims for damages. It was to be composed of an equal number of representatives of the two Governments under a President chosen by agreement. This treaty was observed by Nejd in 1926, whilst the Iraqi Government was unable to prevent the Shammar tribes from making predatory incursions into Nejd from time to time. Relations became strained again in the autumn of 1927, when King Ibn Saud protested against the erection of two fortified police posts at Busaiya and Abu Ghar. By Article 3 of the El Uqair Protocol, the two Governments were not to use the wells near the frontier for military purposes nor to erect fortifications there, and Ibn Saud's Government declared that the erection of these two forts had given rise to serious disquiet amongst the Nejd tribes, who also had news of an intended railway to Busaiya. The Iraqi Government, on the other hand, stated that these were only observation posts in order to enable Iraq to prevent depredations of the Shammar tribes in Nejd, and that the two places, which were 75 and 90 miles respectively from the frontier, hardly came under the terms of the Protocol of El Uqair, which referred to wells near the frontier.

This dispute over the interpretation of the El Uqair Protocol dragged on from the autumn of 1927 and was not settled till February, 1930. It led to serious conflicts which first endangered the peaceful relations of Nejd and Iraq, and later the domestic peace of Nejd. When in February, 1928, Nejd tribes again attacked tribes in Iraq and Kuwait, they were pursued by British air forces which bombarded the headquarters of the attacking tribes about 130 miles south of the neutral zone. King Ibn Saud protested against these operations from the air over Nejd territory, which made it impossible for him to hold his tribes in check. At the end

---

* *Arabia. Agreement with the Sultan of Nejd regarding certain questions relating to the Nejd–Trans-Jordan and Nejd–Iraq frontiers.* (Cmd. 2566, London, December, 1925.)

of February, 1928, rumours were abroad of a Holy War
of all the Nejd tribes against Iraq, Trans-Jordan, and
Kuwait, but they proved to be exaggerated, and it turned
out that King Ibn Saud had succeeded in stopping the advance
of a number of tribes against Iraq's frontiers. In order to
relax the tension Great Britain again sent Sir Gilbert Clayton
to King Ibn Saud. The negotiations did not lead to an
understanding, for the two parties could not agree about the
interpretation of Article 3 of the Protocol of El Uqair.
Sir Gilbert Clayton's appointment as High Commissioner for
Iraq in 1929 brought the possibility of arbitration nearer.
But in 1929 the three tribes who were mainly responsible
for the attacks on Iraq repudiated Ibn Saud's overlordship,
and Ibn Saud was occupied all that year with fighting the
rebels. Not till he had subdued Feisal ed Dawish in January,
1930, was it possible for him to meet King Feisal on
February 23rd on board a British warship in the Persian
Gulf; a treaty of friendship was then concluded between
Iraq and Nejd, and thus hostile relations of many years'
standing came to an end.

IRAQ AND THE LEAGUE OF NATIONS

So it was that ten years' labours laid the foundations
for Iraq's political existence at home and abroad. Iraq
considers her present position as a State to be a transition
stage on the way to her entry into an Arab Federation ; she
knows that she forms part of the rising Arab nation, which
aspires to unity. Only by union can the separate parts of
Arabia so gain strength, politically, economically, and
culturally, as to assert themselves and advance towards a
future of security and growing prosperity. But even her
present position as a State means much to Iraq and,
moreover, to the Arab people and the League of Nations.
The Mohammedan world, with its 250 million souls and over,
which has hitherto been represented in the League only by
Shi'ah Persia, will be more adequately represented when
Iraq enters the League in 1932, and so the League will be
more equal to its mission of representing all peoples. At the
same time as Mesopotamia, Egypt also will join the League.
It is likely that other Mohammedan and Arab States will

follow their example. At the present time the League is regarded in the East as an instrument of colonial policy in the hands of European and American Powers. Its gradual transformation to an all-embracing League of European, American, and Oriental peoples in the near future will strengthen its position in the East. And thus the idea which inspires it, that it should be the outward symbol of mankind's growing sense of unity, will be more nearly realized. Moreover, with Iraq's entry into the League the first of the mandates expires. In this, too, Iraq's example will point the way and contribute to a clearer understanding of the mandatory idea.

Besides this world-wide significance, the development of the youthful kingdom from the point of view of international law has a special significance as expressing the change that is coming over British Oriental policy. In 1929 the British Labour Government took a step no less bold than that taken by the Liberal Campbell-Bannerman Ministry in 1906, when it gave full self-government to the two Boer Republics that had been annexed only a few years earlier after a ruthless war. Conservative circles in England feared the secession of the Republics. Yet it proved that the liberal action and the trustful grant of freedom led not to a slackening but a strengthening of the British imperial idea. The Liberal Government had adopted such a policy only for those parts of the Empire that were inhabited by white races. The Labour Government, by its policy in Egypt, Iraq, and India, has extended it likewise to parts inhabited by other races and that opens a new chapter in the history of the relation of the colonial Powers to Eastern peoples.

X

THE ARABIAN PENINSULA

THE STAR OF IBN SAUD

THE IDEA AND ITS PROTAGONISTS

THE scene of Arabia's history in the first decade after the World War is laid in two different areas, divided from one another and yet with something more than merely geographical contact : the mandated territories detached from the former Ottoman Empire, where European organization and technical science exercised an increasing influence, and Central Arabia, still definitely dominated by Islam and Bedouin customs, where Ibn Saud erected a powerful kingdom that has shown a growing readiness for modernization. The past decade has been as eventful for the Arabian peninsula as for several other parts of Eastern Europe and the Orient. The struggle between Great Britain and Turkey for influence in Arabia, conducted from the Red Sea and the Persian Gulf, was decided by the issue of the World War. Great Britain was in a position to draw Arabia into her sphere of influence at the very time when the primeval trade routes through Arabia recovered their importance thanks to the motor-car and the aeroplane.

But although Arabia thus reappeared on the stage of world politics, the vast desert tracts did not invite conquest. The object of securing communications must be achieved by diplomatic not strategic means. With this in view British policy advanced in various directions from its three bases. From Aden Great Britain tried to penetrate the Yemen and, by establishing herself on the coast, to dominate the hinterland. She had set up a protectorate of nine small Sultanates round Aden, over which the Yemen claimed suzerainty. On the north-western frontier of the Yemen she sought to strengthen the principality of Asir against it ; here the ruler was Mohammed Ibn Ali el Idrissi, a Mohammedan scholar of great renown, a Moroccan by birth, whose great-grandfather had founded the dynasty in Sabya.

239

In 1915 Great Britain recognized Asir's independence, and in January, 1921, she ceded to the Idrissi the port of Hodeida, which the English had occupied after the World War and which gave San'a, the capital of the Iman Yehya of Yemen, access to the sea. The English had already given their ally, the Idrissi, the Yemen's other port Luhayyah. This meant not only that the Yemen was surrounded by powerful enemies on the north and south, but also that it was deprived of its access to the sea and thereby of its chief source of revenue and the opportunity of economic and fiscal progress. The attempt to cut off the coastal plain from the mountains and hinterland of the Yemen was based upon the same kind of policy as the attempt to cut off the Mediterranean coast from Gaza to Alexandretta from its hinterland. After the death of Mohammed Ibn Ali in 1923 family quarrels among the Idrissi brought about the break-up of Asir, so that the Yemen was able to recapture Hodeida and the coast, and from 1925 onwards the Yemen managed to assert itself more and more against Britain and to preserve its independence, although, indeed, the dispute about the Protectorate of Aden was still unsettled in 1930.

The territories on the Persian Gulf had been coming more and more under British influence by means of treaties with the several Arab principalities along the coast, and their administration was subject to the Indian Government and the India Office. Using these territories as a base, Great Britain tried to reach an understanding with the Emir of Nejd, Abdul Asis Ibn Abdur Rahman Ibn Feisal es Saud, of the Wahabi dynasty of Ibn Saud, and to make him a tool of British policy. Ibn Saud, who had restored his ancestors' kingdom as a young man soon after the turn of the century, had won his independence of the dynasty of Ibn Reshid on the field of battle during the first decade of the century ; the latter dynasty had established a kingdom north of Nejd in Jebel Shammar, with Hail as capital, about the middle of last century, and had included Nejd in their dominions. In 1913 Ibn Saud conquered the Turkish Province of El Hassa on the Persian Gulf, and thus came in contact not only with the sea, which gave him his first opportunity of collecting a regular revenue by means of tariffs, but also with English policy. On December 26th,

1915, the English managed to conclude a treaty with Ibn Saud, recognizing him as an independent sovereign within his own territory and at the same time establishing a British Protectorate, so that Ibn Saud and his successors were pledged not to pursue a policy prejudicial to Great Britain's interests and not to enter into relations with any other Power. In the latter years of the War, Philby was British Plenipotentiary at the court of Ibn Saud, who maintained a benevolent neutrality during the War and received in return the considerable subvention of £5,000 sterling a month. His wise policy of reserve placed him, as it proved, in a stronger position in his relation to Great Britain than his rival Hussein Ibn Ali, Sherif of Mecca. Whilst the India Office had endeavoured to penetrate the Arabian peninsula in British imperial interests from the Persian Gulf, the Foreign Office tried to attain the same goal from the Red Sea. Its policy was directed from the Arabian Bureau in Cairo, with Sir Henry MacMahon, the British High Commissioner for Egypt, at its head, and Thomas E. Lawrence, Gilbert Clayton, Ronald Storrs, and Gertrude Bell attached to it. Hussein, trusting to British promises, had allowed himself to be persuaded to revolt against his Turkish overlord and to embark on a struggle side by side with Great Britain for his own and all Arabia's independence, without first assuring the precise fate of the Arab territories after the World War and the Allies' victory by means of binding treaties. His troops formed the right wing of the British Army on its advance north-east from the Suez Canal, and with Aqaba as their base they conquered Trans-Jordan and Syria as far as Damascus. But when Hussein afterwards required the fulfilment of the British promises the response fell short of his expectations, and the dream of Arab freedom and unity, for the sake of which he had revolted against the Caliph, was, it seemed, destined to be realized in such a distorted form as to mock the hopes of 1916. When Hussein's demands became too inconvenient, Great Britain withdrew her protecting hand from her former ally, and he promptly fell a prey to Ibn Saud, who knew better how to bide his time patiently and save his strength, and who had not roused the hostility of a large part of the Islamic world by open rebellion against the Sultan Caliph.

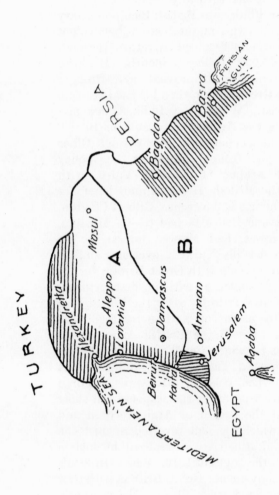

TURKEY

MEDITERRANEAN SEA

Alexandretta

Mosul °

Aleppo °
° Latakia

PERSIA

° Bagdad

A

Damascus °

Beirut °
Haifa °

Amman °

Jerusalem °

B

Basra °

PERSIAN
GULF

Aqaba °

EGYPT

||||||| French Territory (Mediterranean Coast from Acre to Mersina)

A   "   "   Sphere of influence in the Arabian Kingdom

///////// British Territory (Haifa and Southern Mesopotamia)

B   "   "   Sphere of influence in the Arabian Kingdom

======= International Territory (Palestine)

But although British policy had partly determined the fate of Arabia in the past fifteen years, yet Arabia was still first and foremost the home of Islam. The sacred books of Islam bore the Arabic tongue to all the educated classes from Morocco and Nigeria to China and Sumatra. The yearly pilgrimage gathered tens of thousands in Arabia from west and east. A Mohammedan turns his face towards the Holy Places in life and after death. He cannot be indifferent to Arabia's fate. Much as the various reforming movements of the present day in Islam have imbued it with a nationalist spirit, yet historical tradition and an international religious sentiment still live and make the world of Islam a reality still, with its centre at Mecca. In the States of the Arabian peninsula, Islam is the basis of the whole of public life ; the Nejd of Ibn Saud, the Yemen of Imam Yehya, the land of Idrissi, and the Hejaz of King Hussein were at bottom theocracies in which canon law governed political life and the honour in which rulers were held depended partly on their religious knowledge and wisdom. Precisely the two Arab kingdoms which have proved stable and have to-day won the undisputed hegemony of the Arabian peninsula, Ibn Saud's Wahabi State and the Imamate of the Yemen, have drawn their strength from the religious zeal of their people and the leadership of rulers who preserved the purity of the faith and inspired their followers with its fire. The Imam is the head of a Shi'ah sect, the Zaidites, who form the backbone of his State, but are only in a minority compared with the Sunni population. It is true that the Sunni world regards Ibn Saud's Wahabis as heretics, but they are strictly orthodox Sunnis of the Hanbali cult, whose rites are the most uncommon and the strictest among the four Sunni sects. Essentially the Wahabis represent a sternly Puritan reform movement which, like Protestantism, reverted to the original Islam of the Bedouins in Mohammed's day, opposing the later abuses of saint-worship and the refinements and luxuries which they regarded as heathenish ; and this they did not in order to proceed to further construction, after sweeping away the abuses and checking the process of petrifaction, like such Mohammedan reformers as Mohammed Abdu's disciples in Egypt or Mehmed Said Halim Pasha's in Turkey ; but they regard every word dating from that time as absolutely binding, and no others. The influence of the Arab rulers in the peninsula depended upon their piety and their religious standing. The Imam of Yemen is regarded by the members of his sect almost as a holy man, one who leads a life of rigorous purity. King Hussein's position was due less to his own great learning and his venerable age than to his descent from the Prophet and his character as hereditary guardian of the Holy Places. Whilst the Imam Yehya served Islam as the framer of his country's domestic policy and King Hussein as the framer of its foreign schemes, Ibn Saud was wise enough to make Islam a living and life-giving factor in the structure of his kingdom and to make use of the forces inherent in it in order to extend his dominion and win the sympathies of the Mohammedan world. With the help of religion he succeeded in overcoming the fundamental difficulties which the Bedouin character presented in his work of building up a State. The reason why the Bedouins were eternally poor, why they carried on endless feuds for the possession of wells and pastures, why they lacked the love of home and country, and why they were such an incalculable factor in matters of religion, was to be found in their nomad life. Ibn Saud's far-seeing wisdom saw the chain of cause and effect and he realized that in order to erect a lasting political structure and at the same time to organize a standing army, he must settle the Bedouins. Racially and religiously the Bedouins formed a unit. What was needed was to make them conscious of their unity, to organize it as a stabilizing influence in the State capable of bridging over traditional tribal hostilities. Mohammed had managed to do so by imbuing the tribes with an intense inner religious life which endowed them with new vigour and gave their thoughts and aspirations a fresh direction. Ibn Saud trod the same path. He regarded his first mission as one of domestic policy, to overcome ignorance and tame the rude manners of the Bedouins by inspiring religious fervour, by spreading the doctrine, by imbuing them with the fear of God and with a new outlook, and by the fraternizing power of an all-uniting faith. A prerequisite of this mission within his own frontiers was the settlement of the Bedouins so that they came to feel attachment to the soil. And so the politico-religious Brotherhood of the Ikhwan arose and became the protagonist of the Wahabi kingdom.

These missionary labours at home were completed in an amazingly short time. Upon them were built up the missionary labours abroad which now began and which established Ibn Saud's hegemony of all Arabia in half a decade and made him, like his ancestor Abdul Asis II Ibn Saud 120 years earlier, master of the Holy Places. The first Wahabi dominion of the Holy Places had been of but brief duration. In those days Islam would not tolerate the heretics and iconoclasts who had destroyed all the centres of worship and of the cult of the saints which to them was idolatry. The first Wahabi kingdom collapsed, supported only by the religious zeal of Puritan reformers. Thanks to Ibn Saud, the second was to be based on surer foundations. Religious reform reached beyond itself in politico-social measures and in the consciousness of a mission not only Islamic but national and Pan-Arab.[110] At the end of the first decade after the World War Ibn Saud had begun to overstep the narrow limits of his own origin in the soil of Central Arabian religious enthusiasm, and had started on the road towards modern State organization on a national basis. His ideal of uniting the Bedouins of his own country had expanded, even during the World War, to the ideal of uniting Islam, and after his conquest of the Hejaz and the failure of the Pan-Arabian Congress in 1926, it gave place to the ideal of uniting Arabia.

King Hussein of the Hejaz had been the first to put forward publicly the ideal of Arabian unity, of the creation of a State embracing all Arabians. The idea had first taken shape some quarter of a century earlier in the heads of a few Syrians, who looked to Mecca even then as Arabia's centre of unity and longed for the return of the Caliphate to the city of its origin. At the beginning of the World War there were negotiations between Syria and the Hejaz about a joint struggle against the Turks side by side with the Allies in order to liberate Arab territories. Modern nationalist ideas united with romantic visions and dynastic interests. Only a few years earlier the political union of the Arabs on a modern basis would hardly have seemed even an unlikely dream. Arabia was only a geographical term. It was Hussein's merit that he was the first to illustrate to the Arabs, if only for a few years, the possibility of realizing that dream. Hussein's rising in 1916 and his proclamation that he aimed at Arab unity and freedom, a bond embracing all Arabs and ignoring the social distinction of Bedouins, fellaheen, and town-dwellers, and the religious difference of Mohammedans and Christians, acted as a powerful stimulus in rousing the Arabs' will to be a nation. With all Hussein's weaknesses, in spite of his lack of political realism, and his tendency to exaggerate his own merits and the importance of his dynasty, we must yet allow that his action exercised a great influence on future developments. His was the first Arab State which, though itself yet involved in the semi-darkness of mediaeval autocracy, was nevertheless recognized as a member of the community of nations and was invited to join the League of Nations as an original member. But Hussein's personality was not equal to his historical mission, and the solid political groundwork for its accomplishment was lacking. He had believed too blindly in Great Britain's promises. The vision painted by his desires had carried him away. He awoke too late. Just the most valuable parts of the Arabia to whose unity he aspired, the Mediterranean coastal strip, had been differently disposed of meanwhile by the Allies to serve their own interests. Hussein refused to sign the Peace Treaty of Versailles and the League of Nations Covenant, which would have meant sanctioning the destruction of Arab unity. He remained faithful to his ideal, but he lacked strength to realize it once he had embarked upon the insurrection against the Turks, relying on the promises of the Powers. He refused to accept the greatly curtailed goal which Great Britain offered him later. And in so doing he not only missed Arabian unity and freedom, but lost his own realm. The Hejaz, the first Arab State to enjoy international recognition, became a province of Nejd and King Hussein was driven into exile. Great Britain was glad to get rid of an inconvenient ally after he had done what was required of him in the World War, and was not without guilt in his fall. But the idea to which King Hussein first gave shape politically did not fall with him. Ibn Saud entered into his heritage. He is a really great statesman, and he knows that a conglomeration of favourable circumstances, such as Hussein believed to have found in 1916, may go far to set up an idea as the goal of policy and so to render it constructive and effective, but that for its realization it must await the time when the actual

foundations are laid in the external world, although the idea
will act as a driving force. Ibn Saud, by a slow process of
modernization, may create a kingdom which will, perhaps,
serve as a focus for an Islamic religion imbued with new
ideas, but it will certainly be one focal point in the ellipse
of the Arab movement of national union, whose other focal
point lies in the Hither Asian mandated territories.

THE STRUGGLE FOR LEADERSHIP

The history of the first five years after the World War
in Arabia is occupied with the struggle of Ibn Saud and
Hussein for the hegemony of the Arabian peninsula. Great
Britain had partially fulfilled the promises made to Hussein
in 1916 by placing his sons, Feisal and Abdullah, on the newly
erected thrones of the British mandated territories,
Iraq and Trans-Jordan, so that Ibn Saud felt himself encircled
on three sides by his rivals. In addition to dynastic rivalries,
there were religious differences and memories of the Wahabis'
conquest of the Hejaz 120 years earlier, their rule there and
their expulsion. To the Wahabis Mecca, with its worship
of the saints and its licentiousness, was as much an object
of horror and detestation as the papal Rome of the
Renaissance to the early Protestants. It would be an action
pleasing to God to purify the place. To Hussein, on the other
hand, the Wahabis were heretics who scorned and destroyed
customs sanctified by centuries of usage and the general
opinion of Islam. Ibn Saud prepared for his ttacak on
the neighbouring States by religious propaganda amongst the
Bedouin frontier tribes, which he won for the cause of the
Ikhwan. He scored his first great success at the oasis of
Khurma on the caravan route from Mecca to Riyadh, the
capital of Nejd, three days' journey from Taif, the summer
residence of the Sherif and notables of Mecca. In 1917 the
majority of the inhabitants and the Governor of the oasis,
the Sherif Khalid Ibn Luwai, went over to Ibn Saud. When,
in 1919, Hussein tried to recover the oasis a battle was fought
at Turabah, about seventy kilometres south-west of Khurma,
ending in a decisive victory for Ibn Saud. Both places now
remained in his possession, and the road to Mecca seemed to
lie open before him. But Ibn Saud did not hold that the right

moment had yet come, and he first turned his attention to Jebel Shammar. In 1920 he had already occupied the high-lands of Asir and its capital Abha, and had incorporated it in his territories. During the World War and immediately after it the fortunes of the dynasty of Ibn Reshid in Jebel Shammar had risen to a brief prosperity and he had recovered after ten years the important oasis region of Jauf which Nuri Ibn Sha'lan, the chief of the Ruvalla tribe, had captured in 1909. But internal feuds and rivalries for the throne led to a rapid break-up and after a long campaign Ibn Saud succeeded in capturing Hail in the autumn of 1921. This brought the whole of Central Arabia into Ibn Saud's possession, so that his kingdom bordered directly on Trans-Jordan where King Hussein's son, Abdullah, had been installed as Emir that same year. The two countries still disputed the possession of the districts of Jauf and Wadi Sirhan, which has salt beds of importance to the surrounding markets. It was not till November, 1925, that the Treaty of Haddah decided finally in Ibn Saud's favour, leaving only the north-west corner of the Wadi Sirhan in Trans-Jordan's possession.

Meanwhile, the tension between Ibn Saud and the house of Hussein increased from year to year. An attempt to bring about an agreement between the two rivals in Kuwait under England's presidency failed.[111] Whilst the conference was proceeding King Hussein paid a visit to the Emirate of Trans-Jordan, where his son Abdullah occupied the throne. The two months from January to March, 1924, which the king, already an old man of seventy, passed there marked the climax of his power. He intervened with a vigorous hand in the administration of the country, which his son had neglected, emphasized his authority in Arabian territory, and forced the English, with whom he was still negotiating a treaty, to respect him by his bearing and wisdom.[112] At that time the aged man might have cast the destinies of Arabia in a different mould if his own, and particularly his son Abdullah's, ambition had not induced him to assume the dignity of Caliph, in ill-considered over-estimation of his own greatness, when it fell vacant by the resolution of the Turkish National Assembly on March 3rd, 1924. It seemed that the wheel of history had turned backward. Once more an Arab of the house of Mohammed of Mecca was to lead Islam. But Hussein was not the man for the position, and the times no longer favoured a personal Caliph. The failure of the Conference of Kuwait, the acceptance of the office of Caliph, the sudden cessation of British subsidies to Hussein, and, even more important, to Ibn Saud at the end of March, 1924, all these simultaneous occurrences hastened the issue of the struggle for the hegemony of Arabia. In the autumn of the same year the question of leadership in Arabia was settled. In less than six months Hussein's dream of the Caliphate was dissipated.

Ibn Saud prepared his attack carefully. A congress in his capital of Riyadh in June, 1924, prepared the necessary psychological atmosphere. Feisal, Ibn Saud's son, appealed in a proclamation " to the Islamic World and the Arab nation " and protested in a form characteristic of Ibn Saud's Arab nationalism against Hussein's Caliphate and his claims to the leadership of the Arab nation.[113] The proclamation drew attention to the support promised to Ibn Saud in his repudiation of the predominance of the King of the Hejaz by the Indian Mohammedans, who had never forgiven Hussein his apostasy from the Sultan Caliph. At the congress the Ikhwan demanded the resumption of the pilgrimage which had been stopped since the fight between Wahabis and the townspeople of Mecca in the streets of the Holy City a few years earlier. Ibn Saud, unlike his ancestor Abdul Asis II, who had defied the Islamic world by capturing Mecca in 1800, declared that he would seize the Holy Places only if he had a mandate. This he received from the Indian Caliphate Committee " in order that concord may be firmly established among the Arabs and the power of Islam augmented ".

The Wahabi attack was opened by an advance guard led by Sultan Ibn Bijad, who succeeded surprisingly at the beginning of September, 1924, in capturing Taif, the summer residence of the people of Mecca. The Wahabis massacred the inhabitants of Taif.[114] Panic spread through the Hejaz. Hussein's son Ali retreated with his troops to Jidda, the seaport of Mecca, and the people of Jidda demanded Hussein's abdication, for his despotism and avarice had earned him small popularity among his subjects. Hussein's army was poorly equipped, but that was due not entirely to the king's miserly spirit but also to the fact that, whilst Ibn Saud could obtain arms freely by way of the Persian Gulf, the transport of arms by the Red Sea was forbidden by England under a long-standing convention. It was not till 1927 that Ibn Saud secured the recision of this prohibition in his treaty with England. When the English subsidy was withdrawn Hussein had been forced to tax his people with increased severity, and this had not tended to increase his popularity in the towns. Hussein appealed to England, his ally during the World War, and asked for the dispatch of a few aeroplanes. But England deserted her former ally. Eight years had passed since 1916. The situation in the world as a whole and in Arabia had changed. In proclaiming her neutrality England could justify herself by the fact that the intended treaty had not yet been concluded, and could point to the character of the war as a Mohammedan religious conflict in which she must not intervene.

On October 3rd Hussein resigned his titles. The Caliphate vanished from the picture. His son Ali only adopted the title of king and, moreover, with the limitation that he was to be a constitutional monarch, promising the Hejaz a constitution. Ali was universally beloved on account of his character and great confidence was felt in his abilities. Ibn Saud's aim seemed to be accomplished; but when Ali asked for peace negotiations Ibn Saud, with the approval of the Indian Caliphate Committee, said that Hussein's dynasty must quit the Hejaz; the Wahabis, however, would not retain the Hejaz, for that was an affair that concerned Islam as a whole. Islam as a whole must endow it with a democratic constitution. On October 13th the Wahabis under Khalid Ibn Luwai occupied Mecca and destroyed some of the tombs of the saints and historical places of pilgrimage, which called forth sharp protests, especially in Persia and India. It was not till December 5th that Ibn Saud himself entered Mecca, for the first time in his life, and performed the prescribed pilgrim rites. Ali now only retained Medina, and the two seaports of Yenbo and Jidda, where he had his headquarters. Ibn Saud's war aims gradually changed. At a second congress in Riyadh at the end of October, 1924, he declared his intention of summoning a Pan-Islamic conference at Mecca in the spring of 1925 to determine how the Hejaz should be ruled. As it turned out this conference did not meet for another year, and then under completely altered circumstances. For the time being Ibn Saud emphasized the necessity of making an end of despotism in the Hejaz, knowing that in this the Indian Mohammedans supported him. This alliance between the modern and democratic leaders of the Indian Caliphate Congress and the desert prince contained the seeds of future strife. But at that period the approval of the Indian Mohammedans gave Ibn Saud the support he needed, for a large proportion of the Islamic world was displeased at the occupation of the Holy City by the heretical Wahabis, remembering their first rule over Mecca 120 years earlier. But in December, 1925, Medina and Yenbo fell, and on December 19th the Wahabis entered Jidda. Ali betook himself to his brother Feisal at Baghdad, whilst Hussein, who had first withdrawn to Aqaba, the most northerly seaport in the Hejaz, was taken thence to Cyprus in the middle of 1925 at the instance of England, and remained there till the end of 1930, and then returned to his sons in Arabia in view of his great age and the serious state of his health. In spite of its declarations of neutrality, the British Government took the opportunity to detach the important districts of Maan and Aqaba from the Hejaz and annex them to Trans-Jordan.

As late as October 26th, 1925, Ibn Saud had declared in a Note to the Mohammedan Governments that he did not, in attacking the Hejaz, wish to annex it himself. " The Hejaz is a treasure entrusted to me until the time when its inhabitants choose a ruler of their own who will regard himself as the servant of the Mohammedan world and reign under its auspices." But on January 8th, 1926, by the wish of the Mecca notables, he assumed the title of King of the Hejaz at a service in the Grand Mosque in that city. Before the fate of the Hejaz was finally decided a British Mission under Sir Gilbert Clayton had come to Jidda and negotiated with Ibn Saud in Bahrah, half-way between Jidda and Mecca, about frontier questions between Nejd and the English mandated territories of Iraq and Trans-Jordan. The Treaty of Bahrah dealt with the possible sources of conflict between Iraq and Nejd from nomad incursions across the frontier, whilst the Treaty of Haddah laid down similar regulations for

Trans-Jordan and traced the frontier between the two countries. Only the question of Maan and Aqaba was left open. At that time it did not seem certain who would be the future ruler of the Hejaz. But facts were stronger than theories. Ibn Saud was the only personality capable of introducing firm and authoritative rule in the predominantly Bedouin Hejaz. At the end of 1925 the green Wahabi flag flew for the first time at Jidda side by side with those of European States whose consuls saluted the new sovereign. Ibn Saud, the desert prince, had at last outgrown the bounds of the Central Arabian oases. He was resolved to remain in the new and spacious world opening before him and to hold his own. "On that day the old Arabia died for ever; and a new State was born into the world's family. Progress would be the watchword of the desert fanatics! The story of modern Arabia is nearly ended. Its last phase is a phase of peace and progress, of returning prosperity and steady development on lines strangely modern as seen against the background of Arabian history." *

THE IDEA CRYSTALLIZES

Ibn Saud had solved a problem in an astoundingly short time that had been considered insoluble for centuries, both by the Turks and by King Hussein. The Bedouins of the Hejaz bowed to his authority and within a few months the caravan and pilgrim routes enjoyed such perfect safety, and life and property such freedom from attack, as is hardly found in highly civilized countries.[115] Pilgrim traffic was facilitated and severe measures were adopted to prevent any exploitation of the pilgrims; drinking water was provided, and a motor service established. With these successes Ibn Saud could appear before the Congress of the Islamic world which he had summoned for June, 1926, in fulfilment of his earlier promises. But there was now no longer any question of a decision regarding the fate of the Hejaz, all that was required was to accept the counsel of all Mohammedans how pilgrimage might be facilitated and communications and sanitary conditions improved.

* From *Arabia*, by H. St. J. B. Philby (Benn, 1930), p. 320.

The Congress was held a month after the Caliphate Congress in Cairo which, originally summoned by the Egyptian Ulemas for 1925, did not actually take place till May 13th to 19th, 1926. These congresses are an innovation in Islamic history. For the first time for many centuries the representatives of all Mohammedan peoples gathered together, and Islam as a whole struggled to mould and express a common will. Both congresses were failures. The background of the Congress of Cairo was the Egyptian king's wish for the title of Caliph, rejected by his people, and its task was an impossible one under present circumstances, for there is no Mohammedan ruler with a strong enough personality to restore the Caliphate in its old personal form ; it is, in fact, an institution for which, perhaps, the time is for ever gone. Nevertheless, both congresses were important merely in themselves and as mirrors of all the movements and tendencies, often conflicting, presented to our eyes in all their variety by the ever-shifting picture of Islam as it changes and acquires a new knowledge of itself.[116]

It was not the Caliphate question that formed the background of the Congress of Mecca. Ibn Saud knew very well that " only he may wear the Prophet's mantle who can defend the Prophet's people in all quarters of the earth ", and that that was a task far beyond his power. Although he feels responsible to Islam in the Hejaz, he regards his own peculiar mission as confined to Arab territories. Ibn Saud had to justify his assumption of the title of King of the Hejaz before the Congress which was originally to have settled the whole question of the future of Islam's Holy Land. It was now presented with a *fait accompli*. All that remained to be done, therefore, was to support the existing authority in matters of general interest connected with the yearly pilgrimage. Ibn Saud wished not only to justify himself but to raise his standing in the Islamic world and to make the pilgrimage safe upon which the economic life and public revenue of the Hejaz depend ; he wanted, moreover, to secure the support of all Mohammedans in order to solve certain technical and financial problems in the Hejaz, such as the construction of railways, and to be able to adopt a firmer attitude towards the European Powers on questions of foreign policy, primarily on the administration of the Hejaz Railway and the possession of the Maan-Aqaba district. But although the Congress of Mecca, with its more manageable and limited range of problems, was more successful than that of Cairo, it nevertheless fell short of what Ibn Saud had desired.[117]

As a result of this congress, the Indian Mohammedans, who were disappointed in Ibn Saud, and had wanted to set up an international Islamic administration in the Hejaz, adopted a hostile attitude towards the new king of the Hejaz. Shi'ah Persia also held aloof until 1929, when it too joined the number of the States which had recognized Ibn Saud's Government and entered into official diplomatic relations with him. The first of these had been the Union of Socialist Soviet Republics. Great Britain, Holland, France, Germany, and Turkey followed in rapid succession. Incidents in connection with Egypt's traditional privileges in the matter of the yearly pilgrimage have hitherto delayed her recognition of Ibn Saud's Government, for he did not consider the privileges compatible with the new régime in the Hejaz, but it is likely to come soon. In the autumn of 1926 Ibn Saud's son Saud paid a visit to Egypt and a little later his second son Feisal visited England, Holland, and France, the countries which have the largest number of Mohammedans in their colonies.

But Ibn Saud's chief care was to establish order and good administration in his realm. His ambition was to set up a modern bureaucratic State. The administration of primitive Nejd was sharply divided from that of the Hejaz. It was only the Hejaz that came in contact with the outer world, and from it the fanatical Ikhwan elements were withdrawn. The Mohammedan canon law or Sharia obtains in both countries in all its severity. The thief is condemned to have his hand cut off and the adulterer is executed, but such offences are extremely rare in the country. All the privileges of foreigners have been abolished and they, too, are forbidden to touch alcohol in Jidda. The Sharia law is equally binding on the king and on all his subjects.

In January, 1927, Ibn Saud also assumed the title of King of Nejd and the adjoining territories. The double kingdom was divided into two provinces. Ibn Saud's eldest son Saud was made Viceroy of Nejd, and his second son Feisal of the Hejaz. The Hejaz was granted a constitution which, though it leaves all final control in the hands of the king and his regent, yet provides for an Executive Council and an elected National Council. The Executive Council consists of the Viceroy as President, also responsible for the Ministry of the Interior, the nominated President of the National Council, the Minister of Foreign Affairs, and the Minister of Finance. The National Council consists of thirteen members besides the nominated President; five are elected by the people of Mecca, three each by the people of Medina and Jidda, and one each by the people of Yenbo and Taif. The chief obstacle to the development of the State organization is the shortage of suitable officials. It often happens that merchants in the Hejaz have to be entrusted with official duties. Frequently the Government is driven to resort to the expedient of employing Arabs from other countries [118]; with their help the foundations are being laid of modern educational and public health services, and primary schools have been established in the more important towns. A few students have been sent to Egypt for higher education. Thanks to exemplary conditions of order and security, motor traffic has rapidly increased. The number of motor vehicles plying not only between towns in the Hejaz but also crossing the Central Arabian desert is over fifteen hundred.

Ibn Saud's new position of authority induced Great Britain to revise her relations with him. The treaty of December 26th, 1915, which established a protectorate over Nejd, had long been rendered out of date by the facts of the situation. In the new Treaty of Jidda, concluded on May 20th, 1927, between Sir Gilbert Clayton and Ibn Saud's son and regent for a term of seven years, the earlier treaty was expressly cancelled. The new treaty of friendship recognized the complete and absolute independence of Ibn Saud's realm. One result of this recognition was embodied in a supplementary Note in which the British Government cancelled the prohibition hitherto in force of the import of arms and war material into Arabia. Ibn Saud engaged in the treaty not to attack territories under British protection, and to prevent all hostile action from his kingdom. In an accompanying Note the British Government fixed the frontier between Trans-Jordan and the Hejaz so that Maan and Aqaba were left with Trans-Jordan. In reply to this Ibn Saud answered that he adhered to his own point of view in the frontier question, but was ready to recognize the *status quo* and not interpose in the administration of the disputed region until more favourable circumstances allowed of a final settlement.

Ibn Saud's dominion was further extended by the inclusion of the Emirate of Asir. On October 21st, 1926, he concluded the Treaty of Mecca with the Imam Said Hassan Ben Ali el Idrissi, who acknowledged his suzerainty over Asir and promised to conclude no treaties with other countries without his consent, nor to grant concessions, likewise not to declare war or make peace nor to cede any portion of his territory. Ibn Saud in return promised to protect the Idrissi as ruler of Asir, provided that his decrees were equitable and in accordance with the Sharia.[119] The Treaty expired in November, 1930, when Ibn Saud began to administer Asir as a province of his own kingdom, the Idrissi retaining a titular office under the Viceroy of the Hejaz.

Asir brought Ibn Saud in direct contact with the only remaining independent prince beside himself in the Arabian peninsula, the Imam Yehya of Yemen. The Yemen, it is true, is far smaller than the Wahabi kingdom, but it is the most fertile and thickly populated part of the peninsula ; even in the days of antiquity it played an important part in history ; the Romans knew it as Arabia Felix, and it was the home of powerful States and interesting civilizations. Imam Yehya Ibn Mohammed Ibn Hamid ed Din had succeeded his father in May, 1904, and had begun his reign by stirring up a general revolt against the Turks, at that time suzerains over the country. In 1908 he made peace with the Sublime Porte, which granted his principal demand, the introduction of the Sharia instead of the modern Ottoman code. After a renewed insurrection, peace was finally concluded in 1911. During the World War Imam Yehya remained faithful to the Turks and in consequence of Turkey's defeat he won complete independence at the end of 1918. He succeeded in establishing order throughout the country. Except for a few attempts on the part of Sunni tribes, his authority is undisputed, his despotic rule is feared, and his great piety revered.

In 1919 the English made an attempt through Colonel Harold F. Jacob to enter into regular treaty relations with the Yemen, and again in 1926 through Sir Gilbert Clayton. Both attempts failed. The Imam demanded the cession of nine small Sultanates which Great Britain considered as falling under the Aden protectorate. Between 1919 and 1928 there was constant fighting for the possession of this territory, but hitherto no recognized frontier has been drawn between the Imam's and England's spheres of influence. Italy sought to profit by the situation ; during the World War she had supported Asir's efforts to win independence, and on September 2nd, 1926, she concluded the Treaty of San'a with the Yemen,* recognizing the full and absolute independence of the Imam and providing for the importation of machinery and the supply of scientifically trained personnel from Italy. This treaty did not secure for Italy the advantages that she hoped. It was but an effort without results. Italy was the only European Power to recognize the Imam officially. Otherwise none but the Union of Socialist Soviet Republics and Turkey entered into diplomatic relations with the Yemen, the former sending a Trade Delegation to San'a and Hodeida under Karim Khan Hakimoff in 1929. The Imam, miserly and hostile to all modern institutions, cared only to build up an army. Charles Crane, an American lover of the East who visited the Yemen in 1927, was the first to send engineers and machinery in order to promote agriculture and the construction of roads, and so to lay the foundations of a modernizing activity in this fertile country.[120] But in view of the reactionary fanaticism and ignorance of the Zaidites, these efforts are likely to meet with but slow success.

Ibn Saud's relations with the Imam were correct, though none too warm. He cannot reproach the Imam, like King Hussein, with lack of piety. At the end of 1927 he declared emphatically in a public meeting of notables at Mecca that he honoured the Imam for his God-fearing character, and felt bound to him by ties of regard and esteem. In 1929 there were unofficial negotiations between the two rulers. But they led nowhere, and the improvement of relations

* See *Zeitschrift für Politik*, Berlin, xviii year (1928), No. iii, pp. 179–81.

between the pair, who are not without suspicion of one another, is still a problem for Arabian politicians.

THE NEW ARABIA

But Ibn Saud knows that he must first reduce his kingdom to order before he can increase his power abroad. The Ikhwan, with their warlike religious zeal, played a large part in his victorious campaign in the Arabian peninsula. But the naïve fanaticism of the Ikhwan proved unequal to the task of ruling the kingdom which thus arose. Ibn Saud, with his statesmanlike wisdom, fully realized that. Whilst he was perfectly sincere in his own religious life, he was unlike Imam Yehya in being nothing of a fanatic. The slight put upon the Ikhwan, and the endeavour to impose upon the freedom-loving desert tribes a political organization based upon a strong centralized power, were the underlying causes of the rising against Ibn Saud instigated by Feisal ed Dawish, one of the oldest and most tried of the Ikhwan leaders, with his own Mutair tribe and other allied tribes, a rising which shook Nejd to its very foundations for two whole years. Ibn Saud was accused of having departed from the stern and ancient customs of the desert and its faith. The sons of the desert regarded airships and motor-cars, telephones and engines, not as awe-inspiring instruments of the king's power, but as works of the Devil calculated to destroy piety and faith. The leaders of the rebellion were precisely Ibn Saud's old and faithful paladins from the days of the Ikhwan movement, the Emirs of the oldest and largest colonies where the Ikhwan had been settled, like Feisal ed Dawish who had led the capture of Hail and Medina, and Sultan Ibn Bijad, the leader of the Ataiba tribes who had led the capture of Taif and first ruled Mecca in the name of the Wahabis.[121] The unrest on the Iraq frontier, arising from differences about the fortification of wells near the frontier, came to their assistance. Their attacks upon Iraq were the outcome of a general mood of irritation on the part of the Wahabis at what they regarded as British encroachments upon Nejd, suspecting a scheme for the construction of a railway to be behind them. Ibn Saud shared their mood of irritation, but he wished to avoid any open conflict with Great Britain, and the rebels were trying to involve him in one. Yet he could not but fear that, if he sternly forbade the attacks upon Iraq, the general feeling in Nejd would rise against him. In these circumstances he summoned a conference in Riyadh in the autumn of 1928, in which all the tribal chiefs except Feisal and Sultan, and the religious leaders of the Wahabis were to take part. Before this congress Ibn Saud appeared in a manner characteristic of himself and of the desert. He wished to know, he said, if any among the assembly had complaints to bring against him. He did not ask them because he was afraid of them. " For years I was alone with none but God's help, and so I desire only to stand before Him pure in His sight. . . . Let every man here speak with perfect freedom. I will listen to all criticism and every complaint, and the (religious) law shall judge between us. Free speech is essential to dispel mistrust. I will conceal nothing. Let God punish him on the Day of Judgment who conceals anything. I promise to punish no man who speaks the truth from his heart. If there are differences between us, the Koran and tradition shall decide."

At this congress, too, Ibn Saud's personality won a complete victory. The opposition brought forward their scruples about wireless telegraphy. The Ulemas laid down that the Holy Scriptures, the highest and ultimate authority, contained no pronouncement against the adoption of wireless telegraphy. No less absolute was Ibn Saud's victory on political questions. His policy of peace and restraint towards Iraq was approved and thereby Feisal ed Dawish's active policy of attack condemned. But Feisal did not bow to these decisions. It was 1929 that brought Ibn Saud victory in the desert. He had managed to unite the Central Arabian tribes under the banner of a new Brotherhood movement and the influence of the national watchwords that had by now penetrated to the desert, and this League established his hegemony in Arabia in the course of a decade and made the Bedouins a political factor in the peninsula once more after the lapse of a century. Arabia's future depended on Ibn Saud's victory. The alternative was a reversion to the old desert anarchy, the days without religious faith or history. Ibn Saud mastered the crisis by his superior strategy.

Battle was joined in March, 1929, on the plain of Sibila

not far from Artawiya, Feisal ed Dawish's residence and the oldest of the settlements established for the Bedouins by Ibn Saud. Feisal was seriously wounded and the king, who doubted his recovery, granted him life and freedom. Sultan Ibn Bijad, on the contrary, was brought to Riyadh shortly afterwards as a prisoner and Ghatghat, his and the Ataiba tribe's settlement, was destroyed; it had been the largest and most important of Ibn Saud's hijar or settlements after Artawiya. Meanwhile, Feisal had recovered and gathered his forces near Kuwait. There he was supported by Dhaidan Ibn Hithlein, the chief of the Ajman, and later by his son, and by a Ruvalla chief of the name of Farhan Ibn Mashhur. In November Ibn Saud himself took the field against the rebels, and at the end of December he crushed their forces at Rigai in the Batin Valley. The rebel leaders managed to flee to Iraq territory whence, on Ibn Saud's vigorous demand, they were delivered up to him. By the beginning of 1930 the insurrection was finally quelled.

But his victory had further consequences. It was the occasion of a reconciliation between the two dynasties that have been in the past decade the protagonists of Arabian unity and freedom and whose struggle for the honour of realizing the national ideal has filled the decade. In February, 1930, Ibn Saud and King Feisal of Iraq met on board a British man-of-war in the Persian Gulf, and prepared the way for a treaty of amity between their two countries. From the beginning of their career both princes have recognized the union of the Arab territories and the stimulation of an Arab renaissance as their historic mission. After his meeting with Feisal, Ibn Saud declared in a manifesto to all Emirs in his kingdom that the meeting had united the two neighbour States in the closest bonds of friendship, and served the highest interests of the Arab people. This encounter between the two kings, both sprung from the heart of the Islamic Arabian desert yet led by events to the opposite poles of the Arab world of to-day, is of historic import, although it may be long before there is any certainty when the next step will be taken on that historic road and how the historic mission will be fulfilled. European critics sometimes see Ibn Saud's Mecca, sometimes Feisal's Baghdad, as the focus of the Arab renaissance. Before long Baghdad will be the capital of a State Member of the League of Nations. Iraq is fully organized as a modern State. Nevertheless, the majority of the Arabs, even in urban circles in the border regions under European influence, and the majority of Christian Arab youth, regard the Hejaz as the centre of the Arab renaissance and Ibn Saud as the guardian of Arabia's future.

Under Ibn Saud's guidance the Hejaz is slowly but steadily undergoing modernization. The transition from desert to civilization will be only gradual, not only because of the poverty of the country and the backwardness of its inhabitants, but also because of jealous care for the absolute independence of Islam's Holy Land and the original home of the Arab nation. A dynastic and national consciousness is coming into being, as witness the introduction of January 8th, the anniversary of Ibn Saud's proclamation as King of the Hejaz, as a national festival.[122] The whole realm is intersected with motor roads and all important points are connected by wireless stations. Aeroplanes have been ordered from England and stationed partly at Dar'iyah on the Persian Gulf, partly on the Red Sea. The towns in the Hejaz are supplied with electric power. Wahabi fanaticism is restrained. After quelling Feisal ed Dawish's insurrection, Ibn Saud decreed that only the Ulemas are competent to decide religious questions in Nejd, and they are under the king's influence in Riyadh. He has impressed upon the Wahabis that their religion calls for a brotherly attitude towards other Mohammedans and, indeed, towards all who profess monotheistic religions. The narrow rigidity of the Wahabi community is making way for a wider freedom, influenced by the larger world outside. This is the road marked out by the development of the whole East to-day, a development from which even Central Arabia cannot hold back. A hundred and twenty years ago the mighty stream of the Wahabi movement burst forth from the desert and, unable at that time to control and transform itself, was doomed soon to break against the dykes of civilization and then, flowing back into Inner Arabia, to be choked in the sand ; but when it was revived under Ibn Saud's leadership it showed itself capable of seeking access to the common life of the age, of its religion and its nation. It is in process of finding its place in the Arab national movement of the twentieth century. In a quarter of a century Arabian history (like that of the whole East from Egypt to China) has passed through an immense transformation. Arab national sentiment, hitherto unformed and barely conscious, has advanced in that period along different paths to a national consciousness. It still meets with many obstacles, not only from without but within itself—the conflicting stages of civilization, manners, and customs, dynastic and group interests. As yet nobody can foresee how and when Arabia's national aim of unity and freedom will be realized. But fluid conditions are being stabilized, tangled threads are being disentangled, and it seems that in the future remoulding of affairs in Arabia Ibn Saud will play an important part.

BRIDGES BETWEEN EAST AND WEST

BENEATH the cleavages and differentiation brought about in the Hither East by the War and the Peace, beneath the restless variety, the complex problems, the internal tensions and conflicts, there is no mistaking the historical tendencies and streams of consciousness driving steadily towards unity. This convergence of forces is not new, it is the revival of a past still living and acting in men's minds, in customs and songs, in turns of speech, and in the everyday products of a civilization. Indeed, these territories and peoples have experienced history in recent decades, and that means the moulding hand of destiny; the dynamic force peculiar to Europe and distinguishing that small continent from all others has burst in upon the East. It is a social and economic process spreading and revolutionizing life in its outward aspect. It leaves unimpaired the vitality of this alien culture, the product of different conditions and, for the most part, beyond the grasp even of a European living in the East. And it is precisely the pressure of new development that stimulates that culture to assert and unfold itself. The processes of modern social economy and the conditions of transit are pushing towards the political union of a nation bound by a homogeneous culture. There are still great obstacles: social rivalries between town-dwellers and Bedouins, separation into small States kept apart by the interests of alien and hostile Powers or by dynastic forces But so it was in Germany in the eighteenth and Italy in the nineteenth century. It took decades for the dream of unity and freedom cherished by the patriotic intelligentsia of Germany and Italy to attain fulfilment, influenced by the modern national ideal coming from Western States and urged on by the power of capitalism knocking at the gates and penetrating the land. Decades may pass before the dream of unity and freedom cherished by the Arab intelligentsia is fulfilled. In its modern form it is very recent, a child of the twentieth century, as it was a child of the opening nineteenth century in Germany and Italy. The basis of this longed-for unity is a uniform civilization and uniform customs, common traditions of a great past, and a vital humanist participation, almost forgotten in Europe, in a spiritual heritage, in poetry and religion, songs of freedom and legends that are the common property of the whole educated class. What seems of the past to-day is still of the present to many and may become a rejuvenated and transformed present. Europeans are apt to over-estimate their history because they are its heirs and are at home in it. They forget that its duration is only a few centuries, and that a relatively short period divides the present from a state of barbarism which to-day we can barely conceive and which seems unspeakably far removed. History repeats itself because psychological processes are similar and sociological processes are transferred by the intercourse and contact of civilizations. A nation or a civilization needs impetus and stimulus from without and these reveal themselves in political, cultural, and social tensions, conflicts, and acts of intervention. To-day the Hither East is experiencing all this intensely, tempestuously. The result is an impetus to its political and cultural life which gives promise that it will reach its goal at a not too distant date.[123]

Whilst, therefore, the historical trend in Arab civilization is towards unity, social and cultural contacts are leading Europe and the Hither East nearer and nearer to one another and blotting out the line of cleavage that separated them but a short time ago. Their mutual approach is also nothing new, only the rediscovery of common bonds that once united them, but which Europe has cast off since the Renaissance in her tempestuous advance. The Mediterranean countries still form a homogeneous unit in their geographical formation and the physical mould of their inhabitants, in the character of their landscape and customs. In spite of their different histories, Spain, Southern Italy, and Greece, are more akin to Algeria and Lebanon than to Northern Europe. The roots of European civilization are in the Mediterranean basin. Hellenism, the Roman Empire, the continuation of Greek philosophy, the Biblical legends, scholasticism, and mediaeval rationalism were the common property of Europe and the

Hither East. The Arabs, who inhabited Spain for nearly eight hundred years and were driven out only a little over four hundred years ago, the Saracens in Sicily, the Ottoman Empire linking Europe, Asia, and Africa, all gave political expression to the oneness of the Mediterranean basin.

The advance towards unity proceeds in our day in a different manner. With the close of the Middle Ages leadership passed from the Mediterranean to North-Western Europe, from the trade routes of the Levant to the great new paths across the Atlantic Ocean. It was not only Eastern countries which fell into the background ; they were soon followed by the whole of Southern Europe. The new European civilization that took shape from the seventeenth century onward had its rise in Northern and Western Europe and penetrated thence to the south, south-east, and east of Europe and later to the Hither East, to India, and the Far East. The spread of capitalism, nationalism, and rationalist thought further and further over the earth's surface made the peoples of the whole world more and more members of a single cultural community. New means of transport, especially aircraft, created a new sense of space and time in men's minds. Technical science has opened the way to the most distant lands and travel from continent to continent has increased to an extent undreamt of in the past. To-day it is a representative of Venezuela who presides over the League of Nations Assembly ; to-morrow, perhaps, of Siam or Persia. Very shortly the Hither East will be represented in the League by Egypt and Iraq, perhaps a little later by the Hejaz, which was one of the original members, and by Syria. Politically, socially, and culturally the ties which are drawing together Europe and the Hither East, Occident and Orient, are growing stronger from day to day.

They were symbolized in the deliberations of the International Missionary Council that met in Jerusalem at Easter, 1928. In the *rapprochement* between East and West missions have played a great part during the past century, though not always without incurring hostile criticism. It was through them that cultural penetration took place, they transmitted a new spirit, but likewise they were often the heralds and pioneers of colonial and economic expansion. The missions were Europe's representatives in the East, looking down upon

it and believing that they brought it not only the doctrine
of salvation, but a superior civilization, a life worth living,
the fundamentals of civilization. Indirectly the influence of
the missionaries promoted *rapprochement*, but they stressed
the cleavage, the gulf that yawned between two worlds.
Lacking the historical sense, they saw in Europe and in
Christendom at their present stage of development the
absolute norm of what is good and humane. In this they were
characteristic of an attitude of mind adopted even to this
day by the majority of Europeans in the East, by their Press,
and even by some European chancellories, only that with them
it is more naïve and more remote from any strain of the
divine. It is an arrogance that springs from people's natural
dislike of what is alien to them, and from a lack of any
historical sense or capacity to perceive how social and
cultural conditions and processes are relative and in a state
of growth. Miss Mayo's well-known book on India is only a
typical expression of this attitude, all amazement that there
should still be peoples less gloriously advanced than ourselves
who do not joyfully acknowledge our superiority. Not only
does she lack all power of understanding an alien culture and
grasping that other standards may hold good before God
and the bar of history than those of an American in 1925,
she is even totally ignorant of the none too distant past of
her own race ; but first and foremost she lacks that sense
of humour that would enable her to compare the condition
of the outcastes in India with that of the negroes in North
America. Such an attitude necessarily intensifies the cleavage
instead of hastening a *rapprochement*, which would certainly
be to the interest of the East.

The significant and characteristic quality of the Easter
Congress of Missionaries in Jerusalem was that it tried to
break away from this attitude and to discover new ways
founded upon *rapprochement* and equal rights and future
unity. For just as mankind has reached a critical point, a
parting of the ways, in the general relations between East and
West, so a change has begun in the missionary world that
will radically alter the relations between the peoples and
churches that have hitherto sent out the missionaries and the
youthful Eastern churches and native peoples. At the
International Missionary Congress in Edinburgh in 1910, in

the extreme north-west of Europe, there were only twenty representatives of the coloured races amongst three thousand delegates. In Jerusalem, on the borderland of East and West, more than a third of the participants in the congress were members of the coloured races, and it is worthy of remark that alike in theological questions and in the debates devoted to political and social problems the representatives of the non-white races took the intellectual lead. Missionaries have begun to realize that in the East, and even in Africa, they are confronted with great and ancient civilizations with their own right to existence and a profundity that plumbs the very sources of life. Their task can no longer be conceived as to replace native by European culture, which in the past was often naïvely identified with Christianity, but only to bring about a synthesis of the two civilizations, to preserve what is precious and fruitful in the native culture and to render it still more fruitful. The East has become the schoolmaster of the West, has widened the missionaries' field of vision and forced them into serious self-examination. The naïve relation of Europeans and Orientals has begun to change into the exact opposite. The coloured races, in their awakening consciousness of self and from the vantage ground of their ancient civilizations and more polished customs, have tested Christian Europe as it was preached to them by the example of the nations and peoples who believed in it and were supposed to present a pattern of its manner of life. They soon discovered that in the present day Christianity, as it appears in men's lives, the Christianity voiced by churches and chancelleries, is an apostasy from the doctrine as preached, and that it has often identified itself with utterly contradictory ideas, with nationalism, racial arrogance, imperialism, and the sanctioning of wars. The Christian missions, as the advance guard of European civilization, were in danger of losing their influence on the Eastern races altogether. Only a type of Christianity that took itself and the best heritage of European humanism seriously could hope to hold its own when confronted with the cultural self-realization of the Eastern peoples and the renaissance and fresh vitality of which Islam and the religions of Asia have given evidence in recent years.

Before 1928 the Missionary Congress was primarily a

meeting of the European and American churches and societies which sent missionaries to Africa and the East. At the Jerusalem Congress the representatives of the youthful national churches that have sprung up everywhere among the native populations of Asia and Africa won equal standing. The native Christians in Africa and the East stand without distinction beside their non-Christian fellow-countrymen in the foremost ranks of the nationalist movements in their countries. There is no distinction between them and non-Christian Orientals as regards either object or methods in the struggle for full national freedom. But their Western education, with its primary aim of training initiative, energy, and personality, often enables them to set an example in social welfare work and education, especially that of girls. The growing oneness of mankind forbade the missionary congress of 1928 to confine itself to the affairs of the peoples awaiting conversion. The close co-operation of East and West was declared to be necessary in order to combat barbarism and heathendom amongst both sections of the human race.

The political and social resolutions passed by the congress also breathed a new spirit, though cautiously and tentatively. One moved by the English Bishop Temple invited the Eastern churches to send missionaries to Europe and America in order to impart some of the treasure of their spiritual life to the peoples of the West. " We repudiate," the resolution declared, " any attempt on the part of trade or of governments, openly or covertly, to use the missionary cause for ulterior purposes. . . . Especially must it be a serious obstacle to missionary effort if a non-Christian country feel that the relation of the so-called Christian countries to itself is morally unsound or is alien from the principles of Christ." * The resolution on economic questions declared that public loans and the investment of capital must in no circumstances lead to political control or intervention, and that the development of economically backward countries should be promoted by international public utility societies and their revenues expended on extending educational, public health, and public welfare services in those countries. The missionaries roundly declared that they wished to identify themselves with the

* *Report of the Jerusalem Meeting of the International Missionary Council* (Oxford University Press), vol. i, pp. 484, 489.

people in whose country they were working, and did not, therefore, wish any longer to provide excuses for the diplomatic or armed intervention of white Powers in the affairs of Eastern peoples ; on no account would they ask their Governments for armed protection of their lives and property. The missions' task was to open new vistas and to impress on men's hearts the idea of the oneness of the human race and its united labour for the salvation of mankind. It was not for the mission to divide but to unite, not to point out what is negative in others, but to lay stress on what is positive. How far the missions will proceed to carry their own principles, responsibly, seriously, and with a willingness to put them fully into practice is of less importance than the actual symbolical fact that they have thus turned from a policy of separation to one of *rapprochement*, for their attitude towards the problem of East and West has characterized and guided that of the white races.[124] " The march towards the unity of mankind proceeds visibly enough, and from it spring the great problems of the present epoch in world history ; nay, we even see rise in the distance the shining peaks of man's ultimate destiny." (Ragaz.)

Regarded thus broadly, the struggle between imperialism and nationalism in the Hither East is part of a world-wide process. These territories are so poor and their populations, relatively speaking, so small, that the events here recorded are not in themselves of vital significance in world history, as in China.[125] But just because the scene upon which the historic drama is enacted is easier to survey, the present-day lines of force are more clearly marked. The relation between East and West is changing rapidly in our time. Europe's conscious mind and practical policies have been slow to recognize the change. But in the decade beginning with the Peace Treaties of Versailles and Sèvres and the Conference of San Remo and leading up to Great Britain's treaties with Egypt and Iraq and Syria's democratic constitution of 1930, undoubted progress has been made. The prospect of peaceful progress in the Hither East and a relaxation of its internal tensions depends upon constant adaptation to the process of growth, on a policy free from the entangling arguments of self-interest, a policy of understanding, and a wise and prompt renunciation of intervention.

NOTES

[1] The following table gives the number and net tonnage of the merchant ships that passed through the Canal in 1928 :—

Nationality.			No. of Ships.	Net Tonnage.
British .	.	.	3,315	17,839,359
Dutch .	.	.	617	3,346,870
German	.	.	606	3,283,713
French .	.	.	350	1,919,735
Italian .	.	.	349	1,621,844
Japanese	.	.	157	933,021
United States of America			124	727,159
Norwegian	.	.	149	688,780
Danish .	.	.	72	363,484
Swedish	.	.	66	307,352
Greek .	.	.	90	280,018
Belgian	.	.	40	160,082
Russian	.	.	20	67,819
Spanish	.	.	6	17,802
Egyptian	.	.	8	13,630
Others .	.	.	8	16,116

The proportion of British shipping is still larger, if one reckons ships belonging to the Government and men-of-war. Of these, 104 passed through the Suez Canal in 1928, with a tonnage of 319,475, 77 being British with a tonnage of 284,321. On December 21st, 1926, Port Fuad was opened opposite Port Said on the eastern bank of the Suez Canal. It is recognized that Port Fuad will be of importance in connection with the British occupation of the Suez Canal Zone lying, as it does, on the Asiatic side of the Canal. From Port Fuad a railway line is to be built to Kantara East, the terminus of the railway to Palestine, and on to the Sinai Peninsula and to Aqaba at the north-eastern extremity of the Red Sea in Trans-Jordan. This line, which Lord Cromer already had in mind, would assist the exploitation of the mineral wealth of the Sinai Peninsula and at the same time complete the Hither Asian railway system by the junctions with the Hejaz Railway at Kantara and Aqaba near Maan. (See the *Frankfurter Zeitung*, January 20th, 1927.)

[2] See the proceedings of the Mohammedan Congress at Mecca in Achille Sekaly, *Le Congrès du Khalifat et le Congrès du Monde Muselman* (Paris, Editions Ernest Leroux, 1926, pp. 155–62). The reporter and mover of the resolution was the Palestinian delegate Emin el Husseini, the Mufti of Jerusalem. According to his figures the railway cost 5,012,398 Turkish pounds to build. With the help of Turkish troops the work took seven years. The total length of the main line was 1,307 kilometres, and of the branch lines 652 kilometres. The Government of the Hejaz accuses the Syrian administration in particular of having seized by far the greater part of the locomotives and other

equipment after king Feisal's fall in Damascus in the summer of 1920, leaving the Hejaz only quite a small quantity of useless material.

[3] The Palestine loan in December, 1927, was the first in a mandated territory. Its amount was £4,475,000, repayable by the Palestinian Government from 1942 to 1967, with interest at 5 per cent, and both principal and interest were guaranteed by the British Treasury. The loan was to be used as follows : £1,115,000 for building the port of Haifa and improving that at Jaffa ; £1,000,000 as purchase price to the British Government for the railways in Palestine ; £1,640,000 for railway construction in Palestine, which, however, was largely met before this loan was floated by previous loans issued by the British Crown Agent ; £745,000 for various public works, buildings, and telegraph and telephone installations, and for the cost of raising the loan. Provision had already been made in the Sykes-Picot Agreement (letter from Cambon to Sir Edward Grey dated May 9th, 1916, seventh point) for the construction of the " all-British " railway from Haifa to Baghdad, and again in Article 1 and Article 5, par. 3 of the Anglo-French Agreement of December 23rd, 1920 (Cmd. 1195, 1921). Here the pipe-line, to run parallel with the railway, is also mentioned.

[4] It is 534 miles from Damascus to Baghdad, and takes two days by motor. The Rutbah Oasis is 263 miles from Damascus. In 1926 the Iraqi Government established a police post there, a postal station, and one for the dispatch and receipt of wireless messages. There is also an aerodrome, and a hotel and restaurant. The first motor-car crossed the Syrian desert in January, 1923. In October, 1923, the Nairn Transport Company established the first regular passenger and postal service. Regarding the Company and the route, see the *Frankfurter Zeitung*, August 21st, 1926.

[5] The air service has reduced the distance between London and Baghdad for postal purposes to five days. The flight from Egypt via Gaza in southern Palestine and Rutbah (see Note 4) to Baghdad takes nine hours, and the distance is 900 miles.

CHAPTER II

[6] Lord Ronaldshay's observation is taken from his Anniversary Lecture to the Central Asian Society in London in June, 1909. That of the Turkish Governor-General is quoted by M. Nemchenko, *Nacionalnoye Razmeževaniye Srednei Azii* (published by the Literature Department of the People's Commissariat for Foreign Affairs, Moscow, 1925). There is a great deal more about the process of social and cultural transformation in the East in my *History of the Nationalist Movement in the East* and my *Orient and Okzident*. Helmuth von Glasenapp gives an interesting example of the association of religion and nationalism and the use of religious forms and conceptions in the service of nationalism in a song sung at the twentieth Indian National Congress at Calcutta ; one verse in translation reads as follows : " Thou who guidest the hearts of the nations—Hail to thee, O Lord of India's destiny—Thy call goes forth by day and night—It echoes afar—And Hindu, Buddhist, Sikh, and Jain—Parsee, Mussulman, and Christian—Come from east and west to the steps of thy Lion Throne—Bound together in love they sing thy praise—Thou who leadest the nations to unity—Hail to thee, O Lord of India's destiny."

In such terms does this song proclaim an inter-confessional, national, Pan-Indian piety.

⁷ R. O. Wingate in the *Journal of the Central Asian Society*, vol. xvi, p. 319. Even in economically backward countries like Morocco, religious feeling is changing into national sentiment. D. S. Margoliouth in his lecture on " Ideas and Ideals of Modern Islam " (*Journal of the Central Asian Society*, vol. xvii, i, p. 56, January, 1930) quotes a sentence from Michaud Bellaire (*Archives Marocaines*, Paris, 1927, xxvii, p. 172) : " If, as before, the independence of the land remains the ideal, it is less owing to a religious sentiment than to a sort of impulse of patriotism."

⁸ In the introduction to the *Cambridge Modern History*, when discussing the broad lines of difference between the mediaeval and the modern world (vol. i, p. 2), Creighton says : " In outward matters the great distinction is a frank recognition in the latter of nationality and all that it involves."

⁹ See Richard Hartmann's admirable monograph *Die Krisis des Islam* (J. C. Hinrichs, Leipzig, 1928). Together with his monograph, *Die Welt des Islam einst und heute* (do., 1927) it is the best introduction to the world of political, social, and cultural ideas of present-day Islam. As an orientalist, the author reaches views and conclusions very similar to those arrived at in my *History of the Nationalist Movement in the East* and in the present work from a historical and sociological point of view.

¹⁰ The rise of the new philosophy of life has been traced and depicted in a masterly manner in the sphere of Christian and European civilization by Bernhard Groethuysen in his book *Die Entstehung der bürgerlichen Welt- und Lebensanschauung in Frankreich* (2 vols., Max Niemeyer, Halle, 1927 and 1930).

¹¹ During the autumn of 1928 the well-known leader of the Indian Mohammedans, Mohammed Ali, visited the countries of the Hither East. On that occasion he stated in an interview in the Beirut daily *Ahrar* (see the *Frankfurter Zeitung*, December 4th, 1928) : " We Indians are greatly pleased with the Syrian liberation movement. But your sacrifices and exertions are but the first step on the road to freedom. . . . The day will doubtless come when every (Oriental nation) will live in freedom in its own country. In order that that may be successfully achieved, we Mohammedans must faithfully cherish the true Islam. Do not follow those who tell you that religion is incompatible with modern politics and that it does not lead to a free life. The Mohammedan religion is a progressive religion. If we study the laws of our religion profoundly, we find that they form the basis of European civilization." In the interview he also dwelt on the unchanged intention of the Indian Mohammedans to play an active part in Pan-Islamic politics and to work for a more marked recognition of the oneness of all Mohammedan peoples. Characteristically enough, these pronouncements of the Indian Mohammedan appeared in an Arab Christian paper in Lebanon. Mohammedan sentiment and opinion found transitory political expression in demonstrations, lasting for several weeks, against the world conference of Christian missions in Palestine at Easter of 1928.

¹² See the very informative article by H. A. R. Gibb, " Studies in Contemporary Arabic Literature : III. Egyptian Modernists " in the *Bulletin of the School of Oriental Studies*, London Institution, vol. v, p. III, 1929.

[13] On the subject of this celebration see the detailed account by Michaelangelo Guidi, " Le onoranze al poeta egiziano Shawgi ed il loro significato politico " in *Oriento Moderno*, VII year, pp. 146 ff. The festal week began with the meeting in the Grand Opera House in Cairo. The meeting, consisting of delegates of all Arabic-speaking countries, was dominated by a single emotion which broke spontaneously from the depths of men's souls : " è l'orgoglio dell'anima araba, orgoglio che, in tanta varietà d'individui e di tendenze, trova l'espressione comune in qualche cosa che trascende i confini dei paesi : nell'antico retaggio letterario, che è vanto di tutta la nazione araba, della ummah, se anche la ummah è devisa, e che ora s'impersona in un sol uomo . . . que sembra riunire . . . al canto della sua poesia, le membra disiecta della grande nazione araba." A message from Zaghlul, already ill at that time, intensified the national enthusiasm ; " the words of the message, greeting the delegates from the East and urging brotherly love between all peoples of Arabic speech in all countries, called forth raptures of applause which seemed as if they would never end." " L'incontro di tanti fratelli di sangue e di lingua, cui le vicende della storia hanno separato dopo gloriosi periodi di dominazione, l'unione nel celebrare un patrimonio comune che trascende i confini e unisce la nazione araba e le ricorda, anche nella forma esteriore, gli antichi splendori, l'abile sfruttamento di questo occasioni per opera di dirigenti di accesi fazioni panarabiche, esercitano facilmente il loro potere su una folla. . . ." The poems and speeches delivered were animated by the idea, never quenched in the hearts of the Arabs of all the territories of Northern Africa and Hither Asia, of unity and solidarity inspired by the memory of the past glory of their race.   Characteristically enough it was the Christian Lebanese poet Shibli Mallat whose sonorous verses recalled the magnificence of Arab power : The Arab people subdued the East, and then made speed to conquer the West, " and if Charles Martel's steadfast strength had not checked them, they would have set up their tents and pitched their camp in the very heart of the Western world." " E quest' ultimo verso, quest' allusione ad una possibilità, perduta per sempre, di dominare l'Occidente, provocò nell' uditorio un vero delirio, una tempesta d'applausi." For the first time on such an occasion an Arabian woman also spoke in the name of the Egyptian women's movement. The verses of the poet in whose honour the celebration was held, specially written for the occasion, made a grand and moving conclusion. " Verses in which the pride and sorrow of the Arabs found voice, they who had lost their ancient power, but not their courage, and who all burned with patriotism : ' We are all one in the thought of our native land, we are all consumed with love of our country.' ' Encore, encore,' was the unanimous cry with which the crowd greeted these verses, craving to hear them once again ; and everybody repeated them as they came away from this festival of Pan-Arab nationalism." The festival was followed by a congress in Arabic in which delegates from all the countries took part.   Haj Emin el Husseini, the Mufti of Jerusalem, took the chair and the most impressive speech was made by the Palestinian port Issaf Nashashibi.

[14] For Mrs. Hoda Sharavi's speech at the Women's Congress in Rome and the discussions to which it gave rise in Egypt, see *Oriento Moderno* (Rome, III year, pp. 376–9). Turkey and the Mohammedan peoples in the Soviet Union are radically in advance of the rest, both on the women's question and on that of substituting Latin script

for Arabic. Nobody in Egypt or Arabia thinks of following their example. (There were also isolated attempts to advocate the substitution of Latin script for Hebrew amongst the Jewish population of Palestine. They, too, were repudiated.) In Egypt, however, by the king's desire, two small reforms in Arabic script are under consideration, and these would change its appearance and bring it nearer to the European method. Arabic script has no punctuation marks, and, like Hebrew, no distinction between large and small letters. A commission has been appointed in Egypt to consider rules of punctuation and, at the same time, a prize offered for an essay advocating the introduction of initial capital letters.

[15] On the subject of women's place in modern Arabic literature see Ettore Rossi, " Una scrittice araba cattolica Mayy " (Marie Ziyadah) in *Oriento Moderno* (Rome, v year, pp. 604 ff.). Mayy's writings give clear evidence of the consciousness of unity that binds Mohammedans and Christians together, and also all the various Arab countries. She was born in Narazeth in 1895, a Catholic, the offspring of a Lebanese father and a Palestinian mother ; she afterwards lived in Beirut and came to Cairo at the beginning of her literary career. In her writings she has devoted much space to earlier Arabic authoresses : to the Lebanese Christian Wardah el Yazigi (1838–1924) and the Egyptian Mahommedans, Ishah Ismat Timur (1840–1902), and Malak Hifni Nasef (1886–1918), both of whom advocated the education and social betterment of the Mohammedan woman. All these women were animated by keen Arab patriotism. The first Egyptian author who advocated the emancipation of Egyptian women was Kassim Amin who died in 1908 and whose books were entitled *The Emancipation of Woman* and *The New Woman*. He was a disciple of Jemal ud Din el Afghani and a friend of Zaghlul Pasha, to whom he dedicated *The New Woman*. On the position of women in literature and the press among the Egyptian Mohammedans and Copts and the Syrians over thirty years ago, see Martin Hartmann, *The Arabic Press of Eygpt* (Luzac & Co., London, 1899, pp. 46–50). The first Arabic women's paper in Egypt appeared in 1892, with the title *El Fatat* (*The Girl*), edited by a Syrian Christian lady, Hind bint Naufal. See also the lecture by May Ziadès, " Il risveglio della donna in Egitto negli ultime cento anni " in *Oriento Moderno* (ix year, pp. 237 ff.). In 1905, the first Mohammedan woman was sent to London to be trained, to the indignation of conservative circles at the time ; on her return she became the first Egyptian principal of a teacher's training college. The first Egyptian girl to complete a secondary school course as an external pupil did so in 1906, and afterwards filled important posts in Egypt's educational service. After his return in 1921, Zaghlul Pasha persuaded his wife to appear unveiled henceforth. In 1928, there were 224 girls' schools under the Egyptian Ministry of Education, with 36,600 pupils. There are in addition a number of private schools. The new Egyptian State University has admitted women to study in the Faculties of Medicine, Science, and Arts. In the first year (1928–9) seven women medical students entered.

At the beginning of 1930 lectures on the equality of the sexes roused protest in conservative Islamic circles.

CHAPTER III

[16] See the article by Guido Crolla, " La Siria e la Competizione Anglo-Francese " in *Oriento Moderno* (Rome, I year, Nos. 9 and 10).

[17] See Ameen Rihani, *Ibn Saoud of Arabia, his People and his Land* (Constable & Co., London, 1928, pp. 191–4). On pp. 198 and 199 there is a list of the various hijar in Nejd. *Oriento Moderno* (Rome, IV year, p. 641) prints a correspondence in the paper *El Akhbar* of Cairo on the hijar, the Bedouin settlements. It quotes their number as over 60. A settled life cultivating the soil has not only contributed to establish public order and safety in Nejd, but has made for a deeper understanding of the religion of Islam and counteracted superstition. The rise of the new towns and villages give Ibn Saud an opportunity of sending Islamic teachers there. As regards Artawiya, the oldest of these settlements, see H. St. J. B. Philby, *Arabia of the Wahabis* (Constable, London, 1928, pp. 352, 353).

[18] *Review of the Civil Administration of Mesopotamia* (Cmd. 1061, 1920), pp. 20 and 21. E. Rabbath writes in *L'Evolution politique de la Syrie sous Mandat* (Marcel Rivière, Editeur, Paris, 1928), p. 254 : " Le Bedouin réduit a se deplacer sur des étendues restreints sera amené, si une politique habile lui en retrecit progressivement les coins, à se fixer peu à peu au sol. Il suffira de lui faciliter l'acquisition des terres qu'il occupe, de le pourvoir de semences et de l'aide technique nécessaires, pour que, le besoin aidant, il sente en lui se créer les goûts du sedentaire. Ce que l'enchainement des circonstances historiques ne produit qu'à longue écheance, il semble bien qu'une politique rationelle, rigoureusement réaliste, puisse le provoquer à son tour et le hâter. Par l'instruction en premier lieu des fils des chefs, l'on pourrait influer sur la tribe entière. Mais il s'agira aussi de lui procurer des terrains propres à la satisfaire et surtout de la pourvoir des moyens nécessaires à les faire valoir." On the subject of the Bedouins' efforts at settlement the French Mandatory Government wrote in 1930 : " Il est a remarquer que la tendance a la sédentarisation se manifeste de plus en plus fortement chez les nomades. L'évolution économique du pays les pousse à se fixer, au moins en partie, sur la glèbe. Tous les chefs importants possèdent des terres ou en demandent aux domaines. Ils y font des améliorations : Moudjem, chef des Anèzes du Nord, a une machine à pomper l'eau sur l'Euphrate pour irriguer des terrains et Rakkan, chef des Gbaa, a remis en eau des anciennes canalisations romaines d'une region aujourd'dui désertique." (*Rapport à la Société des Nations sur la situation de la Syrie et du Liban*, année 1929, Paris, Imprimerie Nationale, 1930, p. 77.) Sir Herbert Samuel in his five years' report (Colonial No. 15, 1925, p. 41) mentions the improvement in the position of the Beisan Bedouins as regards the possession of land. Otherwise nothing has been done in the matter in Palestine. In the report on Trans-Jordan, on the other hand, we find (*Report on Palestine and Trans-Jordan for 1929*, Colonial No. 47, 1930, p. 138) : " There is a marked tendency among the nomads to settle. This tendency towards settlement is likely to increase in proportion to the speed with which the Government can allot definite areas to the Beduin."

[19] See Ladislaus Gumplowicz, *Nationalismus und Internationalismus im 19ten Jahrhundert* (Verlag Aufklärung, Berlin, 1902, p. 44). There too, is the following quotation from the *Gazetta Robotnicza* of Kattowitz, November 30th, 1901 : " When Bismarck deluded himself with the notion that he had crushed Polish culture, when he cried that the Polish people were content with the Prussian Government, he did not count with the working classes. To Bismarck and such as him nothing was Polish but what bore the mark of aristocracy. And when the Prussian system succeeded in corrupting and enfeebling the nobility and the clergy, by investing them with honours and offices, all the Pan-German patriots thought Prussia had Germanized Poland. But meantime a new power was growing up, the Polish working masses, oppressed and persecuted for centuries. Their nationalist sentiment is no empty phrase, their resistance to every kind of injustice to their country cannot be bought off for a handful of gold. That is why the cry that the working people should be Germanized means a long and severe struggle."

[20] In 1928, there were twenty-two strikes amongst the Jewish workers, involving 886 strikers. Fourteen of these ended successfully for the workers and three with a compromise. In 1929, the number of Jewish urban workers and employees was 14,916. The Jewish workers' organization has its own sickness fund with hospitals, itinerant clinics, and convalescent homes ; it has also an Education Committee which maintains schools, libraries, evening and itinerant classes, and courses of lectures ; and, further, its own bank.

The first great strike of Arab workers in Palestine was in October, 1925, in Haifa : 100 carpenters and 25 tailors wished for a reduction of the ten to eleven hours' day, and did actually succeed in getting the working day reduced to nine hours after a fortnight's strike. In Egypt, a Socialist weekly appeared in Arabic. The advocate Abdallah Hussein had the intention in 1927 of founding a Socialist party in Egypt. (See *Oriento Moderno*, vii year, p. 140.)

[21] A feddan is rather more than an English acre or four-tenths of a hectare. On conditions in Syria see A. Ruppin, *Syrien als Wirtschaftsgebiet* (Kolonialwirtschaftliches Komitee, Berlin, 1917, p. 32—the name Syria also includes Palestine) : " In order to raise the standard of civilization the State ought to interpose between landlord and tenant with the object of making the tenants owners of the land they rent. That might be done either by the State or a bank with a State concession having a free hand to buy the land from the large landowners and sell it to the tenants for payments over a long term of years, or by a special law obliging the large landowners to make over some or all of their land to the tenants on fair terms, whilst a State Mortgage Bank would have to facilitate the raising of the purchase price by the purchasers." This proposal, however, has not been adopted either in Syria or Palestine. According to Ruppin (p. 64) the average sufficient small holding varies from 9 to 23 hectares according to the fertility of the soil. Rent is generally paid in kind, as a rule one-fifth of the yield, whilst the fellah is often required to pay the whole tithe. Ruppin (p. 67) says of fellaheen cultivation : " It is quite unjust to describe the method of cultivation of the fellaheen as exhaustion of the soil. . . . What makes fellaheen methods seem so much behind European is the primitive implements and the lack of manure. But otherwise the method of working cannot be called primitive, for it respects the law of replacing all material, and obtains with small costs,

not indeed a large yield, but a regular medium yield." On p. 95, Ruppin calculates that the large landowners get from 4 to 5 per cent when they rent their land, in Palestine often not more than 1 per cent, which explains the sales of estates by the large landowners that often rob the tenants of their land.

CHAPTER IV

²² Johannes, Schubert, *Machiavelli und die politischen Probleme unserer Zeit* (Verlag C. A. Schwetschke & Sohn, Berlin, 1927), p. 103 : " Individual egotism is recognized as a vice, and there is a constant struggle to hold it in check. Group egotism, on the other hand, is magnified as the highest virtue. The identification of the individual with the group gives the emotional satisfaction of the ego urge, without the pang of conscience, which accompanies it apart from the group. . . . The way of salvation is a group conviction of sin, which will condemn the egotism and immorality of a race or nation as severely as it does that of an individual." (Herbert Adolphus Miller, *Races, Nations, and Classes : The Psychology of Domination and Freedom*, J. B. Lippincott Co., Philadelphia, 1924, pp. 134, 143.)

²³ Karl Renner, *Marxismus, Krieg und Internationale* (Verlag J.H.W. Dietz, Stuttgart, 1917, p. 161). Of Europe, Herbert A. Miller's observation on pp. 181 and 186 of the above-mentioned work is true : " There is no concept of our times more in need of revision and clarification than that of patriotism. . . . The nation is a growth from innumerable simpler forms, and the growth to internationalism relatively hardly more complex than the growth of nationalism. . . . One of the greatest obstacles to truth and progress is the preaching of a hundred per cent patriotism. Reality demands that we begin to advocate ten to twenty-five per cent patriotism. The 75 to 90 per cent of loyalty that is left belongs to values on our life that are international rather than national. When we get this awareness of vital international interest, it will be as easy to enlarge the emotion of patriotism from its present artificial limits, as it was to get to its present national character from the groups which preceded the present state. If we can stop the immoral and untrue limitation of the area within which loyalty is cultivated we shall eventually find ourselves loyal to international interests which are vital to national life in the same way that we have found national values significant in community life."

²⁴ Guido Crolla in *Oriento Moderno* (Rome, I year, pp. 522, 533) : " There are but few methods in colonial policy, and they recur again and again. As soon as a country wants to extend its influence, it begins to seek support in some social or political section and to link its own interests with those of that section. Whilst skilfully supporting this section against their rivals and supporting their demands, it persuades them that it is acting disinterestedly and only wishes for their welfare. Meanwhile every step taken by this section to win the rights that they desire for themselves is also a step towards colonial penetration by the foreign State and in its interest. But though this is the colonial policy of all ages and all countries, it is not without its dangers. Too numerous favours granted too openly to one section of the population may lay bare the yoke of the colonizing nation and call forth an outbreak of universal scorn."

²⁵ Cyprus complains that she is too heavily burdened financially in the interests of the British Treasury or British officials. Thus

the Memorandum states that with a Budget of £735,000 the expenditure on administration amounts to 57 per cent, and 47 per cent—that is nearly half of the total—goes in salaries. Since 1878 the island has paid a tribute of £92,800 towards the Ottoman debt. As this sum was far too large for Cyprus, the British Treasury made a contribution, fixed in 1907 at £50,000 annually. Of the £92,800, £81,000 was used to pay interest on the English loan to Turkey of 1855 and £11,000 deposited in the Bank of England. Even after England annexed the island in 1914, Cyprus continued to pay the tribute, now no longer properly due, till 1927, when England undertook to make this sum her contribution towards Cyprus's revenue on condition that the Legislative Council voted an annual sum of £10,000 for imperial defence. Cyprus demanded the repayment of the £556,000 which she had paid between 1914 and 1927, and of the £452,000 lying in the Bank of England, credited to a separate account.

[26] *The Near East and India* (London, November 21st, 1929) observed that, as soon as the Cypriot Greeks make up their minds to postpone their demand for union with Greece for some twenty years, " the case for a constitutional change and administrative reforms in Cyprus becomes overwhelming."

[27] The country is poor, mountainous, with little mineral wealth, and a very low standard of life. A certain increase in industrial activity in recent years is shown in the growth of imports and exports :—

Year.	Imports.	Exports.
1913	£619,337	£620,591
1926	£1,570,278	£1,103,571
1929	£1,983,873	£1,635,736

Great Britain occupies the most important place both in regard to imports and exports. In 1928, 44 per cent of the imports came from the British Empire.

The Government's finances are developing equally prosperously :—

Year.	Revenue.	Expenditure.
1913–14	£341,816	£296,165
1924	£593,318	£535,870
1928	£713,753	£679,980

(These figures do not include the tribute, nor the British Government subsidy.) At the end of 1928 the Cypriot National Debt amounted to only £174,107, at a very low rate of interest.

The only two industries of economic importance in Cyprus are silk culture, in which it is the second most important territory in the British Empire, and mining, both of iron ore containing copper, and asbestos. There are also small industries of merely local importance.

[28] There are no troops in Cyprus. Order is maintained by a military police force of 746 men and a country police force of 792 men ; both are indigenous and only the highest commands are filled by Englishmen. The strategic importance of Cyprus was emphasized in the Sykes-Picot Agreement (Letter from M. Cambon to Sir Edward Grey dated May 9th, 1916) and even more so in the Anglo-French Agreement of December 23rd, 1920 (Cmd. 1195, 1921). Article 4 of the latter reads : " In virtue of the geographic and strategic position of the island of Cyprus, off the Gulf of Alexandretta, the British Government agrees not to open any negotiations for the cession or alienation of the said island of Cyprus without the previous consent of the French Government."

[29] Until 1929, education in Cyprus was exclusively under the autonomous control of national or religious groups. Under this system the provision for education was not unsatisfactory. Although it is not compulsory, 47,650 children out of 64,000 between the ages of 6 and 12 attended school. Of the remaining 16,000 some 12,000 were girls, so that amongst boys universal school attendance was practically attained. In 1928, there were 695 Greek primary schools and 262 Turkish in Cyprus. Of a total expenditure of £104,810 the Government contributed £59,000 and the rest was raised by the autonomous bodies. The two Turkish and six Greek secondary schools were also completely under the control of the autonomous groups.

[30] On this whole question see the very informative article by Michael Freund, " England in Aegypten " in Zeitschrift für Politik (Berlin, vol. xix, pp. 743 ff.). This article is an important contribution to the study of the structure of the British Empire.

[31] " Thus the revolutionary instinct of the Polish workers, as of all workers in an oppressed nation, drives them to a naive nationalism." (Otto Bauer, Die Nationalitätenfrage und die Sozialdemokratie, 2nd edition, Wiener Volksbuchhandlung, Vienna, 1924, p. 452.)

[32] On the rise of the nationalist movement in Egypt see chap. vii of my History of the Nationalist Movement in the East and George Young's Egypt (Ernest Benn, London, 1927). After the first flicker under Arabi Pasha in 1881–2, which was speedily quenched, the first beginnings of a nationalist movement were among the urban intelligentsia under the leadership of Mustafa Kemal about the turning of the century. It was not till 1918, under the leadership of Saad Zaghlul, that it became a mass movement embracing the whole Egyptian people. Not till the first decade of the twentieth century was there any conscious Arabian nationalist movement. It is worth noting that from the very outset this movement made the unity of the whole of Arabia its aim and that it included both the Syrian Arabs who were subject to Western influence and the princes of the peninsula. On this subject see chap. ix of my History of the Nationalist Movement in the East, and also Martin Hartmann, " Das neue Arabien " in Beiträge des Kenntnis des Orients (Jahrbuch der Münchner Orientalischen Gesellschaft, 1904–5, vol. ii, pp. 88 ff.), and his book Die Arabische Frage (1909) ; further, Franz Stuhlmann, Der Kampf um Arabien zwischen der Türkei und England (Verlag Georg Westermann, Brunswick, 1916), and Richard Hartmann, Die arabische Frage und das türkische Reich (reprinted from Beiträge zur Kenntnis des Orients, Jahrbücher der Deutschen Vorderasien Gesellschaft, vol. xv, Verlag Gebauer-Schwetschke, Halle a.d.S., 1919). Martin Hartmann wrote in 1905, just when the new Arabian League had issued its first appeals in Syria and Palestine and when the dream of a modern Pan-Arabian empire first began to take shape as a political programme. Amongst the Arab princes at that time Imam Yehya of Yemen, who had just risen to power, then seemed the chosen welder of Arab unity. On the strength and importance of the Arabian nationalist movement both in the peninsula and on the Mediterranean coast see the above-mentioned book by Richard Hartmann, pp. 25 and 26 : " It is obvious that all these divergent elements (the various princes and parties in the Arabian countries) could not find support for their particularist interests anywhere among the Arab people. They were, therefore, obliged to conceal them under the cloak of an idea that had power

of attraction. The very fact that it was chosen as the most effective cloak proves that it does attract, and that there is a widespread Arab national sentiment with power to unite across the barriers of religious creeds. In the Arabian East, too, the age of definite national consciousness has dawned, and that not only in the most progressive regions, but for the whole Arabic-speaking area. When even the autocratic princes of Northern Arabia approach the idea of uniting all Arab lands, perhaps in the form of a federation, that proves that the idea of an Arab nation is already penetrating the peninsula. And that plainly means that the solution of the territorial problems of the country, which are always liable to swell to worldwide proportions because of its geographical relation to world communications, can no longer be sought simply with a view to the interests of the great cosmopolitan commercial Powers, but that the problem must be regarded as a whole, one of the complex of questions concerning Arab nationalities." These words describe the position in 1914. Since then national consciousness has advanced to a degree hitherto undreamed of, both in scope and intensity, in Arabia as elsewhere in the East.

[33] On the subject of England's imperialism and the social and cultural conditions on which it is based, see the fine writings of Schulze-Gaevernitz ; also my article " England, beim Abschied von England " in the *Weltbühne* (Berlin, December 1st, 1925) concluding : " Many people to-day talk of the dissolution of the British Empire. That may come about. But it would not involve the cessation of English influence. England is not Rome. Her own civilization and her virility have not been enfeebled and finally destroyed by the process of empire-building, but strengthened and confirmed in their individual character. Canada or Australia may detach themselves from the British Empire ; they will always need to look to England in order to preserve what is best in themselves. The same is true in a lesser degree of India, and England's other possessions. In her political traditions, which likewise influence daily life, there are elements of a conception of freedom and respect for human dignity without which the evolution of mankind can now no longer be imagined. The scheme of a Pan-Europe without England and Russia would not only involve political dangers but would endanger cultural and intellectual development, if the federation pursued a policy of opposition to England and Russia, instead of seeking their co-operation. It is not only that England and Russia form to-day connecting links with the great Anglo-Saxon and Asiatic worlds and present wide vistas to a Europe internally rent and suffering, but the English and Russians are the two peoples, both living on the borders of Europe, through whom, in different ways, Europe (and other continents) may be spiritually and politically resuscitated and renewed." See also my article " The Fabians " in *Zeitschrift für Politik* (Berlin, vol. xviii, pp. 663 ff.).

[34] On these imperialist methods, which he describes in detail, Richard Schmidt writes in his article on " Die Zukunft des modernen Imperialismus " in *Zeitschrift für Politik* (vol. xviii, pp. 368 ff.) : " It has long been observable how the people in their resolve to win self-determination are checked and defeated at every advance by English and French imperialism ; and the reasons are clear enough. On the one hand, the people are divided ; their united demand for political emancipation and activity is obstructed by differences of class, religion,

and locality ; on the other hand there is the superior power of the dominating State, which makes the most of these domestic complications and seizes every opportunity to postpone the collapse of its selfish domination." In this connection Schmidt then proceeds to a brief criticism of the mandatory system which he regards as an expedient for the defence of the old and customary imperialist traditions.

[35] On the subject of the Armenian problem after the World War see André N. Mandelstam, *La Société des Nations et les Puissances devant la Probleme Arménien* (A. Pedone, Paris, 1925) and Fridtjof Nansen, *Betrogenes Volk* (Verlag F. A. Brockhaus, Leipzig, 1928). See also the admirable periodical *Der Orient. Die religiösen und profanen Lebensmächte des Ostens* (published by Dr. Lepsius' Deutsche Orient-Mission, Potsdam).

[36] Martin Hartmann in his *Arabic Press of Egypt* (Luzac & Co., London, 1899) observes on p. 30, " The Copts, although Christians, are much nearer akin to the Islamic inhabitants of Egypt than to their Syrian co-religionists. Incredible as it may appear, it is nevertheless true, that when the English, upon their occupation of the country, looked for support among the native Christians, the Copts neglected the opportunity and sided with their oppressors (i.e. the Egyptian Mohammedans) with whom they were much more congenial in thought, disposition, and mode of living than with any other nation, and more particularly Europeans." About 1910 it was indeed found possible to create antagonism between Copts and Mohammedans in Egypt. But since the World War the Copts have fought side by side with the Mohammedans in the nationalist movement, and Copts have been among its intellectual leaders. In the delegation that represented Egypt in the negotiations in London in the spring of 1930 two of the four members were Copts, Makram Ebeid, Secretary General of the Wafd, and Wassif Ghali Pasha, the Minister of Foreign Affairs in every Wafd Ministry hitherto ; the latter is not only a Copt and a pupil of the Jesuits, but also the son of the Copt Prime Minister, Butros Ghali Pasha, who was so bitterly hated in Egypt that in February, 1910, he was assassinated by a Mohammedan student. It is significant that among the four reserved points in the declaration of Egyptian independence of 1922 England has included the protection of minorities. To this the Copts have retorted unanimously at a meeting of their leaders in St. Peter's Church in Cairo on May 20th, 1922, that they renounce all minority representation and minority protection in the interest of national unity and the attainment of the national aim. The remarkable text of this resolution is reprinted in *Oriento Moderno* (II year, p. 44). The electoral law for the Egyptian Legislative Assembly drafted by the English before the War provided for Copt minority representation. It is significant that *The Near East* (London, June 8th, 1922) criticized the action of the Copts adversely.

[37] " We have taken advantage of the ignorance, economic innocence and the greed of individual Mexicans and have gone into their country buying vast areas of rich land for a song and then assumed a hateful air of self-satisfied superiority. We are surprised that the Mexicans despise us when we are so much better than they are, and when their hatred engendered by both the past and the present becomes aggressive, many of us advocate taking our advanced civilisation and order into Mexico by means of military force." Herbert A. Miller, op. cit., p. 125. See also Scott Nearing and Joseph Freeman, *Dollar Diplomacy : A Study in American Imperialism* (Huebsch, New York, 1926).

[38] Detailed accounts of the various treaties and promises made by the Powers to the Arabs may be found in Erich Topf, *Die Staatenbildungen in den arabischen Teilen der Türkei, etc.*, pp. 12–23, and in J. de V. Loder, *The Truth about Mesopotamia, Palestine and Syria* (London, 1923, pp. 17–23). On p. 29, Topf writes : " A factor of decisive importance in Eastern politics in addition to . . . is the growing intensity of Arab nationalist sentiment which has been of the utmost importance precisely in the development of Arab States. The fact, speedily and widely realized, that they had simply exchanged a Turkish for an English or French overlord inspired the whole Arab population— Christian and Mohammedan—with profound indignation against the foreign Powers." On the subject of the impression made by the Franco-British declarations on war aims, see the *Review of the Civil Administration of Mesopotamia* (Cmd. 1061, 1920, pp. 126 ff.).

[39] Ernst Reinhard reaches similar conclusions in dwelling on the terminology of Social Democracy in his *Kampf um Suez* (Verlag Kaden and Co., Dresden, 1930). If the League of Nations were to be enlarged to a community really embracing the Eastern peoples, it might win recognition in the East. Hitherto it and also the Permanent Mandates Commission have been regarded simply as a tool to serve the interests of the European Powers. It is of interest that the progressive changes carried out, for instance, by Great Britain in Iraq originated with Great Britain and not with the League of Nations. Moreover, the Permanent Mandates Commission of the League is only entitled to test the application of the terms of the mandates, against which the people of the mandated territories have never ceased to protest, but not whether they themselves are in harmony with the spirit of the mandatory system. Replying to a protest by the population of a mandated territory, Marquis Theodoli, the Chairman of the Mandates Commission, declared on October 30th, 1924, according to a communiqué of the Information Bureau : " A cette occasion, le Président a fait observer que la Commission des Mandats est chargée de veiller à l'application des termes des mandats tels qu'ils ont été arrêtés par le Conseil de la Société des Nations et que la question de savoir si ces termes correspondent à la lettre et à l'esprit de l'article 22 du Pacte dépasse la competence de la Commission." The attitude of the Mandates Commission is influenced partly by its unilateral composition, and also partly by the biassed material which is laid before it verbally and in writing. The Mandates Commission consists solely of representatives of the ruling race, mainly of former colonial Governors and high officials. It would be a great gain if its numbers included, say, an Indian, a Persian, a negro, and a Maori, representatives of races whose experience is not that of colonizing but of undergoing colonization.

CHAPTER V

[40] " King Fuad—remembering the autocratic powers enjoyed by his ancestor, Mehmed Ali, and by successive members of the dynasty down to the deposition of his father, the Khedive Ismail, in 1879, and unmindful of the fate which has recently overtaken autocratic rulers in neighbouring Islamic countries who had sought to stem the tide of democratic ideas flowing in from the West—had not reconciled himself to exchanging the role of a British nominee for that of an Egyptian constitutional monarch." (Arnold J. Toynbee, *The Islamic World since the Peace Settlement*, p. 226). See also the incomparably harsher

account of the relation between king and people in Egypt given by Mme. B. G. Gaulis in *Le Nationalisme Égyptien* (Editions Berger-Levrault, Nancy, 1928).

⁴¹ Arnold J. Toynbee, op. cit., pp. 195, 212, where he proceeds : "That which one unilateral act of the British Government had established, another might undo, if serious provocation were given on the Egyptian side or if other new elements were introduced into the situation." E. W. Polson Newman writes in *Great Britain in Egypt* (Cassell & Co., 1928) : "The establishment of Egyptian independence in 1922 was merely carrying our policy of unreality one stage further, and the change from a Protectorate to an Independent Monarchy was mainly superficial. Although the elevation of the title of Egypt's ruler from Sultan to that of King pleased the Palace clique and a small section of the official classes, the great majority, whose susceptibilities lay in other directions, were far from pacified by this measure. They clearly saw that as far as fundamental considerations were concerned, in which their national pride was at stake, the position was in no way altered. . . . Hence the Declaration of 1922 was far from being a solution of the Egyptian question."

⁴² The Nationalist or Patriotic party (the Arabic name for the party comes from the word *Watan*, fatherland, nation) was founded on October 22nd, 1907, by Mustafa Kemal. It was also favourable to Pan-Islamism and faithful to the Ottoman Caliphate. In recent years it has steadily lost influence. The Liberal Constitutional party was founded on October 29th, 1922, by Adli Yeghen Pasha, but he no longer belongs to it and may, like the late Sarwat Pasha, be regarded as non-party. The party's organ is the daily *Siyassah*, edited by Mohammed Hussein Haikal Bey, and, especially in its weekly edition which has been appearing since 1926, it is liberal and progressive on cultural and religious questions. The weekly edition has developed into an important cultural and literary organ of opinion. The fourth or Union party (the Arabic word is *Ittihad*) was founded on January 10th, 1925. Its President was Yahya Ibrahim Pasha, the President of the Commission that drafted the Egyptian constitution. In addition to the dailies the satirical comic journals attached to the parties play a great part in Egypt. Egypt's two largest and oldest. dailies, *El Ahram* (founded in 1876) and *El Mokattam* (founded in 1889), edited respectively by Dr. Faris Nimr and Dr. Jacob Sarruf, were both started and edited by Syrians, and are non-party informative papers which usually support the Government. Before the War *Mokattam* was markedly pro-English and *Ahram* pro-French.

⁴³ On the Egyptian constitution see George Kampffmeyer in *Mitteilungen des Seminars für orientalische Sprachen* (Berlin, xxvi and xxvii year, second section, Western Asian Studies) ; also Amedeo Giannini : " Gli albori costituzionali in Egitto " (*Oriento Moderno*, Rome, vol. 3, pp. 329 ff.), and " La costituzione egiziana " by the same author (ibid., pp. 1 ff.) ; the text of the Egyptian constitution, ibid., p. 24 ; the text of the electoral law of April 30th, 1923, ibid., p. 66. The next two Egyptian electoral laws, ibid., vol. 4, pp. 535 ff. (that of July 29th, 1924) and ibid., vol. 6, p. 66 (that of December 8th, 1925). A characteristic debate arose about Article 13. Article 149 declares that Islam is the State religion and Arabic the official language. Now Article 13 declares that the State will protect the free exercise of every religion in so far as it does not prejudice the public safety and good morals. A protest was raised by the orthodox Mohammedans, which

was met by inserting the very vague words " in accordance with known customs in Egypt ".

Many observers have thought that the Egyptian Parliament has done good work and that it can well stand comparison with European Parliaments. The calm and discipline of the proceedings is mainly due to Zaghlul Pasha's training in his position as President of the Chamber. In spite of the short time that Parliament was allowed to work undisturbed and the fact that during that time it was occupied with foreign conflicts, it nevertheless made good progress in education, in breathing life into local self-government, in labour legislation, in establishing agricultural co-operative societies and an Agricultural Bank, in improving the lot of the fellaheen, and in taxation and public health ; it endeavoured in particular to bring about improvements in popular education which had been neglected by the administration for forty years. See, too, the view expressed by P. G. Elgood in *The Transit of Egypt* (Edward Arnold & Co., London, 1928, pp. 306–8). The opinion of a supporter of the Wafd deserves notice (*La Patrie*, Cairo, August 11th, 1930) : " One of the blessings of the parliamentary system, in our eyes the greatest, is the liberation of the people in the provinces from the yoke of the feudal lords, who have been free to exploit them with impunity for many years."

[44] On the problem of the Sudan see M. Travers Symons, *Britain and Egypt : The Rise of Egyptian Nationalism* (Cecil Palmer, London, 1925, pp. 131–238). The chief financial burden of the administration of the Sudan fell upon Egypt. The cost of reconquering the Sudan, in which Egyptian troops under British command distinguished themselves, was £E 2,354,000. Of this Great Britain bore £E 800,000 and the Egyptians the remainder. In the succeeding years, until 1913, the Sudan Budget showed a deficit, which was covered by Egypt, Egypt likewise bearing the cost of the Egyptian occupation of the Sudan. Up to 1913 Egypt had contributed £E 5,198,700 to cover the Sudan deficit. The Egyptian occupying army in the Sudan cost the Egyptian Treasury over a million pounds annually, whilst the cost to Great Britain was only £200,000 annually. In addition to this Egypt paid to the Sudan Government for public works in the years 1901 to 1909 alone £E 4,378,000. Lord Curzon stated in the British House of Lords on June 25th, 1924 : " The Sudan would be bankrupt at the moment if it were not for the financial expenditure undertaken by Egypt. If you go to the point of saying that Egypt has no connection with the Sudan at all except that of water, and you eliminate Egypt from any voice or share in the administration at all, the Sudan would be quite unable in the existing conditions, to pay its own way (*Hansard*, House of Lords, June 25th, 1924, Col. 990). See, too, Arnold J. Toynbee, op. cit., pp. 240–1.

[45] Toynbee writes (op. cit., p. 243) : " Englishmen tended to regard the well-governed Sudan of the twentieth century as their exclusive creation and therefore their exclusive affair, to minimize the quantitatively greater . . . contributions which Egypt had made to this achievement, to ignore the vital economic interest of Egypt in the Upper Nile Basin . . . and to push aside Egypt's historical title. Thus Englishmen were as deeply shocked when the Egyptian claim was presented in a militant form, as Egyptians were when they found this claim dismissed off-hand by Englishmen as preposterous. All the elements of misunderstanding and bitterness existed on both sides in 1919, and in five years they combined to

produce violent and tragic consequences." In Egypt a League of Union with the Sudan was formed in 1924. *Oriento Moderno* (iv year, p. 560) publishes a characteristic appeal by this society.

⁴⁶ The Egyptian officials immediately responsible for the murder of the English Sirdar were Englishmen, the Chief of Police in Cairo and Director-General of the European Department of Public Safety. It is certain that the Wafd regarded this murder as an attack made upon itself. See also the account in the above-mentioned book of B. G. Gaulis.

⁴⁷ Cotton growing in the Sudan is already of very long standing. There was a highly developed cotton export industry in the Sudan in the seventeenth and eighteenth centuries. The Egyptians introduced modern methods of cotton cultivation immediately after their conquest of the Sudan in the nineteenth century. In 1913 the English began the execution of the great scheme of development in Gezira, the, triangle formed by the confluence of the White and Blue Nile. The area of Gezira is estimated as five million feddans, of which three million are capable of irrigation. In 1919 the Sudan Plantation Syndicate concluded an agreement with the British Government for the cultivation of 300,000 feddans. The British Government granted loans to the amount of £E 13,000,000. See the British White Book (Cmd. 2171 (Sudan No. 1), London, 1924 : *Correspondence respecting the Gezira Irrigation Project*). See also the *Reports on the Finances, Administration, and Condition of the Sudan in 1923 and 1924* (Cmd. 2281, 1924, and 2544, 1925). The Egyptian Government demanded control of all irrigation in the Nile Valley and the precedence of Egypt's needs over those of the Sudan. Sir W. Garstein had already advocated the same principle in his report in 1904. The important passage is reprinted in Toynbee, op. cit., p. 263, note 1. The British Government did not adhere to it. The Sudan is of importance as the chief source of supply of gum-arabic and ivory, as well as for its cotton. Exports from the Sudan amounted in 1928 to £E 5,634,769, of which £E 4,188,354 went to Great Britain. Imports amounted to £E 6,463,206, and of these Great Britain, occupying the first place, supplied £E 2,250,247. The Sudan Budget balanced and expenditure amounted in 1929 to £E 6,451,000. Compared with this economic advance, the backwardness of education is striking. For some five and a half million inhabitants there are only eighty-one traditional indigenous primary schools with 8,022 scholars, and ten modern primary schools with 1,302 scholars. There are only twenty girls' schools in all with rather less than 1,400 pupils. The Gordon College has 502 students. Here, too, secondary education is relatively in advance of primary. There are in addition 589 native schools under Government control with 17,280 boys.

⁴⁸ On the subject of Mohammed Mahmud Pasha see Elgood, op. cit., pp. 262 ff.

⁴⁹ On the subject of the newly established Egyptian University, see *Oriento Moderno* (vii year, p. 627).

⁵⁰ Lord Lloyd demanded the appointment of Spinks Pasha as Inspector-General of the Egyptian Army, with the right of supervising, appointing, and promoting Egyptian officers ; also the appointment of an English officer as deputy to Spinks Pasha and of an Englishman as Commander of Frontiers and Coasts.

⁵¹ After his return the American Minister, Dr. J. Morton Howell, published a book about his experiences in Egypt : *Egypt's Past,*

Present, and Future (Service Publishing Company, Dayton, Ohio, 1929). It is full of interesting information about the most recent events in Egypt, and, moreover, condemns the system of capitulations. In 1929 the Dictatorship forbade the importation and sale of the book in Egypt.

[52] After Zaghlul's death the Egyptian Government received telegrams of condolence from all parts of the East, including one from King Ibn Saud, who said that " the loss was not only a severe blow to Egypt but to the whole East ". Zaghlul was born in a little village in the province of Gharbiya in Lower Egypt, probably in 1850. He first attended the village school, then the mosque school in the chief town of the district, Dasuk, not far away, and finally the theological university of El Azhar, where he studied for five years and came under the influence of Jemal ud Din el Afghani and those around him who first roused Egypt's national consciousness from its slumber. In 1881 he was appointed editor of the literary pages of the official Gazette. In his articles he attacked absolutism. In 1882 he was appointed Assistant in the Ministry of the Interior and took part in Arabi Pasha's movement. After its suppression he devoted himself to the profession of advocate, studied French and other European languages, and was appointed Councillor in the Court of Appeal in 1892. He pressed for the introduction of better educational methods and the spread of elementary schooling in Egypt, and in 1907 he became Minister of Education, and later Minister of Justice. In 1913 he resigned his offices, as he was opposed to the project for a Legislative Council and demanded the introduction of a democratic parliamentary system. He declared that it was better to have no Parliament at all than a sham Parliament. In November, 1918, he went to the British High Commissioner with Ali Sharavi Pasha and Abdel Asis Fahmi as a delegation to demand the country's independence. That was the beginning of the history of the Wafd. On Zaghlul's great achievement as President of the Chamber, see Elgood, op. cit., p. 303.

[53] Mustafa Nahas was born in 1879 in the same province as Zaghlul Pasha. He had studied at the Cairo School of Law and till 1919 he was a judge. He resigned his office in order to be able to devote himself to politics. In 1921 he was deported with Zaghlul and returned with him in 1923. He was Minister of Transport in Zaghlul's Government. After the fall of the Government he returned to his profession of advocate and secured the acquittal of Mahmud Fahmi Nakrashi and Ahmed Mahir in the trial following the murder of Sir Lee Stack. He then became second Vice-President of the Chamber under Zaghlul. In November 17th, 1927, he was elected to succeed Zaghlul as President of the Chamber.

[54] On the negotiations of 1927 and the draft treaty, see *Papers regarding Negotiations for a Treaty of Alliance with Egypt* (Egypt No. 1, London, 1928, Cmd. 3050). The two passages quoted in the text are on pp. 17 and 52. The Egyptian official publication (Green Book) supplies important supplementary information : *Documents Diplomatiques Relatifs aux Conversations de Saroit Pacha avec Sir Austen Chamberlain en vue d'établir des bases à des negotiations officielles, pour la conclusion d'un traité d'alliance et d'amitié entre la Grande Bretagne et l'Egypte* (Royaume d'Egypte, No. 1 de 1928). See in particular Sarwat Pasha's important prefatory exposé. Sarwat Pasha's statement (p. 52 of the English White Book) is interesting that " the League of Nations meant nothing to him or to Egypt ". This remark of

one who is among the most friendly to Europe among Eastern statesmen is characteristic of the small respect in which the League of
Nations is held in the East. With regard to the negotiations, the
draft treaty, and the subsequent events, see Mustafa Nahas Pasha's
great speech on November 13th, 1928, which has been printed without
mention of the printer : *Dixième Anniversaire du 13 Novembre 1918.
Discours prononcé par S. E. Moustapha El Nahas Pacha à la cérémonie
du 13 Novembre 1928* (36 pages).

⁵⁵ On the subject of the Anglo-Egyptian Agreement on the Nile
water concluded by Mohammed Mahmud, see *Oriento Moderno* (ix year,
pp. 229 ff.). This agreement of May 7th, 1929, made concessions to
Great Britain such as Egypt had never made even during the period
of British dominion. Whereas formerly the Egyptian Ministry of
Public Works had control of the Nile in Egypt and in the Sudan, the
management of irrigation in the Sudan was now left in Great Britain's
hands and Egypt retained only nominal control over the measuring
of the water. Further, the Sudanese Government obtained the right
to carry out irrigation schemes independent of the Egyptian Ministry.

⁵⁶ On the negotiations between Henderson and Mohammed Mahmud
in 1929, see Michael Freund in *Zeitschrift für Politik* (vol. xix, pp. 743 ff.).
The text of the draft treaty is in a British White Paper (Cmd. 3376,
1929). Compare also Mohammed Mahmud's Egyptian Green Book
on the negotiations of 1929. See *Oriento Moderno* (ix year, pp. 573 ff.).
The treaty provided for complete equality of rights between the
contracting parties and changed what had been in part unilateral
obligations on Egypt's part into mutual obligations of both parties.
Both were equally bound to adapt their foreign and military policy
to the common interest. Egypt also secured the right to be represented
at the British Court by an ambassador. British troops were to be
withdrawn to the Canal Zone. The British officers were to retire
from the Egyptian army. English officials were only to be engaged
in the Egyptian urban police force for five years longer.

⁵⁷ The Agricultural Bank was to make loans for seedtime and
harvest, for the purchase of machinery and animals, and to help bring
about a more intensive cultivation ; it was to grant loans to agricultural co-operative societies and to sell seed and manure to the
fellaheen. Its share capital was to be two million pounds, of which
the Government was prepared to take up one half and to guarantee
a fixed rate of interest on the remainder. The Government was also
prepared to grant the bank credit to the amount of six million pounds.
It reserved to itself a corresponding influence upon the management
of the bank, and granted it certain privileges in relation to outstanding
debts and their collection, and freedom from taxation.

In 1930 new life was breathed into the Provincial Assemblies,
which lightened the burden of labour upon Parliament. The Provincial
Councils had begun their activities in 1910. The following facts
indicate their progress. In 1910 the Provincial Council of Menufiya
in Lower Egypt had not a single school or hospital. At that date its
expenditure was about £E 18,000. In 1930 it had reached £E 144,000
and the Council had 63 boys' primary schools, 14 girls' primary schools,
8 higher elementary schools (including one for girls), an orphanage,
a training school for midwives, a number of hospitals and clinics, a
large provincial library, two training colleges for men and women
teachers, and an agricultural college. The rate of advance has been
specially remarkable since 1924.

It is worth noting that in more than forty years of English administration hardly anything had been done for primary education, nor for the improvement of sanitary and social conditions in the villages. In 1917 a Commission on Public Health in Egypt reported on the state of affairs in the country. Since 1924 serious efforts have been made to improve matters. So, too, the development of the Banque Misr, with its purely Egyptian share capital of £E 1,000,000, founded on May 7th, 1920, bears witness to Egyptian initiative. See *Oriento Moderno* (x year, p. 125).

[58] On the negotiations between Henderson and Mustafa Nahas see the British White Book (Cmd. 3573) of May 22nd, 1930. Nahas Pasha secured a number of improvements on the original Henderson draft. Thus the duration of the treaty was reduced from twenty-five to twenty years, the posts of Financial and Judicial Advisers in the Egyptian Ministry were to be abolished with the expiry of the existing contracts, and the British troops, with a fixed maximum strength, were to remain stationed at Ismailia on the Suez Canal only until the Egyptian army was able to undertake the defence of the Canal alone. The negotiations broke down on the question of the Sudan ; Egypt demanded a return to the position obtaining before 1924 while Great Britain, at the instance of the Sudanese Administration, refused the demand. The Egyptians also demanded the right of free immigration into the Sudan for Egyptian subjects. The English insisted that the condominium established in the treaty of 1899 had actually been abolished and that the Sudan was under purely British administration. That the Egyptians would not sanction.

THE MANDATES

[59] Until 1918 Syria included (see A. Ruppin, *Syrien als Wirtschaftsgebiet*, pp. 7–10) the vilayet of Aleppo ; the vilayet of Damascus which was divided into four districts (*Mutessariflik*), Damascus (with the districts of Beqa, Baalbek, Hasbeya, and Rasheya which were later attached to Great Lebanon), Hama, Hauran (with the Jebel ed Druz and the northern part of what is now Trans-Jordan), and El Kerak embracing the central and southern parts of what is now Trans-Jordan ; and the vilayet of Beirut embracing what is now northern Palestine (Samaria and Galilee), and the coastal regions which to-day form part of Great Lebanon or the Territory of the Alawis. The vilayet of Beirut was divided into the districts of Beirut, Tripoli, Latakia, Acre, and Nablus. In addition to these three vilayets there were also two independent *Mutessariflik*—Lebanon, embracing the Lebanon mountains proper and enjoying, from 1861 to 1916, a large measure of autonomy, and Jerusalem, embracing Judæa, the southern part of what is now Palestine. The frontier between the French mandated territory of Syria and Palestine under British mandate was drawn in two treaties ; Cmd. 1195, 1921, and Cmd. 1910, 1923.

[60] Lebanese Christians, and even Maronites, have frequently advocated Syro-Arabian unity, and have been among the pillars of the Arabian and Syrian union movement. Amongst the intellectual leaders of Christian Lebanon who have been pioneers of Syro-Arabian unity including Lebanon, we may mention Khairalla Khairalla, who wrote in his book *Les Regions arabes liberées* (1919) : " The Arabic speaking people in Lebanon, in Syria, in Palestine, in Mesopotamia, and, indeed, over almost the whole extent of the Arabian peninsula,

are moving towards a twofold ideal : unity and independence. If Lebanon, for reasons beyond its own control, is condemned for a time to a certain isolation, the same is not true of Syria and Palestine . . ." The same may be said of Ameen Rihani. About him see Richard Hartmann in *Der Islam*, vol. xviii, No. 3–4, pp. 255–62. During the War, L'Alliance Libanaise d'Egypte, consisting of Christians, was overwhelmingly in favour of the union of Lebanon with the rest of Syria and supported the Pan-Arabian aspirations of the Sherif of Mecca. Especially the President of the Alliance, Iskandar Bey Ammun, took a prominent part in the movement. Under its second President also, August Adib Pasha, the Alliance assumed an anti-French and Pan-Arabian attitude after 1917. Amongst the Maronite leaders Shekri Ganem and the Maronite Patriarch Hoyek opposed Syrian union, the former because he wanted to incorporate Lebanon in the world of Western civilization, the second for religious reasons. It is significant that after Ganem's death in 1930 the Lebanese Chamber declared itself opposed to his view, and that at the same time a strong party of Arabian unity made its appearance amongst the higher ranks of the Maronite clergy. On co-operation between the Hejaz and Syria see *Memories of a Turkish Statesman, 1913–1919*, by Djemal Pasha (Hutchinson, London), pp. 197 ff.

[61] S. H. L. Hoskins, *British Routes to India* (Longmans, London, 1928). In 464 pages the book gives a detailed history of the British policy of imperial communications via Suez and through Hither Asia.

[62] On the Orthodox Church in Palestine see Sir A. Bertram and J. W. A. Young, *The Orthodox Patriarchate of Jerusalem* (Humphrey Milford, London, 1926). Whilst the Patriarchate was in the hands of Greek clergy, the laity, consisting of radical Arab nationalists, were hostile to the Patriarchate and demanded that it should become Arab in character. On this subject see the London *Times* of July 23rd, 1923, and the reports of the first Arab Orthodox Congress held in Haifa from July 15th to 18th, 1923 (*Oriento Moderno*, iii year, pp. 166–169). The Congress demanded that the clergy should become Arab in character and that the whole administration of the Patriarchate should be transferred to the hands of a lay democracy.

[63] The Paris *Temps* wrote in a telegram of January 15th, 1926, referring to the task of the French High Commissioner in Syria : " M. de Jouvenal's duty is clearly marked out : to divide in order to rule. The division is there. The rule begins."

[64] The close relations between the Arabs of the British and French mandated territories were repeatedly revealed. Thus the Palestinian Arabs organized two big sympathetic strikes at the time of the Syrian insurrection, whilst the inhabitants of Damascus gave Lord Balfour a hostile reception in April, 1925, which might easily have assumed dangerous proportions. Lord Melchett was met with a similar reception in Baghdad. During the Syrian insurrection the Syrians enjoyed active sympathy in all Arab countries, as did the Palestinian Arabs after the rising of August, 1929. These events found an echo in all Arab and Mohammedan countries, but particularly in Syria and Trans-Jordan. The French Government's report to the League of Nations on the position in Syria in 1929 states on p. 3 : " Syrian public opinion followed and discussed the events in Palestine in August with passionate interest. Opinion was eager in support of the Arabic speaking population of the neighbouring country, and on this occasion feeling was unanimous without distinction of religion or race, for in various Syrian

towns, and especially in Damascus, the representatives of the Jewish
community took part in the protest demonstrations against events
in Palestine." The British report to the League of Nations for 1929
(Colonial No. 47, 1930, p. 143) says of Trans-Jordan : " The close
connection between the Arabs of Palestine and Trans-Jordan . . .
aroused, on the outbreak of disorders in Palestine, a state of feeling
in Trans-Jordan which threatened a march under arms against the
Jewish population of Palestine. That this great danger was averted
. . . is due mainly to the attitude taken up by the Emir and his
Government who exerted all possible influence. . . ." See also the
report on Iraq for 1929 (Colonial No. 55, 1930, p. 24). Another sign
of the close connection between the Arab movements in Syria and
Palestine is the fact that their interests abroad are represented by a
common Syro-Palestinian Congress. The first congress met in Geneva on
September 1st, 1921, under the chairmanship of Emir Michael Lutfallah.
It demanded the cancellation of the mandates and the withdrawal
of French and English troops from Syria, Palestine, and Lebanon,
the recognition of the independence of those countries and their right
to unite under a parliamentary government and to ally themselves
with the other Arab States. The Congress elected an Executive
Committee with its seat in Cairo and a standing delegation in Geneva.

[65] Toynbee, op. cit., p. 387 : " As the Permanent Mandates
Commission itself pointed out (Minutes of the 5th Session, p. 188,
and of the 8th Session, p. 202–3) the opposition arose out of the
circumstances in which those two mandates (Syria and Palestine)
had been introduced. Notwithstanding certain declarations . . .
during the War and notwithstanding the terms of Article 22 of the
Covenant of the League of Nations, the paramount consideration in
the introduction of these mandates had not been to fulfil the aspirations,
or even to serve the best interests, of the majority of the population
in the territories concerned." And p. 391 : " The Syro-Palestinians
believed that the mandatories, realising that the majority of the
population was against them, had sought to bind certain minorities
to themselves by giving them a position of privilege and even dominance
over their neighbours which they could only hope to retain so long
as the mandatory Powers remained in the country."

[66] In Sir Herbert Samuel's Five Year Report (Colonial No. 15,
1925) he writes on p. 44 : " No attempt was made to control the
expression of opinion. Except for a few weeks after the disturbances
of 1921, there has been no censorship of the press. There have been
no political prosecutions, and no deportations, except of alien
communists, and one temporary expulsion of an Arab of little note in
1921." This state of affairs was only changed after August, 1929,
by the Criminal Law (Seditious Offences) Amendment Ordinance,
1929. Since then a number of newspapers have been temporarily
suspended.

CHAPTER VI

[67] An instructive article on the political history of Zionism from
1908 to 1914 is Ernst Simon's " Der Zionismus und die Jungtürken "
(*Jüdische Rundschau*, Berlin, December 24th, 1929). Zionist policy
sought to win whoever was for the time being suzerain of Palestine—
the Sultan, the Young Turks, England. Achad Haam, on the contrary,
observed as early as 1891 : " We abroad have a way of thinking that

292 NATIONALISM AND IMPERIALISM

Palestine to-day is almost desert, uncultivated wilderness, and that anyone who wishes to buy land there can do so to his heart's content. But that is not in fact the case. It is difficult to find any uncultivated land anywhere in the country. . . . We abroad have a way of thinking that the Arabs are all savages, on a level with the animals, and blind to what goes on around them. But that is quite mistaken. The Arabs, especially the townsmen, see through our activities in their country, and our aims, but they keep silence and make no sign, because for the present they anticipate no danger to their own future from what we are about. But if the time should ever come when our people have so far developed their life in Palestine that the indigenous population should feel more or less cramped, then they will not readily make way for us . . ." (*Am Scheidewege*, Jüdischer Verlag, Berlin, 1923, vol. i, pp. 86 ff.).

⁶⁸ The best account of Achad Haam's teaching, regarded from the point of view of political Zionism, is to be found in Moritz Bileski, *Achad Haam. Darstellung und Kritik seiner Lehren* (published by the Kartell Jüdischer Verbindungen, Berlin, 1916).

⁶⁹ In Zionism, as in the Messianic movements, there is a strong eschatological element, the hope of Geulah, of salvation in the Messianic era, the gathering of Israel's scattered children in the ancient kingdom as an independent State, and the rebuilding of the Temple. This religious phraseology influences the political ideas of some Zionists. But until the coming of the Messianic era the Jewish conception of religious duty is only to colonize the land (*Yishuv Haarez*) which " simply means the material and spiritual reinforcement of the Jewish population of Palestine, the promotion of Jewish immigration, and the raising of the country's standard of civilization, all within the bounds of what is practicable and permissible." See Rabbi Abraham Schlesinger in *Zion* (monthly organ of the headquarters of the *Deutscher Misrachi*, Berlin, August, 1930).

⁷⁰ J. Ramsay Macdonald, *A Socialist in Palestine* (published by the Jewish Socialist Labour Party, *Poale Zion*, London, 1922), p. 16 : " We encouraged an Arab revolt against Turkey by promising to create an Arab Kingdom including Palestine. At the same time we were encouraging the Jews to help us, by promising them that Palestine should be placed at their disposal for settlement and government and, also at the same time, we were secretly making with France the Sykes-Picot agreement partitioning the territory which we had instructed our Governor-General of Egypt to promise to the Arabs. The story is one of crude duplicity, and we cannot expect to escape the reprobation which is its proper sequel. No one who has felt the under-currents of Eastern movements can console himself with the belief that the Arab has forgotten or forgiven, or that the moral evil we committed will speedily cease to have political influence. Our treatment of the Moslems has been a madness." And p. 18 : " If the Balfour declaration of a Jewish national home is not only crude in its form, but impossible in its intention, we must bow to the inevitable and drop it ; but we must be quite certain of our ground before we come to any such conclusion."

⁷¹ See Reports of the Executive of the Zionist Organization to the Twelfth Zionist Congress. I. Political Report (National Labour Press, London, 1921), pp. 12, 22, 24, 30. The negotiations on the text of the mandate are recorded on pages 27 to 33. The Zionists demanded the recognition of their " historic right " and the right of the Jews to

restore Palestine as their National Home ; the English Government refused both demands, and for a time it wished to dispense altogether with the reference to the historic association in the preamble. For the territorial demands of the Zionist Organization, see pages 33 to 39. On the attitude of the British military administration in Palestine from 1917 to 1920, see pages 43 to 55.

[72] For Dr. Weizmann's speech see *The Zionist Bulletin*, issued by the Central Office of the Zionist Organization, London, August 26th, 1919. For a similar speech, ibid., September 9th, 1919. As a retort to him a speech of Israel Zangwill's (ibid., September 16th, 1919), in which he says : " Dr. Weizmann had not asked for a Jewish State. That was called tact, but it was really timidity. It was the abandonment of Zionism. He did not know what a ' Jewish National Home ' meant, if it did not mean a Jewish State." To this criticism Dr. Schmarya Levin answered : " He assured the meeting that the national appetite of the Zionist leader was no smaller than that of Mr. Zangwill. They all had but one aim ; the difference was only that of method." *The New Statesman* (London, September 20th, 1919) commented on Zangwill's speech : " We hope that the extreme Zionists will moderate their enthusiasm and realise that a ' national home for the Jewish people ' and a Jewish State are very different things. The one, with wise administration, will offer the fairest prospect for the Jews who yearn for it. The other will mean disaster for them and for all Western Asia."

[73] For the Colonial Office letter to the Palestine Arab Delegation of March 1st, 1922, see Cmd. 1700, pp. 6 ff. For the first report on the civil administration of Palestine, see Cmd. 1499, pp. 7 ff. For the answer to Cardinal Gasparri, see Cmd. 1708, pp. 4 ff. Sir Herbert Samuel stated before the Permanent Mandates Commission : " The underlying idea pursued by the (mandatory) Government (in Palestine) was that it should deal with the Arabs in regard to their possession of their land, their religion, their development generally, exactly as if no Balfour Declaration had been made at all " (Toynbee, op. cit., p. 404, note 2). See also W. Ormsby Gore's statement before the Mandates Commission on June 30th, 1924 (Minutes of the 4th Session, p. 87), and the speech by Amery, the Colonial Secretary, on April 21st, 1925, to the Palestinian Arabs. The double character of the Balfour Declaration is also emphasized by the Duke of Devonshire as Colonial Secretary in his letter on the formation of the Arab Agency (Cmd. 1989, p. 4). Balfour himself stated in the English House of Lords on June 21, 1922, that the Jewish National Home nowise meant a kind of domination of the Jews over the Arabs (*Parliamentary Debates, House of Lords*, vol. 50, No. 47, col. 1,011). Similarly Ormsby Gore in the Commons on July 4th, 1922 (*Parliamentary Debates, House of Commons*, vol. 156, No. 90, col. 264). The Duke of Devonshire, speaking as Colonial Secretary in the House of Lords on June 27th, 1923 (*Parliamentary Debates, House of Lords*, vol. 54, No. 51, col. 676) said in the name of the British Government : " Again and again it has been stated that the intention from the beginning has been to make a National Home for the Jews, but every provision has been made to prevent it from becoming in any sense of the word a Jewish State or a state under Jewish domination." At the same sitting Lord Grey of Falloden urged that this assurance should be clothed in the form of a more precise definition (cols. 680–82). See also Sir John Shuckburgh's statements as British represenative before the Permanent

Mandates Commission on June 28th, 1927 (Minutes of the 11th Session, p. 110).

[74] " The idea of a Jewish State is repudiated, though it is difficult to see how the success of Zionism could be prevented from ultimately bringing this solution into prominence, and make it a demand difficult to resist." J. de V. Loder, *The Truth about Mesopotamia, Palestine and Syria*, p. 154.

[75] On the attitude adopted by the Vatican, see the Papal Allocution to the Cardinals in the Consistory on June 13th, 1921 (*Oriento Moderno*, I year, p. 81). The case of the Arab Mohammedans was defended before the Wailing Wall Commission in 1930 not only by Mohammedan advocates and delegations from Arabian and other Eastern countries, but also by Arab Christians from Syria and Egypt. The heads of almost all the Christian churches and sects in Palestine (Patriarchs, Bishops, etc.) joined with the Mufti in pleading for the reprieve of the Arabs condemned to death for their share in the disturbances of 1929.

[76] On the subject of the mandate see Amedeo Giannini : " I Mandati Tipo A e la loro natura giuridica " in *Oriento Moderno* (II year, pp. 129 ff.). On the Palestinian constitution see the same writer : " La Costituzione della Palestina " (*Oriento Moderno*, III year, p. 129). The text of the constitution is in *Oriento Moderno* (II year, p. 450) and in the book by Marcus quoted below. See also Manka Spiegel : *Das völkerrechtliche Mandat und seine Anwendung auf Palästina* (Verlag Leuschner & Lubensky, Gratz, 1928) ; J. Stoyanovsky, *The Mandate for Palestine* (Longmans, Green & Co., London, 1928) ; Georg Schwarzenberger, *Das Völkerbunds-Mandat für Palästina* (Verlag Ferdinand Enke, Stuttgart, 1929) ; Ernst Marcus, *Palästina, ein werdender Staat* (Verlag Robert Noske, Leipzig, 1929). The concept of the National Home, never applied before in public law and (see note 73) variously interpreted by the British Government and the Zionists, was applied once again in the case of Armenia. The idea was at first to provide the Armenians, who did not constitute a majority in any part of Asia Minor, with an Armenian State of their own which was to be placed under a mandate, in order to safeguard their existence against the Turkish majority. In Article 88 of the Treaty of Sèvres Armenia was recognized as a free and independent State whose frontiers President Wilson was to define ; and this he did. The area marked out by President Wilson " would have provided a territory capable, from the economic and administrative point of view, of constituting an independent state, though, for years to come, the Armenians could not have risen to be a majority of the population." But it was soon found necessary to drop the idea of an Armenian State, and at the Conference of London in March, 1921, the former frontiers were abandoned on condition that Turkey should be willing to recognize an Armenian National Home. In this sense the National Home implied something less than a State. " The phrase was borrowed from the Balfour declaration promising a National Home to the Jews in Palestine. Its meaning was impenetrably obscure, and while no doubt that was an advantage in a war-time promise, it was already proving very awkward in Palestine now that the occasion had arrived for honouring the bond. The importation of this ambiguity into the Armenian question might therefore be considered a doubtful blessing." But the Armenians did not obtain even that, for they could only have done so if nationalism had never penetrated Eastern consciousness. " But, for good or evil, that momentous event had occurred." (A. J. Toynbee,

A History of the Peace Conference of Paris. Edited by H. W. V. Temperley, London, 1924, vol. vi, pp. 84–7.)

In the matter of its official language, moreover, Palestine has been differently treated from the other A mandates. There the language spoken by the people is either the sole or the dominant official language. In Palestine the indigenous languages are, it is true, also official languages, but they are subordinated to English which is used for the internal purposes of the administration and is everywhere predominant. Moreover, the composition of the Palestinian civil service is markedly colonial in character. The intention expressed by Sir Herbert Samuel in his first annual report of diminishing the number of British officials and substituting natives has not been carried out. In 1921 there were 268 English officials in Palestine ; in 1929 there were 397, that is an increase of 48 per cent. In 1921 there were 2,222 non-English officials and in 1929 3,001, or an increase of 35·5 per cent. Moreover, the English officials filled all the more important posts (S. M. Nemirowski, " Die Zusammensetzung der Beamtenschaft der Palästina-Regierung " in *Palästina*, Vienna, June, 1930).

On the subject of Palestine see Harry Charles Luke and Edward Keith Roach, *The Handbook of Palestine and Trans-Jordan* (Macmillan, London, 1930 ; 2nd edition—the first appeared in 1922 entitled *The Handbook of Palestine*), and *Statistical Abstract of Palestine 1929* (text in Hebrew, English, and German; published by Keren Hayesod, 1930). There is a plentiful literature on Zionism, cited in the bibliography. The head office of the Zionist Organization (Jewish Agency) in London, 77 Great Russell Street, W.C. 1, and its chief financial agency, Keren Hayesod in Jerusalem, are constantly publishing informative literature about the constructive activities of the Zionists in Palestine. We may mention the following pamphlets issued from the head office of Keren Hayesod : *Tel Aviv* (1929), *Hebrew Education in Erez Israel* (1930), and *Jewish Agriculture in Erez Israel* (1930). We may also mention the memoranda presented annually to the League of Nations by the Jewish Agency (*Memorandum submitted by the Zionist Organization to the Secretary General of the League of Nations for the Information of the Permanent Mandates Commission*), and the stenographic reports of XII–XVI Zionist Congress. The Arab point of view has hardly found expression at all in books or easily accessible informative literature. In Palestine there is an English weekly edition of the Arabic Jaffa daily *Falastin*. The *Falastin* Press also issued a pamphlet entitled *The Balfour Declaration : An Analysis*, in the autumn of 1929. There appeared in London in 1921 *The Holy Land. The Moslem-Christian Case against Zionist Aggression. Official Statement by the Palestine Arab Delegation.* This pamphlet has been translated in *Oriento Moderno* (i year, pp. 596–603). A number of memoranda by the Executive Committee of the Palestine Arab Congress and the Syro-Arab Delegation are contained in the publications of the League of Nations. Among others we may mention : *League of Nations. Mandates. Report of the Executive Committee of the Arab Palestine Congress* (C. 3. M. 3. 1921. VI) ; *League of Nations. Draft Mandate for Palestine* (C. 372. M. 260. 1921. VI). See also *Oriento Moderno* (iv, pp. 742 ff., and vi, p. 378) besides the minutes of the sessions of the Permanent Mandates Commission. Compare G. Kampffmeyer, " Die Stellung der Araber zur neuren Entwicklung Palästinas und Transjordaniens " (*Zeitschrift des deutschen Palästinavereins*, vol. 50

1927, pp. 274 ff.) ; Amedeo Giannini : " La questione orientale alla Conferenza della Pace : La question Arabo-Palestinese " (*Oriento Moderno*, I year, pp. 257 ff.). See also the point of view expressed in the King-Crane Report, reproduced in Ray Stannard Baker, *Woodrow Wilson and World Settlement. Original Documents of the Peace Conference* (vol. ii, pp. 205–19, especially pp. 207 ff., Heinemann, 1923).

As regards Palestine's treatment as a British colony in contradistinction to the other mandates, it may be observed that the constitutions of Trans-Jordan, Iraq, Lebanon, and Syria were submitted to the people for discussion and adoption, whilst the Palestinian constitution of 1922 was merely put in force by a royal Order in Council. It can be recalled or altered at any time by His Britannic Majesty, and His Majesty may at any time issue orders and decrees applicable to Palestine (Articles 88 and 89). As in British Crown Colonies, but unlike the mandated territories, the law of 1884 regarding the deportation of colonial prisoners is made applicable to Palestine, as if it were a part of the possessions of His Britannic Majesty (Article 37). The British High Commissioner in Palestine, like the Governor in a Crown Colony, has the right to send Palestinian criminals to other English colonies outside Palestine, but not to Great Britain itself, to serve their sentence, and to deport political suspects to another colony (suspicion alone is enough, no trial is necessary), under Articles 68 and 69. There is no appeal against such a sentence of deportation (Article 70). On the other hand, the " constitution ", which is not entitled a constitution but a royal Order in Council, contains no definition of the rights and liberties of the Palestinians, whereas in all other mandated territories the constitution deals at length with liberty of person, of speech, of assembly and the press, the inviolability of domiciliary privacy and of postal secrecy, and so on. Moreover, this " constitution " is contrary to the mandate. For the latter constantly refers to a Palestinian Government (Articles 6, 7, 11, 17), of which the law knows nothing as it stands in Palestine to-day. (See Ernst Marcus, *Palästina—ein werdender Staat*, Leipzig, 1929, p. 140.) Great Britain has made British colonial law apply in full to Palestine, just as if it were not mandated territory but a colony. Nor do the books on Palestinian public law say anything about the civic rights of the Palestinians (see the interesting section on " Individual Rights and Interests " in J. Stoyanowski's *The Mandate for Palestine*, pp. 236 ff.). It is worth noting that, whereas the Palestinians are thus put in the position of British colonial subjects, they are not so placed in the one respect in which it would be an advantage to them. A Palestinian passport secures none of the privileges attached to a British passport and does not even entitle the holder to enter Great Britain without a visa. The British Government tolerates disqualifications and treatment on quite a different basis in the case of holders of the Palestinian passport from what it allows in the case of other " British protected persons ". George Schwarzenberger (*Das Völkerbundsmandat für Palästina*, Stuttgart, 1929, p. 43) points out that the fact that Palestine does not officially belong to the British Empire involves the advantages for Great Britain and the disadvantages for the Palestinians of " inferior " citizenship. " Only in this way is it possible to exclude the subject peoples from citizenship of the ruling Great Power and to deprive them of the rights attached to citizenship."

[77] In the educational sphere a serious effort was made in 1921 to increase the number of Arabic village schools. But since then the

number of Arabic Government schools in Palestine has remained stationary. At the end of 1929 there were 308 Arabic Government primary schools, of which twenty-nine were girls' schools and 259 were in villages. In spite of the keen desire of the Arab population, barely a fifth of the Arab children get any schooling. The village schools have a curriculum of four years, and the town schools six years. There are some secondary classes, but only one complete secondary school, the so-called Government Arab College in Jerusalem, which is also a teachers' training college. There are no Government secondary schools for girls. There are also a number of private Christian secondary and primary schools, but in these teaching is often in a foreign language ; also a number of private Mohammedan schools. The Jewish school system, on the other hand, is admirably developed with the help of Jewry abroad. All boys and girls receive schooling, and the primary course in towns and villages is eight years. The Jewish school system includes a number of secondary schools for both sexes. One weakness of the Jewish school system is that Arabic is not taught at all in the eight-year primary schools, and is only optional and badly taught in the secondary schools. But it is superior to most other school systems in that kindergartens are everywhere admirably organized ; indeed the teachers are universally eager to introduce modern methods and to perfect themselves in pedagogy.

[78] A decree of December, 1921, governs the religious organization of the Mohammedans in Palestine. At the head is the Supreme Moslem Council in Jerusalem, consisting of a President and four representatives of the several parts of Palestine. The term of office of the original Council ended in 1925, but the fresh elections were declared void. The duties of the Council consist in the administration of pious endowments (Wakf), appointment to religious offices, and the administration of ecclesiastical justice. See *Oriento Moderno* (i year, p. 358 ; ii year, p. 594 ; v year, pp. 479, 641 ; vi year, p. 95).

The Jews in Palestine (see " Jewish Community Regulations ", *Report on Palestine for 1927*, Colonial No. 31, pp. 81 ff.) are organized in the Knesseth Israel, which has a Rabbinical Council, and an Elective Assembly chosen by universal elections, and a National Council chosen by the Elective Assembly. The latter, which has seventy-one members, like the ancient sanhedrim, met for the first time on February 9th, 1931.

[79] These figures of the census of 1927 are taken from the *Statistical Abstract of Palestine* published by Keren Hayesod, p. 88. According to the *Abstract* there are in Palestine, according to an estimate made in 1920, 5,515,400 dunam of cultivated land and 3,389,100 capable of cultivation but not yet cultivated. A dunam was formerly 0·09 hectare and is now 0·1 hectare (a hectare is 2·471 acres. *Translator's Note*). In the report of the Commission of Inquiry into the August disturbances of 1929 (Cmd. 3530, 1930) there is an estimate of about 11 to 12 million dunam, of which 1,200,000 dunam are in Jewish hands. Of these 1,200,000 dunam Keren Kayemeth held 280,000, that is the Land Purchase Fund of the Zionist Organization whose land remains the inalienable property of the Jewish people, its sale being prohibited by statute. A further 374,000 dunam belong to the Palestine Jewish Colonization Association (Baron Rothschild) , and 546,000 are in private hands. Before the War, in 1913, the Jews possessed only 448,000 dunam in all in Palestine. According to the Government Land Register 513,400 dunam were purchased by Jews between 1921 and 1929 for a sum of over £6,000,000. Jewish landed

property constitutes about 12 per cent of the cultivable area and is chiefly in the most fertile districts. The average amount of land necessary for a settler in Palestine is held to be 150 to 250 dunam, if it is not irrigated. According to a census of 1927 there were in Palestine 104 Jewish agricultural settlements with 30,500 inhabitants. By 1930 the number of inhabitants had increased to 35,000. The Zionist Organization itself has founded or supports fifty-six of these settlements with a total of some 7,000 souls, of whom 1,840 are working men and 1,654 women. For their foundation or support Keren Hayesod, the financial organ of the Zionist Organization in its constructive work, has expended £1,350,000 up to June 30th, 1930, in addition to a sum of about equal amount expended by the Jewish National Fund for land purchase and improvement. There has been a specially marked increase in Jewish orange plantations. In April, 1927, they covered 18,000 dunam and in April, 1930, 58,000 dunam. It is said that there are 300,000 dunam in Palestine suitable for orange plantations. Of this area some 115,000 dunam were actually planted with oranges in April, 1930, so that the Jews possessed about half. Only a little over a quarter of the orange-trees had begun to bear fruit in 1930.

There is valuable material about Jewish and general agriculture in the report of the expert commission appointed by the Jewish Agency (*Reports of the Experts submitted to the Joint Palestine Survey Commission*, pp. 741, Boston, Mass., October 1st, 1928) and in the *Report of the Joint Palestine Survey Commission* (Lord Melchett, Felix M. Warburg, Oscar Wassermann, Dr. Lee K. Frankel, pp. 182, London, June 18th, 1928) based upon it. The inquiry showed that if all cultivable land is taken into account there is room in all for 83,000 peasant families, 33,000 on irrigated land.

[80] Leonard Stein, the political secretary of the Zionist Executive, has already called attention to the fact that according to all previous experience it is unlikely that there will ever be a Jewish majority in Palestine, in his *Zionism* (Ernest Benn, London, 1925), pp. 201 ff. " Palestine will find room in course of time for hundreds of thousands of Jewish immigrants ; it will become a country in which the Jews form a much larger percentage of the population than in any other part of the world ; but there is little likelihood of its absorbing them in such numbers as will make than an actual majority." The several censuses and estimates of population in Palestine do not altogether agree, but the general upshot is unmistakeable. The population of Palestine is increasing very fast, much faster than before the War, for public health is better administered and wars and military service no longer claim their victims. According to the Report of the Palestinian Government Health Department for 1929, the population will have doubled in twenty-eight years at the present rate of increase. In 1929 the natural increase was on the average 24·64 per 1,000, amongst the Mohammedans 26·06, and amongst the Jews 22·27. The average birth-rate for the whole country was 51·15 per 1,000, being highest among the Mohammedans (57·74) and lowest amongst the Jews (34·06). The average death-rate for the whole country was 26·51 per 1,000, being highest amongst the Mohammedans (31·67) and lowest amongst the Jews (11·79). A leaflet issued by Keren Hayesod in the autumn of 1930 gives the following estimate of population movements :—

	1920.	1930.
Jews	61,000	172,000
Mohammedans (including Bedouins) .	566,000	697,000
Christians	69,000	82,000
Others	7,000	9,000
	703,000	960,000

The Jewish immigration from 1919 to 1930 is estimated at 109,000 souls, and Jewish emigration at 29,000, so that the net increase through immigration is 80,000 ; contrasted with this is a net decrease of the non-Jewish population through the predominance of emigration of about 8,000. The natural increase of the Jews, however, in the decade 1920–30 was 27,000, that of the Mohammedans without the Bedouins 136,000, of the Christians 17,000, and of the rest of the population 2,000.

The Report of the Government Health Department for 1929 gives lower figures : 919,395 for the total population with 675,774 Mohammedans, 154,330 Jews, 80,225 Christians, and 9,066 others.

According to the estimates for 1920 and 1921 and the censuses since 1922 of the Government (see *Statistical Abstract of Palestine, 1929*, published by Keren Hayesod, Jersualem, 1930, p. 40) Jewish immigration into Palestine was as follows :—

	Immigration.	Emigration.	Difference (net immigration).
1920 . .	10,000	1,300	8,700
1921 . .	9,900	1,200	8,700
1922 . .	7,844	1,503	6,341
1923 . .	7,421	3,466	3,955
1924 . .	12,856	2,037	10,819
1925 . .	33,801	2,155	31,650
1926 . .	13,081	7,365	5,716
1927 . .	2,713	5,071	− 2,357
1928 . .	2,178	2,168	10
1929 . .	5,249	1,746	3,503
1920–29 .	105,043	28,007	77,063

In the first decade after the War the average annual increase of Jewish population through immigration was 7,700 ; for this relatively high figure the record year 1925 is responsible.

The natural increase of the population for the following years (see op. cit., p. 58) amounted to :—

	Jews.	Non-Jews (excluding Bedouins).
1922 . . .	1,371	13,973
1923 . . .	1,966	12,442
1924 . . .	2,427	14,856
1925 . . .	2,183	13,685
1926 . . .	3,517	18,604
1927 . . .	3,195	14,192
1928 . . .	3,478	16,340
1929 . . .	3,707	16,671

(Report for 1929, p. 84.)

The annual Jewish excess of births over deaths has, therefore, been on the average 3,500 in recent years, that of non-Jews 16,000. The annual increase of Jews in the past decade has been between 10,000 and 11,000, and, in spite of considerable immigration, it has remained less than the increase of the non-Jewish population even without counting the increase of the Bedouins, which amounted to something between 14,000 and 16,000 annually.

On page 34 the *Statistical Abstract of Palestine* gives an estimate of the movements of population from July, 1919, to July, 1929, leaving out of account the natural increase of the Mohammedan Bedouins (some 110,000 in number), amongst whom no register of births and deaths is kept. This table gives the increase of the Jewish population as follows :—

By natural increase	.	.	.	23,737
By immigration	.	.	.	73,593
Total	.	.	.	97,330

and of non-Jews :—

By natural increase	.	.	.	137,580
Less excess emigration	.	.	.	8,846
Total increase	.	.	.	128,734

These figures seem to fit the interpretation which Freda White sums up as follows in her book on *Mandates* (published under the auspices of the League of Nations Union, with a foreword by Sir Frederick Lugard ; Jonathan Cape, London, 1926) : " The words National Home are capable of various interpretations. The British Government has consistently held the view that they mean settlement in Palestine of Jews in numbers which will not threaten the prospects of the Arabs." (p. 75). Although the figures for the first decade do not indicate that the Jews will ever be a majority, they have nevertheless increased greatly, not only absolutely but relatively. In the census of October 23rd, 1922, the 83,794 Jews formed 11·1 per cent of a total population of 757,182. If we deduct the Bedouin tribes, numbering about 103,000, the Jews were 12·9 of the settled population. In July, 1929, according to the *Statistical Abstract of Palestine* (p. 33), the Jews were already 18·9 per cent of the settled population. At all events it is an amazing achievement of Jewish energy and Jewish devotion to have succeeded in the course of a decade in establishing some 80,000 new immigrants on a relatively very high standard of civilization in a relatively poor country. The non-Jewish population of Palestine will amount to over one million in about twenty years. On this subject the President of the Zionist Organization, Dr. Weizmann, said in an address to the Central Asian Society on November 12th, 1929 : " Whether it will be half a million Jews, or three quarters of a million, or a million, I know not." (*The Position of Palestine.* Four Speeches by Dr. Chaim Weizmann. Jewish Agency for Palestine, London, 1930, p. 19.)

[81] In order to avoid this conflict certain supporters of Zionism endeavoured, partly, perhaps, in view of the statements of the British Government (see Note 73) to suggest that the Zionists should bind themselves to a voluntary limitation in consideration of the numbers and interests of the Arab population. Thus Emile Vandervelde in his *Le Pays d'Israel* (Editions Rieder, Paris, 1929), especially on

pages 120 f., 122 ff., 125 ff., 197, 203 ; and summing up on page 210 : " In this country, which will remain Arab as to the numerical majority of its population, whilst England will endeavour to keep control of it, there will be a National Home for the Jews which we may hope will be large and prosperous. But we may doubt whether it will resemble the visions of the early Zionists." See also H. N. Brailsford in *The Menorah Journal* (New York, December, 1929), and Tredwell Smith in *The New Republic* (New York, October 30th, 1929), both of whom propose a maximum limit of about 40 per cent for the Jewish population of Palestine. In contrast to these attempts to set a limit, which often strike us as artificial, we would call attention to the endeavours to interpret Zionism, not as a political movement aiming at a majority, but as a spiritual and cultural movement concerned primarily with the creation of a cultural centre, quite apart from all political ambitions and aims, not confined to the establishment of cultural institutions but inspiring the whole of social life and yet not seeking to endanger either the political and numerical or the economic position of the Arabs. In this connection see J. L. Magnes : *Like all the Nations ?* (Jerusalem, 1930) ; John Haynes Holmes, *Palestine To-day and To-morrow* (Macmillan, New York, 1929) ; and William Ernest Hocking, " Palestine an Impasse ? " in *The Atlantic Monthly* (July, 1930). Holmes in particular stresses the great significance to Jewry and to mankind of such a non-political Zionism, but points to the dangers which he considers are involved in political Zionism. See in particular pp. 129 ff., written before the disturbances of 1929, and pp. 250 ff. " But even these moderate Zionists show a disquieting tendency to take for granted Jewish ascendancy. They do not think at all in terms of violence or oppression. Yet they were silent when England and the Allies tore to tatters the nationalistic aspirations of the Moslem world. They have refused the request of the Palestinian Arabs, presented in not immoderate terms, for co-operation in securing some form of popular government, and thus have conspired, as an obstructive minority backed by alien power, to deny to the majority their public rights. And they visualize a future, for the coming of which they are determined patiently to wait and work, when the Jews will be the majority in the land. . . . However temperate the spirit of the Jews in Palestine, however idealistic their expectations of the future, the logic of the policy which they are tempted to follow is repression of a native population, interference with its rights, frustration of its ambitions, with all the inevitable consequences of sporadic rebellion and ultimate civil war. In such policy of force, the whole destiny of Zionism is at stake. It is the one policy, of course, best calculated to precipitate those very chances of destruction which it was instituted to appease." Professor Hocking anticipates similar dangers : " If we could see things as they are in Palestine, we should recognize as axiomatic three things : (1) that nothing like the full plan of Zionism can be realized without political pressure backed by military force ; (2) that such pressure and force imply an injustice which is inconsistent with the ethical sense of Zionism, undermining both its sincerity and its claim ; (3) that every increase of pressure now meets with increasingly determined Arab resistance, within and beyond Palestine. Hence the question which political Zionism must answer is whether or not it proposes to-day, as in ancient times, to assert its place in Palestine by the aid of the sword. . . . That true and attainable Zion is a Zion of culture and faith, not the Zion of political nationalism. It is indeed a bitter thing to the sincere Zionist that his ideal community cannot have in that unique spot of earth its perfect body as well as its perfect soul. What I have to say, I say with deep personal regret. For I went to Palestine seized with the idea of Zionism and warmed by the ardor of Jewish friends to whom this vision is the breath of life, prepared to believe all things possible. I came away saddened, seeing that to strive for the perfect body as things now are, can only mean the loss of soul and body alike. To pursue any campaign for the more vigorous fulfillment of ' the British promise ' is to work blindly toward another bloody struggle involving first the new settlements, then Great Britain, then no one knows what wider area." Holding these views, Hocking then proceeds to advocate a purely cultural and religious Zionism which, it must be confessed, offers no solution of the problem of Jewish economic and political miseries.

CHAPTER VII

[82] Sir John Shuckburgh proceeds : " The special arrangements there (in Trans-Jordan) really go back to the old controversy about our wartime pledges to the Arabs. The point is that the country east of the Jordan falls within the area in respect of which we promised, during the War, to recognize and support the independence of the Arabs. That puts Trans-Jordan in a wholly different position from Palestine. What has been done in Trans-Jordan is to set up an independent Arab administration under the Emir Abdullah, who is the brother of the King of Iraq. We are now in the course of negotiating a treaty with the Emir very much on the lines of the treaty which we negotiated with the King of Iraq and which was accepted by the Council of the League as giving adequate effect, in respect of Iraq, to the terms of article 22 of the Covenant of the League."

[83] Trans-Jordan's frontier with Palestine was drawn in the League Council's resolution of September 16th, 1922. It is reiterated in Article 2 of the Anglo-Trans-Jordan treaty. The frontier of Trans-Jordan and the Hejaz has been fixed provisionally in a treaty between Great Britain and the Hejaz concluded on May 20th, 1927, at Jidda and ratified on September 17th. In a Note accompanying this treaty the British Government declared that the frontier between Trans-Jordan and the Hejaz runs from a point two miles south of the station of Mudanwara on the Hejaz railway and thence in a straight line westwards to the Gulf of Aqaba. The Hejaz Government, however, refused to recognize this frontier and said that they would leave the final settlement to a later date.

Trans-Jordan's flag bears the Arab colours—black, white and green. Most of the Arab States have chosen the same flag, with these three colours in parallel strips, the flag being twice as long as it is wide. The Hejaz, the Kingdom of Iraq, and the Syrian Republic have the same flag. Trans-Jordan and Iraq have also a red triangle on their flag, the colour of the house of the Sherif of Mecca to which the rulers of both countries belong. The different countries are distinguished by the number of stars on their flags. Trans-Jordan's has one white star in the middle of the red triangle, Iraq two white stars in the same place, and Syria three red stars on the central white strip. The Hejaz, as the mother country, has no stars.

[84] The Government expenditure on education rose from £11,820 in 1924–5 to £22,350 in 1929–30. During the same period the expenditure on public health rose from £4,991 to £11,482, on the promotion of agriculture from £1,362 to £6,516. Trans-Jordan has fifty-seven Government schools, of which six are for girls, and one Trade School with 3,794 boys and 643 girls. Four of the schools are of secondary grade. There are also a number of private Christian schools in which the teachers are all Arabs.

[85] Trans-Jordan has an Agricultural Bank, established in 1921, which makes loans to the peasants at 9 per cent for five years. There are Government officials on its Board and also representatives of the peasantry ; the latter are elected by the whole country for the central Board in Amman and for the branches by the people of the districts. Progress has also been made in making social use of the Crown lands. " When the survey of a village or tribal area containing State Domain is finished, the Commission, if the area is small, recommends its sale to the cultivators ; if it is large, the assessment of a fixed annual rent in place of rental tithe. The cultivators gladly accept contracts releasing them from crop estimation and affording encouragement for better cultivation." (*Report on Palestine and Trans-Jordan for 1929*. Colonial No. 47 of 1930, p. 165.)

CHAPTER VIII

[86] See the first part of *L'Evolution Politique de la Syrie sous Mandat* (Marcel Rivière, Paris, 1928, pp. 20 ff.) by Christen Edmond Rabbath, a Syrian who had enjoyed a French education : " But Syria has not always been a closed region in which civilizations and peoples confronted one another. It was not till the seventh century, when the Arabs and Islam made their appearance, that its true history began. Since that event of fundamental importance which has dominated Syria's whole subsequent development, the country has been altogether Arab and Islamic in its life, its speech, its spirit ; thanks to them it has been finally captured by Islam and the Arab nation, and finally lost to Christianity and the West. So long a history has inevitably left a deep impression upon the minds and hearts of the people. . . . The bond of speech is only the most striking expression of a community of less noticeable sentiments and ways of thought which bind the several groups of Syrians, be they who they may, in the depths of their being. . . . Left to themselves, what spiritual and moral life can this Christian community in Lebanon or that Shi'ah sect in the mountains possess, their religion clothed in a language long since dead, merely babbled by a handful of priests who repeat it without understanding it ? And yet we need only glance at the nineteenth century in order to be struck with astonishment at the constellation of Syrian writers of all religions whose Arabic is as pure as that of the desert poets and who wrote to give expression to feelings which seem to have developed late and wholly independent of the religious community to which they belonged. With their pens and their example they preach the unity of all Arabs, Christians and Mohammedans, under a common flag, so as to shake off the dust of the past and to revive a glorious heritage represented as the ideal of the modern renaissance. How can we account for the sudden and irresistable movement which sprang from their teaching, penetrating the masses

and breaking forth in the burning patriotism that marked the last years of Turkish domination, in the Turkish persecution during the World War, in the martyrdom of Mohammedan and Christian leaders on the gallows of Damascus and Beirut, and finally in the frenzied enthusiasm of the people during Feisal's brilliant and, alas, all too brief reign ? And the bloody insurrection of 1925. . . . The men who died at that time were no bandits. A lofty and noble ideal led them to their death and to a defeat which even the least wise of them knew was a possibility, if not a certainty. . . . This fervent moral awakening has given birth to an Arabian national consciousness which makes men's hearts beat high and unites their souls across the religious lines of cleavage. . . . Across four centuries of Ottoman decadence, it picks up the long thread of Arabian history. Across artificial boundaries, for the most part drawn by the greed of alien rulers, it links the Arabs of Syria to those of distant lands. . . ." The book has a foreword by Emir Shakib Arslan, in which he states the Arab attitude towards the mandatory system. Compare *Oriento Moderno*, ix year, p. 55.

Toynbee, in *The Islamic World since the Peace Settlement*, p. 356, stresses the fact that, in view of the Maronites' bitter feelings towards the Mohammedans since the World War, the creation of Great Lebanon was a most unstatesmanlike step.

[87] According to France's report to the League of Nations on the position in Syria and Lebanon in 1925, Lebanon had 597,789 inhabitants in that year ; there were in addition 39,240 emigrants who continued to pay their land tax. Of these inhabitants 178,257 were Maronites, 69,539 Greek Orthodox, 40,414 Greek Catholics, 122,678 Sunni, and 101,637 Shi'ah Mahommedans, 38,940 Druzes, and 32,859 Armenians, almost all of whom had entered the country in recent years. There is no exact census of the inhabitants of Syria as a whole. The population of Syria without Great Lebanon is estimated at about 1,800,000 or 2,000,000. The French official publication *La Syrie et le Liban sous l'occupation et le Mandat Français 1919–1927* gives the total population of Syria and Lebanon as 2,046,817 (p. 29), but adds spontaneously that in all probability this figure is too low. *The Statesman's Year-Book* for 1930 gives the total population of the French mandated territory in 1929 as 2,831,622 ; of these 1,696,638 belonged to Syria, 796,284 to Lebanon, 286,920 to the territory of the Alawis, and 51,780 to the Jebel ed Druz. In Syria (as in Mesopotamia), unlike Palestine, there is no registration of births and deaths. In 1929 there were 7,941 emigrants and 3,515 immigrants, for the most part returned emigrants. Emigration was less than in previous years.

[88] This deliberate policy of partition originated with the first Secretary General of the French Mandatory Administration, Robert de Caix, and with Colonel Catroux. See also the latter's article " Le Mandat Français en Syrie " in the *Revue Politique et Parlementaire*, 1922. According to the French report on mandatory administration for 1925 the State of the Alawis had 277,948 inhabitants, of whom 176,285 were Alawis, 52,778 Sunnis, 35,148 Greek Orthodox, 5,263 Maronites, 1,604 Armenians, 1,112 Protestants, and 4,457 Ismailite Shi'ahs. The Representative Council of the State in 1923 consisted of eight Alawis, three Sunnis, three Christians and one Ismailite.

[89] On the subject of the Lebanese constitution see Hans Kohn : " Die Staats- und Verfassungsrechtliche Entwicklung der Republik Libanon " in the *Jahrbuch des Oeffentlichen Rechts* (vol. xvii, Tübingen, 1929). On the protests of the Lebanese, and, moreover, of just those

who had desired the French mandate most eagerly and defended it most stoutly, see *Oriento Moderno* (iv year, p. 100, and v year, p. 519). The Syrians' own demands are very well summed up in several petitions to the League of Nations, and also in *Oriento Moderno* (ii year, pp. 24, 299, 476, and v year, p. 106) and in the *Islamische Gegenwart* (Berlin, November, 1927).

⁹⁰ Sultan el Atrashi's rising in 1925 was the sixth insurrection on a considerable scale since the inception of the French mandate. The first was led by Amir Faour in 1919 in the Huleh district, the second in the territory of the Alawis and led by Sheikh Salih Ibn Ali, lasting from 1919 to 1921. The third was in 1921 in northern Syria, and was led by Ibrahim Hanano. Sultan el Atrashi had already led an insurrection in 1922 in the Hauran. Of less importance were the rising under Sheikh Ismail Harir in the Hauran and the disturbances in Damascus in 1922. In 1923 Melhem Kasim led a rising in the Baalbek district.

The house of El Atrashi had been leaders of the Druzes since the days of Ismail el Atrashi, who died in 1869. *Oriento Moderno* (v year, pp. 464 ff. and 525) gives the history of the Atrashi family. Sultan el Atrashi had helped Feisal Ibn Hussein to win Syria, and had also taken part in the Arab insurrection against the Turks.

⁹¹ What gave most offence was the French secret intelligence service (Service de Renseignements). The employees of the secret service were all officers, and their influence was especially oppressive because they were also advisers to the District Governors, that is, the local representatives of the mandatory Power. In the country districts this duplication of functions was bound to lead to constant abuses. The Syrians' various complaints have been for the most part enumerated in Elizabeth P. MacCallum's *The National Crusade in Syria* (pp. 16–100), taken from the minutes of the Permanent Mandates Commission.

⁹² Expenditure on the French army in Syria up to the end of 1925 amounted to 2,595 million francs according to Comte de Fels (" Le Mandat Syrien " in the *Revue de Paris* for November 1st, 1926, p. 182). Even in 1929 the French Budget still carried a sum of 271 million francs for the French army in Syria. In addition to the French troops there are Syrian auxiliaries in the mandated territory numbering on January 1st, 1930, 212 officers (95 Syrians) and 9,294 privates (322 Frenchmen). For these Syrian auxiliaries there is a Military Academy in Damascus for the training of Syrian officers. There are in addition Syrian depot troops numbering on January 1st, 1930, over 107 officers (40 French) and 3,520 privates (72 French). The cost of these various auxiliary troops is over 93 million francs, and is borne by the mandated territories. Each state has also its own gendarmerie and police.

In the whole mandated territory there are 357 French officials of all ranks of whom 141 are on the staff of the High Commissioner, 89 in the general administration, and 126 in the separate States. There are 71 officers in the secret service.

⁹³ The census of 1921 showed 50,338 inhabitants of the Jebel ed Druz. Of these 42,680 were Druzes, 4,639 Greek Orthodox, 2,112 Greek Catholics, 674 Sunnis, and 217 Protestants. These figures are very likely too low, but the estimate of 101,000 in *Asie Française* (May, 1921, p. 216) is doubtless too high.

⁹⁴ " The campaigns of 1925 and 1926 proved as savage, devastating, and indecisive as the first two campaigns of the Greek War of Independence, which had begun in a similar fashion when, in April,

1828, a highland chief, the Maniot Petros Bey Mavromikhalis, had taken up arms against the Osmanlis in the Morea." (Toynbee, op. cit., p. 424).

⁹⁵ The leaders of the People's party included the President, Dr. Shahbander, the President of the Chamber of Advocates, Faris Bey el Khury, a Protestant of the name of Taufik Bey Shamiyah, Jamil Mardam, who was one of the leading Christians in Damascus, the advocate Fawzi Bey el Ghazzi, the advocate Ikhsan Bey esh Sherif, Lutfi el Haffar, the President of the Chamber of Commerce, and others. In addition the well-known Damascene aristocratic family of El Bakri took part in the insurrection and fled right at the beginning to the Druzes. The El Bakris had been among the first to support the claims of Emir Feisal of the Hejaz in Syria.

⁹⁶ See *Oriento Moderno*, v year, pp. 575–80. There were demonstrations in Palestine, Mesopotamia, India, and Egypt, where Zaghlul Pasha made an appeal on behalf of the victims of Damascus and himself headed the subscription.

⁹⁷ See Toynbee, op. cit., pp. 435–7. On page 435, note 5, for instance, he rites : " Repeated experiences proved that for the Armenians to lend themselves to the designs of European powers was to court disaster." " The statesmanlike and constructive policy . . . of the Druse commander Zayd ul Atrash, in this matter of religious and communal relations, stands out in striking contrast to the policy of the Mandatory Power."

⁹⁸ In the Report of the French Government to the League of Nations on the position in Syria and Lebanon in 1924 the following passage occurs on the absence of labour and social legislation : " It does not do to be surprised at this lack. It may be accounted for here, as everywhere in the Levant, by the patriarchal nature of society, the indifference of the former Ottoman Government to all social questions, and most of all by the absence of industry on a large scale. With the exception of the silk mills of Lebanon and a few workshops in Damascus there are no factories in the whole mandated territory. The small local industries—mills, tanneries, soap works, and oil-presses—only employ a very small number of workers who share their employer's life." In the Report for 1929 we find on page 4 ff. : " Two tendencies mark the character of the mandated territory : the steady retrogression of certain traditional industries and the gradual development of modern industry in which some of the old trades are revived and which has arisen, on the other hand, in order to satisfy new demands." Amongst the industries that are losing ground the Report mentions weaving in Syria (before the War, Aleppo had 15,000 looms for 40,000 workers, whilst to-day there are only 3,000 with less than 10,000 workers ; and there is a similar decline in Damascus, Homs, and Hama), soap manufactory in Tripoli, and the tanneries of Zahle in Lebanon, where the number of workers has fallen from 2,500 to 150. The principal reason for this lies in the tariff barriers which cut Syria off from its hinterland. But there is also a rapid modernization of industry going on. In Aleppo modern woollen mills and hosiery manufactories with petrol and electric motors are being set up ; similar developments may be observed in Damascus, and in Tripoli there is a cotton mill with over 300 workers. In Aleppo, Antioch, and Alexandretta modern soap works have sprung up, and in Damascus and Lebanon modern tanneries. Of new industries we may mention cement works near Damascus and in Lebanon, besides distilleries,

iron works, and a number of engineering shops. In the modern factories
the average wage is twelve francs a day and the working hours nine
or ten. But this process of industrialization is only beginning. Syria
is still predominantly agricultural. It is of interest that the country's
position as mandated territory involves economic disadvantages. It
was the original idea of the mandatory system to bring advantages
to the mandated territories. But now it has come about that the
mandated territories are bound to grant all members of the League of
Nations most favoured nation treatment, but cannot claim the same
treatment in return. The mandates, therefore, do not protect the
mandated territories, but make them the victims of economic exploitation by the League. See also the above Report by France, p. 16.

[99] Syria's school system is separately organized and administered
in each State. The schools are classified as State schools, native
private schools, and foreign schools (French, American, Danish,
English, and Italian). The following table shows the distribution of
the primary schools in 1929 :—

		Private Schools.	
Territory.	*State Schools.*	*Native.*	*Foreign.*
Syria . . .	272 (27,305)	173 (20,587)	73 (8,811)
Alexandretta .	60 (4,257)	27 (2,685)	18 (1,751)
Alawis . .	98 (5,873)	53 (1,904)	24 (1,456)
Druzes . .	40 (3,133)	43 (1,553)	15 (1,194)
Lebanon . .	159 (12,048)	642 (39,721)	337 (25,803)

The figures in parentheses refer to the numbers of pupils. The foreign
schools are predominantly French. The private schools are for the
most part under the control of the various religious communities.
The following table gives the total number of primary schools :—

Territory.	*Town Schools.*	*Village Schools.*
Syria . .	227 (38,356)	291 (18,347)
Alexandretta .	29 (4,302)	85 (4,491)
Alawis . .	19 (3,259)	156 (6,074)
Druzes . .	3 (610)	95 (5,260)
Lebanon . .	153 (24,717)	985 (52,855)

In the whole territory there are 41 boys' secondary schools of which
only six are Government schools, four men teachers' training colleges,
and nine technical schools. The total of all schools is 1,641, with
119,443 pupils and 550 girls' schools with 59,496 pupils. There are
fourteen girls' secondary schools, six training colleges for women
teachers, and eleven technical schools. There are three universities
in the mandated territory, one under the Government in Damascus to
which the Arab Academy is attached, and two in Beirut, one belonging
to the French Jesuits and one American.

CHAPTER IX

[100] According to the census of 1920, which is, however, of doubtful
accuracy, the Kingdom of Iraq has 2,849,282 inhabitants. Of these
1,494,015 are Shi'ahs, living mainly in the provinces of Baghdad
and Basra, and 1,146,658 Sunnis, mainly in the provinces of Mosul
and Baghdad. There are in addition 87,488 Jews, 78,792 Christians,
and 42,302 belonging to other religious communities.

The Iraq Budget, which was presented constitutionally for the first time in 1922–3, has regularly shown an excess of revenue over expenditure since 1923–4. In the financial year 1927–8 the revenue amounted to 572,97,055 rupees. The surplus since 1923 has been applied to paying off Iraq's share in the Ottoman Public Debt.

Iraq's Budgets have shown the following figures of revenue and expenditure :—

	Revenue.	Expenditure.
1922–3	474,67,077	485,81,922
1923–4	509,40,647	424,26,670
1924–5	527,32,595	464,85,702
1925–6	570,01,934	502,37,845
1926–7	549,50,474	519,21,714

These figures are proof of the fact that the finances of the new kingdom are on a firm basis.

Immediately after the World War attention was directed towards Iraq because it was believed that it had valuable oil-fields. Up to the present time borings in Iraq territory have not confirmed this belief. Nevertheless mineral oil forms the most interesting chapter in Iraq's world economic policy. There are two distinct areas in the history of Mesopotamian oil, one close to the Persian frontier belonging to the district which Persia ceded to Turkey in 1913, and the Mosul area. In June, 1914, the Turkish Petroleum Company was promised a concession by the Turkish Government to work the oilfields in the vilayets of Mosul and Baghdad. The Turkish Petroleum Company had been founded in October, 1912, as a compromise between German interests (the Baghdad Railway) and English. Five per cent of the capital belonged to an Armenian of the name of Gulbenkian, who was to negotiate the concession, 47½ per cent to the National Bank of Turkey, a British bank which made over its share in the spring of 1914 to the Anglo-Persian Company, 22½ per cent to the Royal Dutch and Shell, and 25 per cent to the Deutsche Bank. In the Treaty of San Remo of April 24th, 1920, a Franco-Belgian group took over the share of the Deutsche Bank and after prolonged negotiations between Washington and London, half of the share of the Anglo-Persian was made over to the Near East Corporation in 1923, representing the interests of the American oil companies. Each of the four companies holds 23¾ per cent of the shares. On March 14th, 1925, this company acquired a concession for the whole Iraq territory with the exception of the vilayet of Basra and excluding the district ceded by Persia to Turkey in 1913. These districts were originally included in the concession which the British D'Arcy Exploration Company had acquired in 1901 from the Persian Government, and to exploit which the Anglo-Persian Oil Company had been formed. The Anglo-Persian Company was granted the concession for these districts on June 15th, 1926, until May 27th, 1969. The Anglo-Persian Company formed a subsidiary company, the Khanaqin Oil Company, to exploit the oil-fields situated in Iraq, in particular the Naft Khana oilfield. This company established a modern refinery at Alvand near Khanaqin, sufficient to meet the needs of the local market.

Both companies, the Turkish Petroleum Company—now called the Iraq Petroleum Company—and the Khanaqin Oil Company, are of the greatest economic importance to Iraq. Except for the Government they are the largest employers of labour in the country and have

introduced modern conditions of labour for their workers. They
have invested a large amount of capital in Iraq. They are required
by the terms of the concession to employ Iraqi subjects if at all possible.
The Iraq Government is represented on the management and appoints
a member of the Board of Directors. The Companies pay a large sum
in dues to the Iraq State. The first, which the Iraq Government
received from the Khanaqin Oil Company in 1927, amounted to 1,05,000
rupees for a net quantity of 39,300 tons of crude oil. In 1928 the dues
amounted to 1,65,000 rupess for 61,000 tons. The Turkish Petroleum
Company began experimental borings in April, 1927, in eight separate
districts. At Baba Gurgur they were successful. The question is
whether there is enough oil to make the construction of a pipe-line
over a distance of at least 900 kilometres pay. The pipe-line is to run
straight to a Mediterranean port, either to Haifa or to a port further
north in the French mandated territory of Syria. The borings of
the Iraq Petroleum Company have not fulfilled the hopes cherished
by Iraq for her Budget, and her economic position. The problem for
her was, therefore, to induce the Iraq Petroleum Company to work out
the oilfields more rapidly and to find additional companies to take up
the task. That was possible, for the Iraq Petroleum Company had
not the sole monopoly, but only the right to select twenty-four oilfields
of eight square miles each within the area of the concession. A new
partner in the exploitation of Mesopotamian oil presented itself to
Iraq in the British Oil Development Company, founded in 1927 under
the chairmanship of Lord Wemyss, with the participation of Italian,
Swiss, and German groups. The state of the international oil market
and the rivalry of the separate groups make Iraq's position difficult.
The large English and American oil companies do not favour the rapid
exploitation of the Mosul oilfield, but prefer to retain it as a reserve
in order to avoid increasing the already large supply of oil. See the
Frankfurter Zeitung of September 2nd, 1930.

[101] Iraq has its own domestic, religious, and national problems
which have made themselves felt during the period of political
consolidation, in the first decade of its existence. It is only in Mosul
that there can be any question of a national minority problem. There
are no national minorities in the two southern vilayets of Baghdad
and Basra. All the sharper was the religious cleavage there between
Sunni and Shi'ah Mahommedans in former times. Numerically the
Shi'ahs predominate. Under Turkish rule they were without influence,
as being heretics, and in the Turkish Empire they were only a small
minority. Their numerical importance in present-day Mesopotamia
is enhanced by the fact that the Holy Cities of the Shi'ahs are situated
in Iraq, and that the leading Shi'ah scholars live there, men whose
influence extends to Persia whence many of them come and often
retain their Persian nationality. The Shi'ah question therefore plays
a decisive part in Iraq's relations with Persia. In spite of their large
numbers the Shi'ahs are even now of secondary importance compared
with the Sunnis, for the king and the influential politicians in Baghdad
are Sunnis.

[102] Her treatment of the Kurds has played a similar part in Iraq's
relations with Turkey as her treatment of the Shi'ahs in her relations
with Persia. The other minorities in Mosul present a variety of
ethnographical and religious peculiarities and are of greater interest
to the ethnologist than to the politician. Immediately after the
World War the British administration was concerned for the fate of the

Christian minorities who had been driven from their original homes. Here, too, the British administration made the mistake, like the French in Syria, of forming auxiliary troops with these refugees and using them against the Kurds and other Mohammedans, and so embittering the hostility between them. Amongst these Christian minorities we must mention the Nestorians, descendants of the Assyrians who still speak Syrian Aramaic and carry on a warlike existence in the mountains, with customs not unlike those of the Kurds. The Chaldean Christians are fewer in number, of unwarlike character, and scattered through the cities of the lowlands ; they, too, were formerly Nestorians, but since 1778 they have belonged to the Catholic Church. We should mention further the Kurdish speaking, non-Mohammedan Yazidis, the devil-worshippers, who lead a life of strict isolation in the hills.

The Kurds are an ancient race who speak an Iranian language. There may be some three million of them in all, of whom about a million and a half live in Turkey, 700,000 in Persia, and about half a million in the vilayet of Mosul. During the nineteenth century they have made several attempts to win independence of Turkey, in 1843 under Bedr Khan and in 1880 under Sheikh Obaidullah. After the Young Turk revolution in 1908 a nationalist movement in the modern sense began among the Kurds ; the Kurdish Deputies in the Turkish Parliament were its spokesmen and it led to the initiation of newspapers and clubs and the creation of a literary language. The leader of this movement was Sheikh Abdul Kader, a Turkish Senator, who was hanged by the Turks during the suppression of the Kurdish insurrection in the summer of 1925. At the Peace Conference of Versailles a Kurd, Sherif Pasha, spoke for his people's national demand for independence. The treaty between Great Britain, France, and Italy that was signed at Sèvres on August 10th, 1920, at the same time as the Turkish Peace Treaty, expressly mentions in its preamble that the autonomy or eventual independence of Kurdistan is recognized by the Powers. Articles 62–4 of the Treaty of Sèvres with Turkey defined its frontiers.

[103] See C. A. Hooper, *The Constitutional Law of Iraq* (Baghdad, 1928). For the text of the constitution, its basis and history, see Hans Kohn, " Die Verfassung des Königreichs Irak " (*Jahrbuch des Oeffentlichen Rechts*, vol. xviii, Mohr, Tübingen, 1930), and League of Nations Document, C. 49, 1929, vi.

[104] In a *Memorandum on Policy in Iraq* issued by the British Secretary of State for the Colonies on November 21st, 1929, it is stated that England's conditional promises of Iraq's admission to the League of Nations were viewed with profound suspicion in Iraq : " They served to keep alive the belief, never wholly absent from 'Iraqi minds, that His Majesty's Government had no genuine intention of ever establishing 'Iraq in full independence, and that their real policy was to ' colonise ' the country. . . . As explanations and assurances proved of no avail, His Majesty's Government, on the advice of the late Sir Gilbert Clayton, which coincided with that of his predecessor, Sir Henry Dobbs, decided to examine the possibility of dispensing altogether with the provisos attaching to their promise to support 'Iraq's candidature in 1932. On examination these were found to serve no essential purpose. Great progress had been made during the last few years, and it seemed evident that, in the absence of some really serious and unexpected set-back, 'Iraq, judged by the criteria of internal security, sound public finance, and enlightened administration, would be in every way fit for admission to the League

of Nations by 1932. It was felt, therefore, that a time had come when His Majesty's Government could safely, and with a full sense of their responsibility towards the League, decide definitely to recommend 'Iraq for membership in three years time. The High Commissioner was accordingly authorised to inform the 'Iraq Government, without proviso or qualification, that His Majesty's Government would be prepared to support the candidature of 'Iraq for admission to the League of Nations in 1932.

" The effect of this communication upon the internal political situation in 'Iraq was immediate. Distrust and suspicion gave place to mutual confidence and good will, and, whereas previously no Ministry could be found to take office, a strong and responsible Government has now been formed embracing representatives of the two principal political parties in 'Iraq and anxious to co-operate with His Majesty's Government in the solution of outstanding questions before 1932.

" Clearly a new Treaty will be required to regulate the relations of this country with 'Iraq after that State has become a member of the League of Nations, and the necessary steps will be taken to prepare a draft Treaty for that purpose framed upon liberal lines and based generally upon the recent proposals for an Anglo-Egyptian settlement." (Cmd. 3440, 1929.)

For the text of the Treaty of June 30th, 1930, see Cmd. 3627. See also Elizabeth P. MacCallum, " Iraq and the British Treaties " in the *Information Service* (Foreign Policy Asociation, New York, August 20th, 1930).

[105] See Arnold J. Toynbee, *The Islamic World since the Peace Settlement* (Oxford University Press, 1927, p. 508, note 3). See also *Encyclopædia Britannica* (13th edition, vol. ii, p. 651) : " The Kurdish leaders died with the independence of Kurdistan on their lips. The president of the Turkish court-martial stated later that the Kurdish rebellion had a purely nationalist motive."

[106] The problem of Kurdish education presented various difficulties. Iraq's general educational system is as yet little developed and the proportional share of the Kurds in the schools strikes the Kurds themselves as small. Nevertheless, we can observe a steady progress. At the end of 1925 there were fifteen primary schools in Iraq with Kurdish as the language of instruction ; at the end of 1928 there were thirty schools, and of these two were secondary schools in Erbil and Sulaimaniya. There are great difficulties, for not only has it been necessary to create a literary language, but, since there are no Kurdish schools either in Persia or Turkey, to produce text-books, train teachers, and work out a special transcription, for which it proved necessary to add five letters to the Arabic alphabet. The percentage of Kurdish schools—30 out of 264—is rather less than it should be in proportion to their numbers ; on the other hand the Iraqi Ministry of Education complains that Arabic is not adequately taught in the Kurdish schools.

[107] Iraq's constitution has no special provisions for the rights of minorities. Moreover, the special régime in the Kurdish districts is not enshrined in the constitution. By Article 13 of the constitution, Islam is the State religion ; special provision is made for the liberty of the various Islamic sects and full freedom of conscience and worship is guaranteed to all. By Article 17 Arabic is the official language. Kurdish is not mentioned, nor is Turkish

which is the language of instruction in the schools in Kirkuk. Article 37 expressly states that the parliamentary electoral law must embody provisions for the representation of the non-Islamic minorities. Clause 6 of the electoral law of October 22nd, 1924, provides that, in addition to the number of Deputies to be elected for each *liwa* in proportion to the population, four Christian and four Jewish Deputies are to be elected.

[108] The best detailed account is in Arnold J. Toynbee, *The Islamic World since the Peace Settlement* (Oxford University Press, 1927, pp. 490–531). There is also in the Appendix of the book an excellent map of Mosul, showing the various proposals for the delineation of the frontier.

[109] The Sultan of Kuwait receives an annual subsidy from Great Britain, which has kept a Political Agent there since 1880. The Sultanate consists of a capital, also called Kuwait, with some 50,000 inhabitants, and the surrounding territory within a radius of about 70 miles from Kuwait on all sides ; these frontiers were drawn in the Anglo-Turkish Agreement of 1913, rounding the Sultanate off from a much larger area inhabited exclusively by Bedouins and nominally under the suzerainty of the Sultan of Kuwait. In a treaty between Ibn Saud and Great Britain concluded in December, 1915, and ratified in July, 1916, Ibn Saud engaged to refrain from attack on Kuwait and other regions under British protection, the boundaries of which, however, were to be fixed at a later date. This was never done, and in 1919 a frontier dispute arose between Kuwait and Ibn Saud. In this attack the leader of the Wahabis was Feisal ed Dawish, one of the most warlike chiefs of the Wahabi Ikhwan movement who was thenceforward perpetually involved in fighting on the eastern frontiers of Nejd. The efforts of the British High Commissioner in Iraq to negotiate and fix the frontier failed, but the tension was relaxed for the time being by the death of the Sultan of Kuwait and the election of his nephew, Ahmad Ibn Diabir, as Sultan, who was well disposed towards Ibn Saud.

CHAPTER X

[110] Philby, who probably knows Ibn Saud better than anyone else, bears witness in his *Arabia* (p. 183) to the fact that the Wahabi leader was pursuing a nationalist Arabian aim even before the World War when he considered the question of settling the Bedouins. As early as 1908 or thereabouts his ideal was " nothing less than to uproot and destroy the very foundations of Badawin society, which had endured without the slightest change since the days of Abraham, and to replace them with the concrete of a national spirit on which to build up an Arabian nation. In this way he can justly claim the credit of being the first of all Arab nationalists, but it was only by a few years that he anticipated the nationalist movement that began to stalk abroad, at first uneasily and furtively, through the Arab domains of the Ottoman Empire during the last years of the mediaeval tyranny of Abdul Hamid." See also pp. 227 ff. On the Wahabis see Richard Hartmann, " Die Wahabiten " (*Zeitschrift der Deutschen Morgenländischen Gesellschaft*, vol. 78, 1924, and new series, vol. 3, No. 2, pp. 176–213) ; H. St. J. B. Philby, " Arabia 1926–1929 " (*The Contemporary Review*, London, July, 1929) ; Sheikh Hafez Wahba : " Wahabism in

Arabia, past and present," and H. St. J. B. Philby, "A Survey of Wahabi Arabia 1929 " (*Journal of the Central Asian Society*, London, 1929, vol. xvi, part 4).

In his *Arabia* (p. 224) Philby also bears witness to the tendency of the nomads, observable on all hands, to settle when the opportunity offered. "(There is) one factor of nomad society which was, and had been through the ages, absolutely constant—an inherent tendency to desert the weariness and hopelessness of pastoral occupations for the superior comforts of agriculture if land could be found to settle on." On the Ikhwan, the stress laid upon a brotherhood which blotted out all former hostility of tribe and class, the substitution of the Sharia, the Islamic canon law, for the ancient barbaric tribal customs, the mosque as the centre of the new villages, and the use of the desert wells for purposes of irrigation, a practice hitherto unknown, see p. 225 of the above book.

[111] The Conference of Kuwait was held under the presidency of S. G. Knox, the British Resident on the Persian Gulf, from December 17th, 1923, till April 12th, 1924. On this subject see the British *Report on the Administration of Iraq from April, 1923, to December, 1924* (pp. 45–50), which gives the point of view of the Husseinides, and Philby's *Arabia* (pp. 293 ff. and 299 ff.), which gives the point of view of Ibn Saud ; also *Oriento Moderno* (iv year, pp. 204–8).

[112] On Hussein's negotiations with England see *Oriento Moderno* (iii year, p. 111, 1923, and iv year, pp. 510 ff., 1924). The first attempt made by Lawrence with Hussein in 1921 failed. England transmitted a draft through Hussein's delegates in London in 1923, in which Great Britain engaged to recognize and defend Arabian independence in the Arabian peninsula with the exception of Aden, and also in Iraq and Trans-Jordan, and to help the States in question to a federal union. In Palestine, in accordance with England's previous assurances, nothing was to be done to encroach upon the rights of the Arabs. The treaty assumed the perpetuation of the capitulations, though under another name. The draft was rejected because it deprived Arabia of its access to the Mediterranean (Syria and Palestine) and retained the capitulations. Two later drafts, at the end of 1923 and in June, 1924, dropped the capitulations and contained further concessions on England's part, but they were rejected by Hussein and the Arabs because they, too, adhered to Palestine's special position.

On Hussein's ambitions see "The Congress of the Arabian Peninsula " (*Oriento Moderno*, iii year, pp. 447 ff.) and " The Congress at the time of the Pilgrimage " (*Oriento Moderno*, iv year, p. 600).

On the Arabian nationalism of Imam Yehya of Yemen see *Oriento Moderno*, (iv year, p. 186, and v year, p. 314).

[113] The proclamation ran : " For several years past some of our brothers have arisen in order to demand Arabian independence and to proclaim the necessity of union between the Arab princes. We have praised their endeavours and prayed to God that what they propose may be realized and that he will so lead them as to bring salvation to the Arabs. We have offered them our help in order to make an end of the greed of the foreigners and their intervention in the affairs of Arabia. But they wished to achieve the great work alone, to take the responsibility upon themselves, and to reap for themselves alone the fame of having freed the land of the Arabs. Thereat we said : May God bring about the independence of Arabia, whoever the liberator may be. But hardly had we sheathed the sword

when we saw that this independence was nothing but a protectorate and mandate. . . . Noble Arab nation ! Nejd stretches out its hand to all who work for Arabian independence, supports all who rise for the freedom and unity of the Arabs. Nejd seeks to conquer no land beyond its natural frontiers, but it will admit only the full and genuine independence of all Arab lands, over which none but their own sons shall rule."

[114] The massacre of Taif was exploited at the time by Hussein's anti-Wahabi propaganda. Philby in *Arabia* (p. 305) gives a different account. At any rate, the massacre at Taif was the only case of the kind. For the rest, Ibn Saud controlled his troops with iron discipline.

[115] " Whatever the future may hold in store for Ibn Sa'ud, it is probable that the recording angel will place in the forefront of his achievements the rapid and complete subjugation of anarchy and unrest in the Hijaz, which has astonished a wider audience than that of the pilgrims. To-day there is perhaps no country in the world with a cleaner crime-sheet and a better record of internal tranquillity than Arabia, while no country can boast so small an annual expenditure on police." (*Arabia*, by H. St. J. B. Philby, Benn, 1930, p. 320.)

[116] On the two congresses see Achille Sekaly, *Le Congrès du Khalifat et le Congrès du Monde Musulman* (Ed. Ernest Leroux, Paris, 1926). On the Caliphate in transition see the work of a Mohammedan, A. Sanhoury, *Le Califat. Son Evolution vers une Société des Nations Orientales* (Ed. P. Genthner, Paris, 1926).

[117] The Congress of Mecca met eighteen times between June 7th to July 5th, 1926. Seventy-five delegates took part in it, representing nineteen countries. The Mohammedans of northern Africa, China, and Persia were not represented. The delegates from Turkey, Afghanistan, Egypt, and the Yemen did not arrive till the end of June, nor did they take part in the vote on the resolution demanding the restoration by England of Maan and Aqaba. Both they and the Indian delegates were strict in their demand that Ibn Saud should give a more exact account of the money to be contributed, and that there should be complete ritual freedom. The following are the questions which the Congress debated : public health in the Hejaz ; the cession of the Hejaz Railway and its extension by new lines from Jidda to Mecca with branch lines to Muna and Arafat, from Yenbo to Medina and from Medina to Mecca ; religious endowments from abroad for Mecca and Medina ; ritual freedom for Mohammedans in the Hejaz ; the fate of Maan and Aqaba.

Ibn Saud's attitude can best be explained by quoting a message to the Congress which Hafez Wahba read in his name on June 7th, 1926 :—

" In the name of the gracious and all-merciful God. We thank God that he had led us in the right way, for without his help we should not be here. God's spirit and salvation be upon Mohammed, God's envoy, with his family, his companions, and his disciples. We welcome you and thank you for coming to the Congress. O faithful Mohammedans, this meeting of yours is the first of its kind in form and substance in the history of Islam. We pray to the Almighty that it may be a good beginning and that this Congress may reassemble annually according to the divine word : ' Help one another in all that is good and merciful, and do not help wickedness and enmity,' and that other divine word : ' Take counsel together for your well-being.' " You know that in the past men have paid no heed to the public opinion

of the Mohammedan world. Many States have ruled the Hejaz. There
have been Caliphs and Sultans who have taken an interest in the
affairs of this country. . . . Others have neglected it altogether and
have allowed the Emirs who governed it to commit ruthless deeds,
to spread corruption, and to exploit the inhabitants and the pilgrims
as their ambitions or whims dictated. These abuses reached a climax
when, after the fall of the Ottoman sovereignty, the Hejaz came into
the hands of the Sherif Hussein Ibn Ali, the last of these Emirs. His
despotism, his inability to maintain order and peace in the land, which
he placed under the influence of foreign, non-Mohammedan Powers,
as is proved by official documents and by articles in *El Kibla* (*El Kibla*
was the official organ in the Hejaz under King Hussein, who contributed
to it himself. Ibn Saud replaced it by the newspaper *Umm el Kura*).
. . . When at last the cup was full and the responsible persons in Nejd
were consulted and declared that religion laid the duty upon us of
delivering the cradle of Islam from this man's acts of injustice, we
resolved to fulfil their desire, and we have shrunk from no sacrifice
of blood and treasure to reach the goal. God has granted us victory
at last, and, obedient to our duty to the Almighty and the Mohammedan
believers, we have purified the Holy Places from his (Hussein's) and
his sons' extortions.

" My brethren, you yourselves have seen and have heard from the
pilgrims . . . that the security prevailing throughout the Hejaz
. . . is without parallel in the history of the land, nay, even in many
strong and well-organized States. For that we thank God. In this
security, and with a freedom unrestricted except by the commands
of the Sharia, we invite you to take counsel upon everything that you
hold to be desirable in the religious and civic interest of the Hejaz,
upon the régime to be introduced here which shall inspire confidence
in all Mohammedans, so that the law of the Koran may prevail in the
cradle of Islam and the place where it was revealed, so that the land
may be purified of all the heresies . . . which have been committed
here with impunity, and so that its absolute independence may be
established and secured against all alien intervention. . . . We invite
you to examine all means whereby the Holy Places may become the
truest centre of Islamic culture, a model of cleanliness and hygiene,
and so exemplary a land as shall serve to make Islam rightly
known . . ." For further information about the Congress and Ibn
Saud's address, see *Zeitschrift für Politik* (Berlin, 1928, vol. xviii,
No. 3, pp. 175–8).

[118] The first Minister of Foreign Affairs in the Hejaz was
Dr. Abdallah ed Damluji, an Arab from Mosul, who came as physician
in ordinary to Ibn Saud in 1915. Later he took a leading part in the
negotiations with Great Britain and at the end of 1926 he accompanied
Prince Feisal on his journey to Europe. In 1928 he retired from
office. He was succeeded by a young Syrian, Fuad Hamzah. The
Minister of Finance is a Nejdi, Sheikh Abdallah el Fadhl, who, however,
had lived in Jidda for many years as a merchant in a great way.
Besides these Sheikh Hafez Wahba plays a great part in all Ibn Saud's
negotiations. He is an Egyptian and took part in the Egyptian
struggle for independence from 1919 to 1921, when he suffered imprisonment ; he then resolved to devote his life to the cause of Arabian
freedom and in 1930 he was appointed as Ibn Saud's first Minister
in London.

[119] In 1926 the Idrissi had granted a concession on the Farasan

Islands to the British Asiatic Petroleum Company in return for a loan of £23,000 ; these islands lie off Jisan, the port of the Idrissi's capital of Sabya. Ibn Saud recognized the concession, but took the first opportunity to cancel it when the question arose in 1928 of extending the borings to another island.

[120] On the Yemen and the Iman see Ameen Rihani, *Arabian Peak and Desert*, the account of a journey undertaken in 1922. Rihani gives the number of inhabitants of the Yemen as three million, whilst the Imam in an interview (p. 98) gives the figures as five million. The Iman (op. cit.) regards the whole of southern Arabia (Oman, Hadramaut, and Aden) as legally part of the Yemen. The Zaidites, the predominant Shi'ah sect in the Yemen, to which Imam Yehya belongs, are regarded as the most strictly isolated Mohammedan group.

[121] See Leopold Weiss, " Arabisches Drama " (*Neue Zürcher Zeitung*, March 2nd and 9th, 1930, Nos. 393 and 441). See also " Auf dem Wege zu einem islamischen Kirchenstaat " (*Frankfurter Zeitung*, Abendblatt, June 3rd, 1929) and " Wüstenkonig " (*Frankfurter Zeitung*, August 7th, 1930, Reichsausgabe). See also the interview with Ibn Saud from *El Mokattam* in the *Frankfurter Zeitung*, July 8th, 1930 (Reichsausgabe).

[122] January 8th, 1930, was celebrated in Jidda in a manner characteristic of the new Arabia under the presidency of Emir Feisal, Ibn Saud's son and viceroy. After the military parade there was a banquet, of which *The Near East and India* (London, February 6th, 1930, p. 145) reports : " The tables for the 140 invited guests being set out on four sides of a hollow square in the open court yard, which had been elaborately decorated with electric lights, palm-fronds and green and white bunting, while in the central space two portraits of the king had been set in illuminated frames facing east and west." The Minister of Foreign Affairs made a speech on the four years of Ibn Saud's reign as king, and the Egyptian Ahmed Zeki Pasha answered in the name of the guests. The next day there was a festival at the oasis of Madra on the way to Mecca. There, after addresses and recitations from Arab poets of Syria and Nejd, there were speeches by the doyen of the Diplomatic Corps, the Ambassador of the Union of Socialist Soviet Republics, Nadir Bey Torakolov, and by the British Chargé d'Affaires.

CHAPTER XI

[123] See also Richard Hartmann, " Nationale Bestrebungen der Araber " (*Deutsche Revue*, vol. xlvi, 1921, No. 3, pp. 247–50, and No. 4, pp. 53–62) and R. Strothmann, " Gegenwartsgeschichte des Islam " (*Der Islam*, vol. xvii, 1928, pp. 28 ff.) and R. Strothmann, " Islam und orientalische Christenheit in der Gegenwart " (*Orientalische Literaturzeitung*, April, 1928, col. 245 ff.). Information in French on present-day Arabian literature may be found in the writings of Khairallah T. Kahirallah, in English in the admirable studies of H. A. R. Gibb—he would render a great service by issuing them in the form of a book on Arabian literature from 1860 to 1930— in German in those of G. Kampffmeyer (in *Die Welt des Islam* and *Mitteilungen des Seminars für orientalische Sprachen*, Berlin), in Russian in those of Ignaz Krachkovskii.

[124] On the meeting of the International Missionary Council in Jerusalem in 1928 see the reports in the *Frankfurter Zeitung*, on May 22nd, 1928, and *Neue Wege* (Zurich) of May, 1928. There, too, is the sentence quoted from Leonhard Ragaz. On the subjects of missions and the state of religious policy in the East, see also Paul Schütz : *Zwischen Nil und Kaukasus* (Verlag Chr. Kaiser, Munich, 1930).

[125] On China see Emil Lederer : *Japan-Europa. Wandlungen im Fernen Osten* (Frankfurter Societäts-Verlag, Frankfurt a M., 1929, pp. 212 ff.) : " Many of those who ' know ' China, and who yet have been less conscious of the forces of the present day than anxious, perhaps, to assuage their own unacknowledged fears, have tried to prove by means of analogies from history. . . . But these arguments by analogy prove little to-day, as events have shown, now that the Chinese nation is undergoing such a rapid process of transformation, now that the habits of the politically awakened masses are visibly changing, under the guidance of a group of leaders whose abilities are equal to the task they have undertaken. . . . Nevertheless, none of these difficulties will be insuperable, if the alien Powers refrain from disturbing the process of re-organization, or rather, of spontaneous self-organization, and if in future they abstain from all intervention which must after all prove fruitless in the end. With the rise of a great Power, consolidated within, on Chinese territory—an event whose approach may already be discerned—a new epoch will begin in Asiatic and in world history." On the dissolution of the family in China through the national State and individualism, see *Neue Zürcher Zeitung*, December 22nd, 1930, No. 2,535, and on the modern woman in China see *The Times* (London) December 30th, 1930. Both articles point to conditions which are profoundly significant of the spiritual transformation that the whole East is undergoing.

BIBLIOGRAPHY

THE following bibliography gives a survey of the most important publications used. I have included only books and independent publications. Other sources have been referred to in the notes. Amongst periodicals the most important is *Oriento Moderno*, a monthly published in Rome since June, 1921 ; especially in the early years it gives a complete survey of events, largely in translations from Eastern sources. Mention should also be made of *The Near East and India*, a London weekly, and of the quarterly *Journal of the Central Asian Society*. *Die Welt des Islam* (Berlin), edited by Professor G. Kampffmeyer, contains valuable material, whilst the annual surveys of the Near East prepared by Elizabeth P. MacCallum (Information Service of the Foreign Policy Association, New York) give convenient summaries.

The following bibliography deals only with books treating of developments since the World War. A collocation of the more important official publications on the subject under consideration may be welcome to the reader. The British official publications are issued by His Majesty's Stationery Office, London, and may be obtained from there, those of the League of Nations from the Publication Department of the League of Nations in Geneva and its agencies abroad.

I. OFFICIAL PUBLICATIONS

A Handbook of Arabia. Compiled by the Geographical Section of the Naval Intelligence Staff, Admiralty. H.M. Stationery Office, London, 1921.

A Handbook of Syria. Compiled by the Geographical Section of the Naval Intelligence Staff, Admiralty. H.M. Stationery Office, London, 1921.

Handbooks prepared under the direction of the Historical Section of the Foreign Office. H.M. Stationery Office, London, 1920.
> No. 60. *Syria and Palestine.*
> No. 61. *Arabia.*
> No. 62. *Armenia and Kurdistan.*
> No. 63. *Mesopotamia.*

EGYPT

Cmd. 1131. *Report of the Special Commission to Egypt.* London, 1920.

Cmd. 1592. (Egypt No. 1, 1922., *Correspondence respecting affairs in Egypt.* London, 1922.

Cmd. 1617. *Circular* (to H.M. Representatives abroad) *stating the decision of H.M. Government to terminate the Protectorate and to recognize Egypt as an independent sovereign State.* London, 1922.

Egyptian Indemnity Act and Termination of Martial Law in Egypt. Exchange of Notes. July 5th, 1923. League of Nations, Treaty Series, vol. xviii, p. 312 (see also Cmd. 1998, 1923).

Law concerning conditions of service, retirement, and dismissal of Foreign Officials. Exchange of Notes. July 18th, 1923. League of Nations, Treaty Series, vol. xviii, p. 324 (see also Cmd. 1999, 1923).

Cmd. 2171. (Sudan No. 1, 1924.) *Correspondence respecting the Gezira Irrigation Project.* London, 1924.

Cmd. 2269. (Mr. MacDonald's) *Dispatch respecting the position of H.M. Government in regard to Egypt and the Sudan.* London, 1924.

Cmd. 3050. (Egypt No. 1, 1928.) *Papers regarding negotiations for a treaty of alliance with Egypt.* London, 1928.

Cmd. 3097. *Papers respecting the proposed Egyptian Law regulating public meetings and demonstrations.* London, 1928.

Cmd. 3376. (Draft of a Treaty with Egypt.) London, 1929.

Cmd. 3573. (Negotiations for a Treaty with Egypt.) London, 1930.

PALESTINE

Cmd. 1499. *An Interim Report on the Civil Administration of Palestine during the period July 1st, 1920–June 30th, 1921.* London, 1921.

Cmd. 1540. *Disturbances in May,* 1921. Reports of the Commission of Inquiry with Correspondence relating thereto. London, 1921.

Report on Palestine Administration, July, 1920–December, 1921. London, 1922.

Cmd. 1700. *Palestine. Correspondence with the Palestine Arab Delegation and the Zionist Organization.* (Contains under No. 5 the Statement on British Policy in Palestine, the so-called Churchill White Book.) London, 1922.

Cmd. 1708. (Misc., No. 4, 1922.) *Mandate for Palestine.* Letter from the Secretary to the Cabinet to the Secretary General of the League of Nations of July 1st, 1922, enclosing a note in reply to Cardinal Gasparri's letter of May 15th, 1922, addressed to the Secretary General of the League of Nations. London, 1922.

Cmd. 1785. *Mandate for Palestine together with a note by the Secretary General relating to its application to the territory known as Trans-Jordan, under the provisions of article 25.* London, 1922.

Report on Palestine Administration, 1922. London, 1923.

Cmd. 1195. (Misc., No. 4, 1921.) *Anglo-French Convention of December 23rd, 1920, on certain points connected with the Mandates for Syria and the Libanon, Palestine, and Mesopotamia.* London, 1921.

Cmd. 1910. (Treaty Series, No. 13, 1923.) *Agreement between H.M. Government and the French Government respecting the boundary line between Syria and Palestine from the Mediterranean to El Hamme.* London, 1923.

Cmd. 1889. *Papers relating to the Elections for the Palestine Legislative Council, 1923.* London, 1923.

Cmd. 1989. *Palestine. Proposed formation of an Arab Agency.* London, 1923.

Colonial No. 5. *Report on Palestine Administration, 1923.* London, 1924.

Colonial No. 9. *Report by H.M. Government on the Palestine Administration, 1923.* London, 1925.

Colonial No. 12. *Report by H.B.M. Government on the Administration under Mandate of Palestine and Transjordan for the year 1924.* London, 1925.

Colonial No. 15. *Report of the High Commissioner on the Administration of Palestine, 1920–5.* London, 1925.

Colonial No. 17. *Appendices to the Report by H.B.M. Government on the Administration under Mandate of Palestine and Transjordan for the year 1924.* London, 1925.

Colonial No. 20. *Report by H.B.M. Government to the Council of the League of Nations on the Administration of Palestine and Transjordan for the year 1925.* London, 1926.

Colonial No. 26. *Report by H.B.M. Government to the Council of the League of Nations on the Administration of Palestine and Transjordan for the year 1926.* London, 1927.

Colonial No. 31. *Report by H.B.M. Government to the Council of the League of Nations on the Administration of Palestine and Transjordan for the year 1927.* London, 1928.

Colonial No. 40. *Report by H.M. Government in the United Kingdom of Great Britain and Northern Ireland to the Council of the League of Nations on the Administration of Palestine and Transjordan for the year 1928.* London, 1929.

Colonial No. 47. *Report by H.M. Government in the United Kingdom of Great Britain and Northern Ireland to the Council of the League of Nations on the Administration of Palestine and Transjordan for the year 1929.* London, 1930.

Cmd. 2559. *Convention between the United Kingdom and the United States respecting the rights of the Governments of the two countries and their nationals in Palestine.* London, 1925.

Cmd. 2696. *Palestine and East Africa Loans.* Memorandum explaining financial resolution. London, 1926.

Cmd. 3229. *The Western or Wailing Wall in Jerusalem.* Memorandum by the Secretary of State for the Colonies. London, 1928.

Cmd. 3317. *Dead Sea Salts Concession.* London, 1929.

Cmd. 3326. *Documents relating to the Dead Sea Salts Concession.* London, 1929.

Cmd. 3530. *Report of the Commission on the Palestine Disturbances of August, 1929.* London, 1930.

Cmd. 3582. *Palestine. Statement with regard to British Policy.* London, 1930.

Colonial No. 48. *Palestine Commission on the Disturbances of August, 1929.* Evidence heard, 3 vols. London, 1930.

Cmd. 3686. *Palestine. Report on Immigration, Land Settlement, and Development.* By Sir John Hope Simpson. London, 1930.

Cmd. 3692. *Palestine. Statement of Policy by H.M. Government in the United Kingdom.* London, 1930.

Cmd. 3069. *Trans-Jordan. Agreement between the United Kingdom and Trans-Jordan.* London, 1928. (See also Cmd. 3488. Treaty Series, No. 7, 1930. *Agreement between His Majesty and the Amir of Trans-Jordan.*)

INNER ARABIA

Cmd. 2566. *Arabia. Agreements with the Sultan of Nejd regarding certain questions relating to the Nejd-Trans-Jordan and Nejd–Iraq frontiers.* (Treaties of Haddah and Bahrah.) London, 1925.

Treaty of Friendship and good understanding between Hedjas-Nejd and Great Britain. Signed May 20th, 1927. *Exchange of letters re Manumission of slaves and status of Aqaba.* League of Nations, Treaty Series, vol. lxxi, p. 153. (Also as Cmd. 2591. Treaty Series, No. 25, London, 1927.)

SYRIA

La Syrie et le Liban. Haut Commissariat de la République Française en Syrie et au Liban. Paris, 1922.

La Syrie et le Liban en 1922. Paris, 1923.

La Syrie et le Liban sous l'Occupation et le Mandat Français, 1919 à 1927. Berger-Levrault, Editeurs, Paris et Nancy, 1929.

Rapport à la Société des Nations sur la situation de la Syrie et du Liban. (*Année 1922–1923.*) Paris, 1923.

Rapport à la Société des Nations sur la situation de la Syrie et du Liban. (*Année 1923–1924.*) Paris, 1924.

Rapport à la Société des Nations sur la situation de la Syrie et du Liban. (*Année 1924.*) Paris, 1925. (Also as League of Nations publication : C. 452 (*m*). M. 166 (*m*). 1925, vi.)

Rapport Provisoire à la Société des Nations sur la situation de la Syrie et du Liban. (*Année 1925.*) Paris, 1926.

Rapport Définitif à la Société des Nations sur la situation de la Syrie et du Liban. (*Année 1925.*) Paris, 1926.

Rapport à la Société des Nations sur la situation de la Syrie et du Liban. (*Année 1926.*) Paris, 1927.

Rapport à la Société des Nations sur la situation de la Syrie et du Liban. (*Année 1927.*) Paris, 1928. Imprimerie Nationale.

Rapport à la Société des Nations sur la situation de la Syrie et du Liban. (*Année 1928.*) Paris, 1929. Imprimerie Nationale.

Rapport à la Société des Nations sur la situation de la Syrie et du Liban. (*Année 1929.*) Paris, 1930. Imprimerie Nationale.

IRAQ

Cmd. 1061. *Review of the Civil Administration of Mesopotamia.* London, 1920.

Cmd. 1176. *Draft Mandates for Mesopotamia and Palestine.* London, 1921.

Cmd. 1500. *Final Drafts of the Mandates for Mesopotamia and Palestine.* London, 1921.

Report on Iraq Administration, October, 1920–March, 1922. H.M. Stationery Office, London, 1923.

Report on Iraq Administration, April, 1922–March, 1923 (Colonial No. 4.) London, 1924.

Report by H.B.M. Government on the Administration of Iraq for the period, April, 1923–December, 1924. (Colonial No. 13.) London, 1925. (Also as League of Nations publication, C. 452 (*c*). M. 166 (*c*). 1925, vi.)

Report by H.B.M. Government to the Council of the League of Nations on the Administration of Iraq for the year 1925. (Colonial No. 21.) London, 1926.

Report by H.B.M. Government to the Council of the League of Nations on the Administration of Iraq for the year 1926. (Colonial No. 29.) London, 1927.

Report by H.B.M. Government to the Council of the League of Nations on the Administration of Iraq for the year 1927. (Colonial No. 35.) London, 1928.

Report by H.M. Government in the United Kingdom of Great Britain and Northern Ireland to the Council of the League of Nations on the Administration of Iraq for the year 1928. (Colonial No. 44.) London, 1929.

Report by H.M. Government in the United Kingdom of Great Britain and Northern Ireland to the Council of the League of Nations on the Administration of Iraq for the year 1929. (Colonial No. 55.) London, 1930.

Cmd. 1757. (Treaty Series No. 17 of 1925.) *The Anglo-Iraq Treaty of October 10th, 1922.* London, 1922.

Cmd. 2120. Contains the Protocol of April 30th, 1923, and the four agreements made under the Treaty of October 10th, 1922. The Treaty of 1922, the Protocol, and the four agreements are in the League of Nations Treaty Series, vol. xxxv, pp. 14, 36, 104, 132, and 146.

Cmd. 2587. (Treaty Series, No. 10 of 1926.) *Treaty extending duration of former Treaty,* January 13th, 1926. London, 1926. (Also in the League of Nations Treaty Series, vol. xlvii, p. 427.)

Cmd. 2998. *Treaty between the United Kingdom and Iraq.* December 14th, 1927. London, 1927.

Cmd. 3627. *Treaty of Alliance between the United Kingdom and Iraq.* June 30th, 1930. London, 1930.

LEAGUE OF NATIONS PUBLICATIONS

Mandate for Palestine and Memorandum by the British Government relating to its application to Transjordan, approved by the Council of the League of Nations on September 16th, 1922. (C. 529. M. 314. 1922. vi.)

Mandate for Syria and Lebanon. (C. 528. M. 313. 1922. vi.)

Note on Political Developments in Mesopotamia subsequent to October 1st, 1920. (C. 465. M. 341. 1921. vi.)

Letter from the British Government forwarding the Text of the Organic Law of Iraq. (C. 412. 1924. vi.) (C.P.M. 166.)

Decisions of the Council of the League of Nations of September 27th, 1924, and March 11th, 1926, relating to the application of the principles of Article 22 of the Covenant to Iraq, together with certain Treaties and Agreements. (C. 216. M. 77. 1926. vi.) (C.M. 391.) (Ser. L. of N.P. 1926. vi. A. 6.)

Application of the Principles of Article 22 of the Covenant to Iraq and Administration of the Kurdish Districts in Iraq. Question of the Frontier between Turkey and Iraq. (Extract No. 34 from the *Official Journal,* April, 1926.)

Constitution of Iraq. (C. 49. 1929. vi.) (Ser. L. of N.P. 1929. vi. A. 1.) (C.H.M. 834.)

Mandate for Syria and Lebanon. Questionnaire. (A. 34. 1922. vi.)

Mandate for Palestine. Questionnaire. (A. 38. 1922. vi.)

Minutes of the Sessions of the Permanent Mandates Commission :—
  4 Session, Geneva, June 24th–July 8th, 1924. (A. 13. 1924. vi.)
  5 Session (special), Geneva, October 23rd–November 6th, 1924. (C. 617. M. 216. 1924. vi.)
  6 Session, Geneva, June 26th–July 10th, 1925. (C. 386. M. 132. 1925. vi.)
  7 Session, Geneva, October 19th–30th, 1925. (C. 648. M. 237. 1925. vi.)
  8 Session (special), Rome, February 16th–March 6th, 1926. (C. 174. M. 65. 1926.) (Ser. L. of N.P. 1926. vi. A. 5.)
  Appended comments submitted by the Accredited Representatives of France. (C. 173. M. 64. 1926. vi.)
  9 Session, Geneva, June 8th–25th, 1926. (C. 405. M. 144. 1926. vi.) (Ser. L. of N.P. 1926. vi. A. 18.)
  10 Session, Geneva, November 4th–19th, 1926. (C. 362. M. 248. 1926. vi.) (Ser. L. of N.P. 1926. vi. A. 24.)
  Appended Supplementary Observations of the British Government on the Decisions of the Council concerning the Report of the P.M.C. (C. 64. 1928. vi.) (Ser. L. of N.P. 1928. vi. A. 2.)
  11 Session, Geneva, June 20th–July 6th, 1927. (C. 348. M. 122. 1927. vi.)

12 Session, Geneva, October 24th–November 11th, 1927. (C. 545. M. 194. 1927. vi.) (Ser. L. of N.P. 1927. vi. A. 10.)

13 Session, Geneva, June 12th–29th, 1928. (C. 341. M. 99. 1928. vi.) (Ser. L. of N.P. 1928. vi. A. 9.)

14 Session, Geneva, October 26th–November 13th, 1928. (C. 568. M. 179. 1928. vi.) (Ser. L. of N.P. 1928. vi. A. 14.)

15 Session, Geneva, July 1st–19th, 1929. (C. 305. M. 105. 1929. vi.) (Ser. L. of N.P. 1929. vi. A. 2.)

16 Session, Geneva, November 6th–26th, 1929. (C. 538. M. 192. 1929. vi.) (Ser. L. of N.P. 1929. vi. A. 4.)

17 Session (special), Geneva, June 3rd–21st, 1930. (C. 355. M. 147. 1930. vi.) (Ser. L. of N.P. 1930. vi. A.)

II. BOOK PUBLICATIONS

GENERAL

TOYNBEE, ARNOLD J. : *The Islamic World since the Peace Settlement.* (Survey of International Affairs, 1925, vol. i.) Oxford University Press, London, 1927.

JUNG, EUGÈNE : *La Révolte Arabe.* 2 vols. Librairie Colbert, Paris, 1924–5.

JUNG, EUGÈNE : *L'Islam sous le Joug.* Chez l'auteur, 50 avenue Malakoff, Paris, 1926.

JUNG, EUGÈNE : *L'Islam et l'Asie devant l'Imperialisme.* Marpon et Cie., Paris, 1927.

RIHBANY, ABRAHAM MITRY : *Wise Men from the East and from the West.* Houghton Mifflin Company, Boston and New York, 1922.

LODER, J. DE V. : *The Truth about Mesopotamia, Palestine, and Syria.* Foreword by Lord Robert Cecil. George Allen & Unwin, London, 1923.

STAUFFER, MILTON : *Voices from the Near East.* Student Christian Movement, London, 1928.

TOPF, ERICH : *Die Staatenbildungen in den arabischen Teilen der Türkei seit dem Weltkriege nach Entstehung, Bedeutung und Lebensfähigkeit* Friederichsen, de Gruyter & Co., Hamburg, 1929.

COKE, RICHARD : *The Arab's Place in the Sun.* Thornton Butterworth, London, 1929.

KRAŽIN, W. A. : *Nacionalno-osvoboditelnoye dviženiye na bližnom vostoke.* C. 1. (Siriya i Palestina, Kilikiya, Mesopotamiya i Egipet.) Published by the All-Russian Institute of Eastern Studies, Moscow, 1923.

EMIN, AHMED : *Turkey in the World War.* Yale University Press, Humphrey Milford, London, 1930.

HOSKINS, H. L. : *British Routes to India.* Longmans, London, 1928.

ROHDE, HANS : *Der Kampf um Asien.* Vol. I. *Der Kampf um Orient und Islam.* Deutsche Verlagsanstalt, Stuttgart, 1924.

ANCEL, JACQUES : *Manuel historique de la question d'Orient (1792–1923).* Delagrave, Paris, 1923.

POWELL, EDWARD ALEXANDER : *By Camel and Car to the Peacock Throne.* Century Co., New York and London, 1923.

ACITO, ALFREDO : *L'Oriento arabo. Odierne questioni politiche (Siria, Palestina, Libano, Irak).* Popolo d'Italia, Milano, 1921.

GAULIS, B. G. : *La Question Arabe.* Berger-Levrault, Paris 1930.

EGYPT

PRATT, IDA A. : *Modern Egypt.* A list of references to material in the New York Public Library. The New York Public Library, New York, 1929.

JEHON, D'IVRAI : *L'Egypte Eternelle.* La Renaissance du Livre, Paris, 1922.

ADAM, JULIETTE : *L'Angleterre en Egypte.* Imprimerie du Centre, Paris, 1922.

SHAMSY, ALY : *An Egyptian Opinion. Egypt and the Right of Nations.* Imprimerie Nationale, Geneva, 1918.

SEDKY, M. BAHER : *L'Egypte aux Egyptiens. Griefs, Justifications et Revendications.* Librairie Nouvelle, Lausanne, 1919.

SABRY, MOUSTAPHA : *La Révolution Egyptienne d'après les documents authentiques et des photographies prises au cours de la révolution.* Préface de A. Aulard. T. Vrin, Paris, 1919.

EBEID, W. MAKRAM : *Complete Independence versus the Milner Scheme.* Caledonian Press, London, 1921.

LAMBELIN, ROGER : *L'Egypte et l'Angleterre. Vers l'Indépendance.* Bernard Grasset, Paris, 1922.

CHIROL, SIR VALENTINE : *The Egyptian Problem.* Macmillan & Co., London, 1920.

HAYTER, SIR WILLIAM : *Recent Constitutional Developments in Egypt.* Cambridge University Press, 1924.

HARRIS, MURRAY : *Egypt under the Egyptians.* Chapman & Hall, London, 1925.

SYMONS, M. TRAVERS : *Britain and Egypt. The Rise of Egyptian Nationalism.* Cecil Palmer, London, 1925.

ELGOOD, P. E. : *Egypt and the Army.* Oxford University Press, London, 1924.

YOUNG, GEORGE : *Egypt.* Ernest Benn, London, 1927.

GAULIS, BERTHE G. : *Le Nationalisme Egyptien, 1924–8.* Berger-Levrault, Nancy and Paris, 1928.

NEWMAN, E. W. POLSON : *Great Britain and Egypt.* Cassell & Co., London, 1928.

YEGHEN, FOULAD : *Saad Zaglul.* Cahiers de France, Paris, 1928.

MARSHALL, J. E. : *The Egyptian Enigma, 1890–1928.* John Murray, London, 1928.

ELGOOD, P. G. : *The Transit of Egypt.* Edward Arnold & Co., London, 1928.

HOWELL, J. MORTON : *Egypt's Past, Present and Future.* Service Publishing Company, Dayton, Ohio, 1929.

HILMI, ABBAS : *A few Words on the Anglo-Egyptian Settlement.* George Allen & Unwin, London, 1930.

BEAMAN, ARDERN HULME : *The Dethronement of the Khedive.* George Allen & Unwin, London, 1929.

REINHARD, ERNST : *Der Kampf um Suez.* Kaden & Co., Dresden, 1930.

MO-CHO, LIU : *De la Condition internationale de l'Egypte depuis la Déclaration anglaise de 1922.* Thèse, Lyon, impr. Bose frères et Riou, 1925.

MEYER, GEORGES : *L'Egypte Contemporaine et les Capitulations.* Les Presses Universitaires, Paris, 1930.

HALLBERG, CHARLES W. : *The Suez Canal, its History and its diplomatic Importance.* P. S. King, London, 1931.

PALESTINE AND ZIONISM

(See also the following bibliographies : Peter Thomsen, *Die Palästinaliteratur,* 4 vols. (1915–24), ii half ; Hinrichs, Leipzig, 1927. G. Kampffmeyer, in *Die Welt des Islam,* vol. ix, No. 1, Berlin, May, 1927.)

Zionistisches Handbuch. Edited by Gerhard Holdheim, Berliner Büro der Zionistischen Organisation, Berlin, 1923.

BÖHM, ADOLF : *Die Zionistische Bewegung.* Two vols. Weltverlag, Berlin, 1920, 1921.

SCHLESINGER, ABRAHAM : *Einführung in den Zionismus.* Kauffmann, Frankfurt a.M., 1921.

SOKOLOW, NAHUM : *History of Zionism, 1600–1918.* (Introduction by A. J. Balfour). 2 vols. Longmans, Green & Co., London, 1919.

BALFOUR, EARL OF : *Speeches on Zionism.* Foreword by Sir Herbert Samuel. Arrowsmith, London, 1928.

STEIN, LEONARD : *Zionism.* Ernest Benn, London, 1924.

LATTES, DANTE : *Il Sionismo.* 2 vols. Paolo Cremonese, Rome, 1928.

HOLDEIM, GERHARD : *Palästina. Idee, Probleme, Tatsachen.* Schwetschke und Sohn, Berlin, 1929.

FOSDICK, HARRY EMERSON : *A Pilgrimage to Palestine.* Student Christian Movement, London, 1928.

HELSEY, EDOUARD : *L'an dernier à Jérusalem.* Les Editions de France, Paris, 1930.

Rassejet (Deutsches Heft). Edited by Wladimir Jabotinsky, Berlin, 1925.

MAGNES, J. L. : *Like all Nations . . . ?* Jerusalem, 1930.

WIENER, ALFRED : *Juden und Araber in Palästina.* Philo-Verlag, Berlin, 1930.

WIENER, ALFRED : *Kritische Reise durch Palästina.* Philo-Verlag, Berlin, 1927.

RUPPIN, ARTHUR : *The Agricultural Colonization of the Zionist Organisation in Palestine.* Martin Hopkins, London, 1926.

ROMANO, MARCO : *Problèmes politiques de l'organisation sioniste. Nos rapports avec les Arabes et l'Angleterre.* Ed. Rieder, Paris, 1927.

LA MAZIÈRE, PIERRE : *Israël sur la terre des ancêtres.* Libr. Baudinière, Paris, 1927.

HOROWITZ, P. : *The Jewish Question and Zionism.* Ernest Benn, London, 1927.

CORCOS, FERNAND : *Israël sur la terre biblique.* Jouve et Cie, Paris, 1923.

CORCOS, FERNAND : *A travers la Palestine Juive.* Jouve et Cie, Paris, 1925.

VANDERVELDE, EMILE : *Le Pays d'Israël. Un marxiste en Palestine.* Ed. Rieder, Paris, 1929.

SIMON, LEON, and STEIN, LEONARD : *Awakening Palestine.* J. Murray, London, 1923.

WORSFOLD, W. BASIL : *Palestine of the Mandate.* T. Fisher Unwin, London, 1925.

McCRACKAN, W. D. : *The New Palestine.* Foreword by Viscount Bryce. Cape, London, 1923.

JEFFRIES, J. M. N. : *The Palestine Deception.* Daily Mail, London, 1923.

ASHBEE, C. R. : *A Palestine Notebook, 1918–1923.* Heinemann, London, 1923.

SIDEBOTHAM, HERBERT : *British Policy and the Palestine Mandate.* Ernest Benn, London, 1930.

COHEN, KADMI : *L'Etat d'Israël.* Editions Kra, Paris, 1930.

GRANOVSKY, Dr. A. : *Land and the Jewish Reconstruction in Palestine.* Jerusalem, 1931.

HOLMES, JOHN HAYNES : *Palestine To-day and To-Morrow.* Macmillan, New York, 1929.

GRAVES, PHILIP : *Palestine, the Land of Three Faiths.* Introduction by D. G. Hogarth. J. Cape, London, 1923.

BREUER, ISAAC : *The Jewish National Home.* J. Kauffmann, Francfort-on-the-Maine, 1926

JASTROW, MORRIS : *Zionism and the Future of Palestine. The fallacies and dangers of political Zionism.* Macmillan, London, 1920.

VON WEISL, WOLFGANG : *Der Kampf um das Heilige Land.* Ullstein, Berlin, 1925.

WEDGWOOD, JOSIAH C. : *The Seventh Dominion.* Labour Publishing Company, London, 1928.

TRITONJ, ROMOLO : *Il Sionismo e le sue difficoltà politiche in Palestina,* Rassegna Italiana, Rome, 1924.

MASSIGNON, L. : *Le Sionisme et l'Islam.* Girard et Cie., Paris, 1921.

KALLEN, HORACE MEYER : *Zionism and World Politics.* Heinemann, London, 1921.

KOHN, HANS, and WELTSCH, ROBERT : *Zionistische Politik.* R. Färber, Mähr.-Ostrau, 1927.

Die Araberfrage in Palästina. Freie Zionistische Blätter. Heidelberg, 1921.

LICHTHEIM, RICHARD : *Revision der Zionistischen Politik.* Kommissionsverlag Ewer, Berlin, 1930.

BEILINSON, M. : *Zum jüdisch-arabischen Problem.* Verlag Dawar, Tel Aviv, 1930.

SEIDEL, HANS JOACHIM : *Der britische Mandatsstaat Palästina im Rahmen der Weltwirtschaft.* De Gruyter, Berlin, 1926.

PINNER, FELIX : *Das neue Palästina.* R. Mosse, Berlin, 1925.

COHN, JOSEF : *England und Palästina. Die politischen Grundlagen des Palästina-Aufbaues.* Verlag Kurt Vowinckel, Berlin, 1931.

BENTWICH, NORMAN : *England in Palestine.* Kegan Paul, London, 1932.

ANDREWS, FANNIE FERN : *The Holy Land under Mandate.* 2 vols. Allen and Unwin, London, 1931.

SYRIA

GONTAUT-BIRON, CONTE R. DE : *Comment la France s'est installée en Syrie (1918-1919).* Plon, Paris, 1922.

GONTAUT-BIRON, CONTE R. DE : *Sur les routes de Syrie après neuf ans de Mandat.* Plon, Paris, 1928.

GEORGE-SAMNÉ, DR. : *La Syrie.* Préface de Chakri Ganem. Bossard, Paris, 1920.

PACHA, ABDULLAH SFER : *Le Mandat Français et les Traditions Françaises en Syrie et au Liban.* Plon, Paris, 1922.

MANASSA, GABRIEL : *Les Mandats A et leur application en Orient.* Jouve et Cie., Paris, 1924.

DAVID, PHILLIPE : *Un Gouvernement Arabe à Damas. Le Congrès Syrien.* Marcel Girard, Paris, 1923.

ABOUSSOUAN, BENOIT : *Le Problème politique Syrien.* Edouard Duchemin, Paris, 1925.

GAUTHEROT, GUSTAVE : *La France en Syrie et en Cilicie.* Librairie Indépendente, Courbevoie, 1920.

STEIN, LEONARD : *Syria.* Ernest Benn, London, 1926.

MACCALLUM, ELIZABETH P. : *The Nationalist Crusade in Syria.* Foreign Policy Association, New York, 1928.

BONARDI, PIERRE : *L'Imbroglio Syrien.* Rieder, Paris, 1927.

RABBATH, EDMONT : *L'Evolution politique de la Syrie sous Mandat.* Préface de l'Emir Chekib Arslan. Marcel Rivière, Paris, 1928.

RABBATH, EDMONT : *Les Etats Unis de Syrie.* Imprimerie la Renaissance, Aleppo, 1925.

NAVA, SANTI : *Il Mandato Francese in Syria dalle Sue Origine al 1929.* Cedam, Padua, 1930.

CARBILLET, CAPTAIN G. : *Au Djebel Druse.* Edit. Argo, Paris, 1929.

BOURON, N. : Les Druzes. *Histoire du Liban et de la Montagne Hauranaise.* Préface du Général Weygand. Berger-Levrault, Paris, 1930.

BURCKHARD, CHARLES : *Le Mandat Français en Syrie et au Liban. La Politique et l'œuvre de la France au Levant.* Imprim. Couronny, Nimes, 1925.

LAMMENS, HENRI : *La Syrie.* Imprimerie Catholique, Beirut, 1921.

LA MAZIÈRE, PIERRE : *Partant pour la Syrie.* Baudinière, Paris, 1926.

EL CHERIF, IHSAN : *La Condition Internationale de la Syrie.* Vie Universitaire, Paris, 1922.

KHAIRALLAH, K. T. : *Le Problème du Levant. Les Régions Arabes Liberées.* Leroux, Paris, 1919.

DE FERIET, RENÈ : *L'application d'un Mandat. La France Puissance Mandataire en Syrie et au Liban.* Reveil, Paris, 1926.

ARMSTRONG, HAROLD : *Turkey and Syria reborn. A record of two years of travel.* John Lane, London, 1930.

DE BEAUPLAN, ROBERT : *Où va la Syrie? Le Mandat sous les cèdres.* J. Tallandier, Paris, 1929.

MOUNAYER, NASSIB : *Le Régime de la Terre en Syrie. Etudes historiques, juridiques et économiques.* Librairie Générale de Droit et de Jurisprudence, Paris, 1929.

JOFFRE, A. : *Le Mandat de la France sur la Syrie et le Grand Liban.* Recueil Sirey, Paris, 1924.

PIC, PAUL : *Syrie et Palestine. Mandats français et anglais dans le Proche Orient.* Préface de M. le Général Gouraud. Champion, Paris, 1924.

AYOUB, L. : *Les Mandats orientaux.* Recueil Sirey, Paris, 1924.

McGILVARY, MARGARET : *The Dawn of a New Era in Syria.* Fleming H. Revell Co., New York, 1920.

IRAQ AND INNER ARABIA

COKE, RICHARD : *The Heart of the Middle East.* Thornton Butterworth, London, 1923.

HALDANE, SIR AYLMER L. : *The Insurrection in Mesopotamia, 1920.* William Blackwood & Sons, Edinburgh, 1922.

LYELL, THOMAS : *The Ins and Outs of Mesopotamia.* A. M. Pilpot, London, 1923.

HESSE, FRITZ : *Die Mossulfrage.* Verlag Kurt Vowinckel, Berlin, 1925.

JACOB, HAROLD F. : *Kings of Arabia. The Rise and Set of Turkish Sovereignty in the Arabian Peninsula.* Mills & Boon, London, 1923.

PHILBY, H. ST. J. B. : *The Heart of Arabia. A Record of Travel and Exploration.* 2 vols. Constable, London, 1922.

PHILBY, H. ST. J. B. : *Arabia of the Wahabis.* Constable, London, 1928.

PHILBY, H. ST. J. B. : *Arabia.* Ernest Benn, London, 1930.

RIHANI, AMEEN : *Ibn Saoud of Arabia, his people and his land.* Constable, London, 1928.

RIHANI, AMEEN : *Around the Coasts of Arabia.* Constable, London, 1930.

RIHANI, AMEEN : *Arabian Peaks and Desert.* Constable, London, 1930.

LAWRENCE, T. E. : *Revolt in the Desert.* Jonathan Cape, London, 1927.

LOWELL, THOMAS : *With Lawrence in Arabia.* Hutchinson & Co., London, 1925.

RUTTER, ELDON : *The Holy Cities of Arabia.* 2 vols. G. P. Putna n's Sons, London, 1928.

The Letters of Gertrude Bell. 2 vols. Benn, London, 1927.

BROUCKE, JEANNE : *L'Empire Arabe d'Ibn Séoud.* Librarie Falk fils, Brussels, 1929.

VON WEISL, W. : *Zwischen dem Teufel und dem Roten Meer.* Brockhaus, Leipzig, 1928.

WEISS-SONNENBURG, HEDWIG : *Zur verbotenen Stadt Sanaa.* Eigenbrödler-Verlag, Berlin, 1928.

INDEX